THE ORIGINS
OF ENGLISH
TRAGEDY

Oxford University Press, Ely House, London W. 1

GLASGOW NEW YORK TORONTO MELBOURNE WELLINGTON
CAPE TOWN SALISBURY IBADAN NAIROBI LUSAKA ADDIS ABABA
BOMBAY CALCUTTA MADRAS KARACHI LAHORE DACCA
KUALA LUMPUR HONG KONG TOKYO

J. M. R. MARGESON

THE ORIGINS
OF ENGLISH
TRAGEDY

OXFORD
AT THE CLARENDON PRESS
1967

TO MY WIFE

CONTENTS

ACKNOWLEDGEMENTS

I SHOULD first like to acknowledge my very great debt to the late Professor Una Ellis-Fermor for her encouragement when the planning of this book was at an early stage. Dr. E. M. W. Tillyard and Professor M. C. Bradbrook read parts of the manuscript and made useful criticisms. I am also very much indebted to an adviser of the Clarendon Press for his detailed comments and his considerable patience. Finally, I should like to express my gratitude to the Royal Society of Canada and to the Council of Bedford College, University of London, for the opportunities they gave me for undisturbed research and writing.

INTRODUCTION

THE stage history of tragedy during many centuries has shown
its continuing power over the human mind, but the many
attempts of critics to discover the true nature of tragedy make it
plain that this power is not easily anatomized. The present study
does not claim to have answered the ancient, baffling questions.
It is an inquiry into the origins of tragedy on the medieval and
Elizabethan stages and into the different kinds of tragedy which
that theatre produced. Although the movement from a drama
that was largely ritualistic to fully fledged tragedy and comedy
on a professional stage has been thoroughly documented, there
has not been enough consideration of how and why the popular
religious and romantic drama should have moved toward
tragedy, even though we may understand why learned drama
should have done so. Nor has there been enough thought as to
why several important kinds of tragedy should have appeared
at the same moment rather than one dominant form.

This is a study, therefore, of the tragic potentialities of
medieval and Tudor drama and of the organizing and shaping
principles by which dramatists over a period of time began to
give their work tragic form. Since the nature of mature tragedy
in the high Elizabethan period has been comprehensively studied
in recent years, it should be possible to search in earlier drama
for hints and signs of tragic characters, suggestions of tragic
emotion, embryonic patterns of tragic action, and to consider
whether there was sufficient continuity in the dramatic tradition
for such seeds to grow and develop. It should also be possible to
pick out early examples of the shaping of material in a tragic
direction, in order to discover the how and why of such shaping
and whether the organizing principles themselves were derived
from the source stories, from the stage tradition, or from theoretical discussion.

Such a search backwards into the uncompounded elements of
tragedy will be difficult unless we have an agreed definition or
description of the nature of tragedy. A number of philosophers

and critics have attempted to define the tragic vision of life and the nature of the tragic experience within the drama, and yet there is little agreement. If one tries to formulate a description of tragedy based upon a selection of common qualities that a number of 'classic' tragedies possess, there are other difficulties. These common qualities may be the result of similar social and intellectual pressures acting upon dramatists, actors, and audiences at different periods in the history of western civilization, or they may be the result of a strong literary tradition—Greek tragedy acting upon Seneca, Seneca upon the Elizabethans, both Greeks and Romans exerting their influence upon the French tragedians, and all of these acting upon the moderns. Yet one cannot be sure that the common qualities, so laboriously analysed, are as important as the unique qualities of individual plays. The description of tragedy which follows is pragmatic rather than philosophical, being based upon the common qualities of a number of tragedies and the arguments of several critics who agree on essential points.[1] It is a description which will need to be tested by the particular material of our study.

Tragedy is an intense exploration of failure and suffering in human existence, and frequently also of the destructive impulses which cause suffering. This much will be acknowledged by almost everyone, since without intensity of feeling the power of tragedy in the theatre disappears. In terms of the plot or fable which sets up the situation to be explored, tragedy may be described as a confrontation with destiny. It concentrates upon a series of events leading to disaster, and portrays one or several individuals caught in a process from which there is no escape, once it has been set in motion. Usually this series of events is the result of a clash between human will and some superior law, which is called the will of God, the power of destiny, fortune, or simply natural law, a process of cause and effect. The conflict and the resulting defeat of human purpose can seldom be simplified into moral terms except in the naïve forms of tragedy: human will may be evil, deceived, or apparently innocent and

---

[1] I have been particularly influenced by Willard Farnham, *The Medieval Heritage of Elizabethan Tragedy*; Northrop Frye, *Anatomy of Criticism*; H. D. F. Kitto, *Greek Tragedy*; and Clifford Leech, *Shakespeare's Tragedies*.

good, but in every instance it places itself at the mercy of a train of events which cannot be reversed to the initial point of freedom.[2] A sense of tragic inevitability seems to be common to tragedies from every period and is a part of the haunting spirit of doom which reflects both the courage and the madness of man. The universe or the world also has this atmosphere of doom, forcing tragic choices upon men and driving them to disaster when they have made some error or some gesture of rebellion.

The confrontation with destiny comes about because of some deliberate decision by an individual human being, apparently freely made. The central character of a tragedy may himself choose a course of action, in blindness or ignorance, which is doomed to be fatal, or he may be forced by the actions of another to become involved in a similar process. He chooses a course of action because a crisis faces him in his life and because he is a passionate human being who cannot accept the situation with resignation. Though prophets give warning and cautious friends advise prudence, he is provoked to extreme action, to the risk of life itself, by the great need or desire that fills him, or in reaction against what oppresses him. Here is the essential humanity of tragedy.

I have talked about the central character of a tragedy as the prime source of tragic action and hence of tragic emotion. But there may be two or three major characters in a tragedy, each pursuing his own fatal course, in isolation from the others, or in collision with them. There may also be subordinate characters acting as foils to the main characters, or, in a sense, as extensions of their consciousness, though without the same burden of responsibility. The complexity of tragedy depends upon such interrelationships. However, for the purpose of this definition, I shall continue to speak about the 'central character' of a tragedy as the main embodiment of tragic purpose and emotion.

One of the striking qualities of tragedies from different cultures is the isolation of the central character from his family or his society, an isolation that may be apparent at the beginning of the play, as it is in *Hamlet* or the *Antigone*, but more often develops slowly and powerfully during the course of the action. The

[2] Northrop Frye, *Anatomy of Criticism*, p. 212.

emphasis in classical tragedy and in much Elizabethan tragedy upon the greatness of the tragic hero strongly suggests an anthropological background of the leader sacrificed or cast out of society for his defiance of the gods, which is secretly to be admired for its courage, but feared and publicly condemned for its blasphemy. However, this is by no means the only possible kind of tragic hero, even though it may provide the basis for tragic isolation; the central character may be stubborn and weak, maliciously cunning, or pathetically victimized, and still suffer a similar kind of isolation.

From the point of view of society, those who refuse to accept things as they are, or who attack the normal continuity of society as a disruptive force, deserve to be punished, whether their intentions are noble or evil. From the point of view of the tragic hero, the demands of society are wrong and must meet the headlong assault of the brave or defiant individual. Beyond both of these, in Elizabethan tragedy as in Greek tragedy, is an unchanging law which ensures that error reaps its proper reward and that human purpose is frustrated by its egocentric demands. The isolation of the tragic figure does not mean that he has been wrong and the social group right, but simply that some kind of disorder has been recognized, which must be rectified either in him or through him.

The emotional effect of tragedy, though a powerful experience under special conditions in the theatre, is difficult to analyse, and most critics have had recourse either to Aristotle's catharsis of pity and fear or to some variation upon this. It is clear that we shall not be moved by a tragic crisis or confrontation unless the figures caught up in it are characters with whom we can feel some sympathy, not only as persons like ourselves, but also as characters capable of representing humanity in a wider sense and capable of triumph or suffering. Classical tragedy, medieval narrative tragedy, and much Elizabethan tragedy resemble one another in their concentration upon large central characters who are representative because they are leaders or rulers and can thus take others' burdens upon themselves. They also possess largeness of soul as a corollary of their very greatness and nobility. In classical and Elizabethan tragedy they are given a splendid means for the expression of feeling in the rhetoric of poetry. Characters of lesser stature in Elizabethan domestic tragedy gain their effect through their closeness to average human nature, though they are not denied the ability to feel deeply, nor a degree of eloquence.

What is characteristic of the emotional pattern of a major tragedy is a gradually increasing tension as the action proceeds, which cannot be relieved until the catastrophe is complete. 'Suspense' is an inadequate term to describe the tension, since in almost every tragedy it is deliberately made clear from an early point what the outcome is likely to be. Undoubtedly, fear or terror is one part of this emotional experience, fear at the spectacle of human will in conflict with some larger force whose power it cannot or will not recognize. Pity, too, will be a powerful emotion, especially if there is any hint of innocence in the central character or a sense of nobility undermined or corrupted. Both pity and fear reflect the close involvement of the audience in the tragic situation. The tension is made endurable only because there is some slight degree of detachment in the audience as it recognizes the necessity of what is happening and perceives with a sense of irony the responsibility of the character in bringing such a fate upon himself.

As the tragedy moves toward catastrophe, the interplay of emotion grows stronger, because of the enormous contrast between human aspiration on the one hand and the certainty of its overthrow on the other. Such tensions are relieved suddenly and completely at the moment of catastrophe, as everything that was foreshadowed and feared comes to pass and struggle is at an end. The emotional resolution is usually something more than the relief of tension, the purging of the emotions: there may be an element of exaltation if the tragic experience reveals the courage and endurance of the human spirit under adversity. This form of resolution is regarded as morally superior to others which mingle relief of tension with irony, pessimism, or despair, but the latter emotions cannot be excluded, since they may be more appropriate than exaltation to the emotional structure of an individual tragedy. The emotional effect of a great tragedy is a complex whole to which many different elements in the play contribute. The fierce energy of the passions aroused in the course of the action are always matched by some measure of control, which keeps them in a state of precarious balance and leads to their resolution.

I am aware of some of the inadequacies of this description of tragedy and there are doubtless others of importance that I have not recognized. Nevertheless, it may serve its purpose as a basis for exploration into the impulses that made tragedy possible on the Elizabethan stage and gave it its various forms. I shall not be so much concerned with the history of tragic motives like love, ambition, and revenge as with the appearance in early drama of confrontations between human will and superior law and with the powerful emotions arising out of such confrontations. I shall also need to consider ideas about tragic experience which had some currency at the time and which may have had some influence on the shaping and direction of tragic material.

Well-defined ideas about the nature and form of tragedy were slow to appear, apart from the traditional categories handed down by the grammarians and rhetoricians. But, undoubtedly, from an early period there were certain reasons for the choice of serious, violent, uncomfortable, or seemingly painful subject-matter, and in combination with such choice there was often a typical and appropriate way of handling such material. At first the reasons for dramatizing serious subjects were primarily didactic, and it will be part of our task to study the transformation of such didactic material into tragic patterns of action and emotion. There were other sources, too, for ideas about the nature of tragedy. Not only did the word 'tragedy' gain richly in associations as the works of Seneca and Euripides became more widely known, but the popular chronicles, legends, romances, and collections of *novelle* that contained tragic stories provided attitudes toward those stories which helped to shape them in a tragic direction when they were dramatized. The formative elements in early tragedy derived from a variety of sources, and operated in widely differing ways, according to the awareness or sensitivity of individual dramatists. It is through a study of such formative elements that we may expect to find out something about the different kinds of tragedy on the Elizabethan stage and why several varieties should have appeared at the same time.

Any consideration of the nature and meaning of tragedy in general must begin with the plays themselves. It may be that the study of the tragedies belonging to a single and well-documented tradition will have a particular value in determining by what means and in what different ways the tragic impulse grows to full expression.

I

THE CONFLICT WITH DIVINE ORDER

MEDIEVAL religious drama has been restored in recent years to a place of first importance in the development of Elizabethan drama. A number of studies have been built upon the massive foundations laid by Sir Edmund Chambers to show the continuity of the popular stage as a living tradition from the fourteenth to the sixteenth centuries. It is a tradition not so much literary as theatrical, depending upon methods of production, acting, and conventions of staging for its continuity rather than upon a growing body of texts. The popularity of the religious drama, its long life, and its direct influence upon the popular drama of Elizabethan England is no longer in doubt.

However, the influence of this religious drama upon later tragedy has received only qualified acceptance: the morality plays, it is said, had a direct connexion through the moral histories, but the mystery plays are unlikely to have had much influence of any kind. The fact that every incident with possible tragic connotations is eventually subordinated to the total scheme of redemption and triumph has led to a general rejection of the mystery plays as sources of tragic structure or feeling. By contrast, the connexion of the morality plays with tragedy has long been recognized, partly because of the freedom they displayed to develop away from abstractions toward concrete, historical *exempla*, partly because of what Willard Farnham has described as their increasing severity toward the end of their evolution, with emphasis upon the debasement of human life and upon despair and damnation rather than upon God's total plan of redemption. Nevertheless, it seems to me that the craft cycles ought to be considered just as seriously in any account of developing tragedy, even if their total framework is not tragic. Not only do they portray a universe where suffering and evil exist as facts of experience, but they portray them intensely and without consolation, at least in the dramatic moment of the individual play.

My brief consideration of the principles of tragic art made reference to the recurring conflict in tragedy between human will and a superior law which is either antagonistic to human will or remote and difficult to comprehend. The mystery plays are full of such conflict, though it must be admitted at once that the superior law is equated with the will of God, and that this will is assumed to be just in absolute terms. The various embodiments of human will acting in opposition to the divine will are the tyrants, from Pharaoh to Antichrist; the servants and soldiers who act as their agents and yet represent another brand of human iniquity; and thirdly, those who know good and yet choose evil— the great sinners, Lucifer, Cain, Judas, and, in a somewhat different category, Adam and Eve.

The tyrants are the most obvious examples of human will completely at odds with reality and doomed to failure. As they are usually portrayed, they are symbols of all the forces in the world opposed to good, incarnations of evil purpose, agents of God's enemy, Satan or Mahound. Their motives are not analysed except in terms of the pride of the kings of this world and hatred of God. Yet frequently there are signs of the imaginative recognition of an individual, as if to say that evil wears numerous forms and even tyranny is human in its variety. Pharaoh is not at all like Herod, and Herod is unlike Pilate. Moreover, the same tyrants, the Herods for example, differ considerably from one cycle to another. The Pilate of the Wakefield cycle is a forerunner of the cunning, self-announced villains of the chronicle plays, of Richard of Gloucester himself,[1] whereas the Pilate of the York cycle seems almost virtuous by comparison, though he is shrewd and worldly.[2]

How seriously should the tyrants be considered as symbolic figures representing the evil forces of the universe? There is, of course, evidence to suggest that the tyrants were melodramatic stage figures of considerable popularity and that they were sometimes played for comic effect, particularly on first entrance to a

---

[1] Pilatus: 'I am full of sotelty/ffalshed, gyll, and trechery. . . .', XXII, *The Towneley Plays*, ed. George England and A. W. Pollard, p. 243.

[2] XXXII, *York Plays*, ed. Lucy Toulmin Smith. See also Arnold Williams's discussion of the tyrant plays in *The Drama of Medieval England*, pp. 81–82.

scene. Nevertheless, the plays read in sequence suggest that these characters were overwhelmingly serious in their major effect, that they were intended as embodiments of man's inherent evil, his lust for power and his boundless cruelty. They arouse a sense of fear before the enormity of evil. This emotion reaches a high pitch of intensity because of the presence of the victims—the children of Bethlehem and Christ.

Our main problem is the relationship of the tyrant scenes in the craft cycles to the emotional and conceptual patterns of later tragedy. The tyrants are not in themselves tragic characters. There is no hint in their motivation of any aspiration with which an audience could sympathize, nor is there any of the tragic feeling which a broken hope or a savagely reversed aspiration can arouse. Yet the tyrant scenes do represent something quite fundamental to the tragic experience, since they picture in harsh terms the opposition of human will and human pride to a larger force that will inevitably defeat them. Because this human will is completely evil and the divine force completely good, the struggle between them is too directly moral to arouse any of the complex feelings of tragedy, but it remains a nucleus from which other elements can grow. It contains more than a hint of the struggle between human will and an implacable fate which later tragedy was to explore. When the motivation of the tyrant was elaborated in transitional moral histories like *Apius and Virginia* and *Cambises*, sympathy with, or at least interest in, the fate of the tyrant became a possibility, and the way lay open for the growth of tragic feeling in such tyrant plays as *Richard III*, *Tamburlaine*, and *Macbeth*.

Several of the tyrant scenes in the mystery cycles present the fearful, yet satisfying spectacle of pride and cruelty overwhelmed and punished, and in this spectacle lies some hint of a controlling idea of retribution fashioning and shaping an embryonic plot. The basic plot is an inevitable movement from pride towards failure and defeat. Sometimes this structure is merely suggested by the over-all force of the cycle; sometimes it is explicit within the individual scene itself. Thus it exists in the play of the downfall of Pharaoh, though the tyrant is left comparatively undeveloped.

Two of the Advent plays about Herod present the most complete patterns of retribution to be found in the craft cycles. In the Chester play the slaughter of the infants results in the death of one of Herod's own children, and Herod himself is punished by a horrifying and fatal disease. It is the Hegge play, however, that builds up the greatest contrast between the boastful pride of Herod and his approaching doom. During Herod's feast of celebration the allegorical figure of Mors appears and comments on the folly of the king's pride. Like certain morality plays on the Pride of Life theme, the scene is a dramatized *exemplum*, related to the parable of the man who wished to build greater barns for his rich harvest. But the sermon does not diminish the striking dramatic power of the scene in which Herod eats and drinks at his ease, while the sardonic figure of Death stands in the background, waiting to strike.

As we should expect, there is no complete plot worked out for any tyrant in the sequence of Passion plays, where the double climax must be the Crucifixion and the Resurrection. Retribution is therefore by no means a dominating idea in the craft cycles as a whole. Slight, and dramatically unexpanded, in the play of Pharaoh, the moral pattern of crime and punishment is worked out thoroughly only in the Chester and Hegge plays of the *Slaughter of the Innocents* and in the York *Judas*. In these plays human will directed in enmity against the divine will is not simply represented as a fact of existence, but becomes part of a significant pattern of events leading to defeat and justified punishment.

It is worth remembering that the scenes we have been considering are focused as much upon the victims as upon the tyrants. The tyrant figures represent merely one half of the tyrant-victim or terror-pity combination. As forces standing out against God and all his works, the tyrants are representations of hideous evil, which attacks goodness in this world and demonstrates its power through torture and death. This is clearly a fallen world that is presented to us, a world where human will is often wrongly directed toward cruelty and destruction and is punished accordingly, but a world where the innocent too must suffer, simply because they are born into it. There will be justice for all eventually, but in the meantime, in the world of historical existence, there are tragic events and suffering that are part of the condition of man.

The tyrants are not the only representatives of human will set in opposition to divine will. In the same scenes we encounter their followers and servants, who portray human depravity at a lower level, without the power and self-conscious purpose of the tyrants, but with as much confidence in evil and joy in inflicting pain. The brutality of Herod's soldiers dragging the babies from the mothers of Bethlehem, the casual hardness of the soldiers of Pilate, Herod, and Caiaphas as they torture Christ—these are portrayed in far greater detail than the desire for pathos would seem to require. There is an attempt in such scenes to give expression to certain very harsh facts of experience. They represent the bestial elements in human nature, perhaps something more frightening than bestial—demonic forces which erupt in human nature in every generation. The wall paintings of the Passion scenes which survive in a few English churches portray similar figures, in which a malicious delight in evil is given a visual representation in coarse and degraded human features, and in a leer of the eye or a turning of the lip which is devilish rather than sub-human. Other examples may be found in medieval windows and tapestries, and particularly in a wide variety of carvings in wood and stone.[3]

As natural to fallen man is the comic element that creeps into some versions of the Slaughter of the Innocents, the boisterous delight in evil of Herod's soldiers, their boasting and their cowardice. But the general picture is a dark one. Here, at a level below that of the tyrants, is human will once more seeking its own way, oblivious of a higher power directing universal destiny. One is made strongly aware of human blindness in the face of a totally different scheme of things, which the participants refuse to recognize. The audience must take an ironic view of their self-confident and utterly human wrongness.

These minor characters, soldiers, servants, and other agents of the great tyrants of the mystery plays, are not important enough to the dramatic scheme to form part of a larger structure

[3] M. D. Anderson, *Drama and Imagery in English Medieval Churches.*

of retribution. Even as representatives of crude human will in opposition to providence, they do not play any very important part, and their main function lies in contributing to the atmosphere of a fallen world where brutality and suffering are commonplace. Their most striking descendants are the hired ruffians and murderers who torture gentle innocents and noble patriots in the chronicle plays. But the minor figures in many later tragedies who represent the base metal beneath the façade of human splendour could scarcely have had such a vivid existence without this background in the religious drama.

We have not yet considered the most striking and important examples of conflict between individual will and divine will: these occur mainly at the beginning of each cycle in the Fall of Lucifer, the Fall of Man, and what might be called the Fall of Cain. The only example later in the cycles of a similar conflict lies in the story of Judas. The religious reason for placing these stories at the beginning is obvious. Not only does the Biblical narrative begin in this way, but they serve to explain the necessity for the whole universal drama to follow, of Sin, Incarnation, Redemption, and Last Judgement.

Lucifer, Adam and Eve, Cain, and Judas are alike in setting up their own wills in opposition to God's will. They are all involved in a similar progress of action from a state of blessedness or innocence, with an awareness and experience of the good, to a state of sin, frustration, and despair. Their plays differ from the plays we have been considering heretofore in that they show the whole process of choice, and hence of responsibility, so that the suffering and remorse at the end come as the inevitable consequence of choice. I have no wish to obscure the marked differences between these plays by a series of generalizations, but I believe they have certain features in common which grow out of religious conceptions governing the cycles as a whole. The action of each scene is a temptation and fall, the defeat of the individual will in its struggle with the divine will. Characterization is not developed very far, but far enough to reveal a particular fault or sin which provides the motivating force for the rebellion of the individual: pride, ambition, envy, greed. Because of their knowledge of the good and the warnings they have received against evil, the central characters must accept responsibility for their falls, and in their remorse, blame themselves. Characterization goes far enough, therefore, to permit self-knowledge. The emotional patterns of these plays move from over-confidence and pride (which arouse the ironic sense in an audience) to despair and remorse (which may arouse pity). The endings are completely harsh, set against a background of eternal damnation, with the exception of the Fall of Man plays, where the harshness is modified by hope of eventual forgiveness.

The Fall of Lucifer is the beginning of evil in the universe, and is therefore given considerable stress at the beginning of each cycle. This is the primal example of individual will in opposition to God's will; the conflict is the more awe-inspiring because of Lucifer's greatness before his fall and because of the extent of his blasphemy. One may observe some of the typical elements of medieval tragedy: magnificence of place, supreme confidence in the face of warnings, and a catastrophic fall into misery and remorse, though it is direct providential intervention rather than fortune which brings about the fall. There are variations upon this basic pattern in the different cycles. In the Hegge play there is no actual moment of temptation: at the end of a hymn of worship and praise Lucifer demands that it be directed to him as the worthiest of all. In the York play, however, Lucifer is not immediately evil but undergoes a process of self-temptation as he meditates upon his own brightness and beauty. It is the Chester play that is the most striking of the four in its portrayal of a dramatic conflict of wills. In the dialogue with Lightborne, one of his followers, and in the debate with the other angels, Lucifer becomes more and more outspoken in his pride, until he utters the final blasphemy, proclaims himself greater than God, and ascends the divine throne. His language now attempts to take on the majesty appropriate to the speech of God, but he is suddenly and swiftly cast down to Hell.

The writers of these plays picture the fall of Lucifer as the greatest of all possible tragic falls, from supreme bliss into the darkest depths of misery and pain. Afterwards there is remorse, despair, recrimination, as the devils curse one another and think of revenge. In the York play it is the loss of his own beauty that afflicts Lucifer most intensely, but in all of them the loss of the bliss of Heaven is important. An unusual note in the Chester play is the expression of God's sorrow at the fall of Lucifer, his complaint against pride, and his disclaimer of any wish that it should have happened in this way.

There is undoubted tragic potentiality in these scenes as the great conflict between aspiration and destiny moves to its inevitable close. The pride of Lucifer is ironically turned into complete defeat, his surpassing beauty into ugliness and darkness. In expressing Lucifer's bitter remorse and sense of loss the writers of the mystery plays were at least in some degree aware of the contrast between aspiration and defeat that later generations were to call tragic. Of course, the theological implications are absolutely clear, and there is no doubt of the justice of God or of the necessity of Lucifer's punishment: one does not expect any intermixture of sympathy or pity in the emotional pattern. But the element of fear and the sense of loss remain important factors that the writers of these plays were endeavouring to express.

A similar conflict between individual will and divine will exists in the Fall of Man plays in all the cycles. Adam and Eve are very different from Lucifer as tragic prototypes: their sin is not so extreme in its blasphemy, nor are they self-tempted to the same degree, since part of the blame must be placed on the wiles of a cunning enemy. Though they cannot be as 'heroic' as Lucifer in their rebellion and though their fall cannot have the same grandeur and terror, they have the advantage (for drama) of their humanity, with all its possibilities for human sympathy.

The Fall of Man plays are remarkably alike, so that it is possible to speak of them as if they were a single play. The process of temptation is longer than in the Fall of Lucifer, and more interesting dramatically, since several characters are involved and there are two stages in the temptation. The nature of the temptation is made very plain: if they eat of the fruit of the tree they will become as gods in their knowledge of good and evil. Yet in the moment of aspiration they are aware of the fact that they are disobeying God's direct command, that they are setting their own wills in opposition to God's will. Recognition and the full awakening to the meaning of sin comes when Adam has eaten the apple: at once they are filled with shame and remorse, before God has spoken to them and before the nature of their punishment has been revealed. The great goal they sought is not only far different from what they expected, but terrifying. The tragic irony of their situation is made explicit in God's words to them in the Chester play:

> Thou wouldeste knowe bouth weale and woe,
> Nowe is yt fallne to thee soe,
> Therfore, hense thou muste goe,
> And thy desyer fulfilled. . . .[4]

There are two points I should like to make about the conclusion of this play within the framework of the larger cycle. First, the suffering which results from the struggle between human will and divine will is not merely a physical punishment imposed upon them by God and enforced by the angels: it is even more strikingly an inward suffering as they realize their great loss and their own responsibility. Secondly, several of the Fall of Man plays end without any direct expression of consolation. The audience is aware of the pattern of the whole cycle, of the Redemption of Man and Christ's removal of the dread punishment of death, but this tremendous hope lies outside the scenes I have been speaking of and they end on a note close to despair.

In the Chester cycle Cain's murder of Abel follows at once as a kind of tragic corollary of the Fall. Adam warns his sons to obey God and tells them of his dream of the Redemption to come. Yet we are now in the world of tragic experience, as the fatal quarrel between Cain and Abel makes evident. Adam and Eve return to the stage to lament the death of one son and the damnation of the other as part of their continuing punishment.

There is, perhaps, a more intense expression of despair in the Hegge play than in any other. Eve in her misery can only beg Adam to kill her:

> Alas! alas! and wele away,
> That evyr towchyd I the tre
> I wende as wrecche in welsom way,
> In blake busshys my boure xal be.

---

[4] *The Chester Plays*, ed. Thomas Wright, vol. i, p. 33.

In paradys is plentē of pleye,
ffayr frutys ryth gret plentē,
The gatys be schet with Godys keye,
My husbond is lost because of me.
Leve spowse now thou fonde,
Now stomble we on stalk and ston,
My wyt awey is fro me gon,
Wrythe on to my necke bon
With hardnesse of thin honde.[5]

Adam comforts her as best he can and the scene ends on a note of resignation, though without hope or consolation. Here, as in the other examples I have referred to, a fundamental tragic pattern is evident, of human aspiration in conflict with divine law, and leading to defeat, remorse, and suffering. It does not seem possible to me to understand the tension between despair and resignation in Elizabethan tragedy without some awareness of the strength of these qualities in the religious drama.

The Cain and Abel plays provide us with another striking illustration of the same theme, though with greater variations than are to be found in the preceding plays. The two main characters are almost extreme examples of the two possibilities of human existence, obedience and disobedience, submission to the divine will and rebellion against it. Cain is like Lucifer, Adam, and Eve in desiring to follow his own will, though well aware of the divine injunctions. The whole situation is on a more human level, however, since the warnings against disobedience come from fellow human beings, his parents and his brother, rather than directly from God. More important, his rebelliousness is not some great ambition or aspiration to be like God, but simply irritation with his lot, grumbling envy, and at length sufficient anger to lead him to murder.

This emphasis on Cain's ordinary human situation is perhaps the reason for the strong secular element in the York and Wakefield versions, where Cain's comic servant plays a part disruptive of tragic feeling. Nevertheless, the writer of the Wakefield play has developed the character of Cain so fully that it becomes the first major portrait of a human being in the cycle. In the long

---

[5] *Ludus Coventriae*, ed. J. O. Halliwell, pp. 31–32.

dialogue with Abel his motives are revealed, his complaining nature, and the sources of his growing anger. But this full-scale portrait exists not only for its human reality: it is also developed as a representation of natural human stubbornness and greed, so that the rebelliousness of his will against God's becomes a type of human rebellion in general.

The Hegge cycle, which has very little to say about the fall of Lucifer, considerably expands the Cain-Abel episode and makes it into a tragic scene almost as powerful as the Fall of Man play immediately before. The quarrel scene is carefully built up toward an impressive climax and the characters of the brothers are sketched in lightly but effectively. Cain is annoyed by Abel's insistence on the necessity of a sacrifice and calls Abel fool for tithing of his best. When Cain's sacrifice will not burn, Abel displays a little unholy delight and reminds Cain that he should have chosen the best of his grain for the sacrifice. Cain's anger, which has been growing steadily, breaks loose at this point and leads directly to murder. After the murder, Cain's despair is genuine and is passionately expressed: he is a condemned soul. We are presented with the Fall of Man all over again, this time in terms of rivalry, envy, anger, and murder, which are concrete facts of human experience. The writer has deepened the religious meaning of the episode and gained dramatic effectiveness at one and the same time. The tragic germ lies in the passage of Cain's proud and rebellious spirit into passionate anger and thence into passionate despair which is understandable because of the depth of anger that preceded it. It lies also in the pathos of a victim caught up undeservedly in a violent situation from which he cannot escape. We have moved into a fallen world, where innocence and even positive virtue are no guarantees of security and where men may suffer at any time because of the human condition.

The play of Lamech or Lameth is a rare one in European cycles generally, and most probably it had no influence upon the development of tragic ideas or feeling. Yet its mere presence in the Hegge cycle shows how such a story could be interpreted in the fourteenth century in terms of metaphysical implications rather than of any individual moral lesson. It is a strange story of a curse which comes upon a blind man who does not seem to deserve the malicious trick fortune plays upon him. Lameth is characterized as an old, blind hero, proud of his ancient reputation as a hunter and bowman. In memory of former times he takes his bow and asks the boy who is leading him to set the arrow at a mark, some animal or bird. The boy aims at something skulking in the bushes. When Lameth shoots, he kills Cain. He realizes that God's curse upon the slayer of Cain has come upon him, and in his anger and despair he kills the boy who has directed the fatal arrow. In a sense this scene completes the story of Cain, and no doubt it was intended for that purpose. Yet the fate of Lameth is also important for the duration of the brief scene. His impulsive desire to display once more his prowess with the bow has none of the features of direct rebellion against divine will that characterize Cain's actions. He is blind and ignorant of the consequences of his act; yet he comes into conflict with destiny and must suffer accordingly. His fate and the boy's belong to the realm of tragic experience, however little the tragic implications are developed.

Judas is a character who must have made a far greater impact on the audiences of the day than Lameth or even Cain, because of his central place in the great drama as the betrayer of God. Though there is obviously room in his story for a tragic pattern of temptation, fall, and despair, his particular destiny could scarcely receive much attention in the midst of the stronger feeling and transcendental importance of Christ's Passion. In the Wakefield, Chester, and Hegge cycles, the fatal destiny of Judas is lost in the larger story, at least in the forms in which these cycles have come down to us. The York play about Judas is the most complete in that there is dramatic stress upon his motivation, the act of betrayal itself, and his later remorse. Judas is by no means a heroic rebel against the divine will nor even a strong-minded enemy of the good. As the play presents him, he is covetous, mean, and ignorant of all the larger implications of his actions. The legendary motive of covetousness is enlarged upon in a soliloquy where we discover that Judas will sell his master for 30 pence because such would have been his share had Mary Magdalene's ointment been sold for 300 pence.

Judas' efforts to obtain a petty revenge reach their climax in his bland betrayal of Jesus in the garden, but his triumph soon reveals itself as a disaster. Judas' first repentance is comparatively slight: he returns to Pilate to beg for Jesus' life, hoping to undo what he has done. But the taunts he receives gradually force him to a recognition of the truth—that he cannot buy back what he has sold. He is compelled to recognize that he has betrayed a trust when Pilate laughs at him for suggesting that he should become Pilate's bondman. Though the motivation of Judas may appear crude and naïve, there is no lack of subtlety in the scene as a whole. As it progresses, Judas moves from servility to anger and cursing, from uncertain hope to complete despair. It is then that he faces the full weight of his treachery and knows that he must hang himself. If a *Suspensio Judae* has been lost from the York cycle, the pattern was originally complete.

In summary, we may say that the Judas play represents the struggle and failure of a man who commits a terrible crime to gain a petty revenge and finds that revenge turn to bitter gall in the remorse that overcomes him. It is thus more elaborate in its development than the Cain type of play. However, one should not go too far in describing the Judas play as an early tragedy: such was not the intention of the medieval writer, nor is it the effect that the play produces. There is a pettiness and meanness about the character of Judas which prevents the development of tragic passion, and the legendary motive of covetousness, even when supported by a strong sense of grievance and a desire for revenge, is not big enough to give the story of his fall significance or dignity. Yet the tragic germ is there, none the less, in the struggle of human will against the supreme will which it refuses to recognize, and in the vivid realization of an irreversible damnation.

Though the total dramatic scheme of the mystery cycle is a divine comedy, almost all the scenes take place within a fallen world. In this world, whose nature is quickly revealed to us in *The Fall of Man* and *Cain and Abel*, human will is encouraged by ignorance and sin, a desire for some partial good or false reward, to stand out against divine will. Yet such a struggle leads to eventual damnation in the next world, and frequently to mental anguish and physical suffering in this. The divine will against which man struggles at his peril is more clearly defined and more easily discernible than the background of universal law in Renaissance tragedy: yet they are alike in arousing a sense of tragic inevitability.

The religious certainty that God's universe is a just one and that virtue will eventually be rewarded and vice punished is a basic assumption behind the mystery cycles, since the inevitable conclusion for each cycle is the Last Judgement. However, there is quite a powerful sense of a tragic world in the meantime where prosperity and suffering have little relation to merit. In that world innocents are tortured and murdered and evil men triumph: the suffering of pathetic victims like the mothers of Bethlehem, the children, and Christ himself seems to contradict every conception of the moral law, and outrages human feeling, in spite of the assurances of a higher law which will eventually make everything right.

The play of *Abraham and Isaac* contains in miniature the divine comedy of the whole cycle, in which the tragic moment is swallowed up in a final triumph. Yet the suffering of Abraham and Isaac is undoubtedly real during the time of their doubt and fear. That this was recognized as the tragedy of innocence in a fallen world can be noted in the recollections of the scene in later plays like *Cambises* and *Apius and Virginia*, where the eventual consolation and triumph are much more distant.

The pathos of innocent suffering in *Abraham and Isaac* is one of the most intense emotional moments in the cycles, and obviously requires further consideration in relation to other scenes where emotions associated with tragedy occur. The tension of opposed emotions, so characteristic of Elizabethan tragedy, is rare in the mystery plays. Only in the *Fall of Man* is there a hint of the complex emotional pattern of later tragedy: pity fused with the recognition that Adam and Eve have brought doom upon themselves in spite of clear warnings, that the whole catastrophe must follow inevitably upon Eve's first slight inclining of her ear toward Satan. Our emotional involvement with Lucifer, Cain, and Judas is much less, and hence the element of pity is very weak in comparison with the fear we may experience in recognizing the extent of their defiance of God and our detached satisfaction in their punishment. In other scenes the strong effects of pity and fear are distinguished from each other and focused upon separate individuals, pity upon Abel, the children of Bethlehem, and Christ, fear upon Herod and his soldiers, Caiaphas, the second Herod, and Pilate.

One other element inherited by Elizabethan tragedy from the medieval drama—from craft cycles and from morality plays alike—should be referred to at this point, since it links emotional effect with metaphysical idea. Critics have for long been aware of the mixture of comic and serious action in the mystery plays and have tried to explain the existence of these sometimes incongruous strains in a variety of ways, though generally in terms of the gradual loss of control over the plays by the ecclesiastical authorities. A. P. Rossiter has declared that the 'devilish gusto' of torturers and tyrants, so closely bound up with the agony of their victims, is evidence of two rituals, one of which denies the other—and hence the faith of the cycles as a whole.[6] Allied to the ritual of evil, of cruelty and negation, is a kind of mockery and derision which, Rossiter claims, is descended from the Joculator and the 'comic rejoicings of the folk'. This latter spirit may seem entirely comic, but it is often destructive in its effect, because it is a parody, even a demonic parody, of the serious action.

As a qualification of this point of view something might be said of the medieval craftsman's search for realism and a contact with the world around him, whether it be in sculpture, painting, or drama. Thoroughly aware of the meanness and cruelty of human nature, he did not try to falsify it, nor did his religion ask him to hide it. Though a simple artist, he was probably aware also that the more he stressed the cruelty of those who tortured Christ, the greater would be the pity for the suffering victim. Where we possess early and late versions of the same plays, it is apparent that much of the development has been in this direction or for this purpose.

Yet when this has been said, and when allowance has been

[6] A. P. Rossiter, *English Drama from Early Times to the Elizabethans*, p. 70.

made for the playwright's delight in portraying the trivial and comic concerns of human beings, it must be admitted that not everything has been accounted for. There is a strange spirit in this drama, which is reflected also in the wall paintings and stone carvings of the time. It is said to appear strikingly in the religious drama of Germany and Austria. The English craft cycles are never dominated by this Gothic spirit, any more than the parish church at Winchcombe is dominated by its gargoyles, but some clash of tones is evident.

The episode of Garcio and Cain in the Wakefield play, *The Killing of Abel*, adds an incongruous element to the scene of Cain's despair. Cain's tiff with the angel in the York version is comic enough to have a similar result. In the Hegge play, *The Trial of Joseph and Mary*, the Detractors are so lewd and mocking in their jests and accusations that the purity of Mary is nearly forgotten. And in the Digby *Killing of the Children* Herod's timorous knight, Watkyn, destroys utterly the pathos of the scene. By contrast, the various Noah plays are humorous only in a homely and familiar way and the comedy does no great harm to the religious theme. Even the parody of the Nativity in *The Second Shepherds' Play* is comparatively innocent in effect because the spirit of comedy in the play is so genial and so closely related to normal human nature.

Apparently the comic and realistic scenes which undermine the emotional effect and religious meaning of certain parts of the cycles belong to the later enlargement of the cycles; some of them were undoubtedly added for the entertainment they provided and can have no other justification. The devilish gusto of the scenes of cruelty, however, cannot be explained away by such terms as secularization and degeneration. Though perhaps intensified by later redactors (as in the Wakefield cycle), they seem to have formed a part of the cycles from an early period and to represent something essential in the medieval artist's view of humanity. Whether part of the religious vision of the plays or outside it, that dark view of the depths of evil in the human heart, evil easily released and immeasurable in its effect, is one of the most striking products of the medieval mind. The combination of this dark vision with the destructive ridicule of the fool, the rustic, or the evil detractor forms an important contribution to later tragedy.

What is clear from a close study of the mystery cycles is that the medieval dramatists had learned to do certain things most effectively. They were not attempting to write tragedy, but in the process of representing scenes of suffering and despair, always within the total religious structure, they gave to the dramatic tradition scenes which could be imitated and developed in a tragic direction by later secular dramatists. What was once learned well by the medieval stage did not have to be learned again, and this dictum applies not only to the conventions of acting and staging which have been widely discussed in recent years but also to dramatic situation and characterization. I have pointed out certain scenes of quite exceptional emotional power, not far removed from tragic feeling. These scenes influenced later dramatists because they became part of the language of stage representation.

Let us consider the way in which some of these dramatic situations or episodes have relevance for later tragedy. One example is the pathetic struggle of the innocent and weak against brutal power which on the surface appears to rule the world. The three Marys in early liturgical drama, and Abel, the mothers of Bethlehem, and Christ in the craft cycles, express this struggle in different ways. When later writers chose to represent the cruelty of tyrants and the miseries of the weak, they could scarcely avoid the notable models already familiar to wide audiences. The terror, the pathos, and the anger which fill the scene of Cambises' shooting of Praxaspes' young son are close to the emotional power of the *Slaughter of the Innocents*. I am not trying to prove a direct descent through the evidence of verbal echoes, but I think the placing of such scenes side by side will confirm my view that playwrights built on what had already been achieved and did not have to learn certain dramatic lessons over again. In addition, and more important for our purpose, the serious intensity of such scenes was carried over from the religious to the secular drama.

The first two passages from the mystery cycles are direct evocations of misery and despair, strongly arousing the emotion of pity, though there is also anger and a demand for vengeance:

> *Prima faemina.* Longe lullynge have I lorn!
> Alas! qwhy was my baron born?
> With swappynge swerde now is he shorn
>   The heed ryght fro the nekke!
> Shanke and shulderyn is al to-torn,
> Sorwyn I se behyndyn and beforn,
> Both mydnyth, mydday, and at morn,—
>   Of my lyff I ne recke.
>
> *Secunda faemina.* Serteynly I say the same,
>   Gon is alle my good game,
>   My lytylle childe lyth alle lame,
>   That lullyd on my pappys!
>   My ffourty wekys gronynge
>   Hath sent me sefne yere sorwynge,
>   Mykyl is my mornynge,
>   And ryght hard arne myn happys![7]
>
> Outt! morder! man, I say
> strang tratoure & thefe!
> Out! alas! and waloway!
> my child that was me lefe!
> My luf, my blood, my play
> that neuer dyd man grefe!
> Alas, alas, this day!
> I wold my hart shuld clefe
>   In sonder!
> veniance I cry and call,
> on herode and his knyghtys all!
> veniance, lord, apon thaym fall,
>   And mekyll warldys wonder![8]

In the following passage from *Cambises* one can see that pathos is aroused by the same means—the joy of the mother turned to grief, the long burden of child-bearing become a mockery—and, once again, the grief is mingled with anger:

> With blubred eies into mine armes from earth I wil thee take
> And wrap thee in mine apron white, but oh my heauy hart:
> The spiteful pangs ẏ it sustains, wold make it in two to part.

7 *Ludus Coventriae*, p. 182.
8 XVI, *Towneley Plays*, p. 177.

The death of this my Sonne to see, O heuy mother now:
That from thy sweet & sugred ioy, to sorrow so shouldst bow.
What greef in womb did I retain, before I did thee see?
Yet at the last when smart was gone, what ioy wert thou to me.
How tender was I of thy food, for to preserue thy state?
How stilled I thy tender hart, at times early and late?
With veluet paps I gaue thee suck, with issue from my brest:
And danced thee vpon my knee, to bring thee vnto rest.
Is this the ioy of thee I reap (O King) of tigers brood?
Oh tigers whelp hadst thou ẏ hart, to see this childs hart blood.[9]

The literary elaboration is hardly an improvement upon the intensely dramatic speech of the craft cycle plays, but it is clear that the emotional patterns are intended to be similar.

In later plays, the murder of innocent children and the mourning of mother or father is a familiar situation. That such murders could take place on stage, like young Rutland's murder by Clifford in *3 Henry VI*, is itself an indication of the continuity of the tradition. It is true that the murder of the young princes in *Richard III* takes place off stage, but the vivid report of the murderers is very close to actual representation. In the speeches of mourning, too, one often catches an echo of earlier plays in the same tradition. York's lament for Rutland, for example, suggests the last few lines of the mother's lament in *Cambises*, quoted above:

O tiger's heart wrapp'd in a woman's hide!
How couldst thou drain the life-blood of the child,
To bid the father wipe his eyes withal,
And yet be seen to bear a woman's face?
(*3 Henry VI*, I. iv. 137-40)

The pathos of suffering and the terror of unlimited power in an evil world are part of the heritage of later drama from the cycle plays.

There is another episode in the mystery cycles which is again mainly directed toward the emotion of pity: this is the play of Abraham and Isaac, in which emotional and dramatic power are concentrated upon the unbearable choice of the father and upon the pathetic situation of Isaac. In one of the most highly developed of these plays, the Brome *Abraham and Isaac*, there is a striking

---

[9] *Cambises*, Tudor Facsimile Texts, ed. J. S. Farmer.

use of dramatic irony in the opening passage, in which Abraham praises God for his happiness, and especially for his son, Isaac:

> In my age thou hast grantyd me thys,
> That thys yowng chyld with me shall wone;
> I love no-thyng so myche i-wysse,
> Except thin owyne selffe, der Fader of blysse,
> As Ysaac her, my owyne swete sone.[10]

The easy passage of such a scene into tragic irony is demonstrated in the opening lines of *Apius and Virginia*:

> *Virginius.* By the Gods wife I ioy me, that haue such a treasure,
> Such Gemme and such Iuell, surmounting all measure:
> Such a happy spouse, such a fortunate dame,
> That no blot or staine, can impayre her fame,
> Against such an Impe, and grasse of my tree,
> As cleare doth surmount all others that bee.[11]

At the moment of greatest tension and pathos in the Chester *Abraham and Isaac* the child bids his father to cease torturing him with delay and strike quickly, and begs him also to tie a kerchief about his head to cover his eyes. The scene is repeated in *Apius and Virginia*, though with greater potential feeling because the audience is aware that there is no last-minute reprieve for Virginia or her father. Unlike Isaac, Virginia is the victim of tyranny in a cruel and lust-ridden world, and in this respect she is like the victims of cruelty in other craft cycle plays. In many later plays on the popular stage the pathos of *Abraham and Isaac* is combined with the pathos and brutality of the *Slaughter of the Innocents*, so that the precocious and innocent child, the Isaac figure, faces the cruel murderers of the children of Bethlehem, or sometimes the tyrant himself, Herod transformed into Cambises. A few lines, again from the Chester cycle, will establish the moment of pathos that becomes a striking unit in the emotional pattern of *Cambises*:

> *Isaac.* Would God my mother were here with me!
> She would kneele downe upon her knee,
> Prainge you, father, if yt maye be
> For to save my liffe.[12]

· · · · ·

---

[10] 'Abraham and Isaac', ll. 11-15, *The Non-Cycle Mystery Plays*, ed. O. Waterhouse.
[11] *Apius and Virginia*, Malone Society Reprints, ll. 120-6.
[12] *The Chester Plays*, vol. i, p. 68.

> *Yong childe.* O Father, Father, wipe your face,
> I see the teares run from your eye:
> My mother is at home sowing of a band,
> Alas, deere father, why doo you cry?
> *King.* Before me as a mark now let him stand,
> I wil shoot at him my minde to fulfill:
> *Yong childe.* Alas, alas, Father wil you me kill?
> Good master king doo not shoot at me,
> my mother loues me best of all. . . .[13]

In similar scenes at a later date the part of the child facing torturers or murderers is more elaborate, but almost always it is developed in a way that recalls the part of Isaac in the mystery cycles. Arthur pleading with Hubert in *The Troublesome Reign* and in *King John*, the young king and his brother in *The True Tragedy of Richard III* striving to keep up their courage when in the hands of their enemies, Rutland pleading for his life from the bloodthirsty Clifford in *3 Henry VI*, and Pertillo facing the ruffians in *Two Lamentable Tragedies* are all recognizable descendants of Isaac. 'Descendants' perhaps implies a lineage I should not like to press too far in detail, but it is clear that the dramatic power of such scenes had become established and was being used to good effect in new kinds of dramatic structure, in chronicle plays, chronicle tragedies, and domestic tragedies.

The scenes of Christ's Passion are the most powerful, both as drama and in doctrinal force, in all the mystery cycles. Though unrepeatable in secular terms by their very nature, these scenes contain separable dramatic elements which could be used by later playwrights. Essentially, the Passion scenes represent an innocent victim with dignity and strength of spirit, suffering at the hands of brutal torturers and murderers who act under the orders of men of worldly power. Although the emphasis on innocence suggests pathos as the dominant emotion, the effect is a little more complex than this, since the victim has chosen a course of action knowing full well that it will bring him into conflict with the world. In his own person and office he gathers upon himself the hatred and antagonism of the world.

It is in the chronicle plays that we encounter characters and

---

[13] *Cambises*, Tudor Facsimile Texts.

situations that remind us of this heritage. Woodstock is the outstanding example of the virtuous man whose loyalty and integrity
gather together a storm of abuse and eventually bring about his
murder. The last scene of Woodstock's life, in which the ghosts
of the Black Prince and Edward III appear to him, may seem
quite remote from Christ's agony in the garden, and obviously
bears a closer relationship to the appearance of lamenting ghosts
in the *Mirror for Magistrates*. Nevertheless, the language is filled
with references to innocence and the protecting power of angels
and of heaven:

> I here remain
> A poor old man, thrust from my native country
> Kept and imprisoned in a foreign kingdom.   ·
> If I must die, bear record, righteous heaven,
> How I have nightly waked for England's good,.
> And yet to right her wrongs would spend my blood.
> Send thy sad doom, King Richard: take my life.
>
> (*Enter* LAPOOLE *and the* MURDERERS)
>
> I wish my death might ease my country's grief.
>   (*Woodstock*, V. i. 121–8)

The murder scene that follows takes us forcibly into the very
atmosphere and language of the Crucifixion scenes in the mystery
cycles. The contrast between helpless innocence and crude
brutality in the pay of sinister, worldly forces could scarcely be
more deliberately shocking. So that there can be no mistaking
the context in which the deed is done, the murderers call each
other names ('damned villain', 'hell-hound') which show their
full awareness of the nature of their crime and remind the
audience that this is an outbreak of hellish forces.

Humphrey of Gloucester in *2 Henry VI* is a character like
Woodstock, though much less is made of his death scene. Shakespeare turns our attention instead to the effect of the murder
upon Henry and his court and upon the Commons: a larger
pattern has taken precedence. Nevertheless, we cannot escape
the vision of 'murderous tyranny' which Henry sees in the eyes
of Suffolk immediately after Humphrey's death, nor the effect of
Humphrey's piety and innocence upon the murderers as they
escape from the death chamber. Henry himself, virtuous yet

helpless, the sad commentator upon the evils brought to his kingdom by warring ambition, is murdered in *Part 3* by Richard of Gloucester. Though Richard by this stage has already characterized himself as one who will 'set the murtherous Machiavel to school', and though there is much in him also of the cunning Vice of the moralities who delights in the evil he is able to commit, he is, as the murderer of Henry, related also to the Pilates and Herods of the mystery cycles.

> *Rich.* Think'st thou I am an executioner?
> *K. Hen.* A persecutor I am sure thou art.
> If murthering innocents be executing,
> Why, then thou art an executioner.
>
> (*3 Henry VI*, v. vi. 30–33)

One of the essential threads in the total pattern of these plays is the confrontation between evil, worldly power, and helpless innocence, a confrontation which leads on to the increasing horror of Richard's deeds in *Richard III* and the lamentation of the Queens for the deaths of husbands and children. We are constantly reminded of Henry, Rutland, the young Prince Edward, the Princes in the Tower, in the curses of the Queens upon the tyrant who blasphemes against nature and God in every act:

> A hellhound that doth hunt us all to death.
> That dog, that had his teeth before his eyes,
> To worry lambs and lap their gentle blood,
> That foul defacer of God's handiwork,
> That excellent grand tyrant of the earth
> That reigns in galled eyes of weeping souls. . . .
>
> (*Richard III*, iv. iv. 48–53)

It is a marvellous enlargement of the lamenting mothers of Bethlehem in their outcry against the cruelty of a fallen world.

Henry VI is both victim of the destructive forces of worldly ambition, and incipient rebel against those forces; although not a saint, he is a man of virtuous impulses with a gift for contemplation rather than action. There is the germ of tragic action in his aspiration and downfall. Edward II and Richard II are less like saints, and both display greater energy of rebellious self-will than Henry VI. Yet each of them is drawn at the end into a scene of very considerable pathos, in which their role as victim is stressed. When Marlowe reaches the penultimate scene of *Edward II*, he has brought the sympathy of the audience strongly to bear upon Edward, and presents his royal victim as one who is enduring outrage and torture with dignity and patience. The murder places the helplessness and relative innocence of the suffering victim in striking opposition to the brutal heartlessness of the ruffians and the power-worshipping worldliness of their master, Mortimer. Like Herod in the Chester cycle, Mortimer suffers a complete fall immediately after.

Shakespeare's portrait of Richard II is a complex one, but it has often been noted how he becomes increasingly the victim of power politics as the play proceeds, and more subtly, the sacrificial victim who must die in order to fulfil the destiny prepared for his country. There are several references in the latter scenes of the play to the Christ-like patience of Richard as he endures the jeers and insults of the mob, to the betrayal by Judas, to the helplessness of Christ before his judges, though these are modified by the interplay of different strands of feeling, since some of the images are Richard's own dramatization of his position and are linked by the audience with earlier, very clear statements of Richard's guilt. Richard is neither pure innocent nor complete sinner, but the more dominant strain toward the end is that of the anointed of God, helpless in terms of worldly power, suffering the cruelty of the world.

Richard's long soliloquy in the dungeon gains much of its force from the audience's awareness of the approach of the murderers. Though there is little connexion with Christ's Passion, the speech forms part of a religious pattern that affects the whole scene: the coming of a humble and loyal follower in secret to see his master's face; the striking down of the anointed king by several murderers; the fear of hell which overcomes Exton as soon as the deed is done; and the curse of Cain placed upon Exton by Henry IV when he comes to claim his reward. I think it must be admitted that the tragic conclusion of this play, as of *Edward II*, depends in some degree upon the emotional force and the structure of meaning of the Passion plays.

Among other scenes from the mystery cycles which had an

effect on serious drama of a later date, the tyrant plays were probably the most important. It is not difficult to find evidence that Herod and Pilate lived on in the popular memory as fierce, roaring tyrants, brutal and callous in their power, and impenitent in their crimes. There is a resemblance between these rulers and the King of the World figure who appears in *The Castle of Perseverance* and *Mundus et Infans* in that both are representations of the power in the world opposed to God. The worldly king of the morality plays, however, does not commit any brutal crimes: he is merely the ruler of the world of flesh and temptation.

Apius and Virginia is a product of both traditions, mystery cycle and morality play. In the emotions aroused by the conflict between tyrant and victim, and in the ultimate despair of the tyrant, we can see very clearly dramatic elements from the mysteries. They have been secularized, of course, but they have a religious basis which cannot be denied: the clash between innocence and evil, between helplessness and power, which is futile in a worldly sense and yet of the utmost importance in a transcendent universe. The divine justice which saves Virginius and condemns Apius at the end of the play is in miniature the final Judgement of the craft cycles. The debt to the morality play has long been recognized, particularly in the role of Haphazard, who is a traditional Vice. Bernard Spivack considers it a 'virtue play', carrying on the homiletic tradition of the morality play, though this has been diverted toward the secular themes of fortune, honour, and fame.[14] All this is true, but the fundamental characters, the dramatic situation, and the emotional pattern of the play are closer to *Abraham and Isaac* and *Herod the Great* than they are to the moralities.

Cambises provides us with an even more clearly defined example of a tyrant in the craft cycle tradition. Once more, elements of the morality play are present, particularly in the figure of Ambidexter and the role he plays throughout. But Cambises himself is much more the tyrant of the mystery plays than a worldly king in the Pride of Life tradition. He is arrogant in his power and in his freedom to do what he likes with his subjects, like Herod the very embodiment of this world's enmity

[14] Bernard Spivack, *Shakespeare and the Allegory of Evil*, p. 269.

against God. His history is a simple pattern of crime and punishment, and the punishment is God's vengeance rather than man's.
As in the Herod plays, there is a polarization of opposite emotions,
fear and pathos, the contrast between vicious cruelty and helplessness. Undoubtedly what had already been accomplished so
powerfully in religious drama lies behind the emotional effect of
this play.

It would be foolish to represent the many tyrants of Elizabethan drama simply as direct descendants of the tyrant figure
we have been discussing, even though the dramatic archetype
became well established, first in religious plays and then in
individual Biblical plays and moral histories on the popular
stage. There were too many contributions to tyranny and villainy
from too many different sources for a single tradition to retain
its purity: from Seneca, Thyestes and Nero; from propagandist
treatises and travellers' tales, Machiavelli; from Sir Thomas
More and the chronicles, Richard III; from contemporary
history and legend, Tamburlaine, Selimus, Muly Mahamet,
Alphonsus of Aragon, and other warrior-tyrants. The tyrant
was enlarged as a supreme embodiment of cruelty and power, or
as a figure of unexampled cunning and treachery, or as a creature
of passion and extravagant aspiration. There were even divided
characters, tyrants liable to attacks of conscience, like Solyman
in *Solyman and Perseda* or King John in *The Death of Robert,
Earl of Huntington*. Yet in all these variations upon the theme of
tyranny, playwrights, actors, and audiences seem to have moved
on reasonably familiar ground among conventions that maintained some degree of continuity from the original craft cycle
plays. The tyrant remained a boaster, using hyperbolic language
to express his actual power or his aspirations. He was unscrupulous, treacherous, and brutal, careless of the sufferings of
others and confident in his refusal to acknowledge any limits to
his own will. Above all, he continued to be a representative of
rebellious, demonic forces in the universe standing out in complete defiance against providential rule and moral law. The
religious background is implicit even in Marlowe's reversal of
the convention in *Tamburlaine*, and in other plays that followed it.

One might have expected that the theme of the last group of

mystery plays, the rebellion of an individual sinner against God and his eventual despair, would be the most influential of all upon later drama. In a sense it was, but in an indirect way, because this theme was taken over by the moralities and explored in a series of plays that continued well into the Elizabethan period. Adam is the first Everyman or Mankind, standing for the whole race of man and representative also in his proneness to sin. One remembers how Mankind at the beginning of *The Castle of Perseverance* and in *Mundus et Infans* enters as a helpless, naked creature, Adam once more, though suffering from the effects of Adam's fall.[15] Cain, Judas, and Lucifer, the more blasphemous rebels, may not have had any direct dramatic descendants, but they remained the common property of the dramatic imagination and occasionally provided vivid images of despair and remorse. Thus, in Thomas Lupton's play, *All for Money* (1570), when the damned appear out of Hell as a warning to the living, Judas is prominent among them:

Iudas commeth in like a damned soule, in blacke
painted with flames of fire, and with a fearful vizard. . . .[16]

And in *The Conflict of Conscience* (1581), an academic play by Nathaniel Woodes, the Judas theme lies close beneath the surface in the final scenes.

The actual debt of Elizabethan tragedy to the mystery plays was not the result of direct succession. Nevertheless, the debt exists, because the popular drama began to acquire many of its lasting characteristics in the late medieval period. There came into existence a large body of drama, widely played to great audiences, which dealt seriously with themes of tragic implication, such as the constant presence of evil in human life and its power to corrupt and destroy, and the suffering of helpless victims of ruthless power. In this drama one can observe several of the essential elements of tragedy, though enclosed still within a Christian framework of justice and mercy. Individual characters are free to obey or free to rebel against God and the divine law of the universe. But responsibility follows close upon free will,

---

[15] In *Mundus et Infans* Infans is born in sin, the result of Adam's fall, but he is naked and helpless as he faces his first temptation and in this respect reminds us of Adam.

[16] Thomas Lupton, *All for Money*, 1570.

so that those who disobey must take the consequences of their rebellion. The divine law against which the individual human will is prone to rebel is a superior order, not always apparent to the fallen world, but certain in its eventual operation. In the world the order that exists seems to lie under the power of evil. Evil is crude and vigorous with life, sometimes cruelly funny, but it is never explained away: the mystery of its control over life and the mystery of suffering remain potent forces in this drama.

In terms of form, medieval drama supplied a legacy of archetypal characters of general significance—the kings of the world acting as enemies of God, the sinners who deserted God and suffered remorse and punishment, and the innocent victims of the world's evil. Attached to these representative figures were situations, Biblical or legendary, also of doctrinal significance, but capable of generating strong emotions polarized in the directions of pathos and horror. Popular drama had been through these experiences during the fifteenth century, and had discovered means of exploiting them within the strict limits of the religious cycles. In the sixteenth century it was ready to accept wider ranges of experience and new forms of expression.[17]

[17] It is impossible to make a real assessment of the importance of the miracle plays of the saints and the apostles in the development of tragic themes and emotion, since the evidence has almost completely disappeared. The frequency of their performance in England, the range of their subject matter, their existence as individual plays or as parts of larger cyclic dramas are all matters of doubt. One can merely agree with Professor Craig (*English Religious Drama of the Middle Ages*, pp. 323 ff.) that a considerable number of such plays once existed and that they doubtless provided an important link between religious drama and later secular romantic drama. Such themes as temptation, fall, and repentance, or the heroic perseverance of a saint to the climax of martyrdom, were no doubt the recurring subjects, determining the structure of the action and the pattern of emotion. These plays may have influenced the 'virtue plays' of the children's theatre and the romantic biographical plays of the popular theatre, but beyond this we can scarcely go.

II

FRUITS OF REBELLION: THE MORALITY PLAY

THE morality plays have traditionally been regarded as far more important than either miracle or mystery plays in the development of Elizabethan drama, mainly because it is possible to trace a direct line of descent and illustrate a living dramatic tradition through a whole series of plays which still exist. This view is supported by the fact that late moralities appear in the records of plays presented at court; that there is independent evidence of the production of such plays quite widely in the kingdom, like the well-known account by R. Willis of *The Cradle of Security* in Gloucester,[1] and the description given of the repertory of the travelling players in the manuscript play of *Sir Thomas More*; and that the texts of many of them refer in familiar terms to the conditions of staging in great halls or in open spaces, and the give-and-take between actors and audience.[2] It must be admitted that the survival of so many morality plays is not in itself proof of the dominance of the moral tradition on the stage of the time, since many of the plays seem to have been printed because of the polemical or didactic interests of their authors, who were frequently churchmen or schoolmasters. Equally, the almost complete disappearance of miracle plays and of the early romantic drama is by no means an indication either of their triviality or of their lack of popular support. Nevertheless, the moralities retain a good deal of importance in the history of the drama, because of their obvious vitality, their ability to broaden their range of subject-matter and adapt formal qualities to new demands, and their continuing seriousness of purpose.

Our main concern is not to trace the development of the morality play throughout its long history but to try to discover

---

[1] Robert Willis, *Mount Tabor* (1639). Part of the passage is quoted by M. C. Bradbrook, *The Rise of the Common Player*, p. 126.

[2] D. M. Bevington, *From Mankind to Marlowe*, pp. 38-60.

what germs of tragedy existed in its early forms, and whether they remained dormant or grew large in the later development toward a secular drama. The fundamental theme of the morality play is the conflict between virtue and vice, between divine will and human will, and the consequences of human rebellion. It is generally acknowledged to have been derived from the Psycho-machia as it appeared in allegorical poetry and sermons of the age, the endless warfare between God and the Devil for the soul of man. If man chooses to follow his own way, as tempted by his passions and by the demonic forces lying in wait for him, he comes into direct conflict with the purpose and will of God and moves inevitably toward damnation. But in the early moralities there is always a final movement, through repentance, toward reconciliation with the will of God. There may, of course, be several turns or changes of direction in a single play before the final movement.

One element of our hypothetical tragic pattern seems to exist quite clearly in this generalized form, namely the rebellion of human will against some kind of superior law. This rebellion takes the form of a temptation and the deliberate choice of a course of action to suit the passions of the human individual; eventually, rebellion ends in a full recognition of the disastrous consequences of this choice. So far, the pattern is tragic in nature. However, even though the remorse may approach despair, the tragic development is halted. In some moralities the way back to grace from the low point of despair is treated as fully as the process of temptation and fall.

When the sinner confronts destiny in the form of the clear purpose of God, when he comes to recognize the fatal conse-quences of following his own will in defiance of destiny, there is room for depth of feeling and an approach to the agony implicit in any tragic recognition. This is a tragic moment in a larger structure which is not tragic. Not every morality takes advantage of this opportunity, but *The Castle of Perseverance* lays consider-able stress on the despair of the sinner. The structure of the play is an initial movement toward rebellion, a long movement of repentance and perseverance in virtue, a further rebellion under the temptations of Covetousness, and then the full burden of recognition at the coming of Death. Undoubtedly the intensity of feeling in Mankind's lament near the end is due to his recognition of the full extent of his guilt and the consequences of his rebellion. Scorned by his former companions, in despair over his sins, Mankind dies, and it is only in the epilogue that his soul finds forgiveness as the four Daughters of God determine his fate. The full tragic development of the theme is completed in this world; it is in the next world that it moves beyond tragedy. The audience has watched Mankind's pride and self-confidence in sin with a mixture of sympathy and ironic detachment (knowing the outcome better than Mankind can know it), and the moment of recognition arouses pity even though it fulfils expectation. However, in this play more than in any non-allegorical play of a later date, 'ironic detachment' can only be relative and limited, since the whole concentration of the play forces the action back upon the self of the spectator.

Other general moralities, both humanist and popular, pay less attention to the intense moment of conviction of sin and subsequent remorse and far more to the return of the soul to grace through repentance and discipline. Such are *Mundus et Infans*, *Mind, Will and Understanding*, and *The Interlude of Youth*. Two plays, however, *Mankind* and *Lusty Juventus*, are worth pausing over for the way in which they carry on the particular elements I noted in *The Castle of Perseverance*. *Mankind* has strong elements of popular comedy in it, which make the temptation scenes very effective in theatrical terms. Yet the character of Mankind is carefully drawn, and it is this characterization of a human being that makes the situation represented in the play interesting and moving. Mankind is by no means a mere puppet in the allegorical pattern: from the beginning, he admits his divided nature:

> My name ys Mankynde: I haue my composycyon
> Of a body & of a soull, of condycyon contrarye:
> Be-twyx the tweyn ys a grett dyvisyon.
> He that xulde be subiecte, now he hath the victory.
> Thys ys to me a lamentable story,
> To se my flesch, of my soull to haue gouernance. . . .[3]

[3] J. M. Manly, *Specimens*, ll. 189–94, p. 322.

The temptation of Mankind into rebellion and sin is well motivated and completely credible.

The events leading up to the repentance of Mankind are not shown to us: he merely returns, remorseful and despairing, from his worldly experiences with the vices. Nevertheless, his despair is real enough, even if it is not foreshadowed or enlarged upon. It grows out of his earlier knowledge of the two paths open to man and out of his sense of guilt in having chosen the wrong way. It is also consonant with his character as that was presented to us in the first section of the play. Repentance and forgiveness follow inevitably, as is appropriate in a play which is frequently comic in tone and still firmly religious in its background, but a tragic outcome is within the realm of imaginative possibility.

Lusty Juventus, a Protestant interlude of the reign of Edward VI, narrows the subject down from the whole life of man to the period of youth, and introduces polemical elements from the religious strife of the time. Yet it is by no means remote from the general form of the morality described above. In this play, as in *The Castle of Perseverance*, the representative hero hesitates between two opposed ways of life, and his eventual choice very nearly leads him to complete destruction. The choice of the wrong way, ironically emphasized as such by Satan and Hypocrisy the Vice, appears to Juventus to be proper to his youth and time, but looks forward to the reversal of his awakening and despair. The theme of the play, the rebellion of man's will against God in wilful blindness to the fatal consequences, thus comes fairly close to a tragic statement, and would have this effect if the conclusion were more severe. Even the emotional structure of the play is worked out carefully in relation to the theme: thus Juventus obviously abuses Good Counsel because of his guilt and shame when he comes face to face with his former godly companion, and the despair which he feels close to the end would be impossible without his earlier knowledge of the truth. In spite of its background of religious controversy, the play is a serious working out of the themes and dramatic possibilities of the original Temptation and Fall morality.

The morality play, with its basic theme of a universal conflict between human will and divine will, took on another form at a very early stage in its development, what we may call the Pride of Life morality as opposed to the more familiar Temptation and Fall. There are only a few plays in this group, *The Pride of Life*, *The Cradle of Security*, and *Everyman*, but they may represent a larger group which has disappeared, just as the text of *The Cradle of Security* has disappeared. Although the fundamental theme remains the same, this type of morality has less to do with the Psychomachia and seems more closely related to the Dance of Death. The typical theme of the Dance of Death, whether in poetry or painting, perhaps also in semi-dramatic performances, is the vanity of worldly glory as revealed by the coming of death to a man or a woman at the height of power and prosperity. The figure of Mors in the Hegge play of *King Herod*, standing close behind Herod as he feasts in triumph, is a striking example of the Dance of Death imagery related to a mystery play. The distinctive quality of *Everyman* is that it is concerned with an ordinary human being and not with a magnificent king or great noble in his palace.

The rebelliousness of man is one of the presuppositions of the Pride of Life morality, so that there is no long process of temptation, no series of conversion, fall, and conversion again. The action of the play is climactic rather than extensive, the end of man's life rather than the whole narrative of his spiritual career. The central figure is at the height of his prosperity and boasts with pride of his greatness while his courtiers flatter him. At this moment comes Death (in *The Pride of Life* the King of Life is foolish enough to send a challenge to Death) and the stripping away of illusions and pretensions begins. Worldly possessions, health, and strength disappear, until at last nothing is left between man and God. At this low point of despair Everyman starts the painful journey back toward God's forgiveness; we are also told that the soul of the King of Life is snatched from the fiends at the last moment because of the intercession of the Virgin Mary. But *The Cradle of Security* ends in complete severity: '. . . the desolate Prince starting up bare faced, and finding himselfe thus sent for to judgement, made a lamentable complaint of his miserable case, and so was carried away by wicked spirits. This

Prince did personate in the morall, the wicked of the world. . . .'[4] This severity is possible because the Prince is not representative of mankind in general but of 'the wicked of the world', and because the solemn figures who come to him in the midst of his sport represent not only death but the end of the world and the Last Judgement, as Willis tells us.

It is quite clear, I think, that no great chasm separates this kind of morality from the *de casibus* tradition of medieval tragedy—the pride, the over-confidence in the face of clear warnings about the fickleness of fortune, immediately before a fall into adversity. The two plays with a royal protagonist are particularly close to the *de casibus* form, which always emphasizes the lofty place from which the tragic hero falls.

A moral lesson of some power on the vanity of this world was provided by these plays, but theatrically they seem to have been less capable of development than the other moralities. There is no evidence of any important popular tradition, apart from the fact that *The Cradle of Security* was being played at Gloucester in the 1560s. The clearest use of the theme and allegorical imagery of this type of morality occurs in the first part of Lindsay's *Satire of the Three Estates*, where Rex Humanitas bears some resemblance to the Prince of *The Cradle of Security*, and in Skelton's *Magnificence*, where Magnificence himself is a notable example of pride and luxury cast down into misery. Both plays are considerably enlarged beyond the austerity of the early form for the sake of contemporary allusion and satire, and yet they retain from the older moralities the dramatic image of the splendid king reduced to a wretched condition through his subjection to flattery and sensuality. We shall consider the plays of this group a little later.

But let us return now to the Temptation and Fall moralities and the main line of development. First I must try to summarize some of the changes which scholars have noticed in the moral play during the first half of the sixteenth century. The general form of the morality became particularized for various reasons, some of them related to changing social and intellectual influences from both Renaissance and Reformation, others related to

---

[4] Robert Willis, *Mount Tabor*, p. 113.

developing theatrical tradition, the nature of the audience, and the organization of the acting troupes. The subject of the morality was no longer the whole life of man but a portion of it, youth or age; and it was presented not in the most general moral terms but in relation to specific issues in society, education, or the Church. The plays for production at court and in college halls tended to be political moralities with a strong satiric tone or else plays on the theme of education, the moral categories of virtue and vice transformed into learning and ignorance. Popular moralities written especially for professional troupes of actors, or adapted by them for their own purposes, carried over the old conflict between virtue and vice to a world of pressing social issues —the evils of avarice, the oppression of tenants by landlords, the poverty of scholars, the cunning of the ambitious, and so forth. These popular moralities were spiced with realistic comedy in the figures of the Vices, who became the means of social satire, but there was often a serious strain in the portrait of a wilful and deceived human being hastening to his own damnation.

Two changes call for special attention. The first is the loss in many of the late moralities of a dominating central figure whose temptation and fall is the essential action of the play. Instead of a single allegorical character representing mankind there are characters who persevere in good and characters who fall and persevere in evil, each meeting his appropriate reward or punishment at the end. This tendency has been described as the result of Calvinist influence upon religious thought and the division of mankind into the elect and the damned,[5] but it may also be the natural result of the increasing particularization and concreteness of the morality play as a wider variety of human beings came to be included in the action. The second change is the greatly increased importance of the Vice, not only as tempter and deceiver but also as intriguer and stage manager, so that the plot frequently became a demonstration of his skill. In many plays he became the central theatrical figure, attracting more interest than any other character, as Bernard Spivack has so thoroughly established.[6]

[5] D. M. Bevington, *From Mankind to Marlowe*, p. 152; Bernard Spivack, *Shakespeare and the Allegory of Evil*, p. 245.

[6] Spivack, op. cit., pp. 188 ff.

What happened in these later forms to the germ of a tragic theme, which certainly existed in the early moralities? The late moralities seem closer to tragedy in some respects but further away in others. The endings are frequently severe, as Willard Farnham has pointed out, bringing punishment in worldly form —disease, poverty, and death—upon those who have persisted in sin. But there is a loss as well, the loss of a single, central character who goes through the almost-tragic experience of temptation, rebellion, recognition, and despair. The two worlds continue to exist, this world and a superior one which judges it, and the conflict between human will and divine will is more strongly marked than ever. But human will is not often shown as hesitating between rebellion and obedience: instead, human beings are divided into those who are in accord with the divine purpose and those who are irreconcilably against it. There may be a typical virtuous man and a typical evil man set in contrast with each other, like Just and Lust in *The Trial of Treasure*, or there may be a variety of typical characters and exemplary episodes to illustrate the moral lesson, as in *All for Money* and *Like Will to Like*. In both kinds of play there is a loss of concentration and a loss of emotional power because of the diffusion of dramatic interest among several characters. Of course, if one were looking at these plays from the point of view of comedy, one's summing up might be strikingly different. There are gains in the direction of concreteness of setting, personality, plot development, and comic situation and dialogue.

The tragic potentiality of the early moralities remains in the allegorical fables of worldly man on a downward course, now presented as leading to despair and punishment without hope of recovery. Retribution becomes increasingly important as worldly characters come to dominate the plots of the late moralities, and it is worth noting how this theme develops and expands over a series of these plays. In *Impatient Poverty* a rather incoherent plot nevertheless makes plain the theme that virtue leads to material prosperity and vice to material ruin. The central figure, Impatient Poverty, discovers the operation of these moral laws by going through both types of experience himself, the series concluding in virtue and prosperity. In a second group of plays,

The Trial of Treasure, *The Tide Tarrieth No Man*, and *Nice Wanton*, there are parallel plots, involving virtuous characters and evil characters, which lead unequivocally to rewards and punishments at the end. Some slight hint of the wavering hero of the earlier morality exists in Christianity in *The Tide* and Xantippe in *Nice Wanton*, but in neither case is the hint developed very far. The theme of retribution in the latter plays involves only a selected group of characters; other characters demonstrate the reward of virtue or the possibility of repentance.

In the third group of moralities some virtuous characters remain, but they exist mainly for purposes of good counsel, stern warning, and choral comment: the active characters are the worldly ones, who choose evil and move steadily towards a fatal end. *Like Will to Like* and *All for Money* portray groups of worldly characters caught up in a process of degeneration; W. Wager's plays, *Enough is as Good as a Feast* and *The Longer Thou Livest*, concentrate rather more on a single representative of worldliness persevering in evil to the moment of disaster. In this third group of plays retribution is the dominant theme.

We may ask whether the growing importance of the theme of retribution has any relevance for our consideration of tragedy. The effect of this theme is to stress the working of cause and effect in a moral universe where every deed counts and leads to necessary consequences. The plays declare that any man who disregards the moral order of the universe does so at his own peril. If he follows his own self-will and acts proudly and self-confidently, mocking this moral order, he will in turn be mocked and his self-centred aspirations will lead him directly to ruin. Thus, two movements are possible in the action of such a play: an apparent movement toward success and prosperity, and a hidden but real movement toward disaster, the two set off against each other by irony. The irony is frequently explicit in the half-comic, half-tragic mixture of tones when the Vice makes fun of the deluded figure he is pretending to help.

The theme of retribution ensures that the action has a quality of irreversibility about it, a kind of tragic inevitability from which there is no escape, once man has declared his adherence to a worldly course. The sense of inevitability stems from a chain of direct responsibility: a human being makes a deliberate decision, and from this everything follows. In this respect, plays of retribution differ from those (like the Pride of Life moralities) where fortune is dominant. Fortune specifies only probability, not necessity; the great and powerful man is likely to fall because the world has been given over to the vagaries of fortune and because the great man stands in the most dangerous and exposed position. Similarly, those who are dependent upon the world for the fulfilment of their happiness, like the lovers of the romances and ballads, must expect evil chances and ill fortune to frustrate their hopes.

The tragic experience of these late moralities is centred, as I have said, upon the rebellion, deception, and despair of a representative figure of worldly man. By rebellion I mean that he has chosen to follow his will against the dictates of conscience, the warnings of wise friends, and the canons of belief. His lust, his avarice, his cruelty to the poor are encouraged by the Vice and his evil companions, in scenes which are often filled with farcical action and satiric comment. Yet irony pointing to the dangerous deceptions of the Vice and to the wilful blindness of worldly man is seldom absent. In *The Trial of Treasure* the irony is skilfully developed in a series of asides, as Inclination the Vice mocks Lust for his gullibility while flattering him toward damnation. The following is merely one example from a whole series of such exchanges:

> *Luste.* My Lady is amorous and full of fauour.
> *Inclina.* I may say to you she hath an ilfauoured sauour.
> *Luste.* What saiest thou?
> *Inclina.* I saye she is louing and of gentle behauiour.[7]

The warnings of the virtuous characters and the force of the irony place the rebellious actions of worldly man in their true light.

The recognition of the fatal and damning nature of a sinful way of life comes only at the end. Perseverance in evil is a basic assumption of the theme, and this implies perseverance to the moment of despair, when repentance is no longer possible. There

[7] *The Trial of Treasure*, Tudor Facsimile Texts.

are few hints in these worldly characters of conscience or of any soul-searching which might foreshadow the recognition at the end. They continue in self-confidence and wilful ignorance to the time when retribution strikes, whether it be God's Visitation, Divine Correction, or Severity, and the full weight of recognition is upon them. Two exceptions are Lust in *The Trial of Treasure* and Worldly Man in *Enough is as Good as a Feast*. Lust has an occasional attack of conscience, which looks forward to his moment of recognition and despair at the end and helps at the same time to make him less of an abstraction and more of an individual:

Sturdines. What let the worlde wag, all can not be Juste,
　　　　　Some must Naturall inclination embrace.
Luste.　　All men Juste: no, I remember the sentence of Tully
　　　　　That no man is Juste, that feareth death, pouertie or
　　　　　　　paine,
　　　　　which I do feare all & that marueilously,
　　　　　For fortune is variable I doe perceiue playne,
　　　　　And notwithstanding that Flix possessed great gaine,
　　　　　yet when Paule preached of the iudgement daye,
　　　　　He trembled for feare and bad him go awaye.
Inclina.　Doth such passions often trouble your mynde.
Luste.　　Nay not often, but sometime I doe them finde,
　　　　　But then to the entent to dryue them awaye,
　　　　　I either go to sleape, or els to some playe.[8]

In *Enough is as Good as a Feast*, Worldly Man is actually converted to godliness for a time, tries to continue in virtue, and makes an effort to drive off the old temptations. But he relapses into sin and his final state is worse than his former, in cruelty, avarice, and mockery of the good. It is Worldly Man's earlier knowledge of the divine will that makes his fright at the Prophet's words so convincing. The recognition in this play is a gradual process, and as it advances, so Worldly Man's fear and despair grow more intense.

The final stage of the tragic experience in this group of plays is the reaction of the character to his predicament, once he has realized it, a reaction of despair or defiance. When the figure of worldly man has recognized the fatal choice of the wrong way,

[8] Ibid.

there is little left for him except despair, unless he should join
the vices in cursing the good. In *The Tide Tarrieth No Man* the
moral pattern rules the ending as rewards and punishments are
meted out in appropriate terms. Despair persuades Greediness
to commit suicide, but because Despair's appearance is brief
and because Greediness is entirely evil the emotional effect is
merely that of moral satisfaction. In *Like Will to Like*, on the
other hand, the four rogues who have been encouraged in their
vicious ways by the Vice repent at length in moral speeches very
different in tone from the vigorous, comic language of the early
scenes. The sudden conversions, the grievous laments for their
evil ways, the warnings to other young people and to their
parents, remind one strongly of similar speeches made under the
scaffold by the condemned murderers of Elizabethan domestic
tragedy:

> (*Cutb*)   Woe woorth the houre wherin I was borne,
> woe woorth the time that euer I knew thee
> For now in misery I am forlorne.
> Oh all youth take example by me.
> Flee from euill company as from Serpent ye would flee:
> (*Pierce*) Sith that that by the law we are condemned,
> Let ys call to God for his mercie and grace:
> And exhort that all vice may be amended,
> while we in this world haue time and space.[9]

A few plays, however, contain expressions of despair which
are quite closely related to individual characters and the experiences they have undergone. In *The Trial of Treasure* Lust, like
Everyman, finds his friends departing from him as death and
judgement approach. After Pleasure has gone, Treasure remains
at Lust's urgent request, though without any power to help him.
There is no sign, however, of any spiritual recovery at the end,
such as Everyman experiences. In the last scene of the play a few
ashes and a little rust symbolize the end of Lust and Treasure.

In *Nice Wanton* and *Enough is as Good as a Feast* the concluding stage of despair is also important in relation to the earlier
development of character and action in each play. *Nice Wanton*

---

[9] Ulpian Fulwell, *Like Will to Like*, Tudor Facsimile Texts.

has often been cited as a morality well on the way to the concreteness and particularity of secular drama, because the central
problem of the play, the upbringing of children, is given a firm
location in a family and in society, and because the main characters have been given individual names. The second point should
not be stressed too much, however, since Worldly Shame and
Iniquity are in the old tradition, and such names as Ismael,
Dalila, Barnabus, Xantippe and Eulalia are only at one remove
from the generic under the disguise of Biblical and classical
names. The structure of the play, though simple and economical,
has nothing of classical structure about it; the fundamental
division into two halves is that of the morality play, rebellion
and self-will followed by recognition and despair. In the first
part a series of sketches portrays the delinquent children, Ismael
and Dalila, already well on the way to their life of sin, the unhappy but virtuous brother, Barnabus, and the negligent mother,
Xantippe, who pays no attention to warnings about her children.
In the second part retribution has caught up with the worldly
characters: Dalila is dying from a dreadful disease and is overcome with shame and despair; Ismael goes to the gallows as a
thief and a murderer, unrepentant and cursing Iniquity, who
enticed him into such a life; and Xantippe is driven by despair
to the point of suicide. The ending is severe in that Dalila and
Ismael must die, but Barnabus is able to draw Dalila to repentance before her death and prevent his mother from committing
suicide. Religious requirements take precedence over the working out of a tragic denouement, as of course they should in a play
with didactic intentions.

Nevertheless, the expression of despair in passionate terms
has some importance for the development of tragedy, particularly since it arises from a characteristic situation of the
morality play. This situation is the recognition of the failure of
man's perverted will in a struggle with divine law. The strong
feeling in the play is also convincing in terms of character and
motive: the boldness of Ismael as a boy is the boldness that
makes him curse defiantly on the way to the gallows, and
Xantippe's casual optimism in the first part is credibly transformed into emotional despair in the second.

Wager's play, *Enough is as Good as a Feast*, is the most striking example of the tragic possibilities of the late morality play. As I have already suggested, the final scene of despair is the inevitable outcome of the earlier action of the play, in terms both of theme and of character and incident. The play opens with Worldly Man, 'stout and frolike', proclaiming his self-sufficiency and defending the way of life he has chosen. In a debate with Heavenly Man and Contentation his arguments are worsted and he is converted to godliness, but as soon as the stage is cleared and the vices enter, the counter-movement gets under way. After much comic by-play the vices are organized to action and the campaign against Worldly Man's new godliness is begun in a highly skilful manner. Worldly Man is flattered and deceived into choosing the dangerous course. Thus, when Covetous the Vice and Precipitation have introduced themselves as Policy and Ready Wit, Worldly Man welcomes them warmly under their new titles:

> Policy and redy wit: now the trueth is so,
> There is no man liuing that can spare you two.
> I trust God worketh for me happily in deed:
> To send me all such things wherof I haue need.
> For without a redy wit, who can answere make?
> Without a policy all commodityes wil slake.[10]

There is comic irony throughout the scene, but it is particularly specific in lines like these that underline Worldly Man's self-deception. 'Comic', of course, must be qualified because of the serious issues involved and the threat of damnation which lies in the background.

The next major division shows Worldly Man at the height of his prosperity, enormously confident, cruel to his servants and tenants, and laughing at the warning of the Hireling about God's wrath to come. He has left behind all pretence of virtue and is in full and complete rebellion against God. Busy with plans for building larger barns and obtaining more property by fraud, he is suddenly frightened by the solemn words of Prophet and completely overcome by the vision of God's Plague. He is obviously affected by them so strongly because of his earlier

---

[10] W. Wager, *Enough is as Good as a Feast*, Huntington Facsimile Reprints.

knowledge of the truth and his deliberate choice of the worldly way. His despair grows, as he turns first to Devotion (i.e. Ignorance) and then to Physician for help, and his end is a strange mixture of cries of pain, spiritual despair, and a futile attempt to retain control over his possessions after his death by writing a will. Wager has pictured the final moments of Worldly Man with a fine sense of the character he has drawn, as well as with firm control over his theme.

I have suggested that the theme of retribution does much to give a sense of unity to the action of the play and to direct it toward its proper end. At the beginning it almost appears that fortune will play the major part. When Worldly Man debates the problem of wealth with Contentation and Heavenly Man, the latter argues in the familiar medieval way about the uncertainty of this world:

> As for the treasure that you possesse heer,
> Through ficklenes of Fortune soon fadeth away:
> The greatest of renown and moste worthy Peer,
> Somtime in the end falleth to misery and decay.[11]

A list follows of a number of great kings who fell from prosperity into misery through the 'ficklenes of Fortune', and it appears that Worldly Man will fall in a similar way.

As the play proceeds, however, as Worldly Man rejects the godly life he had briefly undertaken and once more rebels against the law of God, the note of retribution is sounded plainly. The Tenant is sure that 'God wil plague him' for his cruelty and the Hireling warns him to his face. Finally, it appears as a direct condemnation in the words of the Prophet and of God's Plague. The latter's speech looks back over the whole career of Worldly Man:

> Heer thou wicked couetouse person I doo strike,
> Which once on the plowe hadst taken holde:
> But willingly again thou rannest in the Dike:
> Therfore thy plague shalbe doubled seuen folde.[12]

Enough is as Good as a Feast has a number of excellent qualities, which make it a considerable achievement for its period—it is

---

[11] Ibid.   [12] Ibid.

precisely balanced between the abstract and the real; characters and action are selected with economy and controlled by the theme; and the conclusion is uncompromisingly stern. Nevertheless, we should be wrong to praise it too highly, either as drama in its own right or as a kind of embryo tragedy, since didactic considerations still dictate many of its characteristics. As in most moral plays, debate counts for more than action, and moral attitudes are more important than emotion. What action there is tends to be typical or representative, like the oppression of the tenant and the servant by the avaricious master. The action of mystery and miracle plays, by contrast, seems almost startlingly real and individual. Furthermore, there is not much ordinary humanity in the central character: his victims claim our sympathy more than he does, and his downfall cannot touch the emotions greatly, even though some suspense is aroused over his fate.[13]

The Vice, in this as in other late moralities, is a major character, but his relationship to the tragic impulse within the play is less certain. Covetous is on the stage rather longer than Worldly Man, and as stage manager and master of intrigue arouses much of the theatrical interest of the play. However, there is one important distinction between the two main characters: what happens to Covetous in the end matters very little, whereas what happens to Worldly Man is crucial. There is no suspense over the fate of the Vice, since he is merely the instrument of evil and makes no spiritual decision of great import. As expected, Satan takes him off to Hell, congratulating him warmly for the job he has done. But Worldly Man's fate sums up all the urgent meaning and emotion of the theme of the play.

The part of Covetous in *Enough is as Good as a Feast* is typical of the part played by the Vice in most of the late moralities. One vice takes precedence over the others, and he is frequently described as the root of all evil, the very source of the existence

[13] Wager's other play, *The Longer thou Livest the more Fool thou art*, is equally severe at the end, but lacks altogether the element of tragic feeling, because the central character is a fool and is not only ineducable but is incapable of recognizing his situation at the end or of feeling remorse.

of the other lesser vices. (In *Enough* there is a comic contest by which Covetous establishes his pre-eminence in evil.) He becomes the cunning intriguer who initiates and directs the campaign against good and encourages the worldly to persevere in evil. In some of the plays with a variety of characters and episodes he is the unifying factor, both as a dramatic character appearing in almost every scene and as an embodiment of the theme, at least in its negative aspects. Courage acts in this way in *The Tide Tarrieth No Man*, Nichol Newfangle in *Like Will to Like*, and Inclination in *The Trial of Treasure*.

The Vice is a demonic force of evil, an unmotivated destructive impulse, opposed to all order, goodness, and harmony in the world, attaining his ends by flattery, deception, mockery, and clever manipulation of the passions. With his fellow vices, he represents also the degenerate part of fallen human nature in its hatred of the good and its blasphemous defiance of divine law. In this aspect the vices may often be rude, vulgar, and comic in their boisterous animality.

None of these moralities shows much sign of the Vice as a potentially tragic character. He is rather a source of contagion or disease, the disease of evil, which arouses an answering element in a representative human figure and hence is this element in human nature. As such, he becomes a most important part of the limited tragic pattern that exists in these plays: the tempter, the villain, the cunning intriguer who mocks virtue, whispers poison, and stirs up the blood of the main characters at the centre of the tragic action. The same function was to be carried on by Vice-like figures in the later drama.

Bernard Spivack has pointed to characteristics of the Vice in such later villains as Barabas, Richard III, Hoffman, and Iago, and he might well have added Bosola and Flamineo: they embody the destructive rebellion against order and the contagion of evil from this tradition. However, they arouse tragic feeling as characters in themselves only when they are least like the medieval Vice: Barabas when he is first ruined by the Christians near the beginning of *The Jew of Malta*, Richard III in his desperate and courageous defiance of retribution toward the end of the play, Bosola when he tries to leave his destructive role behind him. Except at these moments, they do not seem to be at the focal point of tragic attention, although they are essential to the tragic pattern of each play. They are the original rebels against order in the universe, but are such in full awareness of what they are doing; they do not act ignorantly of the full implications of their actions. Since they are rebels to begin with, there is no need for them to make any fearful decision during the course of the play, nor do they, except for Richard III and Bosola, come round to a point of tragic recognition in the end.

One other division of late morality plays consists of three or four political moralities. Two of these, Skelton's *Magnificence* (1516) and Lindsay's *Satire of the Three Estates* (1540), were written by poets who were also satirists and who ventured into the realm of the morality play in order to use it as a vehicle for social and political satire. *Respublica*, however, and the fragment of *Albion Knight* which survives suggest that the plays by Skelton and Lindsay were not alone in the field, and there are also contemporary references to other plays that aroused controversy because they touched on political and ecclesiastical issues.[14] Their origin, no doubt, could be traced to the Pride of Life moralities if we possessed any intermediate plays, since all of them place a royal figure at the centre of the action, who is deceived by false counsellors and moves away from his wise and virtuous counsellors. In *The Pride of Life* and *The Cradle of Security* this deception leads to the downfall of the proud ruler and his bitter remorse, but in the later plays only Magnificence suffers in this way. The main interest of the political moralities lies in the satire of abuses and the wretched plight of a country ruled by rogues who have flattered the king into believing their lies.

Magnificence is the one play of this group that carries on the original tragic impulse of the Pride of Life morality. Only in this play does the ruler-figure sin greatly and reap despair. The play moves beyond despair as Magnificence is led back toward repentance and forgiveness, but it contains within itself some

---

[14] E. K. Chambers, *The Medieval Stage*, vol. ii, pp. 219-20.

elements of tragedy in the medieval sense of the downfall of a great king. As we might expect from the background of the Pride of Life moralities, the fickleness of fortune is a more important theme than retribution, though the two are linked when Adversity announces that he comes from God.

In the political moralities the warfare between good and evil is translated into political and social terms, mainly for the purpose of satire. This change may not have much relevance for the development of tragedy, but it is an important step toward concreteness and the use of historical material to illustrate a moral theme. Each play is concerned with serious problems of government related to actual conditions of the time, as the later chronicle plays were to be: the obliqueness of approach to contemporary affairs is through allegory in these plays, whereas it was to be through more or less remote history in the chronicle plays. At the centre of each play is a representative prince or ruler whose deception by ambitious or greedy rogues has wide repercussions both for the prince and for his subjects. Such a ruler may be virtuous yet deceived, like Respublica, or sinful and weak, like Magnificence: the chronicle plays were soon to present a variety of each kind. There is no tyrant in the extant political moralities, but the mystery cycles could offer several notable examples of this kind of ruler.

It may well have been the political moralities that provided the stimulus for several plays on great kings and magistrates drawn from secular history and the Bible. One can see that there is no large gap between the political moralities and such plays as *Godly Queen Hester*, *Cambises*, and *Apius and Virginia*, where deceiving ministers, tempter-vices, and other allegorical or representative figures appear at the court of a powerful ruler to disrupt order. These plays and many of the chronicle plays that follow are concerned with a ruler who chooses a certain course of action and must take the consequences of that choice. If he sins gravely himself, as Magnificence does, the punishment will come upon him personally; if he chooses evil advisers or allows them to rule, as Respublica and Rex Humanitas do, ruin may come upon a whole people.

Bale's *King John* illustates in a most interesting way the

transformation of the political morality into the moral history. At first sight it appears to be a political morality like those I have mentioned, modified by a few tentative links with the world of history in the persons of John, Pandulphus, and the Pope. John is a virtuous ruler like Respublica, desiring only the welfare of his people. The widow England reminds us of People in *Respublica* and of John the Commonweal in Lindsay's *Satire*. And Sedition is very much the deceiving and corrupting Vice of the other plays.

Yet there are considerable variations. The plot is not concerned with a good ruler who is deceived by evil counsellors and who allows them to oppress the people to their own advantage. On the contrary, the king is aware of the danger from the beginning, and warns Nobility and Clergy to watch out for the rogue, Sedition. The plot consists of a conspiracy by a number of evil characters against a king who wishes to protect his people. The king fails and the conspiracy succeeds for a time. Only after the death of John and after a considerable time has passed are the rogues driven out and the nation rescued from their oppression.

In the general political morality, if the ruler is deceived he can be undeceived in time, or the rogues can be unmasked and punished by divine intervention: the moral lesson is enforced by a representation of what ought to be, and will be at the final Judgement. Such moralities are based on faith rather than on history. But as soon as an element of history is introduced failure becomes possible, at least temporary failure in the context of worldly existence, because an actual person or an historical situation is being represented.

In so far as it concerns John himself, Bale's play is about the failure of a virtuous hero. In all the moralities yet considered failure has been linked with perseverance in evil and is the product of retribution. But this play admits the possible defeat of virtue in a world given over to evil—not ultimate defeat, of course, but complete enough in terms of ordinary human life. In previous drama this possibility had existed most clearly in the mystery cycles and no doubt in miracle plays of the martyrdom of saints.

Bale himself, through the Interpreter, links his play with the familiar matter of the mystery plays and sermons of the time:

> This noble Kynge Johan, as a faythfull Moyses,
>   Withstode proude Pharo for hys poore Israel,
> Myndynge to brynge yt owt of the lande of darkenesse,
>   But the Egyptyanes did agaynst hym so rebell
>   That hys poore people ded styll in the desart dwell. . . .[15]

John is a Moses figure, albeit an unsuccessful one, pitted against the power of Pharaoh and the forces of darkness. He is also a Christ-like figure, struggling to fulfil his mission while the conspirators under the colour of false religion join forces to kill him: the development of the conspiracy and the desertion of John by all his friends are reminiscent of the Passion plays. John is also the prophet trying to save his people from the power of Antichrist. Bale is said to have been directly influenced by the Antichrist play, *Pammachius*, of Thomas Kirchmayer.

Within the larger structure of the papal conspiracy, the defeat of John, and the eventual triumph of reform, lies the tragedy of John, and it is this that we should consider in relation to other impulses working toward tragedy in the early drama. At the beginning John is confident in his strength against the powers of evil and certain that he can overcome the wrongs of which the widow complains. As the conspiracy against him develops, however, he sees himself deserted by Nobility and Clergy, the strongest forces within the country, and eventually by all his supporters except the old widow herself. Rather than allow her to be destroyed by war, John submits to Pandulphus, knowing that he has failed. His lament at this point has a tragic note, the cry of the innocent individual caught by the iron necessities of an evil world:

> I have sore hungred and thirsted ryghteousnesse
>   For the offyce sake that God hath me appoynted,
> But now I perceyve that synne and wyckednesse
>   In thys wretched worlde, lyke as Christe prophecyed,
>   Have the overhande; in me it is verefyed.
> Praye for me, good people, I besych yow hartely,
> That the Lorde above on my poore sowle have mercy.[16]

---

[15] John Bale, *Kynge Johan*, in *Specimens of the Pre-Shakesperean Drama*, ed. J. M. Manly, vol. i, p. 563.   [16] Ibid., vol. i, pp. 600-1.

He is further humiliated when Treason, whom he has condemned, is pardoned by Pandulphus. His death by poison completes his tragedy.

This is not the end of the play, however. Against the downward movement of John's tragedy is set the upward movement of Sedition and his fellow rogues, who gain full power in the land and gleefully celebrate their victory. Sometime after the death of John, Verity appears as a divine messenger and enforces the repentance of Clergy, Nobility, and Civil Order. The rogues are driven out as the work of reformation proceeds and Sedition is hanged. As a propagandist moral history the play could not be left with the failure of John but had to lead on to the victory of Henry VIII.

There is little precedent in the morality plays for the tragic situation of John. Only in the mystery cycles had there been notable representations of virtuous individuals suffering under the conspiring power of evil in the world. We should probably add to these the miracle plays on the deaths of the apostles or the martyrdom of the saints, and the new Biblical drama which Bale and other reformers across Europe were writing. Radclif's school play, *De Ioannis Hussi damnatione*, as listed by Bale, would seem to have been concerned with a modern martyr, dying more clearly for religious principles than John, but Bale's play is probably unique in relating martyrdom to a political situation.

Whatever its background, the embryonic tragedy of John has some importance in its own right, and is quite distinct in kind from other moral plays with tragic elements in them. Bale makes it quite plain that John's human will is in accord with the divine will which underlies the universe and the whole of history: yet he aspires and is defeated. What is tragic in John's situation is that he sets out to do what he must do against the powerful forces of evil in the world, knowing the danger but believing in the overwhelming justice and power of his own cause. But the order of the evil world is superior and brings about his defeat: it is superior for a time in this world as permitted by God's unknown purpose for the future. The tragic potentiality of this situation is, I think, made very clear within the play, and although it is not developed very far shows that it can exist within a framework of religious belief.

The form of the political morality is also evident in *Godly Queen Hester*, perhaps even more typically than it is in Bale's *King John*. Like the latter play, it has some connexion with the continental Biblical drama, which was concrete and particular in action and characterization, and yet it has an obvious relationship, also, to *Magnificence* and *Respublica*. As in the political moralities, a good king is deceived by an evil minister who gathers great power and wealth into his own hands. The evil minister, like Avarice in *Respublica*, deliberately tells the king of slanderous tales circulating in the realm about his activities, but the king is only the more ready to trust his minister because of his seemingly transparent honesty. Eventually his crimes are revealed, not through divine intervention, but through Queen Hester, who wishes to save her people from extinction. Aman, the evil minister, is punished on the very gallows he had set up for his chief Jewish enemy, an ironic conclusion Marlowe or Middleton might have enjoyed. As Hardydardy reports:

> I meane my master is the fyrste taster
> Of his owne inuencion.
> The gallhouse he made both hye and brode,
> For Mardocheus he them mente,
> And now he is faine him selfe for certaine,
> To play the fyrste pagente.[17]

There is much more about the rise and fall of Aman in this play than there is about the weakness or temptation of the king, and in this respect the morality becomes almost pure villain play. As a result retribution is the dominant theme of the play, retribution for deliberate and self-conscious evil, without any intermixture of admiration or sympathy. Queen Hester declares the uncompromising moral:

> And yet the sernantes that bee vntrue,
> A whyle in the world theyr lyfe may they leade,
> yea theyr welth and worshippe dayly renewe,
> But at the length I asswre you in dede,
> Theyr fauell and falsehed wyll come abrede,
> whiche shall be to them more bytter than gall,
> The hygher they clyme the deper they fall.[18]

---

[17] *A New Enterlude of Godly Queene Hester*, ed. W. W. Greg, *Materialien*, 1904, p. 41.
[18] Ibid., p. 46.

The rebellion against some superior law, the recognition, and the defeat may all be there, but they do not add up to tragic experience, since the sympathetic emotions are given so little scope: the villain merely gets what he deserves and neither in his aspiration nor in his recognition is there any expression of intense human feeling.

Cambises and *Apius and Virginia* carry the exploration of tragic incident and feeling a stage further. They have both received their due in recent years as hybrid plays standing between the allegorical and the historical, between the morality play and the chronicle play. There is little doubt of their relationship to the political moralities, in that both portray a king or ruler who disregards good counsel and is tempted into evil courses by a typical vice-figure; the ruler perseveres in evil and finally meets just retribution. On the other hand, they also descend, as I suggested earlier, from the mystery cycles and the subsequent Biblical plays, where notable examples of cruel tyranny were much more common and more theatrical than in any morality plays that survive. The variety of scene and action in *Cambises*, the large number of characters, the contrasting moods of terror, pathos, and comedy, all show signs of their origin in the popular drama of the mystery cycles. The connexion of *Apius and Virginia* with the Abraham and Isaac plays is also evident.

Cambises has always seemed to the literary historians incoherent and shapeless in dramatic form. There is no apparent co-ordination of the incidents toward a particular end, no developing conflict between the tyranny of the king and any counter-force. The end of the play is an accident, even if it is interpreted as the intervention of Providence. D. M. Bevington, however, has recently given a convincing account of the organization of the play by linking it with the late moralities of the popular school.[19] In his view it consists of a series of illustrative scenes showing the range of Cambises' cruelty and power up to the moment of his fall. There could be no continuing characters in the play, apart from Cambises and Ambidexter, because of the small number of actors a popular troupe could supply, but the device of suppressing one group of characters in order to present

[19] D. M. Bevington, *From Mankind to Marlowe*, pp. 183 ff.

a new group permitted a notable extension in time and space, the kind of extension that the mystery and miracle plays had taken for granted. The seemingly anecdotal quality of the play is thus explained as something more than a crudely simple drama- tization of its source: it is an attempt to encompass the colour and variety of a famous legend with strictly limited means. Even the comic scenes, in Bevington's view, are relevant as 'a secular adaptation of vicious intrigue in the Psychomachia', commenting satirically upon the main action of the play.[20]

Although the idea of a series of illustrative scenes explains in some respects how Preston came to organize his play, he seems to have had little idea of general form beyond that of accumula- tion. The theme of retribution which turns up in the prologue and at several points in the play ought to have helped him to select and shape his material, but it had no important effect on the form of the play.

The legend presented certain tragic possibilities. It begins with the potentially great and noble king demonstrating this greatness in his punishment of the wicked regent. However, he is led astray by his passions to become a complete rebel against the supreme law of the universe. In his confidence and pride he refuses to listen to warnings and commits crime after crime, which leads inevitably to his destruction. All of this is suggested in the prologue:

> Euen so this king Cambises heere, when he had wrought his wil
> Taking delight the Innocent, his guiltlesse blood to spil.
> Then mighty Ioue would not permit, to procecute offence,
> But what mesure the king did meat, ẙ same did Ioue commence
> To bring to end with shame his race, 2 yeares he did not raign
> His cruelty we wil delate and make the matter plaine.[21]

In these introductory lines we are reminded that Cambises was a king who 'cleauing more vnto his wil such vice did immi- tate', and as the play proceeds, as the scenes of bloodthirsty crime accumulate, the note of retribution intensifies. Preston has clearly tried to make of Cambises a tragic hero who takes a

---

[20] Ibid., pp. 187–8.
[21] *Cambises*, Tudor Facsimile Texts.

disastrous course, wilfully blind to the vengeance of God which awaits him. The difficulty with this scheme is that Cambises is so inhuman that all sympathy is removed from him, and the only suspense concerns the way in which the punishment he so richly deserves will come upon him. The emotional effect of the play consists of a series of powerful moments in which the inhuman cruelty of the tyrant is set beside the pathetic helplessness of his victims, but there are too many victims for any one of them to become important to the play as a whole. Preston misses altogether the force of emotion which the rebellion of an individual against destiny can arouse, when the rebellion is credible and capable of sympathy and leads to a recognition of some intensity. Cambises' recognition of the cruelty and blasphemy of his career is accomplished more or less in his last gasp:

> Thus gasping heer on ground I lye, for nothing I doo care:
> A iust reward for my misdeeds, my death doth plaine declare.[22]

Another quality Preston lacks is the ability to find effective language for his moments of crisis.

However, the play has some importance for its exploitation of terror and pathos as ingredients in a tragic history, for its continuation of the great variety of scene, incident, and character which the religious drama had established, and for its limited attempt to find in historical material a serious theme concerning man's destiny.

Apius and Virginia gives the impression of being a much better play than *Cambises*: clearly it is organized on different principles from those of the latter play, in that it is not concerned with a whole series of brief episodes illustrating the career of a tyrant, but with a single, crucial action. In addition, it has the advantage of a source story that is itself concentrated in effect and unambiguous in its meaning. The emphasis on meaning, and the relative unimportance of the comic scenes, may also be the result of the play's origin in the children's theatre rather than in the professional theatre to which *Cambises* belongs.

Apius and Virginia is a double play, as most tyrant or villain plays tend to be: it is about a cruel tyrant, certainly, but it is also

---

[22] *Cambises*, Tudor Facsimile Texts.

about his victims and their suffering. Where the victims of cruelty are numerous, as they are in *Cambises*, dramatic attention is centred upon the tyrant. Here, there are only two victims, Virginia and her father, and they are perhaps more important to the emotional structure of the play than Apius himself. The tragedy of Virginia has little to do with the morality play, political morality, or any similar form: it is much more closely related to the mystery plays about the innocent victims of cruel power, the Children of Bethlehem, and to plays about the slaying of children by their parents, who are bound by vows of obedience, Abraham and Isaac, Jephtha and his daughter. There is strong emphasis upon the purity and helplessness of Virginia in an evil world and upon the agony of her father, which is like that of Abraham before the sacrifice, and is then carried beyond Abraham's agony to the point of despair after the fatal deed has been accomplished.

But to the tragedy of Virginius and Virginia is joined the tragedy of Apius, and one of the main difficulties of the play lies in this combination, the refusal of the author to concentrate upon one or the other. It is his moral concern which prompts him to develop both, one as a notable example of martyred virtue, the other as a notable example of retribution. There is no doubt that the fall of Apius is of considerable dramatic interest. The working of Apius's mind is revealed to the audience—his subjugation by lust, his struggle with conscience (albeit in allegorical form), and the victory of passion over conscience. He is by no means so inhuman and remote from ordinary feeling as Cambises. Towards the climax of the play the opposition between human will and divine is presented in a theatrical way that is highly effective. Disregarding the severe warnings of Conscience and Justice, Apius becomes increasingly confident as his complete frustration and ruin approaches. Although the audience knows that Virginia is dead, Apius awaits her coming with gleeful anticipation, telling himself that if she will not submit, he will stab her to the heart! The language and verse may be crude, but the sense of irony is not:

What is the man that liueth now so neare to doore of death?
As I for lust of Lady faire, whose lacke will stop my breth:

But long I shall not want her sight, I stay her comming heere,
Oh lucky light, lo present heere hir father doth appeare,
Oh how I ioy, yet bragge thou not, Dame beuty bides behinde,
Virginius, where is the maide? how haps thou breakes my minde?[23]

But the irony of the scene is not yet complete. When Virginius
declares that he has killed Virginia to save her honour, Apius
brazenly condemns him for his cruel and unnatural deed and
calls down the anger of the gods upon him:

Oh curst and cruell cankered churle, oh carll vnnaturall,
Which hast the seede of thine owne lym, thrust forth to funerall:
Ye Gods bend downe your yre, do plague him for his deede,
You sprites below, you hellish houndes, do geue him gaule for
    meed:
My selfe will se his latter end, I Iudge him to the death,
Like death that faire *Virginia* toke, the lyke shall stop his breath:[24]

It is Apius the Judge who calls upon Reward and Justice to aid
him in his condemnation of Virginius. They appear at his call
promptly enough, like Banquo's ghost, but they condemn Apius
instead and carry him off to his punishment. The climactic
scene not only completes the moral pattern of the play but also
finishes the story of Apius in an ironic way that is highly
satisfying.

The tragedy of Apius is not carried very far: the moral structure of the play prevents this, and likewise the polarization of
feeling upon the source of fear in Apius and the source of pathos
in Virginia and her father. Nevertheless, the exploration of the
mind of a great sinner, even to this limited extent, is an important
aspect of the play. *Apius and Virginia* is less concrete than
Cambises: the good counsellors are represented as Conscience
and Justice rather than as individual courtiers, and the punishment of the villain is carried out by the traditional figures of
Justice and Reward rather than by an accident which belongs to
the world of nature. There is less variety of scene and action in
Apius and Virginia, less of the crude and vigorous life that marks
Cambises. Yet the play has certain advantages in its greater concentration of feeling upon a few characters in two or three

[23] *Apius and Virginia*, Malone Society Reprints, ll. 1024-9.
[24] Ibid., ll. 1048-53.

climactic scenes, and in its greater emphasis upon the inner minds of the main characters. The writers of serious plays at the middle of the century had learned a good many things from popular and learned religious drama; further lessons were to come from other sources.

From *Everyman* and *The Castle of Perseverance* to *Cambises* and *Apius and Virginia* is a long distance in the history of drama, much longer than the distance from the latter plays to *Doctor Faustus* and *Macbeth*. Yet there is little doubt of the continuity of the moral tradition in drama, with its emphasis on meaningful action directed toward a certain end. The morality play was reshaped for educational, social, and political interests and for purposes of entertainment, and the transformation was sometimes so complete that the solemnity of the original form was lost in vigorous comedy. Nevertheless, the seriousness of the moral play was in accord with the moral and religious temper of English humanism, so there was little chance that this aspect of the tradition would disappear completely.

I have noted an essential element of the tragic situation in the morality play—a conflict between human will and a superior law which is the moral law of the universe, the will of God. The action takes place in a world where moral laws operate and where punishment follows closely upon sin or crime. In this drama there is often a striking contrast between the elation of the hero when he throws aside the bonds of moral authority and his later, despairing, recognition of his mistake. In the early plays the tragic moment is swallowed up in repentance and eventual reconciliation, but in later plays, where representative man is divided into several characters, the figure of rebellious man moves inevitably toward despair and damnation.

In their division of human beings into virtuous and evil characters the writers of the late moralities lost sight of the ordinary human being, capable of good as well as of evil, who had been central in the early plays. This loss should not be underestimated, since much of the tragic potentiality of the morality play had seemed to lie in the predicament of a mixed character like Everyman or Mankind. But the late moralities developed two notable

forms of rebellious human will, which proved to be of considerable importance in later drama. One is the worldly man, greedy
for wealth and power or lustful for pleasure, who denies the law
of God and the laws of society and through cunning tries to bend
the world to his will. With the tempter-Vice who becomes his
agent (as well as the agent of his damnation), he is ripe for
development as a Machiavellian villain, as a Barabas, or even
as a Doctor Faustus. The other form of rebellious human will
lies in the figure of the ruler or king who had dominated the Pride
of Life moralities, and was soon linked with the tyrants of the
mystery cycles in the first plays about Biblical or historical kings
and great nobles. By the very loftiness of his position and by the
peculiar temptations of his birthright—pride, self-assurance,
and luxury—he is tempted to a glorification of his own will
against any greater will or law that might be thought to exist. As
A. P. Rossiter observes, the king-figure had a peculiar fascination for those who lived under the Tudors, since he possessed a
freedom of thought and action unique in human existence.[25]

The Vice, too, became a notable dramatic character in the late
moralities. He is important for the development of plot as a
stage-manager of intrigue and suspense, but for tragedy his
great importance lies in his developing nature as the very symbol
of disorder, a disruptive power representing the forces of mocking cynicism, blasphemous denial, and malicious destruction.
Though not a tragic figure in his own right, he stands for one
element in the tragic pattern which the drama of the age built up
as a vision of existence.

The morality plays expose far more strikingly than any other
drama the problem of the didactic element in literature. In
particular, they raise the question: was it necessary for the
didactic to be eliminated before tragedy could emerge? The
didactic bias in a work of literature means that a pattern has been
imposed upon the work for the sake of some cause outside the
work itself, and that situations, characters, and emotions have
been developed to illustrate and enforce the external cause. By
its very nature the didactic piece demands action from its
auditors rather than contemplation. The morality plays are all

[25] A. P. Rossiter, *English Drama from Early Times to the Elizabethans*, p. 118.

didactic, but there are many variations among them in the degree of didacticism in relation to elements of purely theatrical participation. One may notice a subtle difference between the first morality plays, which show sinners the necessity of following a certain course of action, and later moralities, which exist as warnings to sinners rather than as guides for action. There is still an obvious didactic intent in these later plays, but the audience is able to enjoy a little more detachment in watching what happens to characters distinct from themselves.

The moral intention permitted or even encouraged the development of a shaping principle, like retribution, which could give a moral play direction and emphasis and a sense of inevitable movement toward disaster. But as long as the moral idea came first and everything else was subordinated to proving the necessary truth of the moral idea, there could be no exploration of the intensity of the tragic experience for its own sake. It was the change to historical subject-matter that began to give events importance in their own right, and, at the same time, the individuals involved in those events. When the nature and intensity of the human experience became a matter of greater concern in the drama than the moral idea, then tragedy became possible.

III

TRIUMPHS, SHOWS, AND FURIOUS TRAGEDIES

I T is well to remind ourselves at this point of the large extent and the great variety of dramatic activity that had grown up throughout the country in the later years of the religious drama. The remarkable growth of dramatic activity and the establishment of a professional theatre have been explored in a number of important studies in recent years.[1] Two aspects of this development claim our attention. First of all is the increasing dominance of secular over moral and religious subjects. The secularization of English drama was not a sudden transformation at the end of the Catholic Middle Ages. Dramatic activity at court, in the form of tournaments, mummings and disguisings, masques, and interludes, had always been secular since the entertainments were associated with recreation and festivity. Household troupes of actors, deriving as they seem to have done from minstrels, jugglers, fools, and other entertainers, quite naturally carried on this secular tradition and presented interludes and farces as festive offerings in great hall, guild hall, or inn yard alike. The town companies of actors were probably more closely associated with the religious drama in their origin and no doubt played a larger proportion of miracles and moralities at first, but we know much less about them.[2] The civic pageants, as Glynn Wickham has described them, made an eclectic use of folk legends, moral allegory, national history, and classical myth; again, the occasions for such pageants tended to impress a secular and patriotic meaning upon them.[3] A moral theme was sometimes the substance of an individual pageant, but it was usually subordinate

[1] D. M. Bevington, *From Mankind to Marlowe*; M. C. Bradbrook, *The Rise of the Common Player*; G. K. Hunter, *John Lyly*; and Glynne Wickham, *Early English Stages, 1300–1660*.

[2] Alfred Harbage, *Shakespeare and the Rival Traditions*, p. 6.

[3] E. K. Chambers, *The Medieval Stage*, pp. 171–2; Glynne Wickham, *Early English Stages*, vol. i, p. 63.

to political or patriotic interests. Finally, the religious drama itself became secularized, at least those parts of it which were taken over by the professional troupes of actors and played up and down the country for their value as entertainment. This is not to say that moral themes were unpopular either in the household of a lord or on the village green: suitably mixed with pleasant mirth, they remained a staple element in the dramatic fare offered by the travelling actors, but secular elements, in the form of comic action, individual personality, and narrative suspense, began increasingly to disguise the moral themes of the original, purely didactic, drama.

Secularization implies the second point I wish to make about dramatic activity in the early sixteenth century: the greatly increased range of subject-matter. As the popular demand for dramatic entertainment grew and as individual troupes of actors set out to answer the demand on a commercial basis, the search for suitable play material became a matter of pressing importance. At first, that is during the first half of the sixteenth century, moralities (more or less secularized) seem to have predominated, since there are more records of their performance and more sur- viving texts than of any other form, though we have no means of judging the proportion of such plays to miracle and saints plays and individual plays drawn from the mystery cycles that have since disappeared. In a well-known passage from *Playes Confuted in fiue Actions* Gosson speaks of the romances from the early printing presses being ransacked for plays: *The Golden Ass*, *The Aethiopian History*, *Amadis of France*, and *The Round Table*.[4] These plays were probably contemporaneous with the late moralities. By the time records of titles become reasonably numerous, it is romantic fiction from all over Europe that is being ransacked, the collections of Italian and French *novelle*, and continental comedy (Gosson includes these sources in his same list). There is not much evidence to change the conclusions of Chambers and Harbage that the popular troupes moved from moralities and miracles in the early years of the sixteenth century to romances in the middle years of the century, and then to the

---

[4] Stephen Gosson, *Playes Confuted in fiue Actions* (1582), quoted in Chambers, *The Elizabethan Stage*, vol. iv, p. 216.

novelle and the chronicles in the 1570s and 1580s, as main sources for their dramatic shows. The range of subject-matter was enormously extended.

Court entertainers had always been eclectic in their choice of subject, since the court was willing to accept a wide variety of devices and shows, provided that they were novel and spectacular. In the 1550s we hear of masques of Orpheus, Prester John, the Tower of Babylon, Moors, Amazons, the Greek Worthies, the Triumph of Cupid, Venus and Mars, and many more.[5] No doubt elements of plot and characterization were of slight importance, but the variety of subject-matter pointed to the wide possibilities of the future. The repertories of the children's companies who had been playing at court from the early years of the sixteenth century also expanded rapidly. At first the staple fare of the royal chapels and the grammar schools seems to have been moral dialogues and verbal comedies of wit, but Biblical plays and political allegories in the 1530s reflected the twin influences of Christian humanism and the Reformation. The ban on controversial interludes prevented further development in this direction; however, it did nothing to hinder the natural development of the special talents of the children's companies in presenting shows with songs and dances. Classical myth and legendary history provided the framework for these offerings at court, as a long list of titles suggests; the production of classical plays was already a matter of educational policy in the schools and became a matter of prestige at court in the new cultural atmosphere fostered by humanism. Similarly, productions of classical comedies and tragedies at Oxford and Cambridge were justified for educational reasons, but could be developed into elaborate presentations for the entertainment of a visiting monarch.

The increasing dominance of secular themes and the great extension of subject-matter were obviously important for the development of Elizabethan drama. Yet it is clear that there were losses as well as gains. In the great upsurge of dramatic activity there were factors at work tending to overwhelm the serious themes and moments of tragic feeling of the earlier religious

---

[5] E. K. Chambers, *The Elizabethan Stage*, vol. i, p. 158, n. 1; see also Enid Welsford, *The Court Masque*, pp. 151 ff.

drama. Perhaps the most important of these was the need to entertain, as professional troupes developed on a commercial basis and gradually ousted the amateur players of town and country. At court, likewise, the need to entertain took precedence over idea and didactic purpose when the children's companies began to compete with household musicians and interlude players for royal patronage. In the popular theatre the moralities tended to become low comedy and social satire, and the extension of subject-matter was mainly in the direction of romantic narrative; at court the moralities became verbal comedies with farcical elements, and the extension of subject-matter led to the witty adaptation of classical legends to courtly taste. Only in the academic drama of school and college was there much likelihood of a production of a serious Biblical play or of a classical tragedy.

And yet one can see—from the surviving plays of this transitional period, from the titles of lost plays (many of which can be grouped around surviving plays), from later plays that seem to have descended from a recognizable tradition, and from a few comments by propagandists against the stage—that serious themes and individual episodes of tragic feeling continued to exist. They prepared the way for a native tradition of tragedy which classical theory and neoclassical imitations were unable to submerge.

Among the professional troupes and on the public stage, first of all, one may see the growing importance of what Alfred Harbage has called the biographical play.[6] The biographical treatment of great figures from the Bible led naturally, as we have seen, to a similar treatment of legendary characters from history, with a moral theme as a carry-over to justify the use of such material. *Cambises* and *Horestes* are early examples of this process, and no doubt such titles as 'the history of Caesar and Pompey' and 'the Playe of the Fabii', mentioned by Gosson, belong to a later stage of the same development. There are many other titles in the lists of lost plays that suggest the biographical form: *Tamar Cham, Sir John Mandeville, Machiavel, Constantine, Diocletian, Belin Dun*, and so forth.[7] Celebrations of legendary

---

[6] Alfred Harbage, *Shakespeare and the Rival Traditions*, p. 65.
[7] Ibid.; see also Chambers, *The Elizabethan Stage*, vol. ii, p. 122.

greatness and power, firmly based upon a biographical structure, are evident in *Tamburlaine*, *Selimus*, and *Alphonsus King of Aragon*, and in such historical medleys as *The Famous Victories of Henry V* and *The Battle of Alcazar*. The Induction to *Alphonsus* suggests much of the spirit of this drama:

> And there togither do our best deuoyr
> For to describe *Alphonsus* warlike fame:
> And, in the manner of a Comedie,
> Set downe his noble valour presently.[8]

Biographical plays drew their material from Roman history, English chronicles, and romantic history and legend with equal ease. The central figures were notable examples of honour and magnanimity, or notable examples of villainy, it did not matter which, so long as they were sufficiently famous or colourful to arouse the curiosity of an Elizabethan audience and sufficiently active in their careers to provide a good show.

There was no necessary reason why the biographical play should move in the direction of tragedy, but the dramatization of the lives of the great figures of history was bound to include sooner or later both great tyrants who met disaster and noble heroes who fell to ruin through the fickleness of fortune—Caesar, Pompey, Antony, and Richard III were notable enough examples. Stephen Gosson, a prejudiced witness, of course, suggests that the vanity of the poets in wishing to show their skill with the eloquence of passionate speech was another reason why a historical biography might turn in the direction of tragedy:

For the Poets driue it most commonly vnto such pointes as may best showe the maiestie of their pen in Tragicall speaches; or set the hearers a gogge with discourses of loue; or painte a fewe antickes to fitt their owne humors with scoffes & tauntes; or wring in a shewe

---

[8] Robert Greene, *Alphonsus King of Aragon*, Malone Society Reprints, ll. 108-11. These lines follow the exaggerated praise accorded to Alphonsus by Venus, who speaks the Prologue to the play:

> I do not doubt but long or ere this time,
> *Alphonsus* fame vnto the heauens should clime:
> *Alphonsus* fame that man of *Ioue* his seed,
> Sprung from the loines of the immortal Gods,
> Whose sire although he habit on the earth,
> May claime a portion in the fierie Pole,
> As well as any one what ere he be. (22-28)

to furnish the Stage when it is to bare; when the matter of it selfe comes shorte of this, they followe the practise of the cobler, and set their teeth to the leather to pull it out. So was the history of Caesar and Pompey, and the Playe of the Fabii at the Theatre, both amplified there, where the Drummes might walke, or the pen ruffle. . . .[9]

There were undoubted tragic possibilities in many biographies, particularly in so far as they concerned varieties of honour and courage in an unstable world; however, these possibilities could only be seized upon and developed when writers came to have some notion of what tragedy might be, beyond the mere excuse for 'Tragicall speaches' that Gosson speaks of.

As we noticed above, playwrights for the professional companies newly established in London in the 1570s turned from romance to the collections of *novelle* in their search for source material. Contemporary romantic fiction made an increasingly strong impression after Painter's translation of Boccaccio and Bandello in 1566, followed closely by Fenton's *Tragicall Discourses* in 1567. There were further editions of these two collections, and new tales from the Italian by Robert Smythe, George Turbervile, and George Whetstone, between 1570 and 1580. It is in these years that we begin to notice the first appearance of titles of plays suggesting romantic fiction: *The Three Sisters of Mantua* (1578–9), *The Duke of Milan* and *The Marquess of Mantua* (1579–80), and *Ferrar* (1583).[10] Many of the *novelle* were romantic or comic, but it was obvious that the more violent stories would quickly attract the attention of dramatists because of their theatrical qualities—the hideous cruelty of tyrants or jealous husbands, the pathos of their victims, the cunning intrigues of revengers, and in general the high passions of all those involved in the action. Again, there was no necessary reason why plays based upon the *novelle* should move toward tragedy, but violence and strong feeling were there in abundance, available either for melodrama or for tragedy. With some support

---

[9] Stephen Gosson, *Playes Confuted in fiue Actions*, quoted in Chambers, *The Elizabethan Stage*, vol. iv, p. 216.

[10] E. K. Chambers, *The Elizabethan Stage*, vol. ii: the Earl of Sussex's Men in the years 1579–80 and 1583; the Earl of Warwick's Men in 1578–9.

from the tragedies of Seneca, the revenger of Italian fiction became one of the first archetypal characters of Elizabethan tragedy.

The playwrights turned soon to the English chronicles, to such an extent that Thomas Nashe was able to say in 1592 that the subject of most stage plays 'is borrowed out of our English Chronicles',[11] and it appears that *Holinshed* was dramatized in its entirety. For the popular stage the appeal of the chronicle plays, as of the biographical plays, lay in the careers of famous men, but brought closer to home by their Englishness and often by their military campaigns against traditional enemies. Here again, there were many occasions 'where the Drummes might walke, or the pen ruffle'. The fact that serious themes survived in the chronicle drama may be due in part to the tradition of the allegorical interpretation of historical events, which the civic pageants had implanted in the popular mind, as Wickham claims; it is certainly also due to the interpretations of meaning that playwrights found in Holinshed and Hall and that had been made familiar in *A Mirror for Magistrates* and its sequels. The humanist impulse to make history and history plays a force for moral education, and hence to stress the thematic interest of drama, is clearly expressed in the following passage from Gosson's *Schoole of Abuse*:

The *Iew* and *Ptolome*, showne at the Bull, the one representing the greedinesse of worldly chusers, and bloody mindes of usurers: the other very liuely descrybing how seditious estates, with their owne deuises, false friendes, with their owne swoordes, and rebellious commons in their owne snares are owerthrowne: neither with amorous gesture wounding the eye: nor with slouenly talke hurting the eares of the chast hearers. The *Black Smiths daughter*, and *Catilins Conspiracies* vsually brought in to the Theatre: the first contayning the trechery of Turkes, the honourable bountye of a noble minde, and the shining of vertue in distresse: the last, because it is knowen to be a pig of myne owne sow, I will speake the lesse of it; onely giuing you to vnderstand, that the whole marke which I shot at in that woorke, was too showe the rewarde of traytors in Catilin, and the necessary

[11] Thomas Nashe, *Pierce Penilesse* (1592), quoted in Chambers, *The Elizabethan Stage*, vol. iv, p. 239. See also Harbage, *Shakespeare and the Rival Traditions*, p. 64.

gouernment of learned men, in the person of Cicero, which forsees euery danger that is likely to happen, and forstalles it continually ere it take effect. . . .[12]

The passage. is an interesting illustration of several of the dramatic impulses I have been describing: the interest in romantic stories involving noble qualities of mind set against cunning intrigue and treachery, the histories of famous men whose very names are legends, and the humanistic attempt to draw such histories in the direction of serious moral themes.

There is one other aspect of the popular stage which should not be disregarded entirely. The morality play in its severest form, as a fable of guilt and responsibility followed by retribution, survived well into the 1550s and 1560s in such plays as *Like Will to Like* and *Enough is as Good as a Feast*. The popular interest in the details of sin and violence in an ordinary domestic setting led to the appearance of broadsheets and ballads on contemporary crimes of note, but it was the existence of the late moralities, with their realistic social background and their plain moral themes, which permitted the dramatization of these 'domestic tragedies' in a way that was not merely sensational.

The plays which the children's companies presented at Blackfriars and at court seem to have offered less ground for tragic development than the plays of the adult companies. There is little evidence that they made use of romantic tales of violence or tragic histories, so far as we can tell from titles and a few surviving plays. As George Hunter observes, their special talents were suited neither to the working out of a powerful, single intrigue, nor to the physical action on stage that a romantic tale required.[13] The schoolmaster-dramatists cast wide nets through classical mythology, but most of the plays were probably moral debates, like *Damon and Pithias* and *Fulgens and Lucres*, or somewhat static tableaux with music and dancing. Such titles as *Dido* (Paul's under Ritwise, 1522–31), *Iphigenia* (Paul's, 1571), *Alcmaeon* (Paul's, 1573), *King Xerxes* (Windsor, 1575), and *Pompey* (Paul's, 1581) suggest tragedy, and it may be that our

---

[12] Stephen Gosson, *The Schoole of Abuse* (1579), quoted in Chambers, *The Elizabethan Stage*, vol. iv, p. 204.

[13] G. K. Hunter, *John Lyly*, p. 101.

F

conception of the development of tragedy is severely limited by the disappearance of these plays. However, it seems more likely that the tragic stories of these plays were frameworks for fine sentiments expressed in a series of parallel or contrasting patterns, as *Damon and Pithias* and *The Wars of Cyrus* suggest.

The idealization of the courtly virtues of honour and chaste love make up perhaps the only serious themes with any tragic potentiality in the drama of the children's companies. With such subjects there is always the possibility of some outrage to chastity or of some conflict between honour and love. *The Wars of Cyrus*, containing the pathetic history of Panthea, is a demonstration of limited tragic action within such a play, and no doubt *Timoclea at the Siege of Thebes* was similarly mixed in tone. But, on the whole, the very nature of the boys' companies and the history of their employment at court worked against the development of tragedy in this theatre.

We should also consider briefly the possibilities for tragedy that existed in the greatly increased scope of academic drama in the sixteenth century. This drama was limited to a small, learned audience, closely associated with the schools and colleges, but its influence grew more important as the century progressed. The productions of classical plays at the universities seem to have created a taste for similar plays at the Inns of Court, and through the revels of the Inns of Court reached the courtly audience as well. Similarly, royal progresses to Oxford and Cambridge led to elaborate productions of classical plays or of modern plays which were classical in form and theme—*Palamon and Arcite* at Oxford in 1566 and *Richardus Tertius* at Cambridge in 1580. Rare though such royal performances were, they seem to have made a considerable impression. A more important source of influence lay in the fact that the popular stage, because of its burgeoning vitality, began to draw to it as playwrights impecunious university men who had gained reputations as wits and poets among their fellow students.

At the universities the impulse to produce tragedy was at least as great as the impulse to produce comedy, because of the enormous prestige of ancient tragedy, the appearance of Italian commentaries upon Aristotle, and the accounts of courtly productions of classical tragedy in Italy. When records of college productions become numerous, in the 1550s and 1560s, Seneca shares the honours with Terence and Plautus. In the two festive seasons of 1559/60 and 1560/61 alone, four of Seneca's tragedies were presented at Trinity College, Cambridge.[14] These were the same years when the individual translations of Seneca's plays into English began to appear. Other classical dramatists received little attention on the academic stage: one or two plays of Aristophanes, the *Ajax* of Sophocles (prepared for the Queen though not played), but no Euripides, unless certain titles represent Euripides rather than Seneca.

Following general humanist practice, academic dramatists wrote Latin comedies and tragedies which were sometimes original and sometimes adaptations of plays from the Continent. As we should expect, there were tragedies on Biblical subjects, considered by the reforming humanists as highly appropriate for the loftiest of literary forms: Absalon, Jephtha, and John the Baptist were favourite tragic heroes. William Gager was original in choosing for his plays classical stories that had not been treated by the ancient dramatists in extant plays (*Meleager*, *Ulysses Redux*, and *Dido*). Italian influence is apparent in the adaptation of Italian tragedies like *Progne*, which were thoroughly Senecan in dramatic machinery and rhetoric. By choosing a subject and a tragic hero from comparatively recent English history Thomas Legge made his *Richardus Tertius* into something of a landmark in the development of university drama. Though subject-matter varied widely, formal qualities and style in all these plays tended to be dominated by Seneca.

It was this serious, academic drama in the schools and universities that led directly to such Inns of Court plays as *Gorboduc*, *Gismond of Salerne*, *Jocasta*, and *The Misfortunes of Arthur*, and indirectly to plays like *Locrine*, *Titus Andronicus*, and *The Spanish Tragedy*, which reveal a mixture of academic and popular traditions. Whereas almost all of the university tragedies were Latin plays, these Inns of Court plays were in English. Together, they showed the possibility of adapting Senecan themes and Senecan rhetoric to a variety of subjects from romance and

---

[14] F. S. Boas, *University Drama in the Tudor Age*, pp. 386-90.

history, some of them intimately related to the serious political thought of the time. Although tending to be occasional experiments rather than a continuous tradition, they also developed a sense of the possible seriousness and grandeur of tragedy in English which was to influence the more learned dramatists of the following period.

I have suggested that the new subject-matter the drama was ranging through was by no means inimical to tragedy. There was intrigue, passion, and violence in abundance; indeed, stories were chosen for dramatization because they contained these qualities. But before such material could be transformed from history or melodrama into tragedy, there was need of some conception of what tragedy might be, of ideas of tragedy that might influence writers in the selection and shaping of character, event, and emotion. Academic writers were the only playwrights at the middle of the century and a little later who had tragic models and an idea of tragedy to guide them in the choice and shaping of their material. Though writers of the popular theatre came under the influence of Seneca and the Senecan imitators in the last two decades of the century, for the most part they experimented with serious themes, and the forms appropriate to such themes in the workshop of the theatre, without widely accepted models and without any solid basis of critical theory. That they were able to do so without subservience to the classical tradition is an indication that some general ideas or impressions of the nature of tragedy were current during these years, in addition to the conventional formulas of the grammarians and the rather heady, rhetorical, example of Seneca. It is these general ideas that we must now examine.

No writer, especially a writer for the popular theatre, could altogether escape the force of medieval drama, though Renaissance humanism might incline him to scorn it as superstitious and barbarous. Even Marlowe was aware of its emotional and metaphysical power. And yet medieval drama was not a source of general ideas about tragedy. Although it contained tragic episodes and moments of intense feeling, it offered no means of selecting tragic experiences and shaping and directing them toward catastrophe and recognition. Only in a few late, severe moralities is there a conception of this kind, the theme of retribution, which is moral in its didactic intention and yet capable of giving formal direction of a limited tragic nature to its raw material. Rather, the religious drama provided to the dramatic imagination certain characteristic situations of undeniable tragic force, and a religious vision of the meaning of such experiences. It saw the universe divided between forces of evil and forces of good, and man's nature divided also between rebellion and obedience—a view which seemed to make tragic experience inevitable, even if contained within a larger providential scheme that was not tragic. The predicament of innocence in a world that is defiantly and cruelly evil, and the predicament of the sinner who discovers the nature of his sin and the terror of rebellion against God, became the heritage of the later drama in a number of vivid dramatic images. Of course, one may say that the religious experience of the age made this background available to later dramatists, but the tradition of religious drama was so long-lived and so vital in its development that I think one must admit its direct influence. It is doubtful whether *Doctor Faustus*, *Richard II*, and *Macbeth* could have been written in their present form without a dramatic tradition of this kind.

Ideas about the nature of tragic action came chiefly from other sources, however. One of these sources was undoubtedly Boccaccio's *De casibus virorum illustrium* and subsequent translations and imitations in English. The great motivating force of Boccaccio's collection of tales was the doctrine that Fortune was unreliable and deceitful and that therefore men should put their trust in heaven.

Lydgate expresses this view in *The Fall of Princes*:

> And for hir chaung and for hir doubilnesse,
> This Bochas biddith that men sholde enclyne
> Sette ther hertis, void off vnstabilnesse,
> Vpon thynges which that been deuyne,
> Where-as ioie perpetueli doth shyne
> Withoute eclipsyng in that heuenli see,
> Void off all cloudis off mutabilite.[15]

The passage is reminiscent of the concluding stanzas of *Troilus and Criseyde*. Lydgate's own purpose in tragic narratives

[15] John Lydgate, *Fall of Princes*, ed. Henry Bergen, p. 4.

was more deliberately moral than Boccaccio's or Chaucer's:
he wished to show that disaster was the result of crime, that sin
brought its own punishment in this world. In his view the outcry against Fortune was often a means of disguising the real truth
of retribution:

> But such as list(e)nat correctid be
> Bexaumple off othre fro vicious gouernaunce,
> And fro ther vices list nat for to fle:
> Yiff thei be troubled in ther hih puissaunce,
> Thei arette it Fortunys variaunce,
> Touchyng the giltes that thei deden vse,
> Ther demerites ful falsli to excuse.[16]

A Mirror for Magistrates was designed as a continuation of
Lydgate's *Fall of Princes* into the wide realm of English history,
and, with its sequels and imitations, it became one of the most
popular books of the early Renaissance in England. It helped to
preserve well into the Renaissance the medieval idea that a
tragedy was the fall of a great man into misery and ruin. Yet it
did not take for granted the traditional explanations for such
tragic falls: the collection is a series of explorations into the
reasons for disastrous events, and if the moral scheme of retribution is most prominent, other explanations are also proposed.
Willard Farnham has rightly declared that this work is one of the
great source books of the period for ideas of tragedy.

Fortune rules still in tragic poems in which war is the cause
of the hero's downfall. Though the vengeance of God might
sometimes operate through the fortunes of the battlefield, nevertheless, there are several tragedies, in the *Mirror* collections, of
men who suffer through no crime or sin of their own. There are
other characters, too, like Duke Humphrey, Sabrine, and Cor-
dila, who suffer in spite of their innocence or positive virtue in
a world of harsh and bitter forces.

Yet moral responsibility is more important than fortune. Many
of the tragedies both in Baldwin's original collection and in later
additions follow with considerable care the process of retribution from crime to eventual punishment and remorse.

The repentant ghost of Hastings reveals his guilt in the murder

[16] John Lydgate, *Fall of Princes*, ed. Henry Bergen, p. 201.

of Edward and in adultery with Shore's wife; Buckingham
betrays his guilty association with Richard of Gloucester in the
murder of the young princes; and Mowbray examines the way
in which pride and envy led him toward crime and eventual ruin.
Through the mouth of Mowbray, Baldwin deliberately plays
down the part of Fortune and stresses the concept of retribution:

> I blame not Fortune though she dyd her parte,
> And true it is she can doo lytell harme,
> She gydeth goods, she hampreth not the harte,
> A vertuous mynde is safe from every charme:
> Vyce, onely vyce, with her stoute strengthles arme,
> Doth cause the harte to evyll to enclyne,
> Which I alas, doo fynde to true by myne.[17]

It is very important to notice that retribution is seldom portrayed as a simple and direct process of crime followed by divine
judgement and punishment. The writers of these tragedies frequently describe how a murderer or tyrant brings mental suffering upon himself before any physical punishment from God or
man has touched him. Thus Buckingham tells of the misery in
which he and King Richard lived after their apparent success:
fear of vengeance and the hatred of the people made their lives
almost unbearable. Not only this—a murderer or tyrant may
even help to bring about his own punishment, since his success in
crime develops dangerous qualities. The tragedy of Wolsey, for
example, describes the growth of Wolsey's pride and over-
confidence, which parallels the growth of his power and wealth
and leads inevitably to his downfall. Similarly, in the prose
discussion following the tragedy of Collingbourne, the commentator uses the example of Richard III to point out that
tyrants commonly blind themselves to approaching disaster by
listening only to flatterers. Thus, in a sense, they bring retribution upon themselves.

A difficult question concerning retribution is raised by John,
Earl of Worcester. Is a man responsible, he asks, if he commits
a crime ordered by his king, and can he be punished for that
crime? John defends himself, but admits that God may punish
such a man as well as the king who commanded the crime. In

---

[17] *A Mirror for Magistrates*, ed. Lily B. Campbell, p. 102.

such ways as these the writers of the *Mirror* tragedies opened
up the simple idea of retribution and revealed its possible
complexity.

Finally, one must not forget the debates in these tragic poems,
and in the prose discussions between tragedies, concerning mixed
causes of disaster. A man's ruin may be the direct result of his
sin or crime; yet it may also be partly due to the malice of fortune
or to the ambitious schemes of other men in a world of power
politics and war. Many of the tragedies show quite clearly that
the writers had no wish to simplify the issues and point to a single
cause for a terrible event. Richard II, for example, is made to
admit his sins and his oppression of the people, but the writer
gives some stress also to Richard's bitter condemnation of
Worcester for betraying him, and of Henry for killing him law-
lessly. The tragedy of Shore's Wife might seem an excellent
opportunity for a poet to moralize upon sin and its punishment;
instead, Churchyard balances the conventional moral pattern
with a vigorous defence by Mistress Shore of her conduct and a
plea that her fall was due to a whim of Fortune. Rather sur-
prisingly, Jack Cade meditates on this question:

> Shal I cal it Fortune or my froward folly
> That lifted me, and layed me downe below?
> Or was it courage that me made so Ioly,
> Which of the starres and bodyes grement grow?
> What euer it were this one poynt sure I know,
> Which shal be mete for euery man to marke:
> Our lust and wils our evils chefely warke.[18]

The comment by one of the listeners to the tragedy is worth
quoting: 'By saint mary quoth one yf Iacke wer as well learned,
as you haue made his oracion, What so ever he was by byrth, I
warraunt hym a gentylman by his learnyng. Howe notably and
Philosopher like hath he discrybed Fortune and the causes of
worldly cumbraunce?'[19]

Though inappropriate in Jack Cade's mouth, discussions of
the causes of worldly misfortune enter into the narrative because
this tracing of causes is one of the objects these poets had set for

---

[18] *A Mirror for Magistrates*, ed. Lily B. Campbell, p. 171.
[19] Ibid., p. 178.

themselves. Henry VI, for example, is unwilling to accept any single cause of suffering: human misery may be punishment imposed upon the wicked for sin, or it may be a form of spiritual discipline, or yet again, it may be an illustration of the vanity of worldly glory. The remark of one of the listeners points to the interest of the poet in the subject: 'This tragedy ended, an other said: eyther you or king Henry are a good philosopher, so narrowly to argue the causes of misfortunes: but ther is nothing to experience, which taught, or might teach the king this lesson.'[20]

A Mirror for Magistrates, its sequels, and the tragic narrative poems it stimulated maintained and greatly extended in complexity the medieval idea of tragedy. We should not exaggerate the influence of the *Mirror for Magistrates* upon the development of ideas of tragedy, but there is no doubt that the book was widely read and suggested to many readers that certain episodes in English history were essentially tragic in nature. In addition, it suggested in what ways these episodes were tragic, as we shall see more specifically later on.

It is difficult to distinguish any active tragic ideas (ideas that worked upon the drama of the time) emerging from academic or literary discussion. The traditional definitions of tragedy, as provided by the grammarians and rhetoricians, were well known from an early period, though they had no reference to an actual stage tradition, and were merely a useful means of classification for literary works handed down from ancient times or written in direct imitation of these. Tragedy was at first described in the simplest of terms. A typical rhetorical definition is that of Johannes Januensis, quoted by E. K. Chambers: '. . . differunt tragoedia et comoedia, quia comedia privatorum hominum continet facta, tragoedia regum et magnatum. Item comoedia humili stilo describitur, tragoedia alto. Item comoedia a tristibus incipit sed cum laetis desinit, tragoedia e contrario.'[21] It is obvious that the outward and superficial manifestations of the tragic art were more important to the rhetoricians than any inward idea of what tragedy involved. Yet it was these outward marks of tragedy which continued to be regarded as the distinguishing properties

[20] *A Mirror for Magistrates*, ed. Lily B. Campbell, p. 219.
[21] E. K. Chambers, *The Medieval Stage*, vol. ii, p. 209 n.

of tragedy throughout the Renaissance. Though contributing little to the development of tragedy, they encouraged learned playwrights like Jonson and Chapman to aim at lofty characters, a stately style, and moral sentences of weight and authority. Even the writers of domestic tragedies paid lip service to the tradition by apologizing for the lack of these qualities in their plays.

As the classical tragedies became better known and as Aristotle's *Poetics* came to be studied in conjunction with the Italian commentaries, learned definitions of tragedy grew more sophisticated and more complex. Sidney, for example, spoke of tragedy as 'stirring the affects of admiration and commiseration', though he also described in traditional terms the rules concerning what is appropriate for tragedy—lofty personages, an elevated style, and the observance of the unities. And Fulke Greville revealed his awareness of several different kinds of tragedy in a description of his own intentions in the tragic form:

> Now to return to the Tragedies remaining, my purpose in them was, not (with the Ancient) to exemplifie the disastrous miseries of mans life, where Order, Lawes, Doctrine, and Authority are unable to protect Innocency from the exorbitant wickednesse of power, and so out of that melancholike Vision, stir horrour, or murmur against Divine Providence: nor yet (with the Moderne) to point out Gods revenging aspect upon every particular sin, to the despaire, or confusion of mortality; but rather to trace out the high waies of ambitious Governours, and to shew in the practice, that the more audacity, advantage, and good successe such Soveraignties have, the more they hasten to their owne desolation and ruine.[22]

(It is interesting to see in this passage a contemporary recognition of the dominance of the tragic idea of retribution.)

Nevertheless, it must be admitted that academic and literary formulations of the nature of tragedy had probably less influence upon the actual growth of tragedy on the popular stage than any other source of tragic ideas. Together with Italian and French practice in classical tragedy, they had some effect on the development of the chamber tragedies of the period, but little beyond this.

[22] Fulke Greville, *Life of Sir Philip Sidney*, p. 221.

While these tentative critical explorations were being made, the ancient tragedies themselves were being read and sometimes presented in college halls and elsewhere for restricted audiences. Of the Greek dramatists, Euripides seems to have been the most widely known. His plays were available in a number of complete Latin translations, and several of the plays were given wide currency in the translations of Erasmus and Buchanan. For example, there were at least fourteen editions before 1606 of the versions of *Hecuba* and *Iphigenia at Aulis* by Erasmus, and some eight editions of Buchanan's *Alcestis* and *Medea*. One might suspect that the currency of these particular plays would suggest a form of tragedy in which the emotion of grief is dominant. Only the *Medea* emphasizes the strong motive of revenge. The association of the story of Iphigenia with that of Jephtha's daughter in a Greek university play is an indication that the influence of Euripides worked in the direction of a tragedy of innocence and pathos.[23]

Seneca, of course, had a far greater influence upon learned ideas of tragedy than any of the Greek dramatists or any of the critics; his influence also worked through to popular audiences by translations and a number of imitations on the popular stage. The learned audience derived from Seneca an idea of tragedy as the downfall of a great figure or a whole house because of some curse upon it, some overpowering destiny not to be avoided. Certain of his plays made the issues of tyranny and civil war appropriate themes for tragedy, particularly the *Thebais* and the *Octavia* (as well as the *Phoenissae* of Euripides). As important as total conception was the language in which Senecan tragedy was expressed—the stateliness of diction, the easily recognized patterns of imagery, the rhetorical organization of the speeches.

The English translations of Seneca made the Senecan kind of tragedy familiar to a wider audience beyond the academic world, as Greene's scornful remark makes plain. The comments of the translators, prefixed to the printed texts, reveal that popular ideas of fortune and retribution attached themselves readily to these tragedies and frequently transformed the classical doctrine of

[23] F. S. Boas, *University Drama in the Tudor Age*, pp. 48 ff.

destiny or nemesis. Alexander Nevyle, the translator of Seneca's *Oedipus*, writes thus in an epistle attached to this play:

For I to no other ende removed him from his naturall and loftye Style to our corrupt & base or as al men affyrme it: most bar . . . rous Language: but onely to satisfye the instant requestes of a fewe my familiar frendes, who thought to have put it to the very same use, that *Seneca* hymself in his Invention pretended: whiche was by the tragicall and pompous showe upon Stage, to admonish all men of theyr fickle Estates, To declare the unconstant Head of wavering Fortune, her sodaine interchanged and soone altered face, And lyvely to expresse the iust revenge, & fearful punishments of horrible Crimes, wherwith the wretched world in these our myserable daies pyteously swarmeth.[24]

The catastrophe of the play Nevyle represents as 'A dredful Example of Gods horryble vengeaunce for Sin'.

Thomas Nuce is equally concerned to draw a moral from the *Agamemnon* of Seneca:

> Learne here to lyue a ryght, and know
> > how that thear is a god,
> That well deseruers well rewardes,
> > andd ill, doth scurge with rod,
> For to thys and is thys compylde
> > thys play thou hast in hand,
> In vertues race to make thee run,
> > and vyce for to with stand.[25]

It is only fair to notice that another writer, whose verses are attached to John Studley's translation of the play, has interpreted the action solely in terms of fortune, and that the Preface to the Reader is in agreement with this interpretation. Nevertheless, the very mixture of fortune and retribution is in the tradition of the metrical tragedies. There is a curious epilogue to the play, added by the translator as his own contribution. In a long lament Eurybates condemns the hatred and violence of those who have been involved in this tragic history. It is actually a moral condemnation of the whole long story of revenge.

It is dangerous, as one may see from these examples, to assume that the sixteenth-century readers of Seneca's plays, in Latin or

[24] Alexander Nevyle, *The Lamentable Tragedie of Oedipus . . . out of Seneca*, 1563.
[25] *Studley's Translations of Seneca's Agamemnon and Medea*, ed. E. M. Spearing, p. 9.

in English translation, took away with them a conception of tragedy purely 'Senecan'. They saw in the Senecan plays the spectacle of a large, overpowering character suffering a cata-strophic fall and they delighted in the passion of that character, and particularly in the language of his passion. But they tended to read the meaning of the fable in terms of the tragic ideas that were already familiar to them. Even the academic plays that show the clearest determination to naturalize Senecan tragedy on the English stage are by no means entirely governed by Senecan concepts.

We have one other source of tragic story to consider, one which has not usually been looked upon as a source of any ideas about tragedy, the controlling factors we have been searching for. Nevertheless, it is worth examining the popular collections of Italian *novelle* with our particular purpose in mind, simply because they were so widely read and provided so many plots for tragedies on the Elizabethan and Stuart stages.

When the stories were particularly violent or unhappy, they were usually called 'tragedies' by their translator-editors. Thus as Geoffrey Fenton approached one of the stories in his *Certaine Tragicall Discourses*, he wrote: '. . . I haue here to expose vnto you a myserable accident happening in our tyme, whiche shall serue as a bloddye skaffolde or theaterye, wherin are presented such as play no partes but in mortal and furious tragideies.'[26] It is apparent that the familiar idea of retribution influenced the translators in their attitude to these tales. Most of them proclaim the moral purpose of showing the punishment of sin. Yet readers who accepted such Tragicall Discourses as tragedies were bound to find in them certain qualities unusual in anything else called 'tragedy' in that day. They are most often concerned with violence resulting from rash love or jealousy. The main charac-ters are not people of highest degree but those of middling place. Moreover, although the moral purpose is supposed to be dominant, very often the main emphasis lies upon purely emo-tional effects—horror at the spectacle of malice and crime, and pity for those who suffer. The translators admit these qualities as they describe the stories in their collections. Geoffrey Fenton,

---

[26] Geoffrey Fenton, *Certaine Tragicall Discourses*, fol. 79.

for example, writes as follows about the characters and motives to be found in his tales:

. . . who desyereth to see the follye of a foolishe louer passionynge hymselfe uppon creditt, the impudencie of a maide or other woman renouncynge the vowe of her faythe or honor due to virginitie, the sharpp pennance attendynge the rashe choice of great Ladyes in seekynge to matche in anye sorte wythe degrees of inferior condicion: or who wisheth to bee priuie to th' inconueniences in loue, howe he frieth in the flame of the fyrste affection, and after groweth not onelye colde of hymselfe, but is easelye conuerted into a contrarye shapp and disposition of deadlye hate, maye bee heare assisted wyth more then double experience touchinge all those euills . . . And who takes pleasure to beholde the fyttes and panges of a frantique man incensed to synister conceites by the suggestion of frettynge Jelousye, forcynge hym to effectes of absolute desperation. . . .[27]

The moral stress is apparent in one or two of Fenton's phrases, but more evident is the interest in psychological effects of passion upon his characters.

The heading of one of Painter's tales points to the powerful emotional effect of the story, to the exclusion of other concerns:

The horrible and cruell murder of Sultan Selyman, late the emperor of the Turkes and father of Selym that now raigneth, done upon his eldest sonne Mustapha, by the procurement, and meanes of Rosa his mother in lawe, and by the speciall instigation of one of his noble men called Rustanus: where also is remembred the wilful death of one of his sons named Giangir, for the griefe he conceived to see Mustapha so miserably strangled.[28]

There is no obvious punishment for crime in the tale. This story and others like it represent furious passions and dreadful cruelty as the product of immoderate desires. The translators looked for patterns of retribution wherever they could find them, and brought them to the foreground when possible. Their prefaces and epistles make this interest plain. Yet there were stories where this moral interest had little scope. Fenton, for example, is very much of a moralist, but one of the stories in his collection brings no punishment upon the sinner at the end, so that he is forced

---

[27] Geoffrey Fenton, *Certaine Tragicall Discourses*, The Epistle dedicatorie.
[28] William Painter, *The Palace of Pleasure*, ed. J. Jacobs, p. xci.

to concentrate his moral denunciation within the Preface to the tale.

A Yong Lady in Mylan after she had longe abused the vertue of her youthe and honour of maryage with an vnlawfull haunte of diuers yonge gentlemen becoms an vnnaturall morderer of the frute of her wombe for that shee was for saken of hym who gatt her wyth Chylde.

Hauinge then to treate vpon tragicall affayres procedynge of vnnaturall luste, with *Lasyvivs* disposition, the onlye maister pocke and cheif fountayne from whence distylleth all poysned humors of Infection, ouerflowinge at lengthe the channel of his quiett cours with unrewelye waues of Inordynat crewelty: I meane here to presente vnto you the trewe pattorne of a seconde MEDEA, in the person of a yonge Ladye borne and wantonlye bredd vp in the ryche and populus Cytie of MYLLEYNE. . . .[29]

Not every reader or auditor in the theatre was likely to be as shrewd an observer as Fulke Greville; nevertheless, it is worth noting that he at least was well aware of the qualities of Italian plays, or of plays based on Italian stories, which would make an immediate appeal to an audience—intricacy of plot, emotion, and imagination. As in the passage previously quoted from his discussion of tragedy, he is trying to differentiate his own plays from other tragedies:

Againe, for the Arguments of these Tragedies they be not naked, and casuall, like the Greeke, and Latine, nor (I confesse) contrived with the variety, and unexpected encounters of the Italians, but nearer Level'd to those humours, councels, and practices, wherein I thought fitter to hold the attention of the Reader, than in the strangeness, or perplexedness of witty Fictions; In which the affections, or imagination, may perchance find exercise, and entertainment, but the memory and judgement no enriching at all. . . .[30]

It seems apparent that these violent tales were widely regarded as tragic and that plays based upon them were also quickly denominated as tragedies, though they differed in important respects from plays traditionally regarded as such. Fulke Greville would pick out the dominance of intrigue as their distinguishing characteristic, and this is also the quality Miss Doran has pointed

[29] Geoffrey Fenton, *Certaine Tragicall Discourses*, fol. 62.
[30] Fulke Greville, *Life of Sir Philip Sidney*, pp. 222-3.

to in her account of the different forms of tragedy.[31] Yet one can notice as well two themes which seem to be characteristic of the tragic *novelle*: first, the tragic fall of lovers through sad mischance or the malice of jealous rivals; and second, the accumulation of crime and revenge to the point of total destruction of all those involved and the exhaustion of evil passions. Each has a characteristic emotional pattern, so much so that frequently the story seems to exist for the sake of the emotion, whether it be pathos or horror. There is considerably less emphasis in this source of tragic story upon moral responsibility and the inevitable working out of retribution.

The Elizabethans were far from occupying themselves with the formulation of 'ideas of tragedy', either on the basis of practice in the theatre or on the basis of their wide reading in native, continental, and classical literature. On the contrary, one may say only that certain attitudes to tragic story became familiar in the literature of the time, and were available to playwrights if they became aware of any need for them in the construction of a play. Moreover, these attitudes or ideas about tragic experience had little chance of remaining unmixed and individual. Because there was no dominant form of tragedy and no effective body of criticism, a would-be dramatist might use two or three of these interpretative, shaping ideas in a single play without being aware of any incongruity.

In some respects the different ideas of tragedy supported one another and readily permitted combination. Both *Mirror* tragedy and the tragedies of Seneca concentrate attention upon a great central character whose agonized recognition of his true state is the focal point of grief and therefore of tragic emotion. *Mirror* tragedy commonly begins with his recognition and looks backward over the process of error and temptation; in Senecan tragedy, the hero is close to the climax of such recognition at the opening of the play and moves rapidly towards it. There is a good deal of emphasis in both types of tragedy on the initial pride of the hero, his lofty position, and his ignorance of the fate that destiny is preparing for him as he blindly follows his own will. However, he is forced to bow before a superior will or purpose,

[31] M. Doran, *Endeavors of Art*, p. 115.

which in Senecan tragedy is destiny itself, but in *Mirror* tragedy is the moral law and the will of God. In *Mirror* tragedy the dominant power is sometimes fortune, but fortune too operates under the rule of providence.

There are seldom such larger-than-life figures in the tragic *novelle*, because of the dominance of narrative and of complex patterns of intrigue. But the cruel tyrants of Seneca—Nero, Lycus, and Atreus—have their minor counterparts in the atheistic tyrants and villains of the *novelle*, and the characters in Seneca overcome by extreme passions of lust or revenge—Atreus again, Phaedra, and Medea—are frequently echoed by characters in the *novelle*: often there is a direct comparison, as I have noted. The peculiar horrors of scenes of torture and murder in Senecan tragedy have something in common with similar scenes in the *novelle*: we are reminded of this by the use of Senecan imagery and rhetoric in plays which are clearly derived from continental fiction, *Tancred and Gismund*, for example, and *The Spanish Tragedy*.

However, there are important differences as well that distinguish these tragic concepts from one another. In Senecan tragedy there may well be some great crime or sin in the background which has brought a curse upon those involved and all connected with them, but the sense of direct responsibility and guilt that informs many of the *Mirror* tragedies is absent in Seneca. In *Mirror* tragedy every deed counts and must be answered for; the operation of universal law is much more rational and directly moral than is the operation of destiny in Seneca, where it remains in the long run inscrutable. Fortune is common to both, and the idea of the instability of high worldly place and prosperity, but fortune is subordinate in each to fate or providence.

The tragic stories of the *novelle* differ quite strikingly from both Senecan and *Mirror* tragedy in placing everything that happens on a human level of explanation. There is no need for a sense of destiny, a fatal curse, or the intervention of providence, when all the action depends upon intrigue and the cunning mind of a villain. The only hint of fortune in such stories lies in the casual chances of life, the accidents which hurt the innocent, the sudden opportunities the villain makes use of, and the only sign of retribution lies in the way evil forces tend to destroy each other, but this too is capable of a human interpretation.

One other type of tragic story in the collections of *novelle* has no counterpart in Senecan tragedy, and there is scarcely anything similar in *Mirror* tragedy: this is the pathetic tale of innocent love crushed by the harshness of the world. It is fortune that brings about the sufferings of such martyrs for love and, although in a sense they are punished for daring to hope for happiness in a world governed by fortune, their responsibility is negligible.

IV

FORTUNE'S OVERTHROWS

AFTER the opening of permanent theatres in London, on a commercial basis that was relatively secure, the drama developed rapidly, so that the major forms of tragedy, comedy, and chronicle play seem to have appeared almost contemporaneously. The achievements of Marlowe, Kyd, Lyly, and Shakespeare were so remarkable that critics have been tempted by their genius to separate them almost entirely from the dramatic tradition that preceded them. Nevertheless, a study of less successful attempts at tragedy belonging to the few decades between 1560 and 1590 should point to those elements in the dramatic tradition which were capable of such development and could be seized upon by major writers. The process of imitation and experiment that went on during those years reveals both the continuity of a tradition and many of the possibilities lying within it.

We have noticed the great extension of subject-matter in this drama, and the inclusion of much heroic, violent, and pathetic material which was at least potentially tragic. Biographical plays about notable heroes, plays drawn from the *novelle* on such themes as love, jealousy, and revenge, and chronicle plays on the violent events of recent or legendary history, possessed the possibilities both of tragic action and of tragic feeling. Moreover, certain very general ideas about tragedy, some of them familiar and well tried, others more novel or more learned, had become current.

Undoubtedly, tragic shaping was not the major concern of many dramatists, apart from those writing for an academic audience. Most of them were engaged in the difficult process of condensing narrative material for the stage in order to present a reasonably credible sequence of events, sometimes with serious moral commentary, often with variety of action and shows enough to satisfy a very mixed audience. If there were any semblance of tragic form, it was more likely to be the result of a certain simplicity or directness of form in the original narrative than of the application of any theory of tragedy. The dominance of a large central character, the working out of a strong line of cause and effect, such as the theme of retribution might suggest, or the development of an intrigue of revenge, were other factors which could give a sense of control and direction to the action. Traditions and models, apart from the morality plays and the tragedies of Seneca, were still lacking.

As a matter of convenience, and without suggesting any necessary chronological priority, I should like to examine first a group of plays that were not particularly adventurous, but which used the familiar theme of inconstant fortune as a background for the tragic action. Fortune had played a prominent part in medieval narrative tragedies and in much of the romantic literature of the same period, so that ambitious men and lovers alike commonly faced a power which displayed a casual disregard for human desire and aspiration. The importance of fortune in the *de casibus* tragedies of Boccaccio, Chaucer, and Lydgate has long been stressed, but it is only recently that its importance in romantic literature has been recognized. In an examination of many of the romances which lie behind the romantic plays of the Renaissance stage, F. J. D. Hoeniger notes particularly the part played by fortune in romances concerned with virtuous heroines suffering severe tests of their chastity, and in romances of wandering, innocent lovers brought close to disaster by the mischances of this world.[1] In both kinds of romance, he observes, there are numerous appeals to pathos. Elizabethan dramatists who moved on from medieval romance to the *novelle* and classical legend and history found many more such stories, where fortune seemed to rule and pathos was powerfully concentrated upon the innocence and helplessness of its victim.

The theme of threatened chastity was a favourite one, sometimes as a minor strain in a play largely devoted to other themes, sometimes as the dominating element of structure and emotion. An early example is *Apius and Virginia*, one of the first plays to

---

[1] F. J. D. Hoeniger, 'The Function of Structure and Imagery in Shakespeare's Last Plays', unpublished thesis, University of London, 1954.

draw its concreteness from classical story, which as we noted above has obvious connexions both with the mystery cycles and with the morality plays. The theme recurs in a subordinate place in Peele's *David and Bethsabe*, in the boys' play, *The Wars of Cyrus*, where Panthea suffers from the wiles and threats of Araspas, and in *Tamburlaine II*, where Olympia outwits the powerful Theridamas by suicide. In *Solyman and Perseda*, however, the theme is a major one, as it is also in *Edward III* and *The Death of Robert Earl of Huntington*. *James IV* presents an interesting variation in that fair Ida, the object of the king's lust, does not suffer at all, but simply resists his constant suit and marries the man she loves; it is the queen, Dorothea, who is forced to flee and is almost fatally wounded in a struggle with a hired murderer.

It is characteristic of these plays that their emotional patterns should be strongly polarized. The heroine commands the sympathy of the audience as she seeks to preserve her honour to the point of death, and there may be considerable pathos arising out of her suffering. Yet a fearful interest attaches itself to the tyrant also, who is elaborated into a dramatic character of some importance through the demonstration of his divided mind, the conflict between conscience and desire. As early as *Apius and Virginia* the tyrant is drawn as much more than a mere caricature of lust, and Solyman, Edward III, and King John in *The Death of Robert* are developed considerably further. There is a doubleness about these plays which the theme seems to require: each possesses two centres of emotional interest, and two careers to be worked out to their moral or tragic conclusions. In *Edward III* the conclusion is moral and patriotic, and *James IV* is very similar. In *The Death of Robert*, however, the movement of the play is tragic for the heroine: Matilda escapes the pursuit of John only in death, and John, faced by the spectacle of the suffering he has caused to Matilda and other victims of his cruelty, becomes a repentant and humble figure. In *Apius and Virginia* and *Solyman and Perseda* the tragic possibilities of the theme are applied to both tyrant and victim: the heroine preserves her honour through her willingness to die, and the tyrant who has brought this about is appropriately punished, in the earlier play through divine intervention, in the later play quite characteristically by human revenge.

Yet here, as in the other plays I have mentioned, doubleness persists in two respects: first, in what Northrop Frye has called a polarization of the emotions of pity and fear upon separate characters without any character to take up the middle ground between them,[2] and second, in a division of themes such that the fall of the virtuous heroine apparently depends upon fortune, whereas the fall of the evil tyrant depends upon retribution and the moral law. (*Solyman and Perseda* is complicated by the fact that the love of Perseda and Erastus is also a major theme of the play, but the bitter frustration of their love is blamed upon fortune's enmity.) There could be no effective means of resolving this difficulty except through a deliberate concentration upon one main character or the other—upon Macbeth and the theme of retribution, or upon the Duchess of Malfi and the theme of innocence and dignity in a world of terrifying evil. But the writers of these early plays were not yet able to escape from the habit of introducing a diversity of themes and characters for their individual moral or theatrical value.

Have the tragic plays or tragic episodes I have mentioned any importance in the contemporary exploration of the possibilities of tragic drama? Of the two main characters in this theme of threatened chastity, the tyrant, because he is the more active, comes closer to embodying the central tragic situation of human rebellion against the general scheme of things. Striving to attain his will, he meets ultimate frustration and defeat. Yet in spite of some attempts to represent division of mind in Apius, King John, and Solyman, the plays show little success in embodying a tragic theme in the figure of a tyrant. His defeat or death has little meaning beyond that of punishment for an ill course of life, and he achieves only a limited tragic recognition, a recognition of the necessity of punishment. The experience of the heroine-victim is of a different kind: she attains a degree of dignity in death which is denied to her assailant. When she becomes aware of the full dread of her situation, she accepts the necessity of death, but with a sense of the power of virtue to overcome death and a

[2] See Northrop Frye, *Anatomy of Criticism*, p. 210.

knowledge in the midst of her bitter suffering that her fame is secure among men and with God. This is true, in different degrees, of Virginia, Olympia, Perseda, and Matilda.

> *Matilda*. Oxford, for gods sake, to my father write
> The latest commendations of his childe:
> And say, Matilda kept his Honours charge,
> Dying a spotlesse maiden vndefilde,
> Bid him be glad, for I am gone to ioy:
> I that did turne his weale to bitter woe.
>
> Sinke earth to earth, fade flower, ordaind to fade:
> But passe forth soule vnto the shrine of peace. . . .[3]

It is because these plays or episodes are celebrations of virtue that this element of triumph beyond death exists in them.

The attainment of dignity in death has its importance for tragedy because it presents in dramatic form an attitude to catastrophe quite different from the moral severity of the theme of retribution. Pathos, dignity, and a hint of some eventual triumph beyond the vanity of the world are bound up together in the tragic conclusion. This combination was not to remain the unique property of the virtue plays, however. Love's martyrs were frequently associated with religion's saints and martyrs in the literature of romance, and we should not be surprised to find similar parallels in tragic plays on the theme of love. *Solyman and Perseda* is an interesting example of the double theme of martyred love and martyred virtue, since Perseda is a victim in both senses. The triumph of Love over Death is suggested in the epilogue: although Death proclaims his victories at the end, Love departs with the words, 'I go, yet *Love* shall never yield to *Death*', and undoubtedly this is a major effect of the play.

There is one other element of importance to tragedy which stands out clearly from these plays. Apius, Solyman, and King John, and to a lesser extent David, Araspas, and Theridamas, are vivid illustrations of the limitless power of passion to control and destroy a human being, a power so great that it is impossible for conscience, duty, or the codes of society to have any restraining effect. This is the power of evil which innocence must face in

---

[3] Antony Munday, *The Death of Robert Earle of Huntington*, Tudor Facsimile Texts.

all its weakness, and there are graphic scenes in the plays, like the rigged trial of Erastus and the devilish temptation of Matilda in the nunnery, to drive the contrast home. It is fortune which places an innocent victim in the power of evil, but fortune is an inadequate word to sum up the implications of such scenes. The writers show an awareness of the mystery of a scheme of things where evil can reach unbelievable depths and where virtue has little power. In *The Death of Robert* the speech of Bruse upon the walls of Windsor after the murder of his mother and brother is elaborately developed not only for the sake of pathos but also to declare the mystery of human evil.[4] It is an awareness that owes much to the religious tradition of the Middle Ages and to the religious drama which had tried to bring such evil within the scope of its interpretation.

I should not like to suggest that there is any major achievement in tragedy among the plays I have been discussing. There are too many faults of style and structure in each of them, as well as more fundamental difficulties over theme, direction, and shaping. *Apius and Virginia* is a hybrid play, neither pure morality nor pure mimesis, and interesting chiefly as revealing at an early stage the problem of more than one tragic issue, without a resolution in favour of any one of them. *Solyman and Perseda* has moved well beyond the stage of the hybrid play, but it likewise presents several tragic dilemmas—the love of Erastus and Perseda in a cruel world that alternately assists and frustrates their love, the conflict between lust and friendship in Solyman's mind, and the theme of threatened chastity as Solyman uses his power to possess Perseda. Kyd (if he wrote the play) has not succeeded in exploring very far the tension and conflict in Solyman's mind, and Solyman as a result cannot carry the tragic burden of the play. Nor are the lovers very satisfactory for this function, since they must share the tragic pattern with Solyman and since they are far more passive characters than the tyrant. The double-

> Shall I againe
> Set open shop, shew my dead ware, deare bought,
> Of a relentlesse merchant that doth trade
> On the red sea, swolne mightie with the bloud
> Of noble, vertuous, harmelesse innocents?
>   (Munday, *The Death of Robert Earle of Huntington*)

ness of emotional structure and of theme discussed above is the result of insufficient clarity of purpose and a lack of concentration. The theme of revenge, introduced near the end of the play, comes too late to draw its parts together.

The Death of Robert Earl of Huntington has a tragic atmosphere, contains several murders, and is filled with scenes of high passion, cruelty, and pathos. Chettle and Munday have written an exceptionally crowded play in an age of crowded plays. They have concentrated mainly upon 'the lamentable Tragedie of chaste Matilda', and yet the first part of the play is entirely concerned with the plot of Doncaster and the Prior against Robin Hood, and Robin's death, a tragedy of fortune inasmuch as Robin has been betrayed by fortune into the hands of his enemies. In the second and longer portion of the play John's lust for Matilda is broadened into a political theme—the effect of a ruler's lust and cruelty upon a whole people as civil war erupts and a series of terrible events follows. The conclusion of the play is divided between the pathos and dignity of Matilda's death, the moral theme of John's repentance, and the patriotic theme of the need for unity before a French invasion. The diversity of interests in the play, and the resolution of the tragic issues at the end in order to satisfy moral and patriotic needs, prevent our total absorption in the conflict between Matilda and John and greatly dilute the tragic effect. The contribution that these plays made to the contemporary understanding of tragic experience must be weighed against such faults as I have described.

Lust is the primary motive enforcing a sequence of tragic actions in these plays. It would be surprising if love had not also turned up as a tragic motive at an early stage, if only because of the large number of romances and *novelle* concerned with this theme and the famous stories of great lovers of antiquity, at a time when such stories and romances were providing so much of the material for the stage. In the romances lovers are frustrated and separated by the mischances of fortune. There may be much pathos in these stories, but generally they conclude with the overcoming of all dangerous obstacles and the reunion of the lovers. The trials of such lovers appear in *Common Conditions*,

The Rare Triumphs of Love and Fortune, and *The Weakest Goeth to the Wall,* and in the romantic comedies of Greene and Shakespeare. The theme of love from the romances is turned mainly toward comedy, though the threat of tragic action remains in the background and genuine pathos is a strand in the pattern of emotion. The form of the tragi-comedy is implied by this background.

In the collections of *novelle,* on the other hand, the aggressive and cruel forces opposed to love are embodied not so much in fortune as in jealous tyrants, feuding families, and possessive fathers, though fortune is still involved in making the lovers subject to the evils of the world. In the *novelle,* as in the older romances, there is always the chance that the obstacles of jealousy and malice will be overcome and the lovers be triumphant at the end, but those stories which belong to certain 'days' in Boccaccio's series, or to certain collections wholly tragic in nature, look forward from the beginning to the pathos of lovers dead in the very flower of their youth. The classical stories, from Virgil's Dido and Plutarch's Antony to Seneca's Phaedra, are concerned much more with the consuming and destructive power of love and its inevitable catastrophes.

There were soon some strange combinations of ideas about the meaning of the tragic experience of love. Romance and *novella* literature, as I have said, tended to stress the youth, innocence, and ultimate pathos of their lovers and the cruelty of capricious fortune, rather than any overmastering destiny or providential punishment for sin. However, both these latter conceptions derived some strength from the growing interest in Seneca and the French and Italian Senecans and from the moral attitudes of Christian humanism in its English Protestant setting. Learned dramatists writing for university or courtly audiences introduced Senecan interpretations of human experience to stories drawn from the *novelle* and the chronicles, and added moral reflections with a religious basis. Even the translators of Italian fiction spoke of their heroines as Phaedras and Medeas, and provided in prefatory matter stern warnings about God's punishment of sin, though the original stories had little of this atmosphere about them. Robert Smythe's *Straunge, Lamentable, and Tragicall*

Hystories is one of the most moral of such collections in its denunciation of the particular vices which the stories represent, as Thomas Newton's Epistle to the Reader makes plain: 'For certaynelye the view and consideration of the accidentes that haue dryuen others (for notoryous enormyties committed, and lose lyfe lewdely lead,) vpon the rufull rockes, and sandy shelues of lamentable losse, and doleful decaye, is in my opynyon a good document for vs to beware of semblable folly, & to keepe our selues within the prescripte boundes of modest behauyour.'[5] Yet the fourth story, described· in the title as follows, 'The Marques of Ferraria, without hauing regarde to fatherly loue, caused his owne Sonne to be beheaded, for that he was found in Adultery with his faire Mother in law, who lykewyse lost her head in Pryson, by his commaundement',[6] though reminding us of the Senecan parallel in this 'second Phedrya', leads up to a moment of intense pathos, which the moral condemnation at the end cannot obliterate:

These two Patients being executed, whylst men were preparing of rych and accustomable funerals, they were broughte into the base Court of the Pallas, to the ende all the world should see and beholde the cause of their death, that yet renewed the teares and complaynts of men, as well for the one as for the other, bewayling the one for hys worthynesse, the other for her curtesye, and them both for their great bewtye, and youth, wherein they were, for as yet, the more aged of them, had not attayned the age of two and twenty yeares.[7]

Gismond of Salerne represents the combination of these different influences in an interesting way. It is the earliest surviving play in English on the theme of love: the *Romeo and Juliet* mentioned by Arthur Brooke in his Preface to *Romeus and Juliet* (1562) may well have been similar in theme and treatment, and was perhaps its model.[8] *Gismond of Salerne* is, of course, an Inner Temple play, somewhat removed from the main stream of the popular drama. It has the advantages of neo-Senecan form, a certain economy of action and characters, concentration upon

---

[5] R. Smythe, *Straunge, Lamentable, and Tragicall Hystories*, To the Reader.

[6] Ibid. iv.

[7] Ibid. iv.

[8] I. Ribner, 'Then I Denie You Starres: A Reading of *Romeo and Juliet*', *Studies in the English Renaissance Drama*, p. 269.

a single subject, and an attempt at eloquence of expression through the rhetorical development of the set speech. However, it has the typical disadvantages, also, of excessive formality, stereotyped and rigid characterization, and rhetorical dialogue constantly tending to become monologue.

The influence of Seneca upon the framework of ideas in the play is as marked as it is upon the scene structure and rhetoric. The figure of Cupid represents the overwhelming force of love to seize and destroy any human being who comes under its power, and close on his heels comes nemesis, in the shape of furies from hell who rise to punish not only the lovers for their unchastity but also the father who acts as agent for the furies. Like some of the Italian neo-Senecans and the English humanists who translated Seneca, Wilmot and his colleagues identify the ancient concept of nemesis almost completely with the moral concept of retribution for sin:

> Furies must aide, when men will ceasse to know
> their Goddes: and Hell shall send reuenging paine
> to those, whom Shame from sinne can not restraine.[9]

The choruses proper and the speeches of such choral figures as Cupid and Megaera present the moral and the Senecan points of view quite forcibly, but the episodes with their dialogues and monologues retain much of the original emphasis of Boccaccio's story upon the human emotions of the three main characters. Gismond complains of the passing of youth and beauty and longs for the natural human love of the married estate. Sympathizing warmly, Lucrece puts her case to Tancred and receives an angry reply, full of possessiveness and jealousy. The effect upon Gismond, who has already fallen in love with Guishard, is violent, and pity for her misery is aroused by Claudia's report. Although the lovers never appear together in the play except in dumb show, their courage and dignity in facing the furious passion of Tancred and in resolving for death, without regret or fear, must lead an audience to sympathize with them strongly. Even the messenger's report of Guishard's death, with its many echoes of Seneca, reinforces the sense of the lover's youth and

---

[9] R. Wilmot et al., *Gismond of Salerne*, IV. i. 42–44, in *Early English Classical Tragedies*, ed. J. W. Cunliffe.

courage and the pity of his death. As Gismond receives her lover's heart in a cup of gold and drinks the poison she has prepared, we are brought close to the atmosphere of the original story, the pathos of lovers overcome by the cruelty of the world.

As in the 'trial of virtue' plays, pathos is qualified by the courage and dignity with which the lovers prepare for death. They are love's martyrs, in spite of the condemnation they received earlier in the play. In this world their fame will be remembered in a single tomb and epitaph, 'that all louers may rue this mornefull case'; and in the world beyond their souls will be reunited. As Gismond declares just before she takes poison:

> Ah Lord, wth what more sweter companie,
> or more content, or safer may I proue
> to seke to passe to places all vnknowen,
> than thus wth thee? For I am sure euen here
> doest thow yet stay, and tarry me thine owne.
> Thy soule abideth me to be thy fere,
> and lingreth in this place for me, I know.[10]

This combination of pathos, dignity, and a sense of some greater value beyond the vanity of this world is ultimately at odds with the Senecan and retributive tones that dominated the earlier part of the play. It is a distinctive mark of the play, which links it with the plays on the theme of chastity.

I have said little about Tancred's part in the drama. In the main, he is the great obstacle to the fulfilment of the lovers' desires, summing up in his person both family pride as a father and the morality of society as a king. He is therefore a formidable figure, even without his Senecan enlargement into a furious tyrant and revenger. The single touch of psychological realism in his portrait, deriving from the original story, which allows him to be something of a tragic character in his own right, is his possessiveness, his desire to have Gismond for himself after her first husband has died, to care for him in his old age and close his eyes in death. As a Senecan revenger he is much less human, but here too there is a tragic element in that the revenge recoils upon himself and forces him to destroy himself. Perhaps it was a recognition of this element that led Wilmot in his revision of the

---

[10] Ibid. v. ii. 51–57.

play to enlarge the final scene and show on the stage the putting
out of eyes and the self-slaughter of Tancred. But it has the effect
of destroying the pathos of Gismond's death, and upsetting the
balance of the original play, where Tancred's part remained
subsidiary.

I have already spoken of *Solyman and Perseda*, in relation to the
'trial of virtue' theme, as a play which has more than one centre
of tragic interest. One of its themes is the tragic frustration of
love, or the constancy of love and the inconstancy of fortune.
As in *Gismond of Salerne*, the great obstacle to the lovers' desires
is embodied in a single character who is also involved in a tragic
pattern of action, and, even more clearly than in the earlier play,
he takes over much of the dramatic interest. In the early scenes
Erastus and Perseda are constantly frustrated by fortune and
Erastus complains bitterly against their fate. There is a characteristic scene of fulfilment of desire at the centre of the play, but
it is presented ironically, like similar scenes in *Gismond of Salerne*
and *Romeo and Juliet*, as being subject to the whim of fortune
and the malice of the world. In his moment of bliss, Erastus is
unaware that the choral figure of Fortune has promised otherwise:

> And doubt not to, but Fortune will be there,
> And cross him too, and sometimes flatter him,
> And lift him up, and throw him downe againe.[11]

However, the pathos of the lovers' separation and death is almost
completely lost in the tragedy of Solyman's fall through the
revenge of Perseda. Throughout the play attention has been
divided between the Erastus–Perseda relationship, lovers struggling against the tyranny of a cruel world embodied in the figure
of Solyman, and the Solyman–Perseda relationship, lustful
tyrant against chaste heroine. In his second capacity Solyman is
enlarged beyond the scale needed for the tragic love story of
Erastus and Perseda, and at the end is the dominant tragic
character.

One of the curious features of the play is its resemblance to the
Renaissance debate upon a problem of honour or love: in the

[11] Thomas Kyd, *Solyman and Perseda*, II. iii. 15–17.

Induction, Love, Fortune, and Death argue the question as to
which one should act as chorus to this tragedy, and the action
proceeds as a series of illustrations of their separate powers. But
there is no exploration of the nature of love as it affects Solyman,
as well as Erastus, and no strongly felt analysis of the evil passions
of Solyman and his followers. The superficial element of debate
in the background of the play adds nothing to its tragic meaning
and may be one reason for its lack of dramatic urgency and
feeling.

There is little in the earlier plays to suggest the greatness of
Shakespeare's achievement in *Romeo and Juliet*, nor can one say
that *Romeo and Juliet* is the product of a dramatic tradition, so
tenuous and slight is the appearance of the theme of love in
tragedy up to this time. Shakespeare did not need *Gismond of
Salerne*, nor even the early *Romeo and Juliet*, to suggest either
theme or treatment. He found his subject in the romantic literature of the age, already translated from an Italian *novella* into a
narrative verse tragedy. The achievement of the play lies in its
marvellous lyricism and the transformation of the action and
feeling of the poem into scenes of great dramatic immediacy,
both of these the product of Shakespeare's own rapid development as a poet and a dramatist. Nevertheless, it is essentially the
same kind of tragedy as we have been considering: it has little
to do with the theme of retribution, so powerful in the chronicles
and the *Mirror* tragedies, nor with the careful working out of
patterns of cause and effect enforced by such motives as ambition
or revenge.

In atmosphere and feeling *Romeo and Juliet* is close to the
tragic tales of love in the *novelle*, where youth and innocence are
in conflict with the cruelty of fortune and the malice of the world
of experience. Shakespeare does not describe the love of Romeo
and Juliet as lust that deserves to be punished, nor as a destructive passion of the Senecan kind, which carries the seeds of doom
within itself. In this respect the play differs from Brooke's poem,
with its moral accretions, and from that part of *Gismond of
Salerne* which is peculiarly Senecan. Their love is sudden,
immoderate, and desperately impatient to secure its end. Yet
its vehemence is due simply to their devotion to something

beyond all normal considerations and cautions, in comparison
with which nothing else matters. The lovers in the earlier plays
may be equally devoted, but how much more completely Shakespeare makes us believe in his!

The strength of their love is a measure, too, of the rebellion
of Romeo and Juliet against a scheme of things which denies
them fulfilment—the world of feuding, hatred, and murder,
given over to the cruel deeds of men and the senseless happenings of chance. The lovers reach out toward happiness and refuse
to admit their subjection to the world of fortune and the world
of evil human passions. The same striving, the same rebellion
against the enmity of the world, occurs in the earlier plays, as
we have seen. Then quite suddenly, with the death of Tybalt,
they are totally involved in this world, subject both to its accidents
and its malice. They continue to defy this world, but there is no
escape.

Destiny, fortune, and providence are all referred to at various
points in the play, and we must ask whether these terms are
merely functions of characterization, or whether they represent
a serious interpretation of meaning, as they do in *Gismond of
Salerne*. There seems to be a fundamental incongruity between
what the lovers perceive as a hostile fate from the very beginning:

> . . . for my mind misgives
> Some consequence, yet hanging in the stars,
> Shall bitterly begin his fearful date
> With this night's revels . . . ,
>
> (I. iv. 106-9)

and what the prince recognizes at the end as the hand of Providence, punishing the parents through the children, and para-
doxically killing their joys with love:

> Capulet, Montague,
> See what a scourge is laid upon your hate,
> That heaven finds means to kill your joys with love!
> (V. iii. 291-3)

The two points of view are difficult to reconcile because the
providential wisdom of the conclusion seems so remote from
anything which the lovers experience in the midst of their

passion. One might expect Providence to work toward reconciliation through love, as Friar Lawrence indicates at an early
point in the intrigue:

> For this alliance may so happy prove
> To turn your households' rancour to pure love.
>
> (II. iii. 91–92)

But the ironic way in which this end is brought about is scarcely
proof of divine care. Fortune appears to rule in a cruel and
malicious way: Romeo cries out against 'this day's black fate'
when his attempt at peace-making has led to Mercutio's death,
and even Friar Lawrence exclaims 'Unhappy Fortune' when
the letter to Romeo is not delivered.

The most powerful scenes of the play impress upon us the fact
that Romeo and Juliet, once love has seized them, have become
subject to a world of evil passions, cruelty, and violence, where
accident or ill chance can frustrate human purpose beyond hope
of recovery. This is the world that Fortune rules. Through their
suffering the lovers come to realize and accept this, and yet they
hold fast to love. Their strong resolution for death is their
rejection of the fallen world, parallel to, though not encompass-
ing, the Christian's rejection of the world of vanity:

> O here
> Will I set up my everlasting rest
> And shake the yoke of inauspicious stars
> From this world-wearied flesh
>
> (V. iii. 109–12)

The tragic recognition which the fathers attain is not, in the
end, so far removed from that of the lovers. They see that the
fallen world in which fortune acts cruelly is their own creation.
They see clearly at last how the law of hatred and violence
operates, and its tragic results. A universal law has involved them
all, the guilty and the innocent alike, in its stern working out:
'All are punish'd.' Reconciliation comes too late for them as
individuals—they are close to the grave and Montague's wife is
already dead—as it is too late for Romeo and Juliet, and yet it is
necessary as the very symbol of what they have learned. All of
this is expressed briefly and simply, so as not to draw attention

away from the pathos of the lovers' deaths. There is only a hint at the end that good may grow out of evil and that this, perhaps, is the source of consolation. The seeming opposition between fortune and providence in the play disappears in this final view of a world ruled by fortune and the evil passions of men, but subject in the long run to the laws established by providence. The lovers and the fathers move beyond the realm of fortune in different ways, but this does not invalidate the experience of either.

To return briefly to the central tragic movement of the play: in spite of the tendency toward pathos as the dominant emotion, because of the nature of the theme and the innocence of the main characters, *Romeo and Juliet* is clearly a distinctive form of tragedy in its own right. I have spoken of tragedy as an intense representation of defeat, when those who act because of some strong passion or great desire come into conflict with a superior law or scheme of things that denies them fulfilment. Usually they act in ignorance of the true nature of this conflict or its full implications until it is too late: recognition comes after the agony of defeat and suffering. As rebels against fate, Romeo and Juliet stand at the innocent end of the spectrum, reaching out in passionate desire for the fulfilment of their love. The fate against which they must struggle is all that is enforced by their environment, the suspicion and hate which rule the world around them. Their rebellion is imprudent, hasty, and in some respects blind to the forces arrayed against them, and yet in the end, when they have recognized defeat, their defiance is mature and complete. This defiance of the lovers, and their allegiance to something greater than the attainment of human happiness, reveals that there are two kinds of superior law in the play, one dominating and compulsive, enforcing the tragic action and the catastrophe, the other remote and scarcely discernible except briefly at the end. The sense of its presence, however, is strong enough to throw the other into perspective and show that the world of human evil and indifferently cruel chance is not the final law of existence.

If we try to regard the tragedies of love as a group, it is quite apparent that none of the earlier plays is a complete tragedy in the

sense that *Romeo and Juliet* is, because there is little human
reality in the characters of the lovers and therefore little intensity
in their tragic predicament. Yet one can see that the distinctive
kind of tragedy that *Romeo and Juliet* represents also exists in the
earlier plays, that the tragedies of love and the 'trial of virtue'
plays prepared the way for this kind of tragedy. Like the heroines
of the 'trial of virtue' plays, the lovers rebel against a world of
evil passions and harsh obstacles to happiness and adhere to
values of greater worth than life itself. As a result, the pathos of
the catastrophe is qualified by a sense of strength and dignity,
and the utter defeat of the lovers' desires is mixed with some
slight hint of triumph, in a characteristic emotional pattern. The
earlier plays also lay stress on fortune's enmity and the opposition
of the world as two different aspects of the same cruel antagonism, which often aid each other in order to bring about
disaster. However, there is nothing in the earlier plays to suggest
either the intensity of Shakespeare's exploration of this experience, or the difficult balance he achieves at the end between
fortune, human responsibility, and providence.

Fortune in a traditional sense played a prominent part in a
number of early plays in which the tragic motive is ambition.
The fickleness of fortune and the vanity of worldly hopes, a
commonplace in medieval literature, remained important in
works which influenced Elizabethan tragedy directly, in many
of the *Mirror* tragedies, for example, in the chronicles, and in the
choruses of Seneca's tragedies. Yet for several reasons this theme
of the conflict between ambition and fortune did not take up a
dominant place in tragedy. It must have seemed old-fashioned
and exhausted as a mode of interpreting the violent changes in
human affairs even by the middle years of the sixteenth century,
when both history and the *Mirror* tragedies were concentrating
upon linked series of cause and effect and upon the operation of
universal moral laws in human affairs. War might still be a matter
of fortune's hazard in the *Mirror* tragedies, but the most vigorous
and interesting of these tragédies were concerned with intrigue,
the clash of one type of character with another, the relation of
character to event, and the causal connexion between crime and

punishment—all of this much more useful to the dramatist than
the simple contrast between high prosperity and abject misery,
which was all that the traditional tragedy of fortune had to offer.

Early stage plays in which fortune is ranged against ambition
suggest the truth of these observations: we seldom find a 'straight'
treatment of the theme except in minor tragedies within a larger
structure, but rather a number of variations upon the theme.
Indeed, some of the variations turn the theme upside down. Two
or three plays have survived which seem to be quite close to the
traditional subject of the brittleness of worldly glory, the downfall of great figures through the inevitable turning of Fortune's
wheel: *Thomas Lord Cromwell*, *Sir Thomas More*, and *The
Wounds of Civil War*. But Cromwell is a cautious climber, fully
aware of the dangers of high place, rather than the proud and
over-confident victim of fortune we might expect. More is the
unwilling holder of high place, with religious scruples against
worldly pride and vanity. In the third play both Marius and
Scilla are ambitious heroes, but each tries to avoid the pride of
success and reduce his vulnerability to fortune's possible enmity.
Much more striking variations upon the theme occur in plays
like *Tamburlaine* and *Selimus*. In the former the traditional falls
of great kings and emperors through the fortunes of war are
used to emphasize the daring rebellion of Tamburlaine himself
against old ideas of fortune's supremacy. In *Selimus* fortune is
the element of chance in human affairs that presents opportunities of all kinds to those who know how to make use of them:
if Tamburlaine overcomes fortune through sheer will, Selimus
outwits fortune through his alertness and cunning.

Many plays which contain subsidiary tragedies of fortune are
left without any kind of integration. A play that hinges on both
fortune and retribution may simply alternate these interpretations, as if the writer were trying to find the appropriate moral
for each episode without any thought for the whole. In *Locrine*,
for example, the history of Albanact is pure tragedy of fortune,
as Albanact, the brave and virtuous hero, is struck down by
the invading forces of Humber. The history of Humber which
follows is developed at first as a tragedy of fortune, with a typical
protagonist, proud and over-confident, heading for disaster.

Even the ghost of Albanact, though seeking by now a Senecan vengeance, is constrained to cry out against fortune when he sees Humber so deceived before his fall:

> See how the traitor doth presage his harme,
> See how he glories at his owne decay,
> See how he triumphs at his proper losse,
> O fortune vilde, unstable, fickle, fraile.[12]

But when Humber is defeated and driven to despair and suicide, the moral that is drawn is plainly one of retribution. The ghost of Albanact now declares:

> Loe here the gist of fell ambition,
> Of usurpation and of trecherie
> Loe here the harmes that wait upon all those
> That do intrude themselves in others lands,
> Which are not under their dominion.[13]

In the second section of the play the history of Locrine is worked out carefully and thoroughly as a tragedy of retribution, and this dominates the action. Yet there are still subsidiary tragedies of fortune, like those of Elstrid and Sabren. The despairing cry of Elstrid before her death is a *locus classicus* of the idea of fortune:

> O fickle fortune, O unstable world
> What else are all things that this globe containes,
> But a confused chaos of mishaps?
> Wherein as in a glasse we plainly see,
> That all our life is but as a Tragedie.[14]

However, it has little connexion with the idea of providential rule and moral law which governs the action in the latter half of the play, and is obviously simply the expected and appropriate comment upon Elstrid's fate.

Subsidiary tragedies of fortune are not all like these—merely conventional episodes in plays that have some other basis for thought and feeling. Some are very carefully planned in relation to the structure of the whole: thus, in one type of play, they have

---

[12] *Locrine*, Malone Society Reprints, ll. 1089-92.
[13] Ibid., ll. 1675-9.
[14] Ibid., ll. 2116-20.

the function of revealing the kind of world the central characters are reacting against or denying with all the power and cunning at their disposal, as we may see very clearly in *Tamburlaine* and *Selimus*. Such plays picture the falls of lesser characters through fortune's enmity in order to make the defiance of fortune by the main characters more striking. *Tamburlaine I*, for example, is a reversal of all that the traditional theme had made familiar and expected. The enormous pride and self-confidence of Tamburlaine, his defiance of fortune and the gods, seem to mark the typical attitude of fortune's intended victim in exaggerated form. Other characters in the play opposed to Tamburlaine constantly expect his downfall, and Zenocrate, when she finds the bodies of Bajazeth and Zabina, expresses her great fear:

> Those that are proud of fickle empery
> And place their chiefest good in earthly pomp,
> Behold the Turk and his great emperess!
> Ah, Tamburlaine, my love, sweet Tamburlaine,
> That fightst for sceptres and for slippery crowns,
> Behold the Turk and his great emperess!
>
> (v. ii. 290–5)

Marlowe uses the traditional language and feeling to arouse admiration and awe for the hero who has nothing but contempt for the lessons of human experience.

Tamburlaine Part II is less single-minded than Part I and there is a different balance of dramatic forces within the play. In several of the main episodes we are made aware of conflicts other than that between Tamburlaine and fortune. The war between Orcanes and Sigismund leads up to the utter defeat of Sigismund in a way that suggests the intervention of a law of retribution. Orcanes is impressed by the swiftness of the Christian God in avenging dishonour, though Gazellus remains convinced that ' 'tis but the fortune of the wars'. The element of doubt expressed in this disagreement between them is part of Marlowe's refusal to draw dogmatic conclusions from experience. The episode of Olympia works in another direction to show a firm allegiance to honour and a contempt for fortune utterly unlike Tamburlaine's frontal attack on fortune's power.

In the central scenes of the play something of the momentum

of Part I is carried on as Tamburlaine maintains his ascendancy over fortune. But the emphasis has shifted: the struggle with fortune no longer seems to matter so much. Tamburlaine is faced now with the one element of human experience he cannot evade, and his grandiose speeches about attacks on the gods and the fates melt away before the fact of human mortality, Zenocrate's and his own. We recognize a change of tone in the laments of his great lieutenants, since they regard his approaching death as a reversal of all that his stars had enforced for so long. Hence, at the end, triumph over fortune is mingled with defeat, the defeat of the unbounded aspirations of his mind.

The two parts of *Tamburlaine*, as it has so often been said, make up an epic biography rather than a tragedy. In Part II there is no powerful concentration upon Tamburlaine's meeting with destiny, which is ultimately his confrontation with death. Too many other episodes and themes are introduced, and the element of triumph remains too strong throughout most of the play to allow the growth of tragic feeling. Nevertheless, in his intoxication with the splendour of Tamburlaine's greatness of mind, Marlowe developed to an extreme form an essential ingredient of tragedy, the rebelliousness of an individual against a scheme of things which seeks to deny or suppress his great desire. Tamburlaine's absolute and complete rebellion against normal human limitations, against fortune, against whatever laws may exist, provided a prototype for the rebellious will of many later tragic heroes.

Selimus presents us with another battle between human will and fortune, though not quite in the same exalted terms. Fortune is often enough spoken of as a goddess with her traditional wheel, but is regarded in practice by the villains of the piece simply as the element of chance. Selimus as fortune's antagonist does not, like Tamburlaine, belong to a different order of beings from ordinary humanity. Although he proclaims his superiority to fortune and scorns the old, religious, warnings about retribution in this world or the next, and although he acts in complete defiance of all normal codes, it is through his cleverness and unscrupulous villainy that he succeeds. *Selimus* is well on the way to being the villain play in which fortune is merely chance and the villain is an opportunist who makes use of every opening that chance allows him:

> Will fortune favour me yet once againe?
> And will she thrust the cards into my hands?
> Well if I chance but once to get the decke,
> To deale about and shufle as I would,
> Let *Selim* never see the day-light spring,
> Unlesse I shuffle out my selfe a king.[15]

Selimus is by no means a tragedy, but it contains tragic episodes involving a number of minor characters. As I have suggested, these episodes have the direct function of revealing a world which Selimus is intent upon denying altogether. The innocent characters who suffer most severely cry out against fortune, but it is plain that the fortune from which they suffer is the clever villainy and opportunism of Selimus and Acomat. The complete success of Selimus at the end of the play, and the promise of a sequel which 'shall greater murthers tell', is a reversal of traditional ideas of fortune's fickleness and a reversal, too, of any law of retribution for crime. It appears that the theme of fortune is introduced into the subsidiary tragedies only to throw the main action of Selimus's manipulation of fortune into greater relief.

There is another way, even more important for the growth of tragedy, in which minor tragedies of fortune may become an integral part of a play. They may reveal one aspect of a world where several orders of experience can be observed existing together in a complex relationship. For example, it may be a world where all men are subject to fortune and the historical processes of cause and effect, but at the same time a world where some men make themselves subject, through sin or crime, to moral laws that take precedence over the general law of fortune. It is often dramatic irony which makes such complex attitudes explicit. Thus Mordred in *The Misfortunes of Arthur* resembles Selimus in his denial of all law beyond the individual will, but his reasoned defence of 'chance' as the determining factor in human life is ironically placed against a background of destiny and punishment for sin which has been vividly presented to the audience by ghost and dumb show from the beginning of

---

[15] *Selimus*, Malone Society Reprints, ll. 1539-44.

the play.[16] In another play, *The Battle of Alcazar*, which is also classical in its mode of presentation, the Moor's radical naturalism is ironically viewed against the growing force of stern retribution. His outcry against fortune is very different in effect from Captain Stukeley's, which is a genuine complaint against fortune's overthrows. The most obvious example of such irony in a play which is not academic and classical occurs in Marlowe's *Edward II*: Mortimer's complaint against fortune at the moment of his downfall is completely at odds with the general atmosphere of retribution which hangs over him and with the specific accusations of the young king:

K. Edw. Third. Hence with the traitor, with the murderer!
Y. Mor.   Base Fortune, now I see that in thy wheel
         There is a point, to which when men aspire,
         They tumble headlong down; that point I touch'd,
         And, seeing there was no place to mount up higher,
         Why should I grieve at my declining fall?

                                        (v. vi. 57–62)

In each of these plays the irony depends upon the superiority of one interpretation of existence over another, but it does not destroy the inferior interpretation, the agnostic view of fortune, since it is true up to a point and has some basis in human experience. In *Edward II*, for example, the normal historical processes of cause and effect act powerfully throughout most of the play and they are constantly modified by accidents of the world of fortune—the chances of war, by which the barons are sometimes successful and Edward and his party sometimes successful; the headwinds that prevent the escape of Edward to Ireland; the very recognition of the king's party by a Welsh mower. At the end the tension between fortune and retribution, as they affect Mortimer and as they affect Edward, is resolved in favour of retribution, but the world of fortune continues to exist.

The chronicle plays in general are filled with the clash of intrigue and the striving of ambition against ambition, violent human effort worked out on a naturalistic basis; they contain

---

[16] Thomas Hughes, *The Misfortunes of Arthur*, II. ii, in *Early English Classical Tragedies*.

also the risks of chance and the accidents of war, fortune's over-throws, which often mock the most determined human effort and seem mysterious or else completely random; yet many of them move beyond the realm of fortune toward some hint of eventual justice in human affairs. They are tentative in their exploration of the meaning of events and the responsibility of individuals for those events: the various elements I have mentioned are brought together in each play in different relationships. In the three parts of *Henry VI*, for example, Henry represents in his own career and in his attitude to what happens to him a medieval conception of fortune: the world is a place of sad mishaps, where greatness is continually liable to fall, where evil is unhampered and innocence must suffer terribly. At one point in Part III Henry tries to hand over the rule of the kingdom to Warwick in order to forestall fortune's envy of the great by keeping his head low. Most of the other characters, however, represent the energy and will of agnostic man in their willingness to take a chance with fortune for the sake of power. As crime leads to crime, however, each one remembered and pressing toward its appropriate punishment, the idea of fortune fades and a sense of retribution grows: the series of plays moves toward its con-clusion in *Richard III*. These attitudes exist together in the four plays, and it is only gradually that one of them, retribution, becomes dominant.

Richard II is the best example of the linking of fortune with other themes to present a complex interpretation of a tragic career. Dover Wilson, in his Introduction to the play, states that the wheel of fortune is constantly in Shakespeare's mind through-out the action, that it 'determines the play's shape and structure, which gives us a complete inversion'.[17] At the beginning, Dover Wilson continues, Richard is at the high point of the wheel's turning and exhibits the typical characteristics of a person in that dangerous position. The wheel begins to turn and Richard falls, almost passively, as if there is nothing he can do about it, while Bolingbroke rises, 'borne upward by a power beyond his voli-tion'.[18]

[17] *King Richard II*, ed. J. Dover Wilson, p. xx.
[18] Ibid.

It is true that the structure and feeling of the play are strongly influenced by the traditional concept of fortune. Richard sees himself as the victim of fortune and links himself with the unfortunate kings and nobles of the past who have suffered through no fault of their own. There are obvious echoes of the *Mirror* tragedies of fortune in his farewell speech to the queen:

> Think I am dead, and that even here thou takest
> As from my death-bed thy last living leave;
> In winter's tedious nights sit by the fire
> With good old folks, and let them tell thee tales
> Of woeful ages long ago betid;
> And ere thou bid good night, to quit their griefs,
> Tell thou the lamentable fall of me,
> And send the hearers weeping to their beds.
> For why, the senseless brands will sympathize
> The heavy accent of thy moving tongue,
> And in compassion weep the fire out,
> And some will mourn in ashes, some coal-black,
> For the deposing of a rightful king.
>
> (v. i. 38–50)

This is largely a dramatization of himself as an innocent victim of the deceit of fortune and the malice of ambitious men. Yet it is a view which has some validity. Fortune does work against Richard in hindering his landing from Ireland and in dispersing his army. In a larger sense it works against him as an inevitable law of change, so that men's hearts are turned away from Richard and toward Bolingbroke without sufficient cause. The contemptuous reception of Richard by the London crowds is a vivid representation of the fickleness of fortune identified with the fickleness of the mob.

At the same time, the audience is not meant to see Richard only as an innocent victim. He is presented as an impulsive and reckless weakling, subject to the whims of flatterers, unable to control his quarrelling nobles, and seldom able to follow a consistent course of action for long. He is self-indulgent, wilful, and more inclined to follow the dictates of emotion than those of reason. Shakespeare has worked out with considerable care the process by which weakness of character brings disaster upon itself in a situation of crisis. In action, Richard is a robber of other men's goods and disregards his primary duty, the welfare of his kingdom. From this point of view Richard's dramatization of himself as fortune's victim has an ironic quality which reminds us of Mortimer in *Edward II* and Mordred in *The Misfortunes of Arthur*, though the irony is subtler.

There is one other important element in the play that cannot be neglected, the ritualistic quality apparent in the inversion of the coronation rite, such images as the clouding over of the sun and the withering of the rose, and the suffering of Richard toward the end of the play in his role as anointed king rather than as neglectful and worldly ruler. The larger destiny of the kingdom is involved in a series of events that seems necessary and inevitable in the short term, but which will lead to civil war and endless suffering before the evil of the deed has been worked out and reconciliation is possible.

The theme of fortune, then, is only one among several important themes in the play. Of the greatest importance is the fact that these different modes of interpretation are not set down side by side as simple alternatives; they grow one out of another, so that none needs to be discarded, but the range of significance appears to deepen as the play moves on. Yet they are all based firmly upon a literal level of action which is comprehensible in its own terms of character, politics, and war. The measure of *Richard II* as complete tragedy I should prefer to leave until we have considered the tragic concept of retribution.

We have seen little evidence that an idea of fortune could shape tragic material into a conflict and catastrophe of some power. Many of the direct references to fortune in chronicle plays and early tragedies are merely conventional recollections of an earlier tradition. Yet there are plays in which the idea of fortune's fall remains a vital strand, referring either to the mysterious tides of change which seem to affect individual human lives and whole societies, or to the random happenings of chance that disturb in their turn the expected sequences of cause and effect. By retaining the tradition of fortune in such vital senses as these the writers of such plays showed their awareness of the complexity of causes for tragic events. They qualified the rigour of moral interpretations and underlined the mystery still remaining in supposedly transparent processes of cause and effect. Whether such a principle of uncertainty was to be important for Eliza-bethan tragedy we have still to see.

V

'GOD'S REVENGING ASPECT'

WILLARD FARNHAM has advanced the claim that the gradual clarification and strengthening of the idea of retribution was one of the basic factors in the development of Elizabethan tragedy, because it provided a means of giving significance to violent action and of linking events together in a chain of cause and effect.[1] Tragedy did not develop only along this path, as we have noted already, but it is one of the important directions to be considered. In the chronicles retribution was frequently a major theme, and its various manifestations were imaginatively explored by the contributors to the *Mirror for Magistrates*. On the considered and eloquent advice of many humanists, classical tragedy was read through moral blinkers; the translators of Seneca added scenes when they felt that the original play had not been explicit enough in this regard. Many of the translators of the Italian *novelle*, also, sought out suitable tales among the collections for their own moralizing reflections. On the popular stage retribution had been a familiar concept for a long time in the religious drama, associated with spectacular tyrants like Pharaoh, Herod, and Antichrist, and with the great sinners from Adam and Cain to Judas Iscariot. It had also become a major theme in the morality plays as they grew away from abstraction toward the direct representation of life.

There is no difficulty about the reasons why learned dramatists should have emphasized this theme. The moral concern of English humanists led them to Italian critics and dramatists, who had elaborated the tenets of Horace and Aristotle and illustrated the moral purpose of literature in their tragedies.[2] To the English humanists tragic drama was serious and moral by

[1] Willard Farnham, *The Medieval Heritage of Elizabethan Tragedy*, pp. 162, 193, and 232.

[2] Representative passages occur in R. Wilmot's letter 'To the Worshipfull and learned Societie' affixed to *The Tragedy of Tancred and Gismund* (1591-2), in George Puttenham, *The Arte of English Poesie* (I. xv), and in Sidney's *An Apology for Poetry*.

its very nature, and these qualities were the justification of its existence. It was inevitable that such a view of the nature of tragedy should combine with the moralizing tendency in English historical writing to produce plays with a striking concentration upon the theme of retribution.

In the realm of popular drama the humanist reasons for adopting a moral pattern in tragedy had much less force: there was no overpowering desire to imitate classical drama according to the dogmas of the Italian critics. Nevertheless, the prestige of classical tragedy and of notable productions at court and in the universities must have had some effect, if only because of the competition among adult companies to obtain the patronage of the court. The main sources of a moral patterning of events in the popular drama, however, lay in the obstinate persistence of the morality play and in the emphatic moral attitudes running through the subject-matter upon which the stage drew—the English chronicles, many of the *novelle* as translated and commented upon in their English editions, romances like the *Arcadia*, and the ballads and the broadsheets.

Let us look briefly, first of all, at two or three of the academic plays where the theme of retribution plays a major part, and try to judge the importance of this theme in shaping their tragic direction. *Gorboduc*, *The Misfortunes of Arthur*, and *Locrine* have the outward characteristics of Renaissance classical tragedy and in each there is an attempt at some kind of classical form, though *Locrine* has certain popular elements absent in the other two. They are thoroughly moral in the Senecan-humanist manner in that every crime leads to its appropriate punishment, and they are filled with sententious commentary on the action. Yet there are distinct differences in their use of the theme of retribution. *The Misfortunes of Arthur* comes closest to the Senecan idea of nemesis. The initial dumb show and the ghost of Gorlois reveal the origin of the tragic action as a curse laid by the gods upon the whole issue of Uther Pendragon because of his 'unlawful heat and love'. The curse has worked itself out through succeeding crimes and sins by which the victims of the curse have damned themselves. As the play begins, the final moment of retribution has arrived, and reveals itself as the fatal strife between father and

son, Arthur and Mordred. There is no escape from the doom
which the gods have settled upon the house of Arthur.

The authors of *Gorboduc*, on the other hand, preferred to stress
the tragic effect upon a whole people of Gorboduc's initial folly
in dividing his realm. Although mistakes are punished by crimes,
and these in turn punished by further crimes, it is the process of
social retribution which is most important in the play—the effect
on the dynasty and on the nation as a whole. We have noticed
already that *Locrine* is a mixed play, part tragedy of fortune, part
tragedy of retribution. Yet even as a tragedy of retribution the
play is by no means single in effect, since it has two main characters in whom the theme is embodied. Humber, the first of these,
deserves to fall because of his unlawful ambition as an invading
enemy and usurper of power. His ruin comes about quite simply
through the fortunes of war. Locrine also deserves punishment
because of his unlawful lust, but his punishment is worked out
in a very different way, as the direct consequence of his sins. By
giving way to lust Locrine divides the kingdom and raises up
enemies against himself: thus the process of retribution is made
to seem the natural outcome of human passion and political
struggle. *Locrine* is like *Gorboduc* in this respect, but the suffering of individuals is of more importance in *Locrine* than it is in
the earlier play.

Do the academic tragedies show that the theme of retribution is capable of tragic development? There are signs that it
has this potentiality, but its development is hindered by major
faults of structure and style in the plays themselves, which prevent the successful representation of such a theme in terms of
human experience. Thus Gorboduc is a great character who
clearly must suffer because of his stubborn refusal to heed good
advice and his insistence on following his own will. He seeks a
certain limited good, but through his wilfulness releases passions beyond anything his imagination can foresee, and fails
utterly. The resemblance to Lear is striking at the beginning,
but Gorboduc does not approach the depths of experience that
Lear goes through on his way to self-awareness and an awareness
of the human condition. The agony of the individual, whether it
is Gorboduc's or that of any of the lesser characters, is neglected

for moral lessons and social propaganda. Only Porrex is given an opportunity to express his despair after the deed of violence. The moral idea takes precedence over the human experience.

The Misfortunes of Arthur has the advantage of concentration and a sense of climax. In neo-Senecan fashion, Hughes fills in the background of sin and crime through the devices of dumb show and ghost and directs our attention to the state of mind of his three major characters immediately before the conflict which brings disaster to them all. He is fairly successful in picturing Arthur's division of mind, forced to war against his own son, and in describing Mordred's alternations between unrepentant villainy and intuitions of disaster. Nor does he neglect Arthur's final grief and despair, his recognition of the fulfilment of the curse, and his acceptance of his destiny. However, the devices from Senecan and neo-classical tragedy, which ought to have been subordinate to these central dramatic issues, instead obscure them: there is too much of dumb show, ghost, and chorus, and there are too many confidants and counsellors. Hughes is a 'desperate imitator', as Cunliffe says.[3] He is always trying to strain the pitch of horror through the use of Senecan imagery, and he is unable to give much reality to his formal and imitative portraits of character.

Even less needs to be said of *Locrine* because its major fault is so obvious. The historical process is far too important, preventing any tragic concentration upon a single issue or a single character. If the writer had drawn his material together around Locrine, he might have written an effective tragedy of retribution, since Locrine is a mixed character, neither simple hero nor simple villain, who brings his doom upon himself. The process by which Locrine damns himself, allowing his courage and greatness to be overcome by the strength of his lust, is represented with considerable success, but the tragedy of Locrine occupies only part of the last two acts. There are too many other 'tragedies' in the play, and, as I have already pointed out, a tendency to shift between fortune and retribution as the occasion demands.

These academic plays show, I believe, that retribution is one means of taking an individual through a traumatic experience to

[3] J. W. Cunliffe, *Early English Classical Tragedies*, p. xci.

a final point of recognition or awareness by which he is forced to accept his fate. It is perhaps significant that the major figure in each play is a character possessing many great qualities, which help to make the shock and despair more credible. Tragedy lies, I have suggested, in the defeat of human hopes or aspirations when the individual confronts a destiny he has not been able to foresee. If the character is capable of greatness, then he is also capable of a shattering defeat; however, such a reversal can only have a powerful effect upon an audience when the mode of expression is adequate. Unhappily, none of the writers of these plays was able to achieve a successful fusion of theme and concrete experience, largely because of faults inherent in the forms they imitated.

There were many precedents for the theme of retribution on the popular stage, both in the mystery plays about Biblical tyrants and in the late morality plays, where pride, worldliness, and blasphemy were severely punished. Early moral histories like *Apius and Virginia*, *Godly Queen Hester*, and *Cambises* were firmly based on retribution as a result of this tradition. However, there was no widespread and automatic transposition of this theme to chronicle material when history plays began to appear on the popular stage. Some dramatists, perhaps influenced by the romantic drama of the preceding two decades, seem to have been much more interested in fact than idea, in the spectacular events associated with some great figure than in the reasons for those events or the moral to be drawn from them (*The Famous Victories*, *Jack Straw*, *Edward I*). However, one group of plays at the very beginning of the chronicle play's development— *Henry VI*, *Edward II*, *Woodstock*, and *The Troublesome Reign*— reveals a major attempt to come to terms with the political and moral ideas of Hall's *Chronicle* and the *Mirror for Magistrates*: in these plays, as E. M. W. Tillyard, A. P. Rossiter, and others have shown, there is a remarkable selection and shaping of historical events in order to trace the processes of cause and effect and to suggest patterns of meaning beyond the events themselves.

Only one of these plays, *Edward II*, can be called a tragedy, and it happens to be a play in which the theme of retribution is dominant. In the rest many other themes take precedence—indecisive leadership, the ferocity of competing ambitions, the dangers of factions within the state, the disaster of civil war. But these plays are not attempts at tragedy, even though they do contain some fairly prominent individual tragedies, like those of Duke Humphrey, King Henry, and Woodstock: the larger movement of history remains more important than the tragic experience of the individual human being. There were two subjects in the chronicles which seem to have led in a few plays to an emphasis on retribution and hence to some kind of tragic pattern: one was the fall of a tyrant; the other was the fall of a weak king, worldly and neglectful of his duty because of the influence of flatterers and upstarts. Both subjects have a political interest, going back at least as far as *Cambises* and *Magnificence*, but it is the moral issue at stake which allows concentration upon the fate of a single individual—his pride, his ignorance, and his final, agonized recognition of the truth—and hence makes the tragic experience possible.

One can see quite clearly in the last two parts of *Henry VI* how the theme of retribution gradually becomes more important as ambition clashes with ambition and one crime generates another, crime punishing crime. Although individual retribution is important, the series of plays also broadens out into a tragedy of social retribution, so that a whole society, disordered with hatred and violence, requires cleansing. But it is the emergence of Richard of Gloucester as a dominating character that first gives the theme of retribution enough scope to govern the whole action of a play. Richard quite deliberately chooses the evil way, denying both the mandates of society and the laws of God. It is his ambition and his cunning which provide the drive, suspense, and excitement of *Richard III*. Yet opposed to the forceful energy of Richard's rise to power is the growing threat of retribution, expressed at first in the curses of the lamenting queens and then in the flow of power toward Richmond and the sense of divine support for Richmond's cause. Richard must suffer punishment as a villain in his own right and as the veritable embodiment of the evil that has afflicted them all.

It is a familiar story how Shakespeare, against the strength of this pattern, developed the character of Richard so that an audience becomes interested in the methods of his double-dealing and begins to look at other characters through Richard's mocking and cynical eyes. For the first time in English drama a tyrant is made interesting, an audience becomes involved in his fate, through his very villainy. Instead of a struggle with conscience as the obvious way of making a tyrant into a human being, something that was attempted as early as *Apius and Virginia*, now the rather stern and limited emotional pattern allowed by the moral theme of retribution is complicated by dramatic irony. One level of irony is controlled by Richard himself, since it depends on his manipulation of events and characters to his own advantage. A deeper level of irony lies in the manipulation of Richard by destiny or providence for its own purposes. Richard thinks of himself as an agnostic rebel and Machiavel in charge of his fate; however, in a way unrecognized by himself, he is made into an instrument by which those who have sinned must suffer punishment. Moreover, he himself makes it impossible that he should enjoy his goal once he has attained it, and, in a remarkable way, he prepares his own doom. The limited emotional pattern of a severe tragedy of retribution is modified by such irony as this, which allows both admiration and pity to become strands in the total effect.

The True Tragedy of Richard III is worth comparing with *Richard III* from the point of view of retribution. The Richard of the former play is a forthright villain from the start, describing in soliloquy both his own cunning nature and his evil plans. Like Selimus, Humber (in *Locrine*), and Mordred, he is aware of the power of fortune, but is willing to take a chance with her, perhaps rule her by his cleverness and will. Yet this Richard is not continually at the centre of the action as Shakespeare's is, nor are we constantly being dazzled by his cleverness and malicious wit. Other characters, like the young king and his brother, are more important than they are in *Richard III*, and Jane Shore is allowed a tragic fall in her own right.

After he has won the crown, Richard finds that he has little pleasure from the golden circlet or the power it represents. He is troubled by conscience, he sees his friends leaving him, and he becomes a prey to a multitude of fears. He is first rattled, then fearful, and at last terrorized by his bad dreams and the growing power of his enemies. Far more than anything in Shakespeare's play, this is the mode of *Mirror* tragedy, which stressed the power of retribution as mental torture as well as physical defeat and death. Richard's page makes the appropriate comment:

> But he must thinke this is the iust revenge
> The heavens have powred upon him for his sinnes. . . .[4]

If there is any sympathy wrung out of the audience for Richard, it is due to the portrait of him in his final days:

> The hell of life that hangs upon the Crowne,
> The daily cares, the nightly dreames,
> The wretched crewes, the treason of the foe,
> And horror of my bloodie practise past,
> Strikes such a terror to my wounded conscience,
> That sleepe I, wake I, or whatsoever I do,
> Meethinkes their ghoasts comes gaping for revenge,
> Whom I have slaine in reaching for a Crowne.[5]

Though it is not one of Macbeth's speeches, there is a hint here of that combination of weariness and moral despair which we associate with Macbeth's final period.

There are several reasons why *The True Tragedy* seems less satisfactory as tragedy than Shakespeare's *Richard III*. The moral pattern which the theme of retribution imposes is much more direct and unqualified in *The True Tragedy*. Richard is a monster without the brilliance of mind that forces us to admire Shakespeare's villain-hero; he deserves drastic punishment, and achieves it in the form of mental torture and physical ruin. The ironic pattern of the desperate effort for a goal that turns out to be worthless is strongly marked, but remains subordinate to the moral theme and does not affect our emotional reaction to the catastrophe to the same extent. Fundamentally, the aspiration of the hero is evil in both plays, but we are led to admire and sympathize with Richard's tenacity and opportunism in Shake-speare's play, so that his aspiration takes a greater hold on the

---

[4] *The True Tragedy of Richard the Third*, Malone Society Reprints, ll. 1781-2.
[5] Ibid., ll. 1874-91.

imagination. Its frustration and defeat is consequently more moving.

It appears from this comparison that when the theme of retribution is centred upon an evil or villainous character, it may suffer certain disadvantages as a tragic concept if it is used in a way that is too direct and morally rigid. In this regard, there are three well-known plays which may help us to distinguish the potentialities for tragedy of the theme of retribution—*Doctor Faustus*, *Macbeth*, and *Sejanus*. In each play the central character takes certain steps which seem to invite punishment; he is ready, in fact, to risk the vengeance of God or the doom of fate to get what he wants. The plays are all fables of a kind, centring upon single figures who desire greatly, take action toward the fulfilment of their desires, against the whole basis of belief of the society in which they live, and, in so doing, prepare for themselves a dreadful punishment. Although from the beginning they partly realize the possibility of such a doom, they hope to escape. There is no escape, and there is a shattering contrast between what was hoped for and what is attained.

Doctor Faustus is a variation upon the figure of Mankind in the moralities, though he takes a more deliberate and conscious step toward evil than his dramatic forebears usually did. Sejanus and Macbeth are great criminals of the tyrant-usurper category, who have their roots in the tyrants of the mystery plays, the *Mirror for Magistrates*, and such moral tragedies as *Cambises* and *The True Tragedy of Richard III*.

Although these plays can be called tragedies of retribution, there are some significant differences between them. *Macbeth* and *Doctor Faustus* are inward plays, imaginative explorations of what it is like to discover that the worldly goal, so desperately desired, cannot satisfy when it has been attained. Above all, these plays are imaginative explorations of the experience of despair. *Sejanus* is much more of an outward play, a play of the surface. The political intrigues are cleverly worked out; and very skilfully portrayed, also, are the shifting loyalties of men and women in a tyrant-dominated state. Sejanus himself, however, is so thoroughly evil that we can believe in no inner tension before his early adventure into crime, and no remorse or despair at the end. Retribution, therefore, affects the minds and souls of Doctor Faustus and Macbeth; only a public lynching can deal with Sejanus.

The plays we have been considering reveal both the possibilities and the limitations of the tragedy of retribution. Rebellion in such a tragedy means confronting and defying, not an unknown destiny, but a universal moral law, the infringement of which is invariably punished. Because the moral law is accepted as necessary and just, an audience is unlikely to be much in sympathy with this kind of rebellion, except perhaps covertly, and there is a danger of a complete lack of emotional involvement, of any sense of terror or pity, as the action unfolds. The plays suggest that this difficulty can be overcome only if the aspiration of the tragic hero is made to seem enormously powerful, so that the audience understands its control over him and partakes of its power. In *Doctor Faustus* and *Macbeth* Marlowe and Shakespeare are completely successful in communicating the blinding force of the ambition that drives each character on, and hence in revealing the agony of the final despairing recognition. In *Sejanus*, however, this quality is lacking.

Another consequence of the theme of retribution is the strong sense of inevitable movement to disaster. One cannot deny the power this sense of certain doom gives to each play, particularly as the blindness of the tragic hero to the true direction of his course permits a striking use of dramatic irony. Yet it is a limiting factor as well, since the weight of the moral pattern, the inevitability of the outcome, makes the whole process seem too tightly controlled and almost mechanical. In *Richard III* and *Sejanus*, particularly in the former, the certainty of direction is varied by means of irony which is not always at the expense of the villain, since he very often seems to be controlling the action for his own ironic delight. Marlowe was unable to solve the problem in *Doctor Faustus*: the calls to repentance and the suggestions of inner debate are not urgent enough in the middle section of the play to make that section a vital alteration of the tragic movement, and the farcical scenes are simply complete breaks. In *Macbeth* Shakespeare does not try to avoid this aspect of the tragedy of retribution, but uses it as a main element of tension

and tragic feeling: there is no doubt of Macbeth's final damnation, since every move Macbeth makes to try to escape punishment and the loss of his crown leads him more surely toward his
doom. The overwhelming ironic tension of the play lies between
Macbeth's desperate struggle for safety and peace of mind and
the audience's awareness of its complete futility. It is because
the audience understands and shares Macbeth's experiences at
each stage of his way, in spite of moral outrage, that it is able to
comprehend beforehand the agony of Macbeth's final recognition. By this means Shakespeare turns necessity into a dramatic
virtue. The tragic possibilities of the theme of retribution are
more fully realized in *Macbeth* than in any other play, but the
achievement is a conquest over difficulties.

I have suggested that the theme of retribution may also be
concerned with weakness of character and the kind of judgement
such weakness brings down upon the individual. We should
expect this from the chronicles and from the *Mirror for Magistrates*, where sufficient examples were displayed for all to reflect
upon. Some of the chronicle plays and romantic histories contain such tragedies in subordinate form. Thus in *The Battle of
Alcazar* the tragedy of Sebastian of Portugal is an essay in this
form, whereas the play as a whole is concerned with the retribution which the villain, Muly Mahamet, brings upon himself as
a result of his intrigues and crimes. The various plays that retell
the history of King John (*The Troublesome Reign*, *King John*,
and *The Death of Robert, Earl of Huntington*) are also sketches
of a tragedy that might have been written and never was. No
dramatist seems to have been able to work through the historical
material of John's reign under the control of a tragic concept to
give it concentration and intensity.

Yet the task of writing the tragedy of King John would not
have been impossible for the writers of this age (political and
religious considerations aside), since there are two plays,
generally recognized as tragedies, which have central figures
as ambiguous and unheroic as John himself: *Richard II* and
Edward II. If there is any hesitation about calling *Richard II*
a tragedy, it is because the fall of Richard is set off against the
rise of Bolingbroke, and the rise of Bolingbroke suggests the

continuing action of history. Nevertheless, the tragic impulse is strong in the play and works toward some sense of finality.

To what extent does the theme of retribution provide a controlling tragic idea for this play? Certainly there is much stress in the first half upon Richard's sins against the ideals of public duty, loyalty, and justice, because of his dependence upon unworthy favourites. John of Gaunt's dying speech and the commentary of the gardener in the third act seem to enforce the necessity of retribution. As in many other chronicle plays, the process of retribution is worked out in naturalistic terms: Richard's faults of character provoke trouble in the kingdom and yet prevent him from dealing with it effectively. Bolingbroke, on the other hand, has the ambition and the vigour to take advantage of every weakness that Richard displays. The outcome could scarcely be other than it is.

Yet the force of retribution is strictly limited in this play. For one thing, Richard's sins are given much less emphasis than they might have been, as a comparison with *Woodstock* or *Edward II* makes plain. In the second part of the play references to the evils of his reign become obvious parts of Bolingbroke's propaganda for his own cause. Richard is given no scene of remorse at the end: he is more victim than sinner. The latter portion of the play is about worldly power playing cruelly with anointed kingship, and the religious images which had seemed vain-glorious when Richard first returned from Ireland must now be taken seriously:

> Though some of you, with Pilate, wash your hands,
> Showing an outward pity: yet you Pilates
> Have here delivered me to my sour cross,
> And water cannot wash away your sin.
>
> (IV. i. 239-42)

Shakespeare had already done something like this in the three parts of *Henry VI*, where Henry is the saint-like victim of the unscrupulous ambition of others, and at the same time is responsible through his faults of character for many of the ills crowding in upon his realm and himself. However, with its multitude of characters and events, *Henry VI* lacks the concentration of tragic experience that we find in *Richard II*.

The somewhat ambiguous fate of Richard as sinner receiving his due punishment, and yet as Christ-like victim suffering the cruelty of the world, raises an urgent question about what kind of superior order exists beyond the world of nature. Punishment appears to fall upon Richard because he refuses to act justly and disregards the most solemn warnings; punishment is promised also for Bolingbroke and for the entire kingdom through the prophetic mouth of Carlisle. Yet the certainty of a divine order must be qualified by two or three elements of uncertainty. There is no immediate protection for Richard when he calls upon God's name in his grief, nor does his punishment seem just when compared with the much more remote and hardly specific punishment of Henry IV. A second point is that the law of change in earthly kingdoms governed by indifferent fortune seems almost as probable an interpretation of these events as any providential order. When Bolingbroke rises, Richard must fall, and Bolingbroke in his turn will suffer because of his exposed position. Shakespeare seems deliberately to avoid the simple or direct interpretation of tragic events: what happens is neither a moral process of punishment following upon sin, nor a series of accidents and unlucky chances, nor a materialistic account of power politics, but something of each. There are hints of a destiny beyond all these, leading the nation through the tragedy of civil war to an eventual reconciliation; however, it remains inscrutable in its actual mode of working. The different interpretations of events are true on different levels, according to the limits of our knowledge. And yet, because Richard's character and his desperate situation are presented with dramatic immediacy and intense feeling, Richard's fall is able to arouse the response we associate with tragedy.

Edward II resembles *Richard II*, but it is not a 'public tragedy' to the same extent. There is less of the communal *auto* about the play,[6] because the state of the kingdom matters less and the audience is less closely involved in a national sense than it is in *Richard II*. Certainly there are numerous references to the wretched condition of England, but they are highly prejudiced references, with a specific dramatic function in that they are part

---

[6] Northrop Frye, *Anatomy of Criticism*, pp. 283-5.

of the barons' attempt to browbeat the king. *Edward II* is less of a history play than *Richard II* in one other respect also: at the end, there is little suggestion of continuing action, but rather a sense of finality. The tragedy of Edward and his barons is concluded and the new reign is something else altogether.

The theme of retribution, as Marlowe develops it, is transformed almost completely into terms of politics and war, that is, into terms of historical necessity. Given a man with a character like Edward's, an opposition of proud barons, and an historical situation in which the barons could wield effective power more easily than the king, these events were bound to follow. The sense of cause and effect is very strong indeed. If this is so, we may ask whether the moral factor remains strong enough to permit us to call the theme 'retribution' and not 'the survival of the fittest'. It is true that the moral issue of the play is by no means simple and clear-cut. Marlowe has deliberately presented the rights and wrongs of both sides: if Edward is foolish, wasteful, neglectful of his duty, the barons are arrogant, scornful of the king's right, and over-confident. The irony of the situation in which both sides call upon God to justify the right is strikingly illustrated in several passages.

But there is a middle way, presented through the character of the Earl of Kent, which preserves the moral theme both in terms of the order and welfare of society and in terms of universal moral law. Kent is able to see the just claims of both sides, as well as their follies and crimes, and strives to find a way of compromise. At the end of the play, when Kent has been executed and a crime of far greater import than any other in the play has been committed—the murder of Edward—the young prince is introduced to speak categorically for justice. The theme·of retribution is worked out in naturalistic terms, but it is retribution nevertheless, because we are forced to admit that what happens to Edward and to the barons is just and right as well as the inevitable consequence of their follies and quarrels. The return to order at the end of the play throws the disorder and injustice of the whole of the preceding action into relief.

Although retribution is a prominent theme in *Edward II* and controls the general shape and direction of the tragedy, it is not the whole of the play, any more than it is in *Richard II*. The experience that Edward passes through does not lead him to a recognition of his past sins and follies and consequent remorse: rather it leads him to a sense of fortune's power, a realization that the greatest person in the realm may fall and his will lack all authority, that the crown as symbol means nothing when power has passed from it. Like Richard II, he must face the fact of his human weakness and the fading of regal splendour. The final scenes show this passage from magnificence to degradation even more vividly than the end of *Richard II*. Marlowe, like Shakespeare, allows us to see the tragic fall of the king from more than one point of view, each with its own kind of validity.

As tragic hero, Edward has generally been regarded as a weak and pathetic character who gains our sympathy only through the progressive blackening of the character of Mortimer and Isabella. Yet his part as the focal point of the tragic experience runs throughout the play, and he must be seen as one who rebels against powerful forces trying to crush his sense of his own rights and needs. Though unheroic and hardly admirable in any respect, he acts on the basis of his belief in himself as a king, and faces boldly a world of power politics and war which seeks to limit his freedom and authority. This self-assertion is more important as a tragic motive in the play than any hints of lust or perversion. It is true that he wishes to use his freedom to have whatever favourite he chooses near him, and his dependence upon a favourite for love is a main trait of his character. Nevertheless, the issue of the play turns upon his authority and freedom as king. His rebellion is not only a strong reaction against the world of political alignments and military power, but a rebellion also against the order of justice and duty for which Kent and the young prince speak. Yet he scarcely recognizes the superior power of this order of being, though it punishes both him and the barons at the end. His failure and his recognition of defeat both lie in the limited world of history: he is given no glimpse of the eventual justice that transcends his own tragic story. This lack of final knowledge in the central character is by no means a defect in the play; on the contrary, it allows a strong current of pity to run toward him. The tragic effect of *Edward II*, as of

Richard II, depends on the emotional tension that exists between pity for the tragic character in his predicament and a strong sense of its inevitability.

This discussion suggests that there is little doubt of the importance of retribution as an organizing principle in many serious or tragic plays, particularly plays from the tradition of the moral history. The theme of retribution implies that the universe is governed by moral law and that any infractions of that law will be punished accordingly. When the infraction is serious enough, as it is in *Richard III*, *Doctor Faustus*, and *Macbeth*, the moral law is made evident by swift and decisive action. However, in other plays, where crime and sin are not so offensive, the moral law seems much more remote: there is some kind of order which ensures the punishment of the most guilty and the eventual triumph of good, but it works slowly and in obscure ways. The audience experiences the disturbance of recognizing what is just and unjust at the same time, what is terrifying and yet inevitable, through the sequence of events and the characters of those concerned. Though retribution is a moral concept, the didactic pressure to make events conform to the idea is gone, even in the most severe of these plays: instead, there is a genuine exploration of the experience itself, whether it be one of grief, despair, or damnation.

Although they differ so markedly among themselves, these plays are tragedies because they concentrate upon the conflict between human will and destiny, particularly the process of aspiration and defeat. The strong motives enforcing a confrontation with destiny are represented with immediacy and power and the experience of defeat is imaginatively intense. In all of them, though in differing degrees, there is a strenuous balancing of opposed emotions, of pity and terror with ironic detachment and a sense of necessity. The tragedy of weakness is of particular interest, since one may see in it the clearest signs of qualities which were to be of great importance in later tragedy—the analysis of character in relation to tragic action, and a fundamental questioning of meaning, the weighing in the balance of more than one interpretation of a disastrous series of events.

VI

THE WEB OF EVIL: VILLAIN TRAGEDY

IT would be surprising if violent melodrama had not appeared very early on the Elizabethan stage, because of the large number of stories in the popular collections of *novelle* which portrayed lust, jealousy, ambition, and revenge. Such stories inevitably implied the frustration of passionate desires and often led to a series of murders. The increasing knowledge of Seneca from the 1560s onward resulted in an association of the more violent and horrifying of his plays with the contemporary tales of passion and revenge. Beyond these immediate influences, there lay in the tradition of the religious drama notable portraits of bloodthirsty tyrants and of Vice-like intriguers or villains who had given certain forms of evil a powerful embodiment on the stage.

The crime and revenge tradition got a spectacular start on the English stage with a group of plays in the late 1580s and early 1590s—*The Spanish Tragedy*, *Titus Andronicus*, *The Jew of Malta*, *Richard III*, and possibly the early *Hamlet*. These were popular plays which produced a notable progeny because of their sensational theatrical qualities. It is obvious that they have certain elements in common: thus, they depend for much of their effect upon violent and shocking crimes to which the major characters react with passion; villainous characters of exceptional cunning and cruelty set the plot in motion; and the pattern of the action is a process of crime followed by a process of retribution, usually in the form of revenge. *The Jew of Malta* and *Richard III* differ from the others in that dramatic attention is concentrated almost entirely on the villain-heroes. The villain in *The Jew* is driven to evil by revenge, but this motive seems to give way, as the play proceeds, to pure malice. Richard III is motivated by ambition, but once again malice or a simple hatred of the good becomes as important as the original motive. In both plays the action is controlled by the intrigues of the central characters, who are dedicated wholly to evil.

The Spanish Tragedy and *Titus Andronicus*, by contrast, are plays in which there are double strands of action: interest is divided between the criminals, cunning Machiavellian figures, and the victims, who suffer at their hands so desperately that they must react violently and seek revenge by any means in their power. Both are the exuberant products of young dramatists who wished to show whole narratives of violence, sequences of crime and revenge, in all their details. Many later revenge plays keep this double interest in crime and revenge, criminal and revenger: we are aware of it in *Hamlet* and in Marston's play, *Antonio's Revenge*. Yet in these plays it is clear that the main dramatic attention has shifted to the revenger. The villain play of *The Jew of Malta* type and the revenge play of *The Spanish Tragedy* or *Hamlet* type came rapidly together, and in most of the following plays the revenger is the villain-hero.

The atmosphere of horror and violence, the strong passions, the networks of villainous intrigue in the first group of revenge and villain plays owe much to the source stories from which they are derived and to the Senecan drama. But it is also clear that representations of violent and destructive forces in these plays have their roots in the native tradition of popular drama. Medieval religious drama gave great prominence, as we noticed earlier, to certain large, archetypal characters representing the force of evil in the world. They were usually tyrants, kings of this world, cruel, proud, and at enmity with God. Pharaoh, Herod, Pilate, the second Herod, Caiaphas, and Antichrist were sometimes farcically presented, but more often they seem to have been serious embodiments of cruelty and of a supreme hatred of innocence and goodness. When the theme of rampant tyranny was carried over into secular drama, as in *Cambises* and *Apius and Virginia*, the villains of the craft-cycle plays survived, and with them the powerful contrasting emotions of horror and pathos. The association of worldly power with enmity toward God slipped easily into plays about Moorish or Asian villains who worshipped 'Mahound', and attacked the virtuous just as Herod, Caiaphas, and Pilate had done. Muly Mahamet in *The Battle of Alcazar* recognizably combines elements from the native religious tradition with the new romantic material.

The Vice of the morality play was a more prolific and important progenitor of evil characters in later melodrama and tragedy, and had more to do, also, with the shape of the action in this drama than the tyrant figure I have been discussing. 'Evil' is rather a portentous word to use of some of the disguises in which the Vice appeared: he could embody anything from the most damnable temptation at one extreme to practical jokes and mischief at the other. Yet he never lost his role as a representative of disorder and of fundamental enmity against the good. In his more serious aspect the Vice is tempter, seducer from the path of virtue or duty, accuser, and sometimes satiric moralist. The action in which he is involved is always an intrigue, which he carries on with guile and cunning, though often simply as an opportunist with an eye for mischief. In this aspect he was easily assimilated into the part of the villain of romantic history or Italian fiction.

His role as intriguer is clearly demonstrated in *The Rare Triumphs of Love and Fortune*. This is a tragi-comedy whose action several times approaches tragedy because of the fierce passions of the main characters, but it is prevented from becoming such by the gods, who have set the whole affair going as an experiment. A servant in the household, Penulo, is the traitor of the piece, a self-conscious villain who informs the audience of his attitude in asides and soliloquies.

Hermione, a banished lord, is seeking through Penulo to gain access to his lady, Fidelia:

> *Hermione.* Penulo I yeeld my life into thy handes,
> *Penulo.*   Ye, doo sir, as now the matter standes,
> *Hermione.* Holde Penulo and I will looke for thee,
> *Penulo.*   You will not looke for them that come with me.
> *Hermione.* I will be gone and liue to see my deere.
>
> Exit.
>
> *Penulo.*   Doo so sir and perchaunce be neuer the neere.[1]
>
> *Penulo.*   Heigh merely tricke, am I not a knaue for the nonce,
>   That can dispatch two arrandes at once?

·   ·   ·   ·   ·

---

[1] *The Rare Triumphs of Love and Fortune*, Malone Society Reprints, ll. 538–43.

Then tantara tara we shall haue good play.
I like such a knaue so can tickle them all,
To set noble men at brabble and braule.[2]

An unusual mixture of villainy and class consciousness! One
quality that was to remain in many villains of the later drama,
both tool villains and villain heroes, was this delight in cunning
and a gleeful acceptance of evil, which had its main source in the
Vice of the moral tradition.

The extra dimension, the Vice as embodiment of the demonic
force of evil, is scarcely evident in Penulo, but it is prominent
enough in Edricus, the major villain in the chronicle play of
Edmund Ironside. Edricus is a self-conscious villain, and on a
number of occasions explains his nature to the audience:

They Cannot so desemble as I Can
Cloake, Cosen, Cogge and flatter wth the kinge
Crouch and seeme Courteous promise and protest
saye much doe naught in all thinges vse decept. . . .

hee that had hard my story from the eand
how manie treasons I have practised
how manie vild thinges I have brought to passe
and what great wonders have bin Compassed
by this deepe reachinge pate would thincke I wis
I had bine bound apprentice to deceipt
and from my bearth daye studied villanie. . . .[3]

There is something of the Machiavellian villain in Edricus, but
he reminds us from time to time of his medieval ancestry:

Therefore of the Two I love Canutus best
yet I Can play an Ambodexters parte
and sweare I love, yet hate him wth my harte. . . .[4]

Edricus supplies the clue for the later development of this archetypal character on the popular stage: it was through the assimila-
tion of the Vice into villainous characters from history and
fiction or romance that the Vice lived on. Bernard Spivack has

[2] Ibid., ll. 670-1 and 679-81.
[3] *Edmond Ironside*, Malone Society Reprints, ll. 290-3, 300-6.
[4] Ibid., ll. 329-31.

811650   K

traced the descendants of the medieval Vice in such villain-heroes as Barabas, Richard III, Hoffman, and Eleazor (in *Lust's Dominion*), and in a large number of antagonist-villains from Edricus to Iago.[5] In his new role he remained the driving force behind a network of intrigue, the destroyer of order, the mocker of the good, and frequently retained his function as a cynical commentator on the actions of other characters. The tyrant and the brute ruffian were usually involved in simpler patterns of strong emotional content as images of cruel power directed against pathetic innocence. One of the major distinctions between the morality plays and the craft-cycle plays lies in this difference between the images of evil that they provided to the dramatic tradition.

As drama became more versatile, as it began to use historical material from the Bible and from various chronicles, classical and modern, the concrete images of evil developed in range and variety. The chronicles and the romances provided notable examples of such passions as lust, ambition, and revenge, and sins and crimes ranging from simple deceit to hideous forms of murder. At first these concrete images of evil emerged from a distinct moral background. Writers chose certain episodes from history because they demonstrated the working of the moral law in human affairs: this is true of *Apius and Virginia*, *Damon and Pithias*, *Cambises*, and the classical tragedies from *Gorboduc* onward. Yet it was soon obvious that dramatists were as much interested in the colour and excitement of violence in the lives of large characters from history or legend as they were in the moral pattern. Not every event in *The Battle of Alcazar*, for example, is there because of its place in a moral design.

In the chronicle plays the most important of these new areas of experience was obviously that of power politics and war, with its basic driving motive, ambition. In *2 Henry VI* the Duke of Suffolk and Richard Plantagenet are preliminary sketches for Richard III, and the pattern of action in which these characters are involved is the one to become so familiar later on, a series of intrigues and crimes in furtherance of ruthless ambition. *The Battle of Alcazar*, *Alphonsus King of Aragon*, *Tamburlaine*, and

---

[5] Bernard Spivack, *Shakespeare and the Allegory of Evil, passim.*

Selimus carry the process a stage further by moving in varying degrees beyond the bounds of the moral framework which was dominant in the chronicle plays proper. The central characters of these plays are set up for our admiration as well as for our condemnation, and it is clear that new influences are at work.

We have come, in fact, to the great rebels of the Renaissance, and to an attitude of mind usually associated with the name of Tamburlaine. In the Tamburlaine figure, Marlowe, Greene, and other contemporary writers encountered something which seemed to satisfy one of the questing impulses of the age—a man of enormous stature, who was capable of over-throwing conventional ideas of possible and impossible, together with conventional codes of morality. Even if such a man was a 'scourge of God' and the veritable image of cruelty and power, nevertheless there was something to be admired in his tremendous egotism and his ruthless handling of opposition. Both Thomas Fortescue and George Whetstone, considerably more orthodox in their general attitudes than Marlowe, were inclined to praise Tamburlaine rather than blame him in their accounts of his career. Thus Fortescue, after a full account of his ruthlessness, sums up his career: '. . . where on all men accorde, that he neuer sawe the backe or frounyng face of fortune, that he neuer was vanquished, or put to flighte by any, that he neuer tooke matter in hande, that he brought not to the wished effect, and that his corage, and industrie neuer failed hym to bryng it to good ende.'[6] But on the stage only poets like Marlowe and Shakespeare succeeded in arousing admiration for a Tamburlaine or a Richard III. The great rebel and breaker of codes soon degenerated into such cynical opportunists as Selimus and Alphonsus: the Tamburlaine figure became merged with the Machiavellian character in the popular imagination.

A whole accumulation of attitudes and activities, usually of a pernicious or damnable nature, was associated with the name of Machiavelli in the Elizabethan mind, but it seems probable that Italian villains of popular fiction and travellers' tales were a more potent source of so-called Machiavellian qualities than were the works of Machiavelli himself. Subtle and cunning

[6] Thomas Fortescue, *The Foreste*, Ch. 14.

deceit, utter ruthlessness, and a driving, evil will—these were
the unmistakable signs of the Italian villain. The change that
overtook the word 'policy' between *Respublica* and *The Jew of
Malta* is an indication of the growth of this form of villainy. In
Respublica 'policy' had still a good connotation, since Avarice
chooses it as his disguise when Oppression chooses the name of
Reformation and Adulation the name of Honesty. Avarice speaks
thus of his choice:

> The Name of policie is of none suspected,
> Polycye is ner of any cryme detected,
> So that vnder the Name and cloke of policie
> Avaryce maie weorke factes and scape all Ielousie.[7]

In *The Jew of Malta* 'policy' has become associated with deceit
and intrigue, and the ability it implies is one of the chief attributes
of the Machiavellian villain. Barabas sums up his career:

> Thus hast thou gotten, by thy policy,
> No simple place, no small authority.
> I now am governor of Malta.
>
> (v. iii. 27-29)

In the plays of Kyd and Marlowe it is obvious that the master
portraits of villainy were modified by another major influence,
that of Seneca. Perhaps the distinctive contribution from
Senecan tragedy to the Elizabethan tragedy of blood was the
representation of an overpowering passion for revenge, leading
to a crime of almost unbelievable horror. The *Thyestes* and
the *Medea* were the plays of Seneca which seem to have made
the greatest impact on the Elizabethans: here they found the
atrocious deeds of revenge and the terrifying note of delighted
satisfaction with which the revenger contemplated his deed.
Dramatists drew from Seneca large characters dominated by
great forces of passion as well as the rhetoric to express such
passion. One can see the Senecan type of villain in academic plays
like *Roxana*, or Inns of Court plays like *Gorboduc*, in which
Ferrex and Videna play Senecan parts. In *The Misfortunes of
Arthur* Mordred carries the Senecan burdens of villainy and
of a curse upon his house. On the popular stage *The Spanish
Tragedy* and *Titus Andronicus* both work up to catastrophes in

Camp's

HOME
office
& school

100
INDEX CARDS

4 IN. x 6 IN.   RULED

Camp Manufacturing Co.
Baltimore, Maryland 21230

which the peculiar Senecan mixture of horror and self-satisfaction is strikingly evident.

The dramatization of violent action and destructive passion probably received its major impetus, not from the native tradition of popular drama, nor from the chronicles, nor from Seneca, but from continental fiction. In the late 1570s and early 1580s we begin to notice in court records the titles of plays obviously based upon Italian *novelle*, and it was not long before such fiction became the major source for dramatic plots. One may agree in general terms with Fredson Bowers's thesis that the Elizabethans found in Italian fiction the revenger who carries on an intrigue with incredible cunning to gain his purpose, that they were fascinated by this figure of the imagination and invented many horrifying variations upon the type.[8] Yet the cunning revenger is by no means the only figure of evil, nor is revenge the dominant theme, in the English collections of Italian stories. 'Certaine Tragicall Discourses written oute of the Frenche and Latin by Geffraie Fenton' are in the main elaborate warnings against the extreme passions of love which drive men to adultery and murder. We are more likely to find here 'The Ympudent Love of the Lady of Chabrye wyth her procurer Tolonio, together wyth the detestable morders committed betwene them' than a story of a notable revenge. Painter included in his wide-ranging collection similar stories of unbridled passion, though revenge is also a common theme. In Painter we find as well the monstrous lusts and cruelties of tyrants from Phalaris to Aristotemus, written in terms that were to suggest a different kind of villain tragedy, easily associated with Seneca and with the tyrants of the craft-cycle plays:

The horrible and cruell murder of Sultan Selyman, late the emperor of the Turkes and father of Selym that now raigneth, done upon his eldest sonne Mustapha, by the procurement, and meanes of Rosa his mother in lawe, and by the speciall instigation of one of his noble men called Rustamus: where also is remembred the wilful death of one of his sons named Giangir, for the griefe he conceived to see Mustapha so miserably strangled.[9]

[8] F. T. Bowers, *Elizabethan Revenge Tragedy*, p. 51.
[9] William Painter, *The Palace of Pleasure*, p. xci.

Tyrants, revengers, lustful seducers, and less villainous persons who give way to sin because of the overwhelming power of love— these are the characters that abound in the Italian stories, and all of them were to find their place in the drama of the Elizabethan and Jacobean stage.

There are many suggestions in the early translations of the Italian stories of the ironic patterns of these stories, an awareness of the way that evil turns back upon itself. Although there may be a moral element in this final achievement of justice, the moral note is often subordinate to the pleasure which the completion of an ironic pattern arouses. Two of the four tales in Robert Smythe's *Tragicall Hystories* of 1577 are concerned with cruelty and tyranny, and in both the irony of the conclusion is emphasized. For the second, the narrator observes: 'Mark how he himselfe made the Net wherein he was intangled, and whetteth the knyfe where on he myserably ended his lyfe.'[10] The whole process of the ironic reversal is pointed out for us with nice rhetorical emphasis by George Whetstone in one of the stories in *The Rocke of Regard* (1576):

... thus was he occupied in prouision of brauerie against his marriage day, he had no thought how *Rinaldo* wold be auenged of his trecherie, ouerthrow him in combat, weare his weedes, marrie his wife, and vse his prouision of pleasure, for yᵉ honor of his own wedding: he wold not see secret hate yᵗ lay hid in *Gilettas* louing lookes, as yᵉ snake lurkes in yᵉ sweet grasse: his blinde affection made him forget the villanie he had offered *Rinaldo*, so that pricke of conscience could moue him to no repentance. For hauing reacht yᵉ height of his desires, he made her the instrument of his destruction, by whose dishonest seruice, he attained this shew of preferment, I mean *Rosina*, Gilettas waiting woman. . . .[11]

This is tragi-comedy, and there are no serious reflections on the meaning of it all to hinder our enjoyment of the ironic reversal. In later comedy and tragedy, and especially in villain tragedy, similar ironic reversals flourished mightily, aiming at no more than a special kind of theatrical pleasure. But there were moralists in the 1580s and early 1590s ready to echo Robert Smythe's comment quoted above, and make the additional point that the ironic

10 R. Smythe, *Straunge, Lamentable, and Tragicall Hystories*, iii.
11 George Whetstone, *The Rocke of Regard* (The Castle of Delight), p. 55.

twist at the end of the story is the exact justice of Providence. George Whetstone has something to say about the matter in a chapter of *The English Myrror* headed 'Of the disposition and destruction of Atheists, machiuillians and Timepleasers':

But the reprobate Atheists contemne all religion, feare no God, and although they faine to please all men, yet they trulie loue not their owne kindred: for bee it to depose their Soueraigne, to spoile their Countrie, and to murther their dearest friendes, if they see likelihood in thier Treasons, they giue consent, if hope of aduauncement, they first set hand to their sword. But you monsters of humanitie, that as drunken with the strength of your owne wittes, and are bewitched with the hopefull successe of your pollicies, esteeme it for sound counsaile that I giue you to vnderstande, that the eternal, whom you neither feare, loue, no do acknowledge, seeth all your wicked pollicies in his vengeance, and frustrateth them with his mercie, he searcheth the reines and heartes, and will giue to euerie man according to his works. If you dig a pit to burie the innocent, looke to fall into it your selues: if you rayse a gallowes to hang them, be you sure, that you shall suffer thereupon: if you edge your sword to pearce their hearts: trust to it your own intrailes will be the sheath thereof. What you doe, or would doe vnto them shalbe done vnto you. *Hamon* set vp a payre of gallowes to hang *Mardocheus* the Iew, and he and his tenne sonnes, did die thereon. . . . If you *Atheists* regard not these examples in scriptures because you studie not the sacred Bible, looke into the examples of prophane Cronacles and histories of time, from whence you fetch you pollicies and cunning experiments: and you shall see in all ages, howe God returned the mischiefes of the wicked, into their owne bowels.[12]

This is fairly conventional, and corresponds in moral tone to the kind of comment which the translators added to the more violent of the Italian stories. It does not approach the subtle interplay of revenge and counter-revenge in the later plays, the building of one irony upon another in a great cumulative structure, as in *The Revenger's Tragedy*. Nevertheless, the foundations of the ironic villain drama can be observed in this passage— the horror of the actual deeds, the enormous confidence of the villains, which leads them to overreach themselves ('drunken with the strength of your owne wittes'), the nicely calculated punishment, which is here unmistakably divine justice, though it was later to seem most often the ironic justice of fate.

[12] George Whetstone, *The English Myrror*, pp. 241-2.

A brief summary like this of the background of villainy on the English stage can do little more than suggest the complexity of the theme of evil. It is pointless to try to estimate the relative importance of each 'source', except with regard to an individual play, and even then the task may seem impossible. Yet one can see that the materials for a tragedy of blood or a tragedy of evil existed in abundance, and that modes of shaping these materials into horrific or ironic patterns were present within the very source materials.

The shaping of the villain plays can be observed in the structural elements which a number of them have in common; and this shaping, in turn, is some indication of the idea or concept governing selection and purpose. For example, there is one structural element that makes the villain plays seem remarkably similar: they generally begin with some striking incident which explains the motive of the villain-hero, or a direct statement by the villain about his nature. In earlier plays the direct statement was all that was necessary: it had been well enough understood from medieval times that certain dramatic characters were completely the servants or agents of the infernal powers. Richard III and Iago are villains of this kind, announcing their evil natures quite gratuitously and making plain from the beginning their alliance with the powers of darkness. *The Jew of Malta* differs, however, in that there is a crucial event at the beginning of the play which makes understandable the passion for revenge which overwhelms Barabas. In *Hoffman* and *The Revenger's Tragedy* the crucial event has already taken place before the opening of the play's action, but it is vividly present in the first scene of each play as the villain-hero meditates on his wrongs and considers his revenge.

Intrigue is the natural outcome of this initial declaration of evil purpose. We know as soon as Richard III makes his opening soliloquy that 'here's a plotter!' and we watch for his opening move. As with Richard, so with all the other villains. Absorbed in evil, they work and plot alone, though there may be tool villains like Lorrique in *Hoffman*, almost as expert as their masters in finding devious paths to an evil end. These villains represent the strong force of the individual will set up against society and the rest of the world. This is not to say that the rest of the world is good in contrast with the blackness of the villain. On the contrary, the world the villain is dealing with is likely to be hypocritical, as it is in *The Jew of Malta*, or thoroughly corrupt in the manner of the court in *The Revenger's Tragedy* or *Women Beware Women*. One of the remarkable features of the development of this kind of play is the gradual darkening of the world in which the villain lives and against which he acts. In *The Jew of Malta*, *Richard III*, and *Hoffman* (as in *Hamlet*, *The Spanish Tragedy*, and *Antonio's Revenge*) there are evil lusts and passions among the major characters, but there are also virtuous characters and others of ordinary mixed qualities. In later plays, however, the colours darken and a satiric, nightmarish world becomes the dominant background for the machinations of the villain.

The villains are opportunists in their plotting and deeds. They may have long-term objectives in view, such as a crown or some terrifying revenge, but, because they work alone, they must take advantage of every opening, no matter how trivial. At the beginning of *The Tragical Reign of Selimus* Selimus makes a long speech on the greatness of ambition and the folly of all virtue and religion, but his main point is the necessity of catching occasion when it offers. Later, he identifies occasion with fortune:

> Will fortune favour me yet once againe?
> And will she thrust the cards into my hands?
> Well if I chance but once to get the decke,
> To deale about and shufle as I would:
> Let *Selim* never see the day-light spring,
> Unlesse I shuffle out my selfe a king.[13]

Eleazor, an arch-villain among villains, makes a similar speech near the opening of *Lust's Dominion*, in metaphors of some originality:

> Old time I'le wait bare-headed at thy heele,
> and be a foot-boy to thy winged hours;
> They shall not tell one Minute out in sands,
> But I'le set downe the number, I'le stil wake,
> And wast these bals of sight by tossing them,
> In busie observations upon thee.

[13] *Selimus*, ll. 1539-44.

Sweet opportunity I'le bind my self
to thee in base apprentice-hood so long,
Till on thy naked scalp grow hair as thick
As mine: & all hands shal lay hold on thee,
If thou wilt lend me but thy rusty sithe,
To cut down all that stand within my wronge,
And my revenge.[14]

The villains have the advantage of disguise and surprise, but because they are lone wolves they must wait for an opening which will give them their chance. Usually the course of events provides an opportunity the villain is quick to seize upon, and it appears for much of the play as if fortune is in covert alliance with evil. This is the kind of world the villain believes in, a world governed by chance, which will give him scope for his activities.

In spite of the variety of intrigue, there is some similarity in the shapes of the plots in different villain tragedies. After the opening dedication to villainy and the seizing of some initial opportunity of dangerous potential to the victim, the villains move through a series of successes, their activities increasing in scope and their schemes in complexity as they proceed. An obvious fault of *The Jew of Malta* is that the activities of Barabas, while numerous enough to give him malicious satisfaction, seem to dwindle in scope in the middle section of the play. But Hoffman moves on from simple revenge to a much more elaborate revenge, complicated by ambition and lust. Vindice takes great delight in the increasing number of schemes he has his fingers in, and Lussurioso's instructions to Vindice to kill himself (in another disguise) represent a triumph of this kind of complexity. In *Lust's Dominion* Eleazor cannot be satisfied with mere power or mere revenge, but must have supreme power and a supremely exquisite revenge.

The complication of evil schemes in these plays is no mere element of structure, but a direct representation of the proliferating power of evil. New lusts and passions are stimulated, further characters are involved in temptation and crime, and new victims are drawn into the vortex of evil power. The structure in this respect mirrors the development of the theme.

How is this pattern of proliferating evil held together, and how does it come to a conclusion? As Miss Bradbrook has pointed out,

[14] *Lusts Dominion*, I. ii.

the unifying power in structure and theme is dramatic irony.[15]
Irony is a basic theatrical quality in the villain play because of the
way the villain's activities depend upon deceit and role-playing.
However, the villain is usually himself caught up in an ironic
process before the end: his cunning fails him at the last; he is
over-confident, overreaches himself, and falls victim to the cunning of others. At this point the irony adds another dimension
to the theme, suggesting that the world may be other than the
villain thought it to be, or, at the very least, not controllable in
all its details by his cunning.

One may easily see the importance of the ironic structure in
The Jew of Malta and in *Hoffman*. In both plays the villain-hero
is given a strong motive for revenge at the beginning, which is
gradually transformed into an obsessive lust for revenge for its
own sake, an all-embracing malice, the desire to strain villainy
to its uttermost extent. In both plays the villain betrays himself
through over-confidence in his own cleverness, so that, in a sense,
the embodiment of destructive forces in the play destroys itself.
There is little need to comment on the ironic structure of *The
Jew of Malta*, which has a sardonic, almost farcical quality about
it that has often been noted. A similar atmosphere exists in
Hoffman, which has a powerfully ironic structure growing out
of the activities of Hoffman, and his helper, Lorrique. The
ironic pattern of the play is made particularly striking through
its language. For example, after a series of dreadful events,
Saxony and Duke Ferdinand talk of fortune. As Ferdinand
speaks, he is about to take a poisoned cup prepared for him by
his foolish son, Ierom, at Hoffman's instigation:

> *Fer.* Good fortune after all this sorrow, *Saxony.*
> *Sax.* O worthy *Ferdinand,* fortune and I are parted,
>   she has playd the minion with mee, turn'd all
>   her favours in to frownes, and in scorne
>   rob'd mee of all my hopes, and in one houre
>   o're-turnd mee from the top of her proud wheele.
> *Fer.* Build on one fortune, shee's a fickle dame
>   And those that trust unto her spheare are fooles.[16]

---

[15] M. C. Bradbrook, *Themes and Conventions of Elizabethan Tragedy*, pp. 165, 167,
and 227 ff.

[16] Henry Chettle, *The Tragedy of Hoffman*, Malone Society Reprints, ll. 1542-9.

Hoffman's plan succeeds: Ferdinand and Ierom are both poisoned, and Hoffman is left undisputed heir of the dukedom. Again he plays his part as arch-hypocrite while Ferdinand addresses him with his dying words:

> For thee alas I perceive this plot was layde;
> But heaven had greater mercy on thy youth,
> And one my people, that shall finde true rest
> Being with a Prince so wise and vertuous blest.[17]

The phrases about 'fortune' and then about 'heaven' would be conventional under these circumstances were things as they seemed. Chettle keeps the conventional terms and greatly intensifies the ironic effect, since they are so wildly inappropriate to what is actually happening.

There is no doubt of the powerful ironic tone of the play, constantly pointed as it is by ambiguous language. But the irony is completely in the service of clever and subtle intrigue and seems to have no relation to any larger scheme of things: it is contained within the world of the play. When the victims of Hoffman eventually discover the truth, those victims who are still left alive, they plan their own revenge upon him:

> Besides, Revenge should have proportion,
> By slye deceit he acted every wronge,
> And by deceit I would have him intrapt;
> Then the revenge were fit, iust, and square,
> And t'would more vex him that is all compos'd
> Of craft and subtilty to be outstript
> In his owne fashion, then a hundred deaths.[18]

This ironic reversal is the climax of all the ironic reversals that have gone before rather than the intervention of some power of justice. Hoffman is outwitted by the world of intrigue, deceit, and revenge which he himself has created.

The ironic structure of *The Revenger's Tragedy* is complex and taut, like that of *Hoffman*, and depends partly on the cunning

[17] Henry Chettle, *The Tragedy of Hoffman*, Malone Society Reprints, ll. 1618-21.
[18] Ibid., ll. 2200-6.

plots of a revenger who takes a gleeful delight in the wit of his schemes. But there are major differences between the two plays. Vindice is much less the total manipulator of the action than Hoffman is, clever and subtle villain as he may be. As well as revenger, he is the satiric observer on what happens around him, like Malevole, Flamineo, and Hamlet, though more violent in his denunciations than any of them. The ironic structure of the play is therefore complicated by the varied roles Vindice plays. There are scenes of splendidly theatrical irony, growing out of Vindice's disguises and deceptions, scenes that Vindice enjoys because Tourneur has made him an ironist, conscious of the shifting differences between appearance and reality, and ready to use ambiguous language to sharpen his enjoyment. But the irony runs deeper than this. Scene after scene shows the contrast between the splendour and dignity of the court, the pretence of justice, and the ugly reality beneath the surface. As the action moves forward, the irony is not merely a static series of contrasts but becomes an intense process of destruction in the clash of one evil ambition against another. Hippolito says of Lussurioso, in words that might apply to them all: 'How strangely does himselfe worke to vndo him.'[19]

As the various lustful or ambitious individuals destroy in order to fulfil their desires, it becomes apparent that the destructive forces so unleashed will destroy one another, evil cancelling out evil, to the final reversal of all the powerful driving desires of the play. This is the striking ironic pattern that reveals Tourneur's use of a tragic idea to control his material.

At this point we may ask what Vindice's part is in the ironic scheme or the tragic idea. As a shrewd and cynical commentator on everything that happens, he is able to point clearly to the way that evil passions lead to self-destruction. He is also agent and tempter in this very process, tainted by what he condemns with so much disgust. Gradually, he loses the objectivity and the freedom of the satiric commentator: the black comedy of the whole series of situations is spiced with the irony of his increasing involvement, which he cannot recognize. When the body of the Duke is discovered and one of the courtiers speaks conventional

[19] Cyril Tourneur, *The Revenger's Tragedy*, IV. i. 71.

words of comfort to the Duchess, Vindice's aside is sharp, yet more highly charged than he himself recognizes:

> *Nobl.*　　　　　Madame all sorrowes,
> 　　　Must runne their circles into ioyes, no doubt but time
> 　　　Will make the murderer bring forth him-selfe.
> *Vind.* He were an Asse then yfaith.[20]

Vindice is an ass when he confesses to the just Antonio that he and Hippolito were the murderers of the Duke. In his pride, he misjudges Antonio, a just person whom he takes at less than his full value. It is a lapse of judgement characteristic of Vindice's growing cynicism throughout the play, and, ironically and justly, he destroys himself.

Tourneur calls attention at the end not so much to the restoration of an order which has been broken as to the completion of an ironic pattern, the rounding of a circle doomed to reach that conclusion. The end of the luxurious vices of the flesh is death, nothingness, but so is death the end of that destructive cynicism which can take delight only in acts of destruction. Tourneur controls the strong feelings of horror which the language and action of the play generates, the obsessive fascination with the power of evil, and its multifarious intrigues, by an all-pervading ironic structure.

In *The Atheist's Tragedy*, too, the ironic structure is more than simply a device of great theatrical power—it is a means of expression for the basic theme of the play. And the theme, as in other similar plays, is that evil reveals its enormous power whenever it is given an opportunity to act, but ends by destroying itself, since its primary impulses are destructive. In several distinct ways, however, the ironic structure of *The Atheist's Tragedy* differs from that of *The Revenger's Tragedy*. It is more obvious, but not so complex in its organization. For one thing, the society presented in this play is a mixed society, made up of characters of very considerable virtue as well as some of doubtful honour and others of extreme evil. There is little, therefore, of the ironic contrast between a glittering society and its hidden depraved appetites, which was so important an element in *The Revenger's*

---

[20] Cyril Tourneur, *The Revenger's Tragedy*, v. i. 167-70.

Tragedy and which gave occasion to Vindice's bitterest comments. Moreover, although D'Amville and Borachio are gleeful villains who enjoy hugely their schemes for plunder and murder, their intrigues are carried out against the honourable and the virtuous, so that we cannot enjoy, as we did in *The Revenger's Tragedy*, the subtle irony of a deception of the lustful and vicious, whose very sins lead to their fatal blindness.

Finally, the great atheist, D'Amville himself, does not remain villainously true to his nature to the very last, but begins to suffer mental punishment before the end of Act IV. He is maddened by fears and visions in a way that links him with the despairing heroes of the tragedy of retribution, Macbeth and Richard III. The outer, all-inclusive irony of existence, which was tentative and obscure in *The Revenger's Tragedy* until the very end, becomes in this play part of a severe moral framework that explains the irony and makes it almost crudely obvious. D'Amville believes in nothing beyond the material universe; yet Nature turns upon this worshipper, striking down his sons and making his accumulated wealth useless to him. The irony of this process of frustration is emphasized by both words and events, as at the moment when the death of his son, Sebastian, is announced:

> *D'Amville.* Thus while the simple honest worshipper
> Of a Phantastique prouidence; groanes vnder
> The burthen of neglected miserie;
> My reall wisedome has rais'd vp a State,
> That shall eternize my posteritie.
>
> Enter Seruants with the body of SEBASTIAN.[21]

The complete reversal in the concluding scenes of the play is emphatically carried through with striking irony, as the whole of the action comes into perspective. Unfortunately the final moment is grotesque. D'Amville's inability to save the lives of Charlemont and Castabella after he has done his utmost to destroy them (and he wishes to save them in order to learn the secret of a contented mind) has something of the quality of Bosola's belated attempt at goodness in *The Duchess of Malfi*.

---

[21] Cyril Tourneur, *The Atheist's Tragedy*, v. i. 53–58.

But when he tries to act as executioner to the condemned pair and strikes out his own brains instead, we are reminded of the naïve, vengeance-from-on-high endings of the early tragedies of retribution. The fundamental theme of the villain play, that evil is its own destruction, has some strength in this play, but in the end it is subordinated to the doctrine of providential intervention, and the irony of evil's self-destruction becomes the laughter of Providence at the ridiculous confidence of an atheist who does not know he lives in a moral universe. As its ironic structure reveals, *The Atheist's Tragedy* is as much tragedy of retribution as it is villain tragedy.

There are at least two more tragedies we should consider with others of this group because of similarities of theme and because of the use of ironic structure and language in the expression of theme. There were a good many villain plays on the Jacobean stage, but for the most part they were concerned with villainy simply as a sensational theatrical device. In *Women Beware Women* and *The White Devil*, however, passions like lust, ambition, and revenge reveal their consuming power to destroy all that stands in their way, and in the end destroy themselves. Theme and fundamental ironic pattern are therefore like those of *The Revenger's Tragedy*. And yet these plays are not quite villain tragedies in the sense in which I have been speaking of the form. There is no intriguing cunning villain who manages the action of the play as a whole. Instead, there are whole groups of characters engaged in a variety of intrigues to attain their different satisfactions. These intrigues clash with each other and finally cancel themselves out.

Women Beware Women does not, like *The Revenger's Tragedy*, present us suddenly and strikingly with the contrast between surface splendour and hidden corruption. It is only gradually during the course of the first act that we become aware of the nature of this society. The love-in-poverty of Leantio and Bianca has something ideal about it, and yet Leantio's love is obviously tainted with jealous fear as he arranges for Bianca to be hidden from the great world. His suspicions of court life, too, suggest a society where thefts of honour are commonplace. Following scenes soon reveal the nature of this society, where a worldly marriage is being arranged and where an incestuous love seems about to break the limits of restraint. Finally, an exchange of glances during a great procession looks forward to the Duke's seduction of Bianca.

Lustful passions have already been stimulated and are ready to break out. It is Livia's willingness to act as bawd, first of all between her brother, Hippolito, and Isabella, and then between the Duke and Bianca that loosens restraint and allows the passions their full play. She takes on these duties not with the gleeful malice of the revenger-villains, but with a mixture of delight in her own cleverness and a kind of wry self-awareness that she is aiding the sexual pleasure of others and not her own. The seduction scenes are remarkable evidence of Livia's cunning, her delight as an ironist in the situations she has helped to devise, and are at the same time evidence of a society where pleasure alone provides the rules of conduct and honour is satisfied by concealment. Bianca enters this world, aware of its hypocrisy as well as of its worldly advantages, and proceeds upon her course with a kind of defiance, calling Livia a 'damn'd bawd', yet accepting her new way of life for whatever she can get out of it.

By now a striking ironic contrast has been built up between the wealth, splendour, and ceremony of the court and all its handsomely dressed creatures and the corruption of evil passions under the surface. Middleton presents us with a complete view of these contrasting states in the great middle act of the play, first in personal terms as Leantio comes home to his small house, completely unaware of the change in Bianca, and then during a banquet at Livia's house where all the main characters are brought together. Images of fair show and of rottenness beneath link these scenes together:

> When I behold a glorious dangerous strumpet
> Sparkling in beauty and destruction too,
> Both at a twinkling, I do liken straight
> Her beautified body to a goodly temple
> That's built on vaults where carcasses lie rotting. . . .[22]

---

[22] Thomas Middleton, *Women Beware Women*, III. i. 95–99.

> . . . all preferment
> That springs from sun and lust it shoots up quickly,
> As gardeners' crops do in the rotten'st grounds;
> So is all means rais'd from base prostitution
> Even like a salad growing upon a dunghill.[23]

Though passions are high in the latter scene, there is a kind of suspension or poise about the action, because for most of them lust is being satisfied. It is only Leantio's dedication to hate that suggests an unstable element.

, A slight touch upsets the equilibrium. Leantio boasts to Bianca of his worldly success through Livia's love and swears that he will plague her. His words set off a chain reaction that leads to his own death, Livia's fury, and the clashing revenges of the final act. Only the deaths of the Duke and Bianca are separate in some degree from this chain of events. What is remarkable about the process of destruction, as of the earlier scenes of seduction, is the skill with which Middleton has built up an interlocking pattern of irony. We are never allowed to forget that the various disasters that befall the individual characters grow out of their own choices, that each brings his own punishment upon himself. When Bianca becomes the Duke's mistress, Leantio realizes that what he has stolen has now been stolen from him:

> O equal justice, thou hast met my sin
> With a full weight! I'm rightly now opprest,
> All her friends' heavy hearts lie in my breast.[24]

When Bianca discovers that Livia is in love with Leantio, her comment is 'Why, here's a bawd plagu'd home!'[25] Livia herself realizes a cruel ironic justice in the killing of Leantio by Hippolito. She says to Isabella:

> Look upon me, wench;
> 'Twas I betray'd thy honour subtlely to him,
> Under a false tale; it lights upon me now.—
> His arm has paid me home upon thy breast,
> My sweet, belov'd Leantio![26]

23 Thomas Middleton, *Women Beware Women*, III. ii. 47–51.
24 Ibid. III. ii. 94–96.
25 Ibid. IV. i. 77.
26 Ibid. IV. ii. 73–77.

In the masque of death at the end of the play Livia acknowledges, as she dies,

> My subtlety is sped, her art has quitted me;
> My own ambition pulls me down to ruin.[27]

These momentary recognitions of the meaning of what is happening prepare the way for Hippolito's dying speech, which looks back over the whole action of the play and is a sudden illumination of its meaning. As Hippolito declares in his suffering,

> . . . man's understanding
> Is riper at his fall than all his lifetime.[28]

He can see now that

> Lust and forgetfulness have been amongst us,
> And we are brought to nothing . . .
> . . . vengeance met vengeance,
> Like a set match, as if the plagues of sin
> Had been agreed to meet here altogether. . . .[29]

The deaths of Bianca and the Duke are separated from the other deaths that take place during the masque, no doubt deliberately, since Bianca and the Duke are the great examples to whom all men look, as the Cardinal has said. The irony of evil's self-destruction is powerfully present in their death scene. One of the attendant lords observes:

> See, my lord,
> What shift sh'as made to be her own destruction![30]

He is referring to her last desperate effort to ensure that she is poisoned, but his words have a wider application to Bianca's dangerous rise in the world and her plotting in search of security.

A severe moral note is also present in the final scene, because of the downright language the Cardinal has used in condemning the lust of the Duke and Bianca and because of Bianca's final admission of ugliness of soul. Retribution is not the dominant theme at the end of the play, but it is an important one. In addition, we are aware of the reversal of hope and desire, foul lust

[27] Thomas Middleton, *Women Beware Women*, v. i. 173-4.   [28] Ibid. v. i. 193-4.
[29] Ibid. v. i. 187-8, 198-200.   [30] Ibid. v. i. 258-9.

though it may have been, the complete destruction of the worldly hopes, not only of Bianca but of all those pathetic beings who placed their trust in the satisfactions of this world. Bianca speaks for them all at the end:

> Pride, greatness, honours, beauty, youth, ambition,
> You must all down together, there's no help for't. . . .[31]

Bianca's recognition of this descent of human desire into oblivion confirms Hippolito's words and allows pity to qualify the strong sense of necessity at the end. There are factors in the play which tend to give it a predominantly satiric cast—the precise working out of the ironic pattern, for example, and the dissipation of interest among a number of characters—but it moves into the realm of tragedy because of the emotional power of the final scene, which brings the rest of the play into perspective. The irony has its satiric purpose, but it is also a means of looking at human life from a tragic point of view, the contrast between desire and disillusionment.

The White Devil, like Women Beware Women, is not a typical villain tragedy. Although it has cruel and cunning villains like Flamineo, Lodovico, and Francisco among its characters, the major figures, Vittoria and Bracciano, are not villains of this type. Yet the essential theme of the play links it with the others we have been considering. Vittoria and Bracciano are totally involved with the intriguers and revengers in an intricate web of evil. As Flamineo puts it, 'We are engag'd to mischief and must on'.[32] To remove obstacles to the satisfaction of their lust Vittoria and Bracciano are responsible for the murders of Camillo and Isabella, and these acts generate a counter-process of intrigue which leads inevitably to their own deaths. All are caught, except the wily Francisco, in the proliferating web of evil passions.

The ironic structure of the play, in which the theme is embodied, is not so elaborate as it is in Women Beware Women, nor worked out with the same attention to an interlocking pattern of intrigues. Yet it is intricate enough. In the first place there is an immense amount of deception, as one would expect from intrigues that stimulate counter-intrigues, which in turn

---

[31] Thomas Middleton, Women Beware Women, v. i. 260-1.
[32] John Webster, The White Devil, I. ii. 347.

stimulate more intrigues. Nothing is ever quite what it seems on the surface, and this is true of the comic gulling of Camillo at the beginning of the play, where the over-friendly heartiness of Flamineo conceals a severe blow to Camillo's honour, as it is true of the wedding festivities at the end of the play, which not only adorn with inappropriate dignity the fulfilment of Bracciano's and Vittoria's lust but also conceal a revengeful plot of the utmost cruelty. The quarrel and separation of Isabella and Bracciano is made by arrangement to appear entirely her fault; the arraignment of Vittoria seems unjust to the assessors (which it is), whereas the charges against her remain true; and the newly elected pope is made to appear a supporter of Lodovico's revenge when his denunciation has been quite genuine.

However, there is another mode of irony which also affects the structure of the play, and it grows out of this pattern of deception. The major characters give themselves away to their enemies through their own passions, so that they appear to bring destruction upon themselves. Flamineo observes of Camillo 'thou entanglest thyself in thine own work like a silkworm'[33] at an early stage in the gulling. Similarly, but much more seriously, Bracciano and Vittoria fall readily into the trap which Francisco has laid for them through his letter to the house of convertites. Even Isabella chooses unwittingly a mode of death which depends on her continued reverence for the husband who has planned her murder. As Bracciano, Vittoria, and Flamineo come to the moment of death, each is reminded of the appropriateness of his doom. Bracciano, a murderer by poison, is told of the poisons eating away his brains, and Vittoria cries out as she is stabbed:

O my greatest sin lay in my blood.
Now my blood pays for't.[34]

As for Flamineo, he has already pretended to be 'caught with a springe' in the mock death scene; immediately after he is truly caught, having been so intent on punishing his sister that he has neglected to consider other possibilities. He can only complain:

Fate's a spaniel,
We cannot beat it from us. . . .[35]

---

[33] John Webster, *The White Devil*, I. ii. 196-7.
[34] Ibid. v. vi. 240-1.   [35] Ibid. v. vi. 177-8.

The tragic emotions of *Women Beware Women* are aroused by the fact that those caught up in the ironic process of self-destruction realize at the end, quite suddenly and intensely, how they have come to the moment of disaster. This tragic awareness allows pity to modify the ironic sense of necessity which has governed the action as a whole. Something similar happens in *The White Devil*, but the tragic emotions are more powerfully aroused in this play, perhaps because of the greater concentration upon two central figures, Bracciano and Vittoria. As I have already suggested, each of them is forced into an awareness of the final tragic irony of his plight. The power of this moment is intensified because of the emotional interest that has been kindled over their fate at earlier stages of the play. The devouring quality of their love for each other is one element in this emotional involvement, but by no means the most important. Webster seldom allows us to see the lovers together, and when he does, it is a scene in which the seed of murder is sown, or a quarrel scene, both coloured by the sardonic comments of a cynical Flamineo. In the last act the lovers are not shown together before the crisis and they die separately. Bracciano calls out for Vittoria in his agony, but, in the play-acting scene under the menace of Flamineo's pistols, Vittoria, without any intention of doing so, says she will die in order to follow Bracciano.

It is their courage and perseverance in their absolute defiance of society, family, and Church, rather than the power of their love, which attracts the sympathy and interest of the audience during Bracciano's questioning by Francisco and Monticelso, throughout the arraignment of Vittoria, and particularly in the final scenes of the play. Undoubtedly this courage permits some degree of admiration to overcome feelings of moral outrage and horror at the end of the play.

It is a remarkable fact that Webster allows us to feel the tragic mixture of emotions centring upon Bracciano and Vittoria without catering to jaded tastes by an ambiguous handling of the issues of good and evil. There seems to me no doubt whatever that Isabella is a portrait of martyred virtue, and that her death scene is the seal and confirmation of this; also that Cornelia and Marcello are figures of virtue intended to contrast strikingly with the other members of the family, Vittoria and Flamineo. Webster's achievement lies in the fact that he was able to gain tragic power from the fate of three characters, in spite of the weight of moral disapproval and fear these characters arouse.

Flamineo is something of a special case. He is a tool villain in one sense, Bracciano's helper, and yet tempter also, presenting his sister to Bracciano as a dish that he will not be able to refuse. As well as plotter and pandar he is a satiric commentator upon the motives and actions of all he observes, friends and enemies alike. As a villain he is by no means completely in control of the intrigues of the play, particularly in the later scenes, when he is fooled with great success by Francisco as the Moor. Yet one might say without exaggeration that he is an embodiment of the lustful and cynical imagination, a character who reveals and extends the power of evil in the play. His gratuitous slaying of Marcello towards the end is credible only from this point of view.

Vigorous in his language, flamboyant in his gestures, Flamineo is one of the most striking of the play's characters. If he had remained hardened and ruthless to the end, the force of his un-remitting cynicism would have undermined the tragic effect of the play almost beyond repair. But because he is finally affected by the distraction of his mother, and because he comes to a realization of the great gulf of oblivion he must face, he is humanized, and through his courage becomes a tragic figure in his own right.

Are these plays about villainy, and the proliferating power of evil, tragedies in the full sense of the word? Part of the description of tragedy with which I began this study states that tragedy is an intense exploration of failure and suffering, growing out of a conflict between human will and some superior law or destiny. In these villain tragedies there is no doubt whatever about the conflict between individual will and destiny, but there may be considerable doubt as to whether many of them approach an intense exploration of failure and suffering. When failure is a sudden and ironic climax at the end of the play, there is little room for any exploration of its power and meaning. We shall come back to this problem in a moment, since it is bound up with the question of the emotional effect of tragedy.

The central characters in these plays set their own wills against society and the traditional moral law: they seek isolation from all social and moral bonds almost fanatically, being driven by such powerful motives as revenge, hatred, and lust. Very often they believe that they are allying themselves with the real law of the universe, which is a law of chance and the survival of the most cunning. This seems to be Hoffman's attitude, Vindice's to a large extent, Eleazor's undoubtedly, Livia's and Bianca's, and Flamineo's. The world that is portrayed in these plays appears to give evidence for such a belief, since the virtuous are weak and suffer from the mishaps of chance, whereas the cunning are able to take advantage of every opening. Yet in the end there are signs of an order superior to cunning and chance: through some error, or some adversary neglected, even the most powerful and the most cunning of villain-heroes destroys himself.

It seems strictly a moral idea, related to the older idea of retribution and implying a universal order against which the individual has offended. But we cannot quite posit a moral order when there are so few signs of any providential rule of the universe. A demonic power which gives evil its energy and stubborn strength is much more obviously present, and the fate or fortune which allows evil to go so far and infect so many is altogether too malicious in its working to permit any simple view of a moral universe. An unholy glee seems to mock the serious idea of retribution in *Hoffman*, *The Revenger's Tragedy*, and *Lust's Dominion*. Nor is it an acceptable moral view that Providence should match ironic trick with ironic trick in the fulfilment of vengeance, even though there are a few, like Whetstone, who find it appropriate. It is as if God has left the fallen world to its own devices and its own eventual oblivion. The general law against which the lustful or revengeful or malicious human will eventually stumbles is a moral law in so far as it affirms the self-destructiveness of evil. But it seems to exist without any counterpart in a positive sense, affirming the final triumph of the good. We are apparently not in the realm of the Fortunate Fall. Such drama as this implies a sceptical attitude toward traditional ideas of natural law, sceptical enough to throw the balance toward doubt, though not all the way to disbelief.

It is the emotional effect of villain tragedy or the tragedy of evil that is the chief stumbling-block to its consideration as complete tragedy. There is much that is simply melodramatic—suspense based on intrigue, obvious dramatic irony, the sensationalism of accumulating horrors, and the unholy glee of the villain at his success. More than one critic has observed that plays of this kind allow audiences to indulge their suppressed desires for criminal activity. They can sympathize with the villain, enjoy his triumphs, and at the end make an easy peace with conventional morality in the spectacle of the villain punished. But there is little in such a view to suggest the 'intense exploration of failure and suffering' which we have demanded of tragedy, and almost no hint of the mixed emotions of pity, fear, and admiration usually associated with the tragic effect.

In considering this problem, one must make a distinction, first of all, between such villain tragedies as *Hoffman* and *Lust's Dominion* on the one hand and *The Revenger's Tragedy*, *The Atheist's Tragedy*, *Women Beware Women*, and *The White Devil* on the other. In the former, the suspense and major emotional interest are centred upon the villain's success up to the last possible minute, and then upon his sudden, ironic fall. An audience may feel admiration for the villain's cleverness, but this is not great enough to arouse much regret over his fall and punishment or the blasting of all his hopes. Such plays are simply villain plays and can scarcely be considered as tragedies. In the latter group, the emotional patterns are more complex and differ considerably from play to play. The greater seriousness of approach is indicated also by the constant pressure of feeling upon language and metaphor. In *The Atheist's Tragedy* D'Amville's predicament as he moves inevitably toward his ultimate disillusionment and damnation arouses fear and even some small degree of pity, as in the old tragedy of retribution. The necessity of his frustration and fall is evident from an early point in the play and every move he makes can be regarded against this background. In *The Revenger's Tragedy*, *Women Beware Women*, and *The White Devil*, the ironic overthrow of the hopes and desires of the major characters arouses a more severe twinge of tragic feeling. I have emphasized the ironic structure of each of these plays and the way in which such irony not only works in the direction of satire but also gives a strong sense of necessity or inevitable movement toward disaster. The blindness of the characters thus bound to suffer does not arouse the same degree of tragic tension through pity and fear that one finds in other plays, where there is a more sympathetic presentation of character and less sardonic comedy and satire. But one must admit the existence of some tragic feeling of this kind, some involvement with the fate of human beings caught through their passions in a web of evil from which there is no escape. The major characters are evil, they condemn and punish themselves, and yet as they move toward the dark, as the edifice of their passionate desires collapses about them into nothingness, an audience cannot remain indifferent. A final awareness of the vanity of earthly striving at the end of *Women Beware Women* and *The White Devil* gives the main characters in these plays an extra dimension and affects the emotional resolution of each play quite strikingly, making the awareness of the meaning of the tragic experience, or 'tragic recognition', seem to be another of the essential ingredients of tragedy.

The highly seasoned mixture of satiric and melodramatic elements in villain tragedy, and the ironic way in which the whole range of human emotions is treated, hinder the full working out of a tragic catharsis in these plays. They are undoubtedly limited in many respects, and yet, as I have tried to show, they should not all be excluded from the scope of tragedy.

VII

A REALM BETWEEN FAITH AND DOUBT

HAVING considered a form of tragedy which is dependent upon the spreading power of evil and the disordering of the mind of man by the passions of lust and revenge, we ought now to go back and examine other possibilities for tragedy in the late 1580s and 1590s, to which I pointed in earlier chapters. In many of the tragic chronicle plays, and in at least one early revenge play (*The Spanish Tragedy*), the action consists of the attempt of a lofty character to achieve some great desire or justice for himself, and his defeat through errors of judgement, weakness, or ignorance. It is perhaps of importance that the central characters of these plays fulfil the Aristotelian requirements of being men like ourselves, neither completely virtuous nor completely evil, but suffering because of some fateful error they have made. We noted in *Richard II* and *Edward II* a form of tragedy in which there is an intense representation of the defeat of characters who had aspired to follow their own wills, confident that they could impose their wills upon society. But they are not deliberately and viciously evil; their eventual suffering springs from error and weakness of character rather than total rebellion against the divine order. I have described these as tragedies in which the theme of retribution is dependent upon weakness.

In other plays which possess some tragic potentiality, in the old *King Leir*, *King John*, and even the two parts of *Henry IV*, disastrous events stem from mistaken judgement, over-confidence, and pride, rather than from deliberate evil, and tragic feeling is suggested by the failure of some great aspiration and by the humiliation of pride. The central characters are important to these plays as the means of focusing tragic emotion, but society, or the whole realm of the kingdom, is also important in all of them, as the context of the action within which the action is judged. As chronicle plays, they are more public than domestic in their major interest.

The *Henry IV* plays which follow *Richard II* in Shakespeare's canon are not tragedies, and yet they enlarge some of the tragic possibilities of the earlier plays by combining the concept of error and retribution with the large-scale heroic characters of the biographical plays. Henry himself is a much more forceful and energetic character than Henry VI or John or Richard II: he acts decisively and takes responsibility for his actions. In one sense he is a strong king, maintaining the unity of his realm against the attacks of irresponsible rebels who would throw the country into confusion. And yet in another sense his history is an account of retribution striking a usurper and preventing him from enjoying the prize he had gained unlawfully. The character of Hotspur, and the whole history of Hotspur's career in Part 1, is a tragedy of virtue and courage twisted toward the wrong cause and unable to escape the fatal conclusion such a cause demands. The movement of each play is directed away from catastrophe, but the analysis of a complex situation involving two characters of considerable stature was not lost for tragedy. In the plight of Henry there is more than a hint of the tragic situation of Claudius in *Hamlet* and of Macbeth. The relationship of Hotspur and Worcester suggests with some force the tragic relationship of Brutus and Cassius.

It was probably no accident that the first fully developed tragic character of this kind, noble and yet capable of serious error, should be a Roman. Inevitably, dramatists had turned to ancient chronicles for heroic legends of the great men of the past: *The Wounds of Civil War*, *The Wars of Cyrus*, and a lost play, *Caesar and Pompey*, are evidence that such subjects exerted their attraction. It was clear, too, that tragic potentiality lay in some of the most famous of the ancient stories, to such an extent that any writer who chose to dramatize such stories was forced to consider the possible requirements of the tragic form. In Plutarch's *Lives*, moreover, there was not only abundant material for the development of large and striking characters, since this book was essentially biography; there were also suggestions for connecting tragic downfall with errors of judgement or particular weaknesses in otherwise noble characters.

All of this lay ready to hand in the source material and may

explain why one of the first tragedies of 'noble failure' should be
Julius Caesar. Yet this play could scarcely be the one we know if
it had not been for the tradition of the chronicle play behind it,
in which the mixed causes of disaster had been explored and the
paradoxes of existence given intense expression.

On the surface *Julius Caesar* appears to be mainly concerned
with retribution: not any simple pattern of crime and punishment, but retribution none the less, since the murder of Caesar
by his seeming friends demands vengeance. Vengeance is
accomplished quite properly by Mark Antony and Octavius,
Caesar's loyal followers and heirs, with the aid of Caesar's ghost,
which acts as a demoralizing factor on Brutus and the army.
Retribution operates also in a much more subtle way upon the
conspirators through their own characters, through weaknesses
and certain areas of blindness. The single-mindedness of Brutus,
his lack of insight into his own nature or into the characters of
other men, prevents him from seeing how he may be used as the
instrument of conspirators with less worthy motives than his
own. Brutus is thus responsible to a large degree for the punishment he brings down upon himself: the gods act through human
weakness and ignorance.

And yet the issue of the play is not just a simple and clear-cut
moral demand for retribution. Shakespeare could easily have
made it such, if he had wished, with the experience of the
chronicle plays behind him: presenting Caesar as a noble character, and Brutus as much more blinded by self-righteousness and
vanity, much more misled by envious and small-minded colleagues, than he is in the existing play. Or he could have made it
a tragedy of Stoic virtue, like one of Chapman's philosophical
plays, in which the noble and idealistic Brutus is overthrown
by the envy of the other conspirators and the evil plotting of
Antony and Octavius. As it is, the rights and wrongs of the whole
human and political situation are mixed. Individual vanity and
ambition and the stress of opposing forces within the Roman
state are so well analysed in the play that everything that happens
can be explained purely in these terms, without recourse to a
moral concept of retribution enforced by an external power.
There is a resonance between the two interpretations, since

neither blocks the other completely from consideration. When Antony in soliloquy over the dead body of Caesar prophesies:

> And Caesar's spirit, ranging for revenge,
> With Ate by his side come hot from hell,
> Shall in these confines with a monarch's voice
> Cry 'Havoc!' and let slip the dogs of war . . .,
>
> (III. i. 270–3)

the audience is ready to accept this forecast of the future as the necessary consequence of murder, such as destiny requires. And of course Caesar's ghost does rise in the midst of civil war. Nevertheless, the audience realizes very quickly that Antony and Octavius are politically shrewd and ruthless and will spare no effort in letting slip the dogs of war for their own ends.

What happens in the play is credible enough in terms of cause and effect—character, politics, and military power. The course of events gives also a sense of retribution, at least in the latter half of the play, since the demand for punishment appears to be answered and Caesar's ghost is eventually satisfied. But there is behind all this some sense of destiny that is not merely the moral law of an intelligible universe. Caesar's murder is fated, as dream and prophecy and the sympathetic distress of nature reveal. Shakespeare makes no attempt to narrow down the causes of the disaster to one explanation, but allows each to stand as a possible interpretation—retribution, necessity, and fortune—even though retribution in the form of revenge is the most powerful. The increasing complexity of the chronicle plays, the working out in secular terms of the moral and metaphysical explanations of such happenings, has found its true succession here. Some mystery remains at the heart of every tragedy, both as to the reasons why men are driven to extreme action and in the suffering that seems to follow directly upon such passion or action.

The fault of the play lies mainly in the emphasis on revenge for what the audience instinctively feels to be the wrong cause. Shakespeare has given his central tragic character so much humanity and nobility that the carrying through of the revenge theme seems almost a denial of justice. He partly escapes from this difficulty by slighting the revenge theme on a deeper level of the play, and concentrating instead upon the theme of the insufficiency of greatness of spirit in a struggle for worldly success. The issue in the play lies between single-mindedness for worldly ends and a divided allegiance. Those who struggle single-mindedly for worldly ends come out on top: there is little mercy for those who attempt to retain other loyalties. The relevance of this statement to the conflict between Antony and Octavius in a succeeding play is strikingly clear.

The theme of man's insufficiency and blindness is embodied vividly in the mixture of greatness and idealism with vanity and ambition which affects so many of the characters of the play, notably Caesar and Cassius in addition to Brutus. However, the emotional climax of the play comes at the death of Brutus, and emotional tension in the course of the play is mainly concentrated on his temptation, his decision to act, and his subsequent ruin. An audience is deeply involved emotionally and intellectually in his cause, and in the different elements of his nature which promise success or failure. Even so, there is recognition of the fact that matters had to turn out in this way, a detachment which binds the flood of emotions to reality and permits some hint of calm at the end. This is the emotional balance that mature tragedy reveals.

The fulfilment of a certain potentiality for tragedy in the chronicle plays and chronicle tragedies, which found expression in *Julius Caesar*, is also apparent in *Antony and Cleopatra* and *Coriolanus*. These are Roman plays drawn from the same source, and they also depict the failure in a worldly conflict of proud and passionate individuals. In each of them there is a full analysis of worldly factors in a struggle for power, and on this basis the plays are concerned with the divisive effects of love, pride, or honour upon those who seek worldly success as well as personal fulfilment. What seem to the main characters to be closely related goals, naturally united with each other, are tragically separated in each play, since the world has no mercy on those who have allegiances other than to itself. In terms of prudential morality, the main characters make grave errors, which cost them dearly in the subsequent action. They are judged within the context of society, but it is an open question whether the world's judgement is just and fair. Each character holds on to some kind of personal integrity: the individual will, in conflict with society and the greater laws of destiny, has still some worth given to it.

The great conflict in *Antony and Cleopatra* lies between the self-absorption of love and the practical demands of power. Antony can conceive of himself only as fulfilling both sets of demands, not as subordinating one to the other, since he believes that his greatness as a lover stems from his greatness as a warrior and ruler of half the world. However, he is driven by fate to choose between them.

It is simplifying Shakespeare's tragedy very greatly to say that it is founded on a choice which Antony must make between two different worlds, whose ultimate value remains in doubt during most of the play. Nevertheless, Antony's dilemma is in a sense the very source of disaster, since it is his refusal to abandon either world completely which leads to catastrophe. The fact that there is no final and complete judgement between the two worlds of the play is not a sign of Shakespeare's indecision, nor is it a sign of disinterest. On the contrary, the continuing tension throughout the play is a clear pointer to the tragic division between desire and reality in the world of harsh experience. Antony's tragic moment of insight is his complete turning away from the world to love, and love only, in his last hour of life. Cleopatra, too, grows into a knowledge of the difference between desire and reality, which two she had assumed Antony would always be able to draw together. This is a recognition that had seemed utterly beyond her earlier in the play.

It is also a considerable simplification of *Coriolanus* to say that the play consists of two opposed worlds, two sets of values between which Coriolanus is forced to choose. Yet it is clear that there is an opposition in the play between Coriolanus's sense of his own integrity, a personal code of values, and the code of patriotism, duty, and traditional rights, which is social in its origin and in its demands. As in *Julius Caesar* and *Antony and Cleopatra*, Shakespeare has refused to picture one side of the conflict as correct and the other as wrong: there is only a fatal division, which leads to personal compromise and worldly ruin.

Thus, Coriolanus possesses a kind of integrity that makes him self-sufficient, and yet we cannot admire it whole-heartedly because it is so closely bound up with pride and contempt of others. The Roman society to which he belongs displays the virtues associated with duty, patriotic feeling, and family ties, but it is divided into warring factions, each seeking its own interest and ready to use any means of intrigue to gain its ends. In trying to be true to his own nature and to the code of his society, and without understanding the causes of anger and weakness within him, Coriolanus founders in disaster.

The irony of *Antony and Cleopatra* and *Coriolanus* is worth some mention, because of the way it emphasizes theme and affects dramatic tension at one and the same time. Through irony the audience is able to perceive the strength of worldly forces at war with each other, and the striking and fatal ignorance of the individual who is trying to master the struggle, but who has less freedom than he thinks he has. When Antony tries to justify his choice of love, his grandiloquent language is undermined by the rude comments of his Roman officers, or the shrewder, more telling comments of Enobarbus. But the Roman world of politics and the struggle for power also has its critics, notably Cleopatra herself, so that we are not able to take its claims to duty and honour entirely at face value. In fact each point of view tends to act as an ironic focal point for the deflation of the opposite attitude.

In *Coriolanus*, also, the irony aids in the recognition of the division of mind or soul which afflicts the central character, and points the contrast between the two worlds in which he tries to live. Coriolanus is even less introspective than Antony, but like Antony he is subject to irrational forces which rule him almost completely. He regards himself as single and whole, master of himself and of his own fate, but he is constantly played upon both by his friends and by his enemies. The result is his breakdown and a shameful death, neither saviour nor conqueror of Rome. Even in the final scenes of the play, when he bows to Volumnia's plea for Rome, and later reacts so strongly to the gibes of Aufidius, he remains unaware of the impulses that drive him to speak and act as he does.

As in *Antony and Cleopatra*, several attitudes or points of view with regard to the basic issues of the play are set in contrast with one another. It is the ironic sense that allows the audience to perceive how one attitude undermines or deflates another. Thus, there are striking contrasts between the excessive self-sufficiency and contemptuous disregard of other men which drive Coriolanus along his course, the more realistic, moderate attitude of Menenius, Volumnia, and their friends, and the scornful debunking of all these by the tribunes.

Where we might expect the irony to remain single, as it would in a simpler play, contrasting the depth of Coriolanus's illusions about himself and the world in which he lives with the more reasonable views of his friends and family, it becomes double. Evidently we are not expected to accept the point of view of Volumnia and Menenius as the platform of truth from which all other acts can be judged. The ironic mood in which we watch and listen to Volumnia, Menenius, Coriolanus, and Aufidius in the final scenes of the play creates a detached objectivity of mind which some regard as a serious fault in the play. The balance of emotions that belongs to tragedy has been upset by the pre-dominance of one element, the ironic. To some extent we are released from this ironic detachment by the steady march of Coriolanus toward his doom, but there will probably always be doubt whether tragic emotion operates strongly enough in this atmosphere of irony. Only the exceptional stage performance can resolve this doubt.

Two of Chapman's tragedies show some resemblance to the plays I have been discussing, namely *Bussy D'Ambois* and *The Conspiracy and Tragedy of Byron*. Although the two plays are very different in dramatic technique, one being a kind of revenge play, the other much closer to the chronicle play, they both pre-sent a large central character, almost heroic in some of his qualities, who represents a rebellion of the human spirit against limitations imposed by human society, the harsh facts of power, and fortune. The rebellion fails, partly through the weakness or blindness of the individual, partly through the hostile operations of worldly forces, but there is no single, dogmatic interpretation. On the contrary, Chapman suggests some element of mystery in nature's shaping of disproportioned individuals for situations of stress. As in the Roman plays of Shakespeare, dramatic irony sharpens the contrast between two possible views of the central character and the conflict in which he is involved.

Bussy D'Ambois strikes the reader as a play much closer to the revenge tradition than to the chronicle tragedy. However, it is worth pointing out that dramatic interest does not lie mainly with the revenger but with his victim, who struggles to impose his ambitions and desires upon the society around him and fails in the attempt. In its basic theme, therefore, it is closer to *Edward II* than it is to *The Spanish Tragedy*. Bussy is obviously guilty by the code of the society in which he lives, and by the code generally accepted by Chapman's audience, even the aristocratic audience which patronized the boys' companies. Yet the play is not merely a tragedy of retribution. There is something free, magnificent, and proud-spirited about Bussy, which makes all the more striking the meanness and jealousy of his opponents. Morality means nothing to him when set against ambition, and ambition he quite casually tosses aside when he meets with love. Right is very nearly identified with the kind of freedom, courage, and self-sufficiency Bussy stands for, and which the world will not suffer to exist because of its envy and fear. Chapman allows the interplay of these two ideas, the guilt and punishment of Bussy, the greatness and martyrdom of Bussy, and the audience is invited to admit both interpretations to its consciousness.

Chapman was able to achieve this balance partly because of the strength of the Marlovian tradition of the magnificent man, freed from the conventions which cramp and limit the development of the ordinary person. Bussy is a Tamburlaine in his freedom of spirit, though confined and ultimately ruined by his lack of any real power in a world of strongly competing forces. On the other side, Chapman had apparently no strong desire to be the complete rebel and justify the amorality of Bussy as some great virtue.

The open background of the play is stressed by its irony. There is, of course, a good measure of dramatic irony, since Monsieur is something of an ironist and he enjoys playing with fire. However, the more intrusive form of irony, such as exists in *Coriolanus*, is apparent in the somewhat equivocal attitude toward Bussy which the play encourages. Bussy is presented as a man without fear or servility, splendid in many of his utterances, a man who rises in the world solely through the freedom of spirit he seems to embody. Yet he has obvious weaknesses that his enemies are able to discover without difficulty and use for his destruction. The double attitude of irony exists also in the contrast between Bussy's high-minded defence of immorality, and Monsieur's and Montsurry's cynical defence of traditional morality.

As in *Coriolanus*, the centre from which the irony operates remains unfixed. We cannot quite accept the opposition which destroys the hero as the basis for judgement, since there remains a substratum of doubt as to whether Bussy's morality of the free spirit is necessarily inferior to the kind of traditional morality that lies in the care of Monsieur and Montsurry. There is, however, an important difference between this play and *Coriolanus*. Shakespeare reveals in serious terms a conflict between civic duty and loyalty on the one hand and personal wholeness or integrity on the other, but he takes nothing for granted: just as the integrity is compounded of a large measure of arrogance and self-satisfaction, so the civic duty and loyalty is envisaged as at best qualified adherence to a sadly fractured state. Chapman, although treating a theme of similar dimensions, does not give the impression of treating it quite seriously. The absence of reflective soliloquies prevents it from being a play like *Hamlet*, and the large amount of sensational action prevents the direct confrontation of political and moral issues which occurs in *Coriolanus*.

The Conspiracy and Tragedy of Byron is more serious in its treatment of substantial issues, less theatrical and sensational in its form. The two-part play is a study of the conflict between an emancipated individual who is also a great noble and warrior, and the contemporary state represented by the king. The tragic emotion depends largely upon the spectacle of a proud individual in hopeless conflict with a dominant power which he refuses to recognize: the audience is sharply aware of the hero's wilful blindness and self-deception. The balances are weighted against Byron—he must suffer for moral reasons because of his fall into treachery, and for political reasons because he over-estimates his own power and importance in the state. Yet there is no doubt of his courage and largeness of mind, a man so much superior to the informers who betray him.

These two tragedies of Chapman can thus be linked quite closely with the Roman tragedies of Shakespeare and several of the earlier chronicle tragedies in their emphasis on strong patterns of worldly intrigue and the defeat of a lofty figure who sets himself against the world in order to attain some great desire. There is no great clash between forces of good and forces of evil, no terrifying region of darkness within the soul, such as Hamlet or Othello must peer into, but instead a very clear pattern of cause and effect in a conflict between equal or near-equal opponents. These tragedies are also distinguished by their refusal to take sides as to the ultimate worth of the hero's cause or that of his opponents. This open background to the action is reflected in the different interpretations that are possible for the steady movement toward disaster—retribution, fortune, and necessity all seem to be involved in the process. And as we have noticed, the pretensions of the central character, and frequently those of his mighty opposites, are revealed by irony, which is a powerful device for maintaining an attitude of controlled tension within each play. Because of the qualities I have been describing, several of the plays, notably *Julius Caesar* and *Coriolanus*, have been called problem plays rather than tragedies. Certainly the ironic balancing of different points of view suggests such a form. Nevertheless, I believe that tragic emotion arises from the predicament of the central character in each play, emotion which is intensified by the scene of recognition when illusions are stripped off and the grim force of necessity is revealed. Where the ironic pattern is strongest, as it is in *Coriolanus*, the emotional power is less; the opposite is true in *Antony and Cleopatra*.

Without further analysis of well-annotated plays, I should like to stress the fact that the particular qualities we have looked at fulfil the promise of theme and emotion which the chronicle plays and tragedies of the 1590s had suggested as vital components of a tragic pattern. They are all tragedies of the seemingly heroic individual in conflict with society as he tries to attain justice or fulfil the great desire that has driven him to act. The individual believes that he serves society (as warrior or ruler) and that society ought therefore to admit his pre-eminence or support his view of justice and right. Yet not only human society but the very scheme of things seems determined to take advantage of his mistakes and crush him. *Julius Caesar* and the following tragedies carry on a tradition suggested by the chronicle plays of retribution in terms of cause and effect: character influences event, and event in turn has its effect upon character, all this within the realm of nature and without intervention from providence. The tragic hero has submitted himself to the processes of cause and effect in nature and must accept disaster when he fails.

Although the individual is defeated for reasons we can accept as necessary, something enduring in the individual's commitment and perseverance remains important at the end of the play, and this too is a constant factor in the tragic effect.

There are other tragedies of the age which seem to have a superficial resemblance to the plays I have been discussing, in that the central characters are figures of apparent greatness whose tragic careers depend upon ignorance, faulty judgement, and error. They are much more violent, however, in the explosive passions which set the action going. Although these are not villain tragedies, the action stems from some great outrage against human feeling and divine order, which demands an intense reaction in its turn. *The Spanish Tragedy* resembles in some respects the plays I have been discussing, in that it has a central tragic figure who is renowned for his nobility of character and lofty rank, but who suffers because of his inability to cope with the situation in which he is placed. However, it is not a process of retribution that counts in the play: the emotional impact lies in the experience of Hieronimo, who is an innocent person brutally hurt by the cruelty of others. The murder of Horatio is so extreme an outrage against humanity and order that Hieronimo is led to defy both society and the heavens in his suffering.

The deed of outrage is a part of the long tradition of popular drama, where it had been a kind of symbol representing the horror of the fallen world. The revenge plot gave dramatists the

means of developing the random deed of cruelty, with its concentrated emotional power, into a main element of structure.
As we have seen, it was relatively easy to begin a play with some
act of outrage (represented or reported) and move rapidly into a
plot of accumulating villainy under the guise of revenge. Yet in
The Spanish Tragedy, and in *Hamlet*, a strong emphasis on the
horror and injustice of the initial crime, and an even greater
dramatic stress on the suffering of the person affected most
nearly (the blood connexion), enforced a revenge plot which was
a quest for justice, and a revenger who was not a villain.

Let us consider for a moment this kind of revenge tragedy and
try to judge how it differs both from the tragedy of retribution
and from villain tragedy. The demand for revenge, like love, is
assumed to be a passion that it is impossible to resist once it is
given sufficient cause to exist. Destiny imposes the necessity of
revenge upon certain individuals, and when those individuals
are innocent of any part in the original, crucial deed, revenge
becomes an agonizing yet inescapable burden. Hieronimo, like
Hamlet, has no choice apart from revenge, unless it be helpless
inactive grief, or madness. Once a revenger has decided to take
up the dreadful burden laid upon him, he becomes involved in
a necessary sequence of bloody deeds, which at length claims
him as well as other victims, both innocent and guilty. Hieronimo's tragedy is that he is involved in suffering against his will
and is forced to seek justice by his own hands, though he is
physically weak and old, and overcome by the obsession of his
grief. This type of play is therefore strikingly different from the
villain tragedy in which the revenger seizes upon an opportunity
for bloody deeds either because of his direct fury or because of
his natural delight in cunning and cruelty. It differs also from
the tragedy of retribution, in which the decision to act, in order
to secure the object of lust or ambition, is unforced and free and
is not something imposed upon the individual by an external force.

The Spanish Tragedy begins, as *Hamlet* does also, with an act
of injustice so terrible to human feeling that it demands punishment or another deed equally horrifying to be placed in the
scales against it. The revenge that Don Andrea seeks in *The
Spanish Tragedy* does not have this sense of outrage surrounding

it, because it arises merely from an incident in a battle, but the murder of Horatio, as it occurs upon the stage, is a different matter. Almost to the end Hieronimo is obsessed with the icy weight of injustice: he cries out against the heavens for refusing to act, he seeks human justice and is denied a hearing, and he resolves at last to depend only upon the infernal gods. From the same source of feeling arises Hieronimo's agonized need to balance one deed of horror with another. The deed that has been huddled up in silence must be revealed in its full horror by other crimes equally terrible, which alone can make the original crime seem the outrage it was. When the characters in his 'tragedy' are all dead, Hieronimo pulls a curtain and reveals the pitiful body of his son. There is more than a hint in this play, as there is in *Hamlet*, that the public revenge, achieved at long last, is the necessary recompense for the secrecy of the initial crime.

The Spanish Tragedy looks forward to *Hamlet* most obviously, but also to *Othello* and *King Lear*, since all these plays are concerned with the fatal involvement of a passionate character in a quest for justice. They differ from the political tragedies of responsibility in their emphasis on the power of evil in a world where justice had been assumed to exist. It is worth noting that justice and order are the primary assumptions of the tragic heroes, and the breakdown of order is the more effective because of these assumptions. Evil and good are sharply differentiated, and, although all men may be sinful, the destructive power of evil seems to be embodied in particular individuals—Lorenzo, Claudius, Iago, and Edmund.

A second distinctive quality is a corollary of the first. The destructive force of evil leads in each play to words or acts of outrage which seem to herald the overthrow of universal order: the tragic characters break down as a result into distraction and madness, or roll like Othello on the ground in the throes of horrible imaginings. Yet they are not pictured as the innocent victims of demonic powers. Their good intentions and self-justifications conceal the fact that they too are responsive to the evil tides of feeling that have been released in society, are infected by them and will be caught and destroyed along with the more direct embodiments of evil forces.

The imagery placed in Hamlet's mouth shows that his imagination has been strongly infected, that there is in him the same
sickness that affects Claudius and Gertrude. *Othello* is no
demonstration of the easy conquest of innocence by an evil
figure of enormous cunning: it is the conquest of a mind ignorant
in matters of love and ordinary human relationships, suspicious
and ready to be overthrown by another shrewd enough to
realize it.[1] The play pictures the breaking down of Othello's
conscious desire to maintain trust and avoid jealousy, and the
victory over his nature by irrational forces which Iago does no
more than stimulate.

There are characters in *King Lear* more terrifying as embodiments of evil than any in *Hamlet* or *Othello*. On the surface, it
sounds like a bitter drama of ingratitude and the reversal of the
natural order of affection and respect between children and
parents. It soon becomes evident, however, that stronger forces
are at work. The hatred which affects Goneril and Regan so
strongly cannot be explained merely as ingratitude or ambition,
or the desire of two sensible women to tidy up the disorderly
world of their troublesome father. We are close here to a primi-
tive and destructive human impulse—the change in the maturing
child from admiration and love for her father to disgust and
hatred as the powerful king and father becomes the intemperate
old man, ineffectual and impotent. Lear's reaction to his daughters' treatment of him is to rage and curse, and, when he utters
his unnatural curse upon his daughters, he is acknowledging the
power of the same irrational and evil forces over himself. His
breakdown and madness follow inevitably.

It was the revenge play that first showed how a great character
could be overcome by evil tides of feeling in the act of opposing
them and be driven to breakdown or madness. In particular, *The
Spanish Tragedy* demonstrated both the terrible suffering and the
destructive energy of a character driven beyond the limits of his
endurance. In earlier drama there had been notable examples of
pure evil embodied in such figures as the Vice and the Tyrant:
Iago and Edmund are obvious descendants of the Vice, and
Cornwall and Regan of the brutal Tyrant. But the victim forced

[1] F. R. Leavis, *The Common Pursuit*, pp. 136-59.

into distraction or madness by his wrongs seems to be a product
rather of Senecan tragedy, and of such imitations of Senecan
revengers as Videna in *Gorboduc*, and Tancred in *Gismond of
Salerne*, who is overcome by a fury rising from hell.

Because of the power of the destructive forces, and the savagery
of the spectacle of evil, there is an intensity of questioning in
these tragedies that is hard to match elsewhere, basic questioning
of the principles of order and justice in the universe. In the
chronicle plays and tragedies of retribution the action is contained within a framework of order and meaning, but even in
these plays there are moments of questioning, just as there had
been in the medieval craft cycles. Henry VI, meditating on the
field of battle as fathers and sons kill each other, comes to such a
moment. Another occurs in *King John* when Faulconbridge bids
Hubert take up the body of Arthur:

> Go, bear him in thine arms.
> I am amaz'd, methinks, and lose my way
> Among the thorns and dangers of this world.
> How easy dost thou take all England up!
> From forth this morsel of dead royalty
> The life, the right, and truth of all this realm
> Is fled to heaven; and England now is left
> To tug and scamble, and to part by th' teeth
> The unowed interest of proud-swelling state.
>
> (IV. iii. 139-47)

The questioning I have been speaking of is peripheral in the
chronicle plays and early tragedies; in the major tragedies of outrage and revenge it becomes central. The action of these tragedies
is played out against an open background where the ultimate
questions cannot be answered, and in this respect they differ
considerably from the tragedies of retribution. When the murder
of Desdemona is discovered, Othello's words of justification
possess the tragic irony of the cry of Oedipus before he recognizes the truth:

> O, I were damn'd beneath all depth in hell
> But that I did proceed upon just grounds
> To this extremity . . .,
>
> (V. ii. 137-9)

and they arouse almost the same kind of metaphysical disturbance in the minds of the audience. At the end neither a moral nor a deterministic interpretation of the tragic action is sufficient to answer the questions posed by the violence of the language and by the tide of feeling aroused by the climax. The arena of experience stands open to troubled doubt and uncertain judgement.

We have noticed the importance of irony in the political tragedies of Shakespeare and Chapman, where it sharpens the dramatic tensions of each play and at times seems to delineate the very theme. Its nature and its function are similar in this second group of tragedies, though the irony is perhaps more nearly subordinated to the structure of tragic emotion. In each play there is a contrast between the central character's view of what he is striving for, his justification of his own character and purpose, and the wider view given to the audience, which goes beyond this character's limited vision. Hamlet, Othello, Lear—whoever it may be—imagines that he is acting freely, and that he can bring about the end he desires if he can overcome certain obstacles in his way. But it soon becomes apparent that stronger currents are running than he can control, that he is caught up in something he does not understand—as Hamlet is caught up in an assumed madness that very nearly becomes true madness, and Othello, who had proclaimed his freedom from jealousy, becomes the victim of savage impulses he had never recognized in himself. We as audience are able to see this happening and feel strongly the discordant clash between what the major characters believe they are doing and what is actually happening, a far more complex affair. At the end of the play there is some sort of revelation that permits the hero to look back and see the whole struggle from a point of greater detachment, though there is no complete clarification.

The fundamental questioning of the laws of existence that is so important in these tragedies makes the basis of such irony itself open to question. In forms of tragedy where the background is established and accepted, whether it be the providential structure of the tragedy of retribution or the cynical 'cleverness is all' of the villain tragedy, the audience knows where it is, and the dramatist can develop highly theatrical scenes, in which the surface appearance is set in contrast against a vastly different but recognizable reality. In these tragedies, however, the background reality is less certain because various possible interpretations of what is happening are being held in suspense. In such tragedy there may be a powerful and ironic contrast between things as they seem and an underlying reality which is very different, but the assumed underlying reality may itself be an illusion. Thus in *King Lear* the trust and hope which Lear reposes in his elder daughters is set in ironic contrast against another view of those daughters very early in the play: Cordelia makes an ambiguous comment that hides a needle, and the sisters themselves in a moment of intimate conversation reveal their minds. This sort of ironic contrast can exist in tragedies of retribution and pure villainy, but here it goes much further as the play develops. It is not simply a contrast between ignorant virtue and hidden villainy. Lear's ignorance is ignorance of himself as well as of his daughters, and they know more of his character than he does himself.

When we ask what the full reality is, against which Lear's illusions can be measured, there is no clear answer. He is to be given a dreadful experience by way of enlightenment, but we cannot say that it comes about because he lives in a moral universe and is being punished for his pride, bad temper, and wilfulness, nor that it is part of a providential process revealing goodness in the very midst of evil, nor that everything has been determined to follow this course by purely worldly factors— ambition, lust, and cunning in an authoritarian state. It may be all of these working together in a strange and terrible way. We feel the ironic twinge strongly with Lear himself, because we know that most of his assumptions about his family, his kingdom, and the world itself are false, even if we cannot define the assumptions that would be correct. We feel it also with most of the other characters of the play, because we know that they too are deceived and are acting upon false assumptions.

In each of the two modes of tragedy that I have been describing one may see a new arrangement of the Elizabethan constituents of tragedy, a leap forward into a new cohesion of elements that had existed in other forms and arrangements in the dramatic tradition. It is this doubleness that is particularly interesting, the obvious relationships with a dramatic tradition of the past and yet the profound sense of something completely new.

The Roman plays of Shakespeare and Chapman's *Bussy D'Ambois* and *Tragedy of Byron* owe many of their elements of theme and structure to the chronicle plays and the tragedies of retribution. Like the earlier plays, these tragedies are based fundamentally on a process of cause and effect in society which takes its start from the character and decisions of the central figure. The strikingly new element is that this central figure, the tragic hero, is neither tyrant nor weakling, but a person with some claims to greatness and nobility. The imaginative leap to a new kind of tragedy arises from the exploration of the suffering of such a hero, who is neither wholly right nor wholly wrong, who deserves to suffer in the world because of his mistakes, but who is admirable in his perseverance in his own cause. This is tragedy of the realm of nature, in that the disordering of the mind of man by passion or the pride of selfhood are punished by inevitable worldly reactions. The tragic experience of the individual is none the less real, the agony of self-realization and the recognition of errors from which there is no retreat.

One can see the whole tradition of retribution in this type of play, involving choice, responsibility, failure, and despair, but it is no longer retribution as a strictly moral process of sin and punishment, backed up by the power of providence. The background is open, as the irony of these plays indicates, and ultimate values are uncertain. Although the world triumphs, and justifiably so, the individual retains his worth through his final commitment to some kind of inner integrity.

The second group of tragedies, from *The Spanish Tragedy* to *King Lear*, has obviously grown from different roots in the chronicle plays, the English classical plays, and ultimately the religious drama. It is the terrifying passion or crime, the outrage against all concepts of order, justice, and human feeling that characterizes this type of tragedy. This very characteristic is part of the tradition, since deeds of violence and blasphemous outbursts against order and degree existed in the chronicle plays and mystery cycles as striking images of a chaotic, fallen world. But the same characteristic is a mark of the newness of that form: it is a kind of tragedy that depends upon the victim of such outrage, his reaction against the world that has presented such a terrible aspect, and his desperate search for right and justice. There is an imaginative leap from the suffering of the innocent victim, which is strongly pathetic, to the tragic suffering of the victim who struggles fiercely against the forces of oppression, and who is so strongly affected by them that his rational self loses control. The tragic irony of this kind of drama lies in the way the victim himself for a time becomes allied with the destructive forces.

Religious levels of experience are involved more clearly in this form of tragedy than they are in the tragedies of secular retribution. The deed or passion which drives the action toward its fatal conclusion denies the divine law of the universe and is a kind of blasphemy, and the tragic figure who is largely the victim reacts violently and wildly, and becomes involved in guilt before his final submission. There is even a hint in these plays of a realm of innocence, altogether unlike the hideous world of experience. In *Othello* the courtship of Desdemona, as Othello describes it to the Senate, and their meeting on the Cypriot shore after the storm suggest the atmosphere of gentle unsullied innocence, which might have endured in a different state of being. What is idealized in *Hamlet* is a youthful state of innocence and happy relationships within the family. The dream of innocence comes late in *King Lear*, since it had no real embodiment in the past, and is only recognized by Lear after suffering and madness; it is what might have been in his relationship with Cordelia rather than what is.

Are these tragedies therefore based on a religious framework of meaning such as is evident in medieval drama and in many of the chronicle plays? It must be admitted that the tragic characters learn through suffering, that Othello, Hamlet, Lear, and even Macbeth know themselves better at the end and recognize a far greater range of human feeling and responsibility. There is a religious overtone in the final acceptance or submission of the tragic character to what has been decreed. But the experience as a whole is far too terrible for it to be justified in this way as a moral lesson or spiritual discipline. The perverse accidents of fate, whether they involve a dropped handkerchief, Polonius behind the arras, or the outcome of a battle—the 'accidental judgements' and 'casual slaughters' Horatio speaks of at the end of *Hamlet*—cannot be reconciled with a providential scheme. One can only say that, if evil ultimately destroys itself in this drama, innocence suffers terribly, and weakness and error are punished sevenfold. This is the realm between faith and doubt which tragedy explores.

It is one of the paradoxes of tragedy that it should give the satisfaction of a pattern of meaning and at the same time enter the region of doubt, just as it gives pleasure in the midst of pain. The sense of meaning arises from the audience's acceptance of a credible sequence of necessary actions, the doubt from the way in which irony undermines conventional moral explanations of what has happened. Although the catastrophe is recognized as inevitable, the whole background of possible meaning has been opened out into a range of uncertainty. Whether one expresses this quality of tragedy in terms of tension, the balance of op-posites, or paradox, it is a phenomenon undeniably present in the effect of tragedy and seems to be particularly powerful in the last group we have considered. They are metaphysical tragedies, even if they are not specifically Christian.

CONCLUSION

THERE is no incontestable reason why our exploration of the different forms of Renaissance tragedy should conclude at this point, since the Jacobean and Caroline stage continued to work out the potentialities for tragedy that had existed in earlier drama and non-dramatic literature. However, it should be possible by now to see what tragedy's debt to earlier drama and literature was, and how a theatrical background of considerable range made possible several quite distinct kinds of tragedy.

Has the general method of this study been of any value for an understanding of tragedy? The purpose throughout has been to explore the emergence of tragedy from a specific dramatic tradition. Since it is an historical study, attention has been concentrated upon what can be understood in historical terms: in the first place, the development of a theatrical tradition favourable to the appearance of tragedy, and secondly, the transformation of potentially tragic episodes and subjects into the actually tragic, by enlargement and intensification, as well as by other means more difficult to specify.

One must admit that the historical development of the theatre had an influence on the appearance of tragedy. For example, the stage became increasingly committed to the production of large numbers of plays because of the rapid growth of audiences eager for novelty. The demand for plays led to the ransacking of literary sources and to many experiments in the handling of new material, so that the plays actually produced were considerably varied in subject-matter, tone, and style. One can speak also with reasonable assurance about the development of technical skills on the stage itself. There was an obvious growth of practical knowledge in the handling of complex subjects and patterns of emotion: the sophisticated games played with illusion, for example, the skilful management of several intrigues at once, and the interplay of different levels of irony. Of considerable importance for tragedy was the development in the hands of several dramatists of an eloquent means of expression for thought and feeling.

The dramatic tradition not only produced favourable conditions on the stage for tragedy but also provided part of the stimulus for its writing. The stimulus was twofold: first, the use of violent or passionate tales as source material for the drama, and second, the prestige of tragedy because of the humanist emphasis upon Seneca and his Greek predecessors and the widespread imitation of Senecan tragedy in France and Italy. Given the basic story of passion and violence, and the prestige of the form, what then made the actual writing of tragedy possible was the existence of a number of general ideas about tragic form and style, some of them implicit in the original material, others more clearly defined from classical and native sources. It was a background that was vigorous and yet tentative, without the dogmatism of clearly enunciated literary theory and therefore inclined toward the experimental. One can see why it was possible under these circumstances for several different forms of tragedy to appear at the same time.

The second phenomenon we have been concerned with is the transformation of potentially tragic episodes and themes into complete tragic patterns. The direct origins of tragedy are exceedingly difficult to anatomize, since the writing of any tragedy depends upon a unique combination of different elements in the mind and imagination of the playwright, those elements we call psychological and biographical, those which belong to his memory of a literary tradition, those that are a part of his awareness of the living stage itself, and the more general influences upon him of his society and culture. Most difficult of all to grasp completely is the sudden moment of comprehension by which substance and form fall into place and the playwright or poet recognizes with exhilaration the design of the whole. If the act of creation cannot be understood in anything like its entirety, it is at least possible to know a good deal about the constituent elements lying behind it, since there is no hint of *creatio ex nihilo* in this process. It has been a major concern of this study to discover the nature of these constituent elements, including those which are formal principles of dramatic organization.

In medieval and early Tudor drama, and in narrative poems and romances, one can find many of the uncompounded elements of tragedy which reappeared later in new contexts. As we have seen, these uncompounded elements may be representative characters, such as the great tyrants who reveal a fundamental rebelliousness against divine order, or they may be controlled patterns of action, like the stern movement of retribution, or concentrations of emotion, like the overwhelming pathos of innocence suffering under the brutality of power. The transformation of such embryonic characters and situations seems to have come about through an intensification of individual episodes, the tying together of such episodes into a firm structure of action governed by cause and effect, and the enlargement of the context within which such episodes occur.

Some of the changes were natural and inevitable because of theatrical demands and opportunities on a stage which was becoming increasingly mature. But it is also clear that other impulses were affecting writers of the time, so that they were driven to explore the variety and intensity of contemporary experience through the mode of tragedy. The endeavour of playwrights to provide a credible sequence of cause and effect was no doubt a necessary response to the growing sophistication of theatre audiences. It can also be regarded as the playwright's attempt to explore the causes of violent events and bring understanding to bear upon what would otherwise be random or chaotic. Similarly, various playwrights discovered that there were obvious theatrical advantages to be gained in concentrating attention upon the acts, motivation, and emotional reactions of a single character. At the same time some of them were able to see that in such concentration there were opportunities for exploring an individual's experience of aspiration, defeat, and suffering, and that by such means they could gain a form of coherence and emotional intensity which did not exist in late moralities such as *Like Will to Like*, in an academic play like *Gorboduc*, or in most of the chronicle plays. There was an intensification of conflict and hence of emotion in this drama because of the exuberant energy of the age, which glorified the boldness of man in his search after power, glory, love, or revenge, and yet which was checked severely by the weight of forces opposed to such desires in fate or providence, or in society.

Another kind of awareness, an awareness possessed by play-wrights, is apparent in early tragedy and obviously had some-thing to do with the writing of tragedy: this is the complexity of attitude toward the central character that each play reveals. In the chronicle tragedies particularly, plays like *Richard II*, *Edward II*, and *Richard III*, several different views of the tragic characters are given striking dramatic expression, so that it is impossible to accept a simple moralistic view of what is happen-ing. Gerald Else regards this 'double vision' as an outstanding factor in the emergence of Greek tragedy.[1] Its existence in English tragedy is a product of the 'double vision' of the morality plays in which the Vice castigates and burlesques the serious characters, and, beyond this, a very similar quality in a number of the mystery plays. The tragedies of the *Mirror for Magistrates* also encouraged such complexity of attitude because of the choral passages of comment and reflection that separate the individual tales and often take up a different point of view from that of the lamenting ghost.

One further influence upon playwrights of the time is closely related to the growth of a particular awareness such as I have just been describing. It is apparent that the directly moral inter-pretation of violent action which had once kept episodes of cruelty and suffering within a non-tragic pattern had weakened rapidly in much of the dramatic and narrative literature of the time, and that other forms of interpretation—satiric, ironic, and tragic—were beginning to supplant it. No longer is there com-plete certainty as to the causes of worldly events, but moral law must take up a limited place beside the deterministic law of cause and effect and the principle of uncertainty symbolized by fortune. In earlier pages I have pointed to some of the direct sources of these new ideas about the meaning of tragic events. Unhappily, the wider context of thought and feeling which led to the explora-tion of causes and meaning has been beyond the scope of this study. I can suggest only a few of the most obvious factors that influenced writers and thinkers.

In the first place, it is clear that English humanism had stimulated a great deal of intellectual activity in the historical

[1] Gerald Else, *The Origin and Early Form of Greek Tragedy*, p. 44.

field, sometimes to bolster certain useful legends, sometimes to determine the facts of confused and bitter periods of history. Historical writing shows as clearly as the poetical narratives of the *Mirror for Magistrates* the increasingly sceptical, querying mind of the age with regard to human character and event. It was also a time when the sceptical intelligence was being brought to bear upon medieval books of science and natural history, and for that matter upon the classical texts which had frequently stimulated the new approach. The heavens and the earth were being searched with a fresh outlook. Above all, it was an age of increasing debate about fundamental issues concerning the nature of society, the rule of law, and different versions of the Christian faith. These recognizable historical factors doubtless had something to do with that striking quality of Elizabethan tragedy that I have mentioned more than once—the tension that exists between different possible interpretations of suffering and violence, the open background that allows these possibilities to coexist within a play, and hence within the consciousness of an audience. The human individual acts out his cause against a background that is partly inscrutable, and his tragedy lies not only in his stubbornness but also in his blindness, which is never completely wiped away at the end. In Elizabethan tragedy the tragic character recognizes part of the truth at the time of the catastrophe, but the truth which the play presents in its wholeness is complex, and there is scarcely a tragic character from Edward II to Coriolanus who sees more than a part of the meaning of his tragic experience. The rest is for the audience to try to comprehend in the context of the whole play. Such 'partial recognition' is not a fault of the tragedy of this age but a deliberate element of its art in portraying the uncertain boundaries of human experience.

Is scepticism, then, necessary for tragedy? It is clear that there was a general development in the theatre from a theologically based drama to a drama almost completely secular, and that this development took place during a period of considerable disturbance of accepted ideas about nature and society. But whether tragedy and scepticism are related in a causal way is not immediately obvious.

Not every tragic action is worked out against a background of disbelief. Some, like *Doctor Faustus* and *Macbeth*, portray a universal system of order which the individual violates at his peril. Many others, however, represent a world of very long-delayed justice or a world where accounts are ironically settled at some moment ironically appropriate. Sometimes it is a seemingly neutral universe, subject only to the inevitable harshness of cause and effect. What is evident in them all, including *Doctor Faustus* and *Macbeth*, when we compare them with the religious drama and most of the chronicle plays, is a much more powerful and convincing view of the motives that drive men to ultimate decisions and rebellious or violent action. The demands of the individual and the passions that create such demands have been particularized in terms of ambition, lust, or revenge in situations which are explored in detail and can therefore be communicated with much greater intensity. These demands and passions are also enlarged in scope, so that there often seems to be something magnificent about them, even when they are conventionally evil. Hence a tragic conflict between such an individual purpose and a frustrating power immediately becomes possible and the reversal is able to achieve a sense of tragic loss.

By searching into the motives of human action with considerable intensity, and by giving so much value to the passions and desires that move the human will, the open, sceptical mind of the age undoubtedly made tragic conflict possible in this drama. It is doubtful, in fact, whether tragedy could have appeared under any other auspices. Moreover, by undermining the framework of belief with uncertainty or ironic ambiguity the scepticism of the period allowed dramatists to explore struggle and suffering with greater freedom and envisage their meaning over a greater range of possibilities. Thus it is characteristic of Elizabethan tragedy that it should combine a sense of the inscrutability of fate with a sense of the necessity of all that happens. We have found this conjunction in the mystery of that fate which reverses human hopes even when they seem most natural, and which punishes the innocent with the guilty and the guilty more severely than justice would require. The presence of irony is a constant reminder of this fundamental doubt. A general scepticism, in the form of irony, pervades the villain tragedies, also, where justice exists in a highly ironic mode and virtue is little more than an aberration. Though it may not be an essential quality of tragedy, a sceptical attitude toward order and belief strongly affected most Elizabethan tragedies and gave some of them an exceptional power to disturb an audience.

Doctor Faustus and *Macbeth*, as I have said, belong to a Christian framework of belief, and scepticism does not shake this framework to any noticeable extent. But are we justified in calling them 'Christian tragedies'? In so far as the term refers to a process of spiritual damnation in a Christian universe, the loss of what ought to have been saved, its use is accurate enough. Yet it is an ambiguous term and may have no meaning apart from a few plays of this kind. What are we to make, for example, of a play like *A Woman Killed with Kindness*, which leads to the physical death of the central character, and yet has an upward movement of repentance and reconciliation, a veritable triumph in spiritual terms? When the fatal mistake and its consequences are transcended by a spiritual victory, it must be admitted that a play moves away from tragedy toward divine comedy, as *Antony and Cleopatra* does to a limited extent, and as *Samson Agonistes* does almost entirely. Such spiritual victory, which means a reconciliation with law and perhaps a new understanding of law or the divine will, has an important resemblance to the movement beyond tragedy found in an Aeschylean trilogy like the *Oresteia*. Tragic events are brought into a relationship with some larger pattern which draws good out of evil and ends in triumph and order. Aristotle and most Elizabethans would admit such plays into the ranks of tragedy, provided they maintained their seriousness of tone, dignity and expressiveness of language, and weightiness of fable, but in a stricter sense they are religious plays rather than tragedies.

This is not to deny the direct importance for tragedy of the religious drama of the Middle Ages. From the religious drama came a vision of the Fall of Man and the loss of innocence, and powerful images of brutal power and suffering in a world whose evil is man's own creation. The morality plays in their turn added another dimension to the drama, in particular the experience of breakdown, the overthrow of human confidence, and a recognition of ultimate despair. These images and experiences from medieval drama were of prime importance for the emergence of tragedy when didactic and other-worldly elements lost their dominating position in the drama. Though the tragedy of the English Renaissance is not in the main Christian tragedy, there is no doubt that religious levels of experience run through almost all its forms. Without the conception that human aspiration might be fulfilled or that ultimate justice might be achieved in a universe willing to accept such dreams, the poignancy and irony of tragedy would scarcely exist.

I began this study with a description of tragedy drawn from several sources, but not yet tested as a whole against a theory of the emergence of tragedy. At this point we ought to reconsider the main terms of that description, in order to judge whether they have taken on new meanings during the course of this investigation. First of all, the phrase 'an intense exploration of failure and suffering' has not proven to be accurate enough for extensive use, since in many plays the tragic centre of the action and the emotion lies not so much in failure and suffering as in a bold and often heroic confrontation between the individual will and a superior law or destiny. The driving passion that moves Elizabethan tragic characters toward their fatal destiny is one of the most striking qualities of the tragedies we have been considering, even though the causes are so different and the situations so varied in this range of plays. The emotional pattern of Elizabethan tragedy is also vitally dependent upon this element in the drama, the experience of dogged commitment against all odds, a stubborn hanging on to individual will and purpose until some overwhelming climax puts an end to doubt.

The idea of confrontation has allowed considerable insight into the working of tragic plots, but it has had to be extended to include the whole range of human rebellion, from arrogant defiance of the gods to a merely innocent neglect and disregard of the laws which operate in this world. It is clear in this drama that there are many different kinds of self-assertion or rebelliousness against whatever order may exist. Moreover, this confrontation is almost always associated with a fundamental and agonized questioning of order. Such questioning may seek out with fear and trembling some hint of justice or mercy in the universe, or it may express the bewilderment and anger of the defiant individual in the face of a great frustrating force. Whatever its form, the questioning represents the immense disturbance and overthrow of the confidence with which the individual originally took his stand, and leads to the experience of a tragic recognition.

There was also too little stress given to recognition in my original description. As I have said, recognition is linked with the overthrow of an original confidence and pride: it is the poignant moment when the truth is seen in part or in whole, when error must finally collapse. Recognition is therefore the climax, both in terms of the meaning of the play and in terms of its emotion. The tragic character is forced into defiance or into exhausted acceptance. In either case the individual admits the necessity of what has happened but not the worthlessness of his cause or motive, and from this source stems the value given by tragedy to the tenacity of the human will.

The characteristics I have been speaking of may not belong to all forms of tragedy, but they are undoubtedly essential qualities of the tragedy of this age. Tragedy came into existence because of the creative acts of a few playwrights who saw the possible scope of the contending forces already present within the drama, and who conceived the dramatic power of confrontation and recognition. It was an age and society in which the dreams and desires of man seemed extraordinarily great and his determination intensely real. The poets of the time had their own lofty dreams and were infected by the same spirit as touched the adventurers, the scientists, the lovers, the religious prophets, and the seekers after beauty, luxury, and power. Yet it was also an age when the forces arrayed against human purpose and desire seemed more powerful and more inscrutable, because of their complexity, than at any previous time. The strong motivating forces of Elizabethan tragedy, the dreams of its aspiring and struggling heroes, and the unravelling of complex patterns of determining law are a record of some of the most vital forces of that age. It is in tragedy that they are given expression and brought into a system of imaginative order for the mind and soul of man.

BIBLIOGRAPHY

I. PRIMARY SOURCES

Apius and Virginia, by R. B., ed. R. B. McKerrow, Malone Society Reprints, Oxford, 1911.

BEZA, T., *A Tragedie of Abrahams Sacrifice*, Written in french by Theodore Beza, and translated into Inglish, by A. G., 1577.

The Castle of Perseverance, The Macro Plays, E.E.T.S., Extra Series xci, 1904.

CHAPMAN, GEORGE, *Bussy D'Ambois*, ed. Nicholas Brooke, London, 1964.

—— *The Plays and Poems of George Chapman*, ed. T. M. Parrott, London, 1910.

The Chester Plays, ed. Thomas Wright, London, Shakespeare Society, 1843.

CHETTLE, HENRY, *The Tragedy of Hoffman*, Malone Society Reprints, Oxford, 1950.

Cromwell: The True Chronicle Historie of the whole life and death of Thomas Lord Cromwell, London, 1602.

Early English Classical Tragedies, ed. John W. Cunliffe, Oxford, 1912.

Edmond Ironside, or War Hath Made All Friends, Malone Society Reprints, Oxford, 1927.

FENTON, GEOFFREY, *Certaine Tragicall Discourses written oute of Frenche and Latin* by Geffraie Fenton . . ., London, 1567.

FORTESCUE, THOMAS, *The Foreste or Collection of Histories*, London, 1571.

FULWELL, ULPIAN, *Like Will to Like, 1587*, Tudor Facsimile Texts, ed. J. S. Farmer, 1919.

GASCOIGNE, GEORGE, *The Glass of Gouernement*, Tudor Facsimile Texts, ed. J. S. Farmer, 1914.

—— *Supposes and Jocasta*, ed. J. W. Cunliffe, Boston, 1906.

Godly Queene Hester: A New Enterlude of Godly Queene Hester, edited from the quarto of 1561 by W. W. Greg, *Materialien zur Kunde des älteren Englischen Dramas*, Louvain, 1904.

GREENE, ROBERT, *Alphonsus King of Aragon 1599*, Malone Society Reprints, Oxford, 1926.

GREVILLE, SIR FULKE: *Sir Fulke Greville's Life of Sir Philip Sidney*, ed. Nowell Smith, Oxford, 1907.

John of Bordeaux or The Second Part of Friar Bacon, Malone Society Reprints, Oxford, 1935.

KYD, THOMAS: *The Works of Thomas Kyd*, ed. Frederick S. Boas, Oxford, 1901.

Locrine: *The Tragedy of Locrine 1595*, Malone Society Reprints, Oxford, 1908.

Ludus Coventriae: A Collection of Mysteries formerly represented at Coventry on the Feast of Corpus Christi, edited by James Orchard Halliwell, London, Shakespeare Society, 1841.

LUPTON, THOMAS, *All for Money*: A Moral and pitiful Comedie intituled All for Money. Plainly representing the maners of men, and fashion of the world now adayes, London, 1570.

Lusts Dominion; or, The Lascivious Queen. A Tragedie. Written by Christofer Marloe, Gent., London . . ., 1657.

Lydgate's Fall of Princes, ed. Dr. Henry Bergen, E.E.T.S., Extra Series cxxi, London, 1924.

MANLY, J. M. (ed.), *Specimens of the Pre-Shaksperean Drama*, Boston, 1903.

MARLOWE, CHRISTOPHER, *Edward II*, ed. W. D. Briggs, London, 1914.

—— *Works*, ed. C. F. Tucker Brooke, Oxford, 1910.

MIDDLETON, THOMAS, *The Works of Thomas Middleton*, ed. A. H. Bullen, 8 vols., London, 1885–6.

Mind, Will and Understanding, The Macro Plays, E.E.T.S., Extra Series xci, 1904.

The Mirror for Magistrates, ed. Lily B. Campbell, Cambridge, 1938.

More: *The Book of Sir Thomas More*, ed. W. W. Greg, Malone Society Reprints, Oxford, 1911.

MUNDAY, ANTONY, *The Downfall of Robert Earl of Huntington 1601*, Malone Society Reprints, 1964.

—— *The Death of Robert Earl of Huntington*, Tudor Facsimile Texts, ed. J. S. Farmer, 1913.

PAINTER, WILLIAM, *The Palace of Pleasure*, ed. Joseph Jacobs, London, 1890.

Parts Added to the Mirror for Magistrates by John Higgins and Thomas Blener-hasset, ed. Lily B. Campbell, Cambridge, 1946.

PIKERYNG, JOHN, *A Newe Enterlude of Vice Conteyning the historye of Horestes*, London, 1567.

PRESTON, THOMAS, *Cambyses King of Persia*, Tudor Facsimile Texts, ed. J. S. Farmer, 1910.

PUTTENHAM, GEORGE, *The Arte of English Poesie*, ed. G. D. Willcock and A. Walker, Cambridge, 1936.

The Rare Triumphs of Love and Fortune, Malone Society Reprints, Oxford, 1930.

Respublica: An Interlude for Christmas 1553, ed. W. W. Greg, E.E.T.S., 1952.

Selimus: The Tragical Reign of Selimus 1594, Malone Society Reprints, Oxford, 1908.

SENECA: *Studley's Translations of Seneca's Agamemnon and Medea*, edited from the octavos of 1566 by E. M. Spearing, *Materialien*, xxxviii, Louvain, 1913.

—— *The Lamentable Tragedie of Oedipus the Sonne of Laius Kyng of Thebes out of Seneca*. By Alexander Nevyle. London, 1563.

Seneca, His Tenne Tragedies Translated into Englyshe, London, 1581.

SHAKESPEARE, *King Richard II*, ed. John Dover Wilson, Cambridge, 1939.

SKELTON, JOHN: *The Complete Poems of John Skelton, Laureate*, ed. Philip Henderson, London, 1931, rev. ed. 1948.

SMYTHE, ROBERT, *Straunge, Lamentable, and Tragicall Hystories*. Translated out of French into English by R. S. Anno 1577.

TOURNEUR, CYRIL, *The Atheist's Tragedy or The Honest Man's Revenge*, ed. Irving Ribner, London, 1964.

—— *The Works of Cyril Tourneur*, ed. Allardyce Nicoll, London, 1929.

Towneley Plays, ed. G. England and A. W. Pollard, E.E.T.S., 1897.

The Trial of Treasure, 1567, Tudor Facsimile Texts, ed. J. S. Farmer, 1908.

The True Tragedy of Richard the Third 1594, Malone Society Reprints, Oxford, 1929.

WAGER, W., *Enough is as Good as a Feast*, Huntington Facsimile Reprints, ii, New York, 1920.

—— *The Longer thou Livest the more Fool thou art*, Tudor Facsimile Texts, ed. J. S. Farmer, 1910.

A Warning for Faire Women, London, 1599.

WATERHOUSE, O. (ed.), *The Non-Cycle Mystery Plays*, E.E.T.S., 1909.

WEBSTER, JOHN: *The Complete Works of John Webster*, ed. F. L. Lucas, London, 1927.

—— *The White Devil*, ed. John Russell Brown, London, 1960.

WHETSTONE, GEORGE, *The English Myrror*, London, 1586.

—— *The Rocke of Regard*, London, 1576.

WILLIS, ROBERT, *Mount Tabor*, London, 1639.

WILMOT, R., *The Tragedy of Tancred and Gismund 1591-2*, Malone Society Reprints, Oxford, 1914.

WOODES, NATHANIELL, *The Conflict of Conscience*, London, 1581.

YARINGTON, R., *Two Lamentable Tragedies*, London, 1601.

York Plays: The Plays Performed by the Crafts or Mysteries of York on the day of Corpus Christi, ed. Lucy Toulmin Smith, Oxford, 1885.

Quotations from Shakespeare's plays are from *The Complete Works of Shakespeare*, ed. G. L. Kitteredge, Boston, 1936.

II. CRITICISM

ABBREVIATIONS

E.C.	*Essays in Criticism*
E.L.H.	*English Literary History*
M.L.Q.	*Modern Language Quarterly*
P.Q.	*Philological Quarterly*
R.E.S.	*Review of English Studies*
S.P.	*Studies in Philology*
U.T.Q.	*University of Toronto Quarterly*

ADAMS, H. H., *English Domestic or Homiletic Tragedy, 1575 to 1642*, New York, 1943.

ALEXANDER, SIR WILLIAM: *The Poetical Works of Sir William Alexander, Earl of Stirling*, ed. L. E. Kastner and H. B. Charlton, Scottish Text Society, 1921.

ANDERSON, M. D., *Drama and Imagery in English Medieval Churches*, Cambridge, 1963.

BAKER, HOWARD, *Induction to Tragedy*, Louisiana, 1939.

BALDWIN, T. W., *William Shakspere's Small Latine & Lesse Greeke*, Urbana, 1944.

BATTENHOUSE, R. W., 'Chapman and the Nature of Man', *E.L.H.* xii (1945), 87–107.

BEVINGTON, D. M., *From Mankind to Marlowe*, Cambridge, Mass., 1962.

BOAS, F. S., *University Drama in the Tudor Age*, Oxford, 1914.

BOGARD, TRAVIS, *The Tragic Satire of John Webster*, Berkeley, 1955.

BOWERS, FREDSON T., *Elizabethan Revenge Tragedy 1587-1642*, Princeton, 1940.

BRADBROOK, M. C., *The Rise of the Common Player*, London, 1962.

—— *Themes and Conventions of Elizabethan Tragedy*, Cambridge, 1935.

BROOKS, CLEANTH, 'A note on the death of Elizabethan tragedy', *Modern Poetry and the Tradition*, London, 1948.

BURTON, R. M., 'The political tragedies of Chapman and Jonson', *E.C.* ii (1952), 397–412.

CAMPBELL, LILY B., *Divine Poetry and Drama in Sixteenth-Century England*, Cambridge, 1959.

CHAMBERS, E. K., *The Elizabethan Stage*, Oxford, 1923.

—— *The Medieval Stage*, Oxford, 1903.

CLEMEN, WOLFGANG, *English Tragedy before Shakespeare*, London, 1961.

CRAIG, HARDIN, *English Religious Drama of the Middle Ages*, Oxford, 1955.

CRAIK, T. W., *The Tudor Interlude*, Leicester, 1958.

CUNLIFFE, J. W., *The Influence of Seneca on Elizabethan Tragedy*, London, 1893.

DORAN, MADELEINE, *Endeavors of Art*, Madison, 1954.

EDWARDS, PHILIP, 'The danger, not the death—the art of John Webster', in *Jacobean Theatre*, Stratford-upon-Avon Studies I, London, 1960.

EKEBLAD, I., 'The impure art of John Webster', *R.E.S.* ix (1958), 253-67.

ELLIS-FERMOR, UNA, *The Frontiers of Drama*, London, 1946.

—— *The Jacobean Drama, an Interpretation*, London, 1936.

ELLISON, L. M., 'The Early Romantic Drama at the English Court' (Diss.), Chicago, 1917.

ELSE, GERALD F., *The Origin and Early Form of Greek Tragedy*, Cambridge, Mass., 1965.

ENGEBERG, E., 'Tragic blindness in *The Changeling* and *Women Beware Women*', *M.L.Q.* xxiii (1962), 20-28.

FARNHAM, WILLARD, *The Medieval Heritage of Elizabethan Tragedy*, Berkeley, 1936.

—— *Shakespeare's Tragic Frontier, The World of his Final Tragedies*, Berkeley, 1950.

FRYE, NORTHROP, *Anatomy of Criticism*, Princeton, 1957.

HARBAGE, ALFRED, *Shakespeare and the Rival Traditions*, New York, 1952.

HERRICK, M. T., *Tragicomedy: Its Origin and Development in Italy, France, and England*. Urbana, 1955.

HOENIGER, F. J. D., 'The Function of Structure and Imagery in Shakespeare's Last Plays' (unpublished Thesis), University of London, 1954.

HUNTER, G. K., *John Lyly: 'The Humanist as Courtier'*, London, 1962.

JOHNSON, S. F., 'The tragic hero in Early Elizabethan drama', *Studies in the English Renaissance Drama*, ed. J. W. Bennett, O. Cargill, and V. Hall, London, 1961.

KITTO, H. D. F., *Form and Meaning in Drama*, London, 1956.

—— *Greek Tragedy*, London, 1961.

LAWLOR, JOHN, 'Romeo and Juliet', in *Early Shakespeare*, Stratford-upon-Avon Studies III, London, 1961.

LEAVIS, F. R., *The Common Pursuit*, London, 1958.

LEECH, CLIFFORD, *Shakespeare's Tragedies and Other Studies in Seventeenth-Century Drama*, London, 1950.

LISCA, P., '*The Revenger's Tragedy*, a study in irony', *P.Q.* xxxviii (1959), 242-51.

LUCAS, F. L., *Euripides and his Influence*, Boston, 1923.

—— *Seneca and Elizabethan Tragedy*, Cambridge, 1922.

—— *Tragedy In Relation to Aristotle's Poetics*, London, 1928.

McCollum, W. G., 'The tragic hero and Chapman's *Bussy D'Ambois*', *U.T.Q.* xviii (1949), 227-33.

Ornstein, R., 'The ethical design of *The Revenger's Tragedy*', *E.L.H.* xxi (1954), 81-93.

—— *The Moral Vision of Jacobean Tragedy*, Madison, 1960.

Peery, William, 'Tragic retribution in the 1559 *Mirror for Magistrates*', *S.P.* xlvi (1949), 113-30.

Peter, John, '*The Revenger's Tragedy* reconsidered', *E.C.* vi (1956), 131-43.

Ribner, Irving, *Jacobean Tragedy; the Quest for Moral Order*, London, 1962.

—— 'Then I denie you starres: a reading of *Romeo and Juliet*', *Studies in the English Renaissance Drama*, ed. J. W. Bennett, O. Cargill, and V. Hall, London, 1961.

Rossiter, A. P., *English Drama from Early Times to the Elizabethans*, London, 1950.

Salingar, L. G., '*The Revenger's Tragedy* and the morality tragedy', *Scrutiny*, vi (1938), 402-22.

Schoell, F. L., *Études sur l'humanisme continental en Angleterre à la fin de la Renaissance*, Paris, 1926.

Schoenbaum, S., *Middleton's Tragedies*, New York, 1955.

—— '*The Revenger's Tragedy*, Jacobean dance of death', *M.L.Q.* xv (1954), 201-7.

Sewall, R. B., *The Vision of Tragedy*, New Haven, 1959.

Spencer, Theodore, *Death and Elizabethan Tragedy*, Cambridge, Mass., 1936.

Spivack, Bernard, *Shakespeare and the Allegory of Evil*, London, 1958.

Steiner, G., *The Death of Tragedy*, London, 1963.

Thorndike, A. H., *Tragedy*, London, 1908.

Tomlinson, T. B., 'The morality of revenge: Tourneur's critics', *E.C.* x (1960), 134-47.

Tucker Brooke, C. F., *The Tudor Drama*, London, 1912.

Welsford, Enid, *The Court Masque*, Cambridge, 1927.

Wickham, Glynne, *Early English Stages, 1300 to 1660*, vol. i, 1300-1576, London, 1959.

Williams, Arnold, *The Drama of Medieval England*, Michigan, 1961.

Wilson, F. P., *Marlowe and the Early Shakespeare*, Oxford, 1953.

INDEX

Moralities and early Tudor plays are generally listed by title; Elizabethan plays by author, unless they are anonymous. Under subject headings, only main references are listed.

PRINTED IN GREAT BRITAIN
AT THE UNIVERSITY PRESS, OXFORD
BY VIVIAN RIDLER
PRINTER TO THE UNIVERSITY

"All right then. I first met Katie when she was eighteen. She had just left a top-line girls' school and wanted to behave like all the debby friends she'd made there, but she realized that she hadn't quite got the money to do it. Only two choices. She had to make money or marry it. And there were quite a few men—old men"—Holbeck's mobile mouth wrinkled at the corners—"who were prepared to buy her, even at the price of matrimony. She was sensible enough to say no. And she started out on the other route. She had no acting experience, so it was tough going. She got a job as a researcher with one of the independent television companies. A producer who liked her looks—correction, who liked her—wangled her a spot in one of their advertising quickies. And it *was* a wangle. He'd have had to get round Equity rules, but he did it. That was the beginning."

Holbeck stopped. He was looking back seven years, and ome of the things he was seeing seemed not to please him. He said, "You need just one quality to succeed in that ld. It isn't beauty and it isn't brains, though both are ful. It's a rock-hard, chilled-steel determination to suc-. You asked me just now if I liked Katie. I didn't like But I respected her. One day—it was after she'd been ng for about two years and making peanuts out of it ey Ruoff the photographer made an approach. h me, of course. I'd been half expecting it. Katie ying down her age in those early commercials. fourteen or even younger. Girls with small bones ravagant figures can go on doing that for a sur- ong time. Rodney was very interested in young oys. He's known in the trade as 'Rod the Sod.' rilliant photographer and really has got some with the television studios. Katie knew all e asked my advice. I said, 'Steer clear of him. s.' She said, 'If I was able to handle you,

128

ism, an ideal which he had once held himself and which was now slipping out of his reach in the backwater of Hannington.

Mr. Mapledurham, the head of the Documents Division, had been warned to expect him. He examined the photocopy of the letter with expert attention, scratched the back of his neck and said, "A Crossfield Electric, I should say. Not a golf ball, though. The earlier mark."

Ian tried to look intelligent.

"A lot of machines are turning to the golf-ball type now. It might be an Olympia or a Hermes, but I don't think so. We can easily find out. Let's see what we've got. Short 'm' and 'w.' Serifs at top *and* bottom of the 'I.' Lateral at the bottom of the 'T.' That should be enough to be going on with."

Remembering Knott's instructions, McCourt said, "How long will it take?"

"Ten minutes, if the line's clear."

"Ten minutes?"

"That's right. We'll put it on the computer." He was scribbling out a message as he spoke and said to the young man who sat at the other desk, "Feed this into the magic box, would you, Les. Gent wants an answer quickish."

"I'd no idea," said Ian. "I imagined these things took weeks to work out."

"Some things take months. Some things take minutes. That's science for you. If it'd been a Ransmeyer we'd have had a lot more trouble. That's a communal type face, used by a lot of different machines. I'd guess this is a PLX face, which generally means a Crossfield."

"Will it make it easier, or less easy, if it does turn out to be an electric machine?"

"It won't make any difference in identifying the machine. Make it more difficult to peg it down to any one typist. With a manual machine you get variations in

125

pressure. An electric machine smooths them out."

"But if I got hold of another letter typed on this machine, you'd be able to say for certain that they both came from the same machine? Sorry. That was a bit confused, but you see what I mean."

"I see what you mean and the answer's yes. Provided the two samples were typed reasonably soon after each other. Machines develop different peculiarities as they grow older."

"Like people," said Ian.

Soon after that Les came back and said, "You're right. It was a Crossfield Mark Four Electric."

Mr. Mapledurham was consulting a large book. He said, "Crossfield Mark Four. Ex-factory at the end of 1973. Available in the shops early in 1974. I'll make one guess about your machine. It doesn't come from an office. If it had been bashed by an office typist for several years the type face would be a lot more worn. Anyway, this letter wasn't typed by a professional."

"How can you tell?"

"Spacing and alignment. If you wanted a guess, I'd say a private owner. Someone who did a fair amount of typing, but not a professional."

"Thank you," said Ian. "That's going to be very useful."

"Do you want a written report?"

Ian thought about Superintendent Knott and said, "Yes. I'm afraid we shall want a written report. I'll give you the address."

Mark Holbeck's agency occupied the third floor of an eighteenth-century house in Henrietta Street, Covent Garden. It looked across at the Tuscan portico of St. Paul's Church, designed by Grinling Gibbons, from which Samuel Pepys had watched a Punch and Judy show and in which Professor Higgins had met Eliza Doolittle.

Mark Holbeck was a young-old man with a sunburned and freckled bald patch in the middle of an outfield of sandy hair. If you asked what he did for a living he would tell you that he dealt in words and flesh, which meant in the jargon of his trade that he promoted both books and people.

The books were all around him, new copies in bright jackets. They filled every shelf in his office, spilled over onto the floor, occupied the window seats and trespassed onto his table. He shifted a couple off a chair and waved to Shilling to be seated.

"Of course I read all about it," he said. "It was in the later editions of the Saturday papers, and the Sunday papers made a meal of it."

First surprise. Lack of any real evidence of distress.

Shilling said, "She was your client. I imagine it mu have come as a considerable shock to you."

Holbeck looked at him with the suspicion of a sm "Sorry, Sergeant," he said. "No crocodile tears. Natu I don't approve of people who kill my clients. It co ten per cent of their annual earnings. And in Kati that was beginning to add up to a very respectab money. But no personal involvement."

"I wasn't suggesting anything of that sort, s surprised that you didn't seem to mind mu sonal level, I mean."

The two men looked at each other. Eac other up. Holbeck said, "What are you a analysis of her character or a list of

"Both might be helpful, sir."

"I'll do what I can for you, on or

"Yes, sir?"

"That you stop calling me s seem to have picked up from

Shilling grinned and said

126

Mark, I ought to be able to handle him.' And off she trotted to his studio near the Kings Road."

Holbeck paused again, then said, "I'm damned if I know why I'm telling you all this. It must be because you've got such a disingenuous sort of face. You don't look like a policeman at all. When you first came in, I thought you were another hopeful pop star. Sorry."

Shilling was unoffended. He said, "It is a fact that people do talk to me. But not often as usefully as you're doing. So please go on. How did Ruoff get on with her?"

"I'm not sure. He certainly took some wonderful photographs of her—dressed, half dressed and undressed. And peddled them round the studios. Whether he got anything else out of her, I rather doubt. In fact, I'm pretty certain, if anyone got anything out of anyone it was the other way round." He smiled. "I remember I ran into Ruoff at a party about a year ago. Katie was a big property by then and, knowing he had an interest in her, naturally I was ready to talk about her. As soon as I mentioned her name, Ruoff went the color of a beetroot. I thought he was going to burst into flames. He squeaked out, in that funny high-pitched voice of his, 'Don't talk to me about her, Mark. Don't mention that bitch to me. She's a criminal. She's a thief. Why did you ever send her to me?' I had to remind him that it was the other way round. He'd sent for her himself. But he wasn't listening. He was too bloody angry."

"Did you gather what he was angry about?"

"Not exactly. I gathered that she'd lifted some of his property, but done it so cleverly that he couldn't go to the police. You'd better ask him. I imagine you'll be wanting a word with him."

"I'll be seeing him next. Will you tell me something else. That is, if you don't mind. It's rather a personal question."

"You alarm me."

"When you were talking to Katie about this photographer chap, she said, 'If I was able to handle you, I ought to be able to handle him.' Did she mean anything in particular by that?"

"I knew I was talking too much," said Holbeck gloomily. He thought about it. Outside, a motorist tried to go around the Covent Garden piazza the wrong way and got spoken to by the driver of a vegetable lorry.

At last Holbeck said, "All right. Confession is said to be good for the soul. I made a fool of myself. Mind you, I was seven years younger then. And you can take that smirk off your face, Sergeant. This isn't going to be a sex story. No. It was Katie's contract. I've got a standard form, drafted by my own lawyer. When I showed it to Katie she opened those innocent eyes wide and said, 'Oh, we don't need anything like *that,* surely. It's much too legal for poor little me. I wouldn't understand a word of it. If we must have something in writing—you know, about the ten per cent and all that—just give me a bit of paper. I'll jot down what I think we've agreed and we'll sign it here and now.' And she sat straight down and did just that. Ten lines of school-girl handwriting. I've got it in my safe over there. Any time I feel I've been smart I take it out and read it. It's an excellent corrective to self-esteem. Because she'd slipped in a final sentence which said, 'Agreement to be firm for two years and then renegotiable.' "

"And that wasn't a good idea?"

"As far as I was concerned it was a lousy idea. When these kids start out, it's make-or-break and it usually takes a year or two to show which it's going to be. If they're a flop, they want to get out anyway. If they're a success, that's when you begin to get back some of what you've put into them. In fact it took Katie almost exactly two years to make the grade. It was that song that helped. Remember it? 'What Are They Like in Your House?' " He hummed the well-known tune.

"I was at school when it came out," said Shilling. "We used to sing a rather coarser version of the second line."

"Any song which can be perverted is halfway to success. It was short-lived, but it was dynamite while it lasted. It blew Katie up into stardom almost overnight. That's when I hoped she'd forgotten what was written on that paper."

"But she hadn't?"

"She'd made a copy and she'd kept it. She showed it to me sitting where you are now, with a wide smile on her face. She said, 'You realize I can walk away whenever I like, Mark. There are plenty of people would be glad to have me now.' And she trotted out the names of some of my rivals. And that's the way it was from then on. Whenever we had an argument, she'd say, 'All right, Mark. If you don't like it, I'm off.' And then, of course, I'd have to knuckle under. I don't think she actually meant to leave. She just liked having the whip hand. And cracking the whip every now and then."

Shilling thought about this. It opened up a rather startling line of thought. He said, "Are you telling me she had a sadistic streak?"

"That's rather overstating the case. You don't call a kitten sadistic when you see it playing with a ball of string or chasing a leaf."

"No. But I might when it grows up and becomes a cat chasing a mouse. Do you think she tried the same game on with Ruoff?"

"You'd better ask him," said Holbeck. "Only keep upwind of him. When he gets excited he's inclined to spit."

Ruoff's house-cum-studio was in Chelverton Mews, which lies north of the Kings Road. It had three tubs of hydrangeas in front of it and a big white metal knocker in the shape of a bull's head on the scarlet front door. Shilling seized the bull by the horns and knocked. When this produced no response he tried the door, found it unfastened and went in.

A notice on the wall of the entrance hall said, "Studio Upstairs. Excelsior." An enlarged photograph of a human hand pointed upward. Shilling went up. It was one of those tall thin London houses which have their living rooms on the second floor. A further hand pointed up a further flight of steps. Bedroom floor. Further steps—scrubbed and un-carpeted. Above him a murmur of voices. A notice on the door at the top said, "Pray Enter." He went in. It was a small room and was empty.

The wall opposite the door was entirely covered by a photomontage made up of heads, bodies, arms and legs. Some of the heads were upside down. The arms and legs had been arranged into groups in a floral pattern. The effect in that small brightly lit room was hypnotic.

He was staring at it when a door in the left-hand wall opened and a boy came out. He was wearing gray flannel shorts and a cricket shirt. Shilling guessed his age as twelve or thirteen. He said, "Excuse me. I was wondering if your father was anywhere about."

"About what?" said the boy.

"I mean, could I have a word with him."

The boy said, "You'd have to shout pretty loud to do it from here. He lives in Southwark."

"Then I take it Mr. Ruoff's not your father."

"That's right. And I'm not his son."

"Who are you?"

"Me? I'm one of his favorite models. If you've come to have your photograph taken, Rod's in there. Got to be off. Got another engagement."

"How old are you?"

"Ninety-nine," said the boy. "Next birthday. Goodbye for now." He departed and his footsteps went clattering down the stairs. Shilling stood looking after him.

The murmur of voices which he had heard as he was coming up broke out again. It was louder now and came from behind the door in the left-hand wall. Shilling opened it cautiously and looked in. The first impression he got was of blinding light, directed not at him, but toward the far end of the room. Light and heat. The room was overpoweringly hot. It stank vilely of sweat and of some scented stuff which had been splashed about, presumably to hide the smell of the sweat.

On a low stage, bathed in the full glare of the lamps, two young men were engaged in a wrestling match. He thought at first sight that they were naked, but then saw that they were wearing flesh-colored tights. A squeaky voice from behind the lamps said, "Hold it," and the wrestlers froze into immobility. "Left hand a little higher, love. Pull his wrist up behind his back. You aren't really hurting him."

"He bloody is."

"Hold it."

"For Christ's sake, Rod, I'm getting cramp."

"That's it. All right, relax. And shut that bloody door."

Shilling, who could already feel the sweat running down his face, backed toward the door. The voice said, "See what he wants, Louie. But outside. For God's sake, this isn't a public waiting room."

A paunchy man, wearing off-white trousers and a singlet, followed Shilling out into the anteroom and slammed the door. He said, "Mussen come barging in there, chummy. Rod gets very up-tight when he's working. He's artistic, see."

"I'm sorry," said Shilling, mopping his forehead with his handkerchief. "It's very hot in there, isn't it?"

"It's the lamps. You'll get used to it. Turn sideways a moment."

"Why?"

133

"Profile, lad. That's the important thing. Not bad. Not bad at all."

"You've got it wrong," said Shilling. "I haven't come here to have my photograph taken."

"Then what the hell have you come here for?"

"To talk to Mr. Ruoff." Shilling took out his warrant card and slid it across the table.

The man looked down at the card without touching it, looked up again at Shilling and said, "You could have fooled me. I'll tell him." He departed into the studio, closing the door carefully behind him. Then a murmur of voices, which went on for a long time. Shilling composed himself to wait. He was determined on one thing. He was not going into that stinking hothouse again. Minutes ticked by. Then the inner door opened and a small man bounced out. He had pink cheeks and a gray beard which jutted from his chin as though it had been trained in espalier. It waggled when he spoke.

He said, "I've got nothing to say to you. This is a respectable establishment. Regularly inspected. Licensed by the London County Council. Passed by the health authorities and the fire authorities."

"Do the authorities know that you employ juvenile models?"

"I've no idea what you're talking about."

"That boy who just came out of your studio."

"A relative. Paying me a visit."

"He might have been a relative, of course. What he said was that he was one of your favorite models."

"Joking, Sergeant. You know what boys are. They say the first thing that comes into their heads."

"The first things people say are often the truth," said Shilling. "Actually, I didn't come here to talk about your studio. Or only indirectly. The person I wanted to ask you about was Miss Steelstock."

134

Up to that point Ruoff had been standing. Now he came across and sat down, very slowly, at the table opposite to Shilling. He said, "You're referring to Katie Steelstock, of course."

"Yes."

"Who was killed two days ago."

"Yes."

"Apart from the fact that I took a number of publicity photographs of her some years ago, I can tell you nothing about her at all."

"You did a little more than that, didn't you?"

"Meaning?"

"Using your influence to get her a start in television."

Ruoff's babyish mouth opened in what might have been the beginning of a smile. A tip of pink tongue looked out. He said, "Who have you been talking to?"

"I had a word with her agent, Mark Holbeck."

"You mustn't believe all that agents tell you. The only way I influence anyone is by taking beautiful, beautiful photographs. The eye of the camera, Sergeant, which never lies, but seldom tells the whole truth."

The inner door opened and the two young men came out. They had put on track suits. They looked incuriously at Shilling and one of them said, "Anything more, Rod?"

"I'll tell you when this lot come out," said Ruoff. "If they're as good as I think they're going to be, there'll certainly be more." As the door closed behind them he said, "An interesting pair. Cousins. They both have beautiful bodies. Did you know that it was Michelangelo who first exploited the full potentiality of the male body?" He got up. "I'm afraid I can't help you any further, Sergeant."

Shilling got up, too. He said, "What did Katie steal from you?"

He saw the color rising like a tide from the veins of the

neck into the cheeks, turning pink to dark red and red to crimson.

"Who said anything about stealing?"

"Actually it was you. Something you said to Mark Holbeck at a party." Shilling was watching him closely.

"Did I say that? I'd forgotten. It can't have been very important, can it?"

"Possibly not."

"And in any event, if such a thing did happen, it happened years ago. It could hardly affect your inquiries."

"Mark Holbeck said last year. And until I know what she took from you, sir, I'm in no position to judge."

If his forehead was made of glass, thought Shilling, I swear I'd be able to see those brain cells working. He knows damn well what Katie stole. He's thinking it out, in all its aspects. Will it be to his advantage to tell me or not? Will it damage him in any way? Dare he tell me? Dare he *not* tell me?

In the end Ruoff evidently came to some sort of conclusion. He said, "If I do happen to remember, Sergeant, I'll let you know."

And Shilling had to be content with that.

THIRTEEN

Mrs. Havelock came into the operations room at the Hannington police station like a very large liner towing a very small tug. The tug was Sim. She had him fast by one hand.

Knott said, "Please sit down. You too, lad. I gather you've got something to tell me."

"It's Sim here who's got to do the telling." She looked down at her son, who was very pale. "It should be the older boy, Roney, but he wouldn't come, so Sim's got to do it alone."

It took ten minutes of patient questioning to get the story into some sort of shape.

"Just those two occasions you and your brother saw Jonathan and Katie by the boathouse?"

Sim nodded.

"And when you got there they were lying on the grass together?"

"Yes."

"Could you see what they were doing?"

"Not really."

Knott paused. He knew only too well with what delicacy a nine-year-old witness had to be handled.

"O.K.," he said. "They were just lying there. Then what happened?"

"Then they went into the boathouse."

"How did they do that, when the door was locked?"

"Oh, everyone knows how to do that. You just put your hand through that place where the glass is gone and turn the handle. The one on the little door."

Knott nodded. He had read Shilling's report. He said, "What then?"

"There was no point hanging around. We came home."

"Did that happen both times? I mean, going into the boathouse."

"No, that was only the second time."

"How long ago was the first time?"

"I can't exactly remember."

Mrs. Havelock said, "Was it holidays or term, Sim?"

"Holidays. Last holidays. Just before term started."

"That makes it early May," said Mrs. Havelock.

"And the second time?"

"I can't exactly remember. It was before the regatta."

"Long before?"

"Not very long before."

"That would make it early July," said Mrs. Havelock. She had one eye on Sim. He was going to be sick and she wanted to get him outside before it happened. Knott picked up the warning in her eye. He said, "That's fine, Sim. You've done very well. Only one more question. You're nine. Right? Nearly ten. Old enough to know what telling the truth means."

"Oh, yes."

"Because you may have to stand up in court and say all this to a judge."

"Outside," said Mrs. Havelock.

She got him into the courtyard in the nick of time.

Knott had kept Dennis Farr at Reading informed about the progress of the investigation. He had telephoned him each evening and sent him copies of all the interrogation reports. He took this extra trouble because he knew that it would be repaid in cooperation.

As he drove over to Reading he could already see the bones of the Crown case. There were gray areas, to be sure, and shadowy corners, but that was the way with murder investigations. Some points of detail were never cleared up. There were questions which remained unanswered even after trial and conviction. Why should a man who had poisoned his wife with lead arsenite and watched her die in agony keep more than twenty photographs of her pinned up around his bedroom? Why had the college porter who had murdered two girl students wasted long minutes after each killing smashing up their bicycles? These were problems for psychologists, not for policemen. They needed investigation only if they were going to form part of the defense case.

"Not much doubt who did it," said Farr. "The difficulty is going to be proving it."

"As bloody always," said Knott. "Did you fix things for me?"

"Both sound men. And very willing to help. I could see the point of having a word with Cowie, of course. But why the schoolmaster?"

"I want to find out why Limbery was sacked."

"Resigned by mutual agreement was what I heard."

"I don't believe he'd have left the school unless he was forced to. Remember what Katie called him when they had that slanging match? A schoolmaster manqué."

"You might be right. I certainly got the impression he enjoyed working with kids."

"Too thoroughly perhaps?"

Farr said, "I shouldn't have thought there was anything like that. You never can tell, of course. Is it important?"

"It would give us a motive. He's unbalanced. I don't mean mad. But he's got a hair-trigger temper. And Katie had a saw-edged tongue. Suppose she said something to him like 'You're no good to a girl. Small boys are your scene.' He'd lash out without thinking twice about it."

"He'd lash out," agreed Farr, "but that doesn't mean he'd plan a cold-blooded killing days or weeks later."

"That's what I thought, at first," said Knott. *"But suppose we've all been jumping to conclusions.* Suppose that note was genuine. Suppose he really did want to make things up and put things back on their old footing."

"Rolling round on the punt cushions to prove he could do it."

"Right. *But suppose Katie had quite different ideas.* Suppose she planned to spend a few enjoyable minutes telling him exactly what she thought of him. You great big poof, go chase a choirboy. What then?"

"He'd blow his top, no question. But do you think you could make a jury understand it?"

"Twenty years ago—even ten—I wouldn't have cared to try. Nowadays I think they'd take it."

"I suppose you might call that progress," said Farr, "of a sort. Look in on the way back and tell me how you got on."

"It's all right," said Roney. "I told him you didn't want to do it. I told him Mum made you."

"Good," said Sim. They were sitting on the fence at the bottom of the garden. Since Rosina had sneaked up on them they had avoided the veranda. "What did he say?"

"He said O.K. He understood."

"Good."

"What I can't see is why everyone thinks it must be him who did it."

"It could be anyone."

"That's right."

"It could be the rector."

"Or old Mr. Beaumorris."

They considered them. Neither of them seemed plausible murderers. Roney said, "I'll tell you what. What about Mr. Mariner? It could easily be him. He was always hanging round the boathouse."

"I'd rather it was him than Johnno."

"I'll tell you something else. Johnno isn't going to let them arrest him."

"How's he going to stop them?"

"He'll fight them."

"He couldn't fight them all."

"He could. He's got lots of weapons. He showed them to me. He's got a saber and a kukri."

"What's a kukri?"

"It's a thing the Gurkhas have. A sort of curved knife. They used them to cut off Japs' heads."

Sim tried to visualize a row of decapitated policemen.

140

"And a swordstick. And a pistol."

"Did he show you the pistol?"

"No. He's got that hidden somewhere. But I saw the swordstick. It's got a catch just under the handle and you pull it and it comes out—*wheesh.*"

Not decapitated. Impaled. It seemed tidier somehow.

Mr. Ferris, headmaster of Coverdales, was a distinguished scientist, a fact evidenced by the string of initials after his name. He was small and squat and his iron gray hair stood up from out of his head like a crown of thorns. It was clear at first encounter that he was a man you did not take liberties with.

He said to Knott, "I accept your authority to ask me questions. I have an equal right not to answer them."

"That is so, sir."

"I am prepared to answer them on the understanding that anything I say is off the record. That I shall, if necessary, deny that I said it and shall not be asked to give evidence in any court proceedings."

"Quite so, sir," said Knott easily.

"Totally off the record, Superintendent."

"Totally, sir."

"Then suppose you switch off whatever gadget it is you've brought with you."

Knott had noticed the curious object on the desk between them. It was made of black metal and was about the size of a cricket ball. The top was opaque milk-colored glass. Behind the glass a yellow eye moved and flickered.

"It's called an 'Encore,' Superintendent. It records any instrument receiving or emitting electric impulses within a range of about a hundred feet. There are larger instruments with much longer ranges. This is what you might call a pocket model."

"Interesting," said Knott. He slipped one hand into the

side pocket of his jacket and switched off his tape recorder. "To tell you the truth, I'd forgotten I had it switched on." He told this lie without embarrassment.

The yellow eye centered in the glass and stood coldly still.

"Very well, Superintendent. What is it you want to know?"

"I'd like to find out why Limbery was sacked from this school."

"Sacked?"

"So I was told."

"The person who told you that was using an inaccurate piece of shorthand to describe a complex situation. It is quite true that Limbery did not take the initiative in the matter. He was happy here and got on well with the boys. Less well with the girls, but since he did no sixth-form teaching he didn't come across them much. And our pay here is good. Above Burnham Scale."

"Then," said Knott, "if he was happy here . . . "

Mr. Ferris was not to be diverted. He had an explanation to make and he proposed to offer it in the same logical way that he would have explained any natural phenomenon.

"When I said that he got on well with the boys, it would have been more accurate if I had said that he got on too well." Although Knott had not tried to speak, Mr. Ferris held up one hand as though rebuking an importunate student. "And when I say that, I do *not* mean that he made advances to them or interfered with them. Had he done so, he would indeed have been sacked. No. It was more subtle and more difficult. I think the truth of the matter is that he was the same age, mentally and emotionally, as the boys themselves. That is perhaps why he got on with them and not with the girls. Girls become adult more quickly."

Here he paused so long that Knott ventured to say, "That hardly seems any reason for getting rid of him."

"You might not think so. But it had one unfortunate result. If any difference or difficulty arose, regardless of the rights or wrongs of the matter, he *always* took the side of the boys as against constituted authority. This did not make him popular with other members of the staff, who had more old-fashioned ideas about discipline. It came to a head over one particular boy. Another member of the staff wished to punish him. Limbery, I am told, threatened to kill him if he did so."

My God, thought Knott, I wish I could get that tape recorder turned on. His hand was actually in his pocket when he saw the yellow eye on the desk looking at him. He took his hand out again.

"That wasn't something I could overlook. And it was the culmination of a number of smaller instances of this sort of disloyalty."

"Sticking up for the boys against the staff?"

"Trahison des clercs," said Mr. Ferris. "Uncommon in schools, but the bane of our newer universities."

Knott thought about it as he drove back into Reading. He could subpoena Mr. Ferris and despite any promises would have done so without scruple if he thought it would assist the Crown's case. But he had had some unhappy experiences with witnesses dragged into court against their will. They might not tamper with facts, but they managed somehow to put a different slant on them.

What did it demonstrate, anyway? That Limbery had a violent and uncontrolled temper. They knew that already.

"Frankly," said Arnold Cowie, news editor of the Reading *Sun,* "it just wasn't good enough. A lot of descriptive stuff. Flames leaping sky-high. Smoke billowing. Readers don't want that sort of thing. They can imagine it for themselves. They want *facts."*

"And Limbery's account was a bit thin on facts?"

"I could have done it without leaving my house."

"You mean that, literally?"

Cowie thought about it. It had suddenly occurred to him where the questions were leading.

"No," he said. "Perhaps not literally. He reported something the skipper of the local fire brigade said to him. That could have been checked, so he wouldn't have made it up. He was there, all right. But I don't think he stayed very long."

"What makes you think that?"

"Did you read our account—the one we did publish?"

"No. But I'd like to."

"I'll get you a copy." Cowie spoke into the telephone. "It's good stuff. It was sent in by a local stringer. The roof of part of the factory collapsed and trapped two of the firemen inside. The brigade lowered one of their ladders down to horizontal and used it as a battering ram. Smashed a way in through the side of the building. Just got them out in time."

"And none of this was in Limbery's account?"

"Not a word. Nothing but flames and sparks and hot air."

"I see. I wonder if you could give me a few timings. For instance—when did the fire start?"

"I don't know when it started. We heard about it around a quarter to ten. I'd just got back from dinner and the news was on the blower as I got here."

"And you telephoned Limbery at once?"

"Right."

"And he answered the telephone at once?"

"Not at once. He was in his bath."

"But within a few minutes?"

"Right. He said he'd finish getting dressed and go straight out."

"Let's say he left at ten o'clock. How long would it take him to get to Goring?"

144

"Twenty minutes, if he hurried. A few minutes to get over the bridge and through Goring. The paper factory's half a mile out, on the Oxford road."

"I suppose you don't know exactly when the roof collapsed?"

"I might be able to tell you that." Cowie had the stringer's report in front of him by now, three sheets of foolscap slashed by the editorial blue pencil. He said, "We didn't use it all, of course. But I'm sure there was something. Yes. That's right. The rescue effort I was talking about was put on by the Streatley and Goring brigade. Here's what I was looking for. 'The Wallingford contingent, who must have turned out with remarkable speed to be there on the stroke of eleven, were able to help with the latter stages of this courageous rescue.'"

"Then we can place the collapse of the roof at some minutes before eleven. Say between ten and five to eleven."

"That's a fair assumption."

"In other words, Limbery must have left the scene by a quarter to eleven. Having arrived at about a quarter past ten."

"It certainly looks like it."

"And when did he let you have his report? I gather he dictated it over the telephone."

"That's correct. We got it sometime after midnight. We were going to set it up when this other chap steamed up on his motorbike with his much better account. So we scrapped Limbery's." Mr. Cowie smiled thinly. "He still wants us to pay for it."

"Did he say where he was speaking from?"

"From a public call box. It cost him fifty pence. That's one of the things he was complaining about."

Knott thought about it. It was clear that Limbery had told him less than the whole truth. But a man could lie

145

about some things and tell the truth about others.

The news editor was looking at him curiously. He said, "I hope what I've told you has helped."

"It's been most helpful."

"Then if you could—"

"All right," said Knott with a grin which showed all his teeth. "When I'm ready to charge someone you shall hear about it first."

Back at the Reading police station he told Farr what he had found out, skipping most of what Mr. Ferris had told him and concentrating on the timings.

Farr said, "It was a fluke, of course, the fire happening when it did, but he grabbed the chance to give himself an alibi. He could have been back in Hannington by eleven. Easily. The difficulty's going to be to prove it. Everyone round that factory would have been too bloody busy to notice when people came and went."

"I thought about that," said Knott. "And here's where I'll want a bit of help. Limbery told me he phoned in his story from a public call box on the Oxford road. We know he was telling the truth about it being a call box. I had a word with the shorthand typist at the paper who took it down. She heard the tenpenny pieces going in and Limbery cursing every time he had to find another one. At night you get four minutes for tenpence. So we know he was in that box more than sixteen minutes, maybe twenty."

"If his account was any length he'd need all of twenty minutes. You know what these girls are. He'd have to spell all the names for her."

"I'm not questioning the length of time he took," said Knott. "What I was wondering was just where he found a public call box on that bit of the Oxford road. I know it quite well. There are two A.A. boxes, but he's not a member of the A.A. and anyway he said quite clearly a *public* call box. So what I'd like you to do for me is this. Find out from the Post Office what public call boxes there are between, say, Streatley on the east and Pangbourne on the west." Farr got out a map and they studied it. "No. Spread it a little further. Make it a square. Moulsford, Yattendon, Pangbourne, Whitchurch. Then take those two men of yours off the house-to-house inquiry they've been doing at Hannington and put them onto the call boxes."

"Hoping," said Farr, "to find an indignant member of the public who wanted to use a particular box and was kept waiting for twenty minutes."

"Right," said Knott. "The *Sun* can provide you with a photograph. They had one in connection with a personality piece they did about that song he wrote. And I'll bet you a level quid that if we locate that call box it'll be a damned sight nearer Hannington than away out on the Oxford road."

"I don't bet on certainties," said Farr. He said it with such conviction that Knott's head jerked up. He said, "Come on, Dennis. You've got something for me."

"Maybe," said Farr. "Maybe not. I won't know for sure unless you happen to know the make and number of Limbery's car."

Knott thought for a moment and then said, "It's an old Morris Traveller. And the number is ABB 9190 G."

"What a memory!"

"It's not a question of memory," said Knott. He was watching Farr turning over the pages of a police logbook and thinking, I wonder if he really has got something. He's looking very pleased with himself. He said, "Whenever I've got my eye on someone, someone I may want to pull in, I naturally get the number and description of his car. If he makes a break for it, ten to one he'll take his car."

Farr had found the page he wanted and was running his finger down it. He had stopped listening to Knott, who

147

continued placidly. "Then I can put out an all-stations call without wasting any time. Minutes can be precious at a moment like that."

"ABB 9190 G, you said?"

"Right."

"And Limbery drove back across the Pangbourne bridge at some time between twelve and one?"

"Right."

"You're sure about the time?"

"He said he noticed the time on the Town Hall clock."

"Then he's a liar."

Knott said, "Ah-h-h." It was like a letting out of long-held breath.

"That was the night we had a dragnet out to try and pull up the villains who did Yattendon House. Remember? We had blocks on every bridge over that stretch of the Thames. They went on at eleven and didn't come off until three. Here's a list of the cars they checked, Pangbourne bridge. Makes. Registration numbers and times. No ABB 9190 G. No Morris Travellers either."

"Beautiful," said Knott softly.

FOURTEEN

The Coroner said, "You are Charles Knott of 56 Albany Street, St. John's Wood, N.W. 8, a Detective Superintendent in the Metropolitan Police Force, and you are in charge of the police inquiries into this case?"

"I am, sir."

"Have you concluded your inquiries?"

"No, sir."

"I understand it will assist your inquiries if I adjourn the case."

"Yes, sir."

The Coroner directed his gaze on the five men and four women in the jury box and said, "This is an inquiry into the death of Kate Louise Steelstock at a point adjacent to the West Hannington Boat Club premises on the night of Friday, August fifteenth, in circumstances suggesting murder. I shall adjourn the inquest for fourteen days, that is to say until Tuesday September second."

"Witnesses in this case may leave the court," said the Coroner's officer.

The jury, and the members of the public who had packed the room to suffocation, looked baffled. The press, who had expected nothing more, looked bored. A reporter caught Knott as he was making his way out and said, "How's it going, Superintendent?"

"Not too bad, son."

"An arrest imminent?"

"Well now, you'd hardly expect me to be as definite as that, would you?"

This was accompanied by what could have been a wink. The hint could hardly have been more deliberate. The reporter, who had been a long time at the game, said, "Knott's got his teeth into someone. Won't be long now."

Back at the operations room Knott settled into his chair and started to leaf through the brown-covered green-laced folder that Sergeant Esdaile had strung together for him. From his smaller table, Shilling looked across at him. He was remembering like moments in other cases.

"Well," said Knott at last, "so what have we got? We know that Limbery and Katie used the boathouse as a rendezvous for lovemaking. We know that the note found in Katie's bag probably came from him. There's no direct evidence. We haven't traced the typewriter. But there's evidence in the wording of the note itself. We know it was sent by the man who killed her, because he searched for it. First, in her bag. Then, when he couldn't find it there, at her house."

"Sound nerve," said Shilling.

Knott accepted this remark as a criticism. He said, "All right. I agree. It doesn't fit in with the picture we've got of Limbery. But remember he was desperate. He had to have that note. If it was found, he was finished. Next point, he lied about where he was and what he did that night. Why?"

"Obvious answer, because the whole trip was set up to give him an alibi."

"Obvious answers can be right."

Shilling knew what his job was. He was critic. He was counsel for the defense. He said, "You're building up two quite different characters, aren't you? One's a man with no control over his temper who flies off the reel because of something spiteful Katie says to him, hits her on the head too hard and finds himself with a corpse on his hands. The other's the sort of man who could make a plan to get her to that particular spot, taking care to fix himself up with an elaborate alibi first. They don't match."

"I think there's an answer to that," said Knott. "We know, now, that Katie had another side to her character. She liked to have people on the end of a string. So that she could give it a twitch from time to time and watch them dance. There are women like that. Remember Mrs. Huntingdon?"

"Yes," said Shilling with a grimace, "and I remember what her husband did to her when she twitched it once too often."

150

"Right. Now suppose Katie had something on Limbery."

"What sort of thing?"

"Anything. Going too far with a boy, most likely. Her brother was at Coverdales. He could have known about it. And told Katie. She'd have enjoyed tweaking Limbery."

"All right," said Shilling. "But here's another point. If he did send her that note, just how and when did he get it to her? It wasn't sent through the post. And it had to reach her late in the day, or there was no chance she'd bring it with her to the dance. There's only one way he could have done that—"

The telephone interrupted him.

Knott picked up the receiver and listened, with no more than an occasional grunt. At the end he said, "Thank you, Dennis. That sounds very promising. I'll send someone from here to take a statement."

He replaced the receiver carefully and said, "How do you explain this one away? At ten past twelve, when Limbery, according to his statement, was having a snack in that motel on the Oxford road, preparatory to crossing the river at Pangbourne—in an invisible car—he was also occupying a public telephone box on Streatley Common, *south* of the river. To the growing fury of a Mrs. Mason, who wanted to use the phone. She recognized Limbery at once from the photograph. No hesitation. She said, 'When you've watched someone for twenty minutes preventing you from using a telephone, his face gets sort of fixed in your mind.'"

"She sounds a useful sort of witness," agreed Shilling.

Knott had closed the folder and was holding it in one hand. He seemed to be weighing it. He said, "I'd like you to take this lot up to the D.P.P.'s office. You can strip it down a bit. Leave out the photographs and maps, but see that you've got all the statements. Including Mrs. Mason's, as soon as we've got hers. And Dr. Farmiloe's report. And my daily summaries. And a copy of the note we found in Katie's bag. Ask for the Principal Assistant Director in Charge of Southern Region. He's a man called Adlington. He's got three chins and stutters like a machine gun, but he's very sound. I'll tell him you're coming. Give him the file to read and ask if he or the Deputy Director can see me at nine o'clock tomorrow. Understood?"

"Understood," said Shilling. He thought, The old man's playing this one very carefully. Natural enough if he's looking for promotion, I suppose. Bit uncharacteristic, all the same.

A word on the internal telephone brought in Esdaile and McCourt. Both looked as though they had been expecting the summons. The electricity in the air was unmistakable.

Knott said, "I've got jobs for both of you. Ian, I want you to talk to a Mrs. Mason. Here's her address. She's got a statement for us. As soon as you've got it, let Bob have it. Eddie, I want you to get hold of Limbery. He'll either be at his office or his house. Don't make a big occasion of it. Just tell him I'd like him to step round here. If he asks why, be vague. Say that something's cropped up and I want to ask him some questions. Right?"

McCourt said, "Aye," and took himself off. Esdaile hesitated for a moment and said, "What do I do if he won't come?"

"Let's worry about that when it happens," said Knott.

Sergeant Esdaile drew blank at the *Gazette* office and devoted some thought to his next move. To ask a hair-trigger character like Jonathan Limbery to "step round" the short distance from his office to the police station, that was one thing. To ask him to make the journey on foot, under escort, from his house in Belsize Road was quite different. It would have to be done by car. Fortunately the Chief Inspector's car was parked in the yard. Dandridge said, "Certainly you can borrow it. What do you want it for?"

"To bring in Limbery."

"Bring him in?"

"For questioning."

"Well, do it tactfully," said Dandridge.

Be vague, said Knott. Do it tactfully, said Dandridge. Bloody useful advice. If they wanted Limbery, why didn't they go and fetch him themselves? He knew the answer to that one. If there was a cock-up and someone had to carry the can, it was going to be poor old Eddie.

A crowd outside the door of number 17. Something up? No, it was just a gang of boys who had been to pay Jonathan a visit. Tim Nurse, Terry Gonville and the Havelock tearaways. Funny how the kids hung around him all the time. Better give them a minute to get clear.

Jonathan was standing inside his open front window as Esdaile drew up. Some instinct for trouble had made the boys stop and turn to stare. Esdaile cursed quietly. The last thing he wanted was an audience. He started up the front path.

Jonathan said, "What do you want, Eddie?"

"Can I come in?"

"Not until you tell me what you want."

"The Superintendent wants to ask you a few questions."

"Then let him come and ask them."

"He'd be obliged if you'd come round to the station."

"To help the police with their inquiries. Isn't that the correct expression?"

"Well—"

"Well," said Jonathan, suddenly savage, "you can give the Superintendent a message from me. He can go jump in the river. And if he never surfaces again, so much the better. Bad luck on the fishes, of course."

The boys liked this.

Esdaile said, "Look. Be reasonable. I'm not enjoying this either. I'm just obeying orders."

"Who said I wasn't enjoying it?" Jonathan swung one leg over the low sill and climbed out onto the front path. It could now be seen that he was holding a polished black walking stick in his hand, a stick with an ivory handle, which he twisted. The long bright blade came out.

"Now don't be stupid," said Esdaile, backing down the path.

Mrs. Havelock had been out shopping and had stopped to pick up Sim and Roney. She took in the scene in one comprehensive glance. Limbery, Esdaile, the rapt boys, two delivery men, a mother with a child in a stroller and, thank goodness for possible support, Gerry Gonville taking his old cocker spaniel for a walk.

She crossed the pavement in three quick strides and stepped into the telephone box.

"You're trespassing," said Jonathan, "on my property." The blade flickered. Esdaile retreated another step. "I have the right to defend my property, by force if necessary."

"You've got no right to threaten me."

"You've got it all wrong. It's not me who's threatening you. It's you and other pigs like you"—the blade flashed again—"who threaten the peace and privacy of people too timid to stand up for themselves. This time you've picked the wrong victim. Now take yourself off, you great looby."

The point of the blade was flickering in Esdaile's face. He stepped back. One of the watching boys laughed. The Sergeant, angry himself now, plunged forward.

The point of the blade slid through the top of his arm.

The only person who did not seem to be paralyzed into inactivity was Group Captain Gonville. He hitched the loop in the dog's lead over a railing, dropped his walking stick, pulled out a handkerchief, folded it into a pad and clapped it over the wound with one hand while he felt for the pressure point with his other hand.

"If he's hit an artery," he said, "we'll have to put some sort of tourniquet on it until help arrives." He had his back to Limbery and ignored him. "Let's have your tie, Terry."

"Tie?" said his son blankly.

"And quick."

Terry pulled off the school tie he was wearing. Limbery was watching them with a smile on his face. Mrs. Havelock emerged from the telephone box. Before she could say anything they heard the car coming. It cornered with a squeal of tires and stopped.

Knott got out. He moved across without haste to where Sergeant Esdaile was sitting on the pavement, looking pale but angry, his back propped against the garden wall. The Group Captain had got his son's tie into position above the wound and was tightening it. He said, "It's all right, I think. No artery. Better be on the safe side, though."

Knott nodded, picked up the heavy ash-plant walking stick and walked toward Limbery holding it loosely in his right hand.

"Put down that sword," he said.

"Not on your life."

Knott continued to advance. Limbery said, "I've stuck one pig this morning. Let's make it a double."

As the blade came at him, Knott dropped onto one knee and swung the heavy stick in a circle. It hit Limbery with a crack on the outside of his knee. He gave a scream and keeled over, dropping the sword.

Knott straightened up, put one foot on the sword and said to the larger of the two delivery men, "I'll need a hand here."

Together they lifted Limbery into the back of the car.

Knott said, "Sit in with him and see that he doesn't try to do anything silly." He turned to the Group Captain and said, "It might be best if you used the car Esdaile came in to take him to the hospital."

"Will do," said Gonville.

Mrs. Havelock said, "I'll take all the boys home. Climb in, kids."

The crowd dispersed slowly.

FIFTEEN

For nearly two days the second body had been lying half in, half out of the water among the tall rushes. It was on the opposite side to the towpath, the unexplored side of the river, a mile or more below Whitchurch. To get at it you would have had to wade across a backwater and force your way through the thorn bushes and scrub elder; and since no one had happened to do this, the body had lain in peace.

The bow wave from a river steamer had lifted it and carried it into its hiding place. Subsiding, it had deposited it on an underwater snag which had caught the belt of the raincoat and held it. A pair of swans had investigated it with supercilious yellow eyes and had turned away in disgust. So far the carnivores of the undergrowth had left it alone, but they would soon be busy. Unless, of course, another wave floated the body off into deep water, when it would be the turn of fish and the submarine parasites.

The Assistant Director of Public Prosecutions said, "He's saved you a bit of trouble, anyway. No need to think up a holding charge. He's thought one up for you. How's Esdaile?"

"He's all right. A clean flesh wound. He'll be back on the job in a day or two."

"Assaulting an officer in the course of his duty and causing him actual bodily harm. You could hold him on that, while you looked around for more evidence on the main charge."

"I could," said Knott. "But I wouldn't want to. I'd prefer to go the whole way now."

The Assistant Director said, "I agree. I think you've got more than enough to justify charging Limbery with murder. Short of finding someone who actually saw him do it, I really don't see how you could get any more."

"No one saw him," said Knott. "I'm sure of that. Before the moon got up the night was pitch black. And if anyone *had* been passing, I think he'd have killed them, too. It's lucky the Havelock kids weren't by ten minutes sooner. We might have had two other bodies on our hands."

"If that's the sort of man he is," said the Assistant Director, "the sooner we have him under hatches the better. It's your decision, of course. But you can take it that I'll back you all the way on this one."

"Thank you," said Knott.

"And Philip Frost would like a word with you before you go."

The Deputy Director, Philip Frost, brother of Mrs. Steelstock and uncle of Katie, was a portly person with a manner which combined the acerbity of the barrister he had once been with the smoothness of the politicians he had occasionally to deal with.

He said, "I'd like to congratulate you, Superintendent. I read the papers last night. I think you've done an excellent job. I don't know if you realize that it was I who asked the Assistant Commissioner to give you the assignment." He smiled. "I imagine you cursed him at the time."

Knott smiled, too. He said, "I confess I'd have liked one good night's sleep after the Oxford business. However, things seem to have come out all right. I had a lot of help from Sergeant Shilling."

"Bob's a good lad. We shan't forget him. Since we've gone so far so fast, do you think we could get the committal proceedings expedited? Could you be ready in a fortnight?"

"Quicker than that, if you want."

"We'll have to brief counsel. Davenport should be all right for the preliminaries. We'll get Mavor or Masterton for the Crown Court. It'll be at Reading. It won't come on before October at the earliest. That should give you all the time you want to tie up the loose ends. If there are any."

"There are three loose ends," said Knott slowly. "If I can tie up any one of them, I'd say the case really would be defense-proof. First and most important, of course, if that print on the cupboard door above Katie's desk can be brought out sharp enough for legal identification."

"The laboratory are working on it now."

"If we can't get that, I'd like to identify the typewriter that was used. I don't imagine that it was Limbery's own machine. He wouldn't be that stupid, but—"

"Enough if you can show he had access to it. Agreed. What else?"

"The third thing's more difficult. Sergeant Shilling pointed it out to me. Part of the killer's plan must have turned on the probability—maybe simply on the possibility—that Katie would bring the note with her to the rendezvous."

"He certainly expected her to do so. That's why he searched her bag."

"Quite so, sir. But there wasn't anything in the note itself which meant that she *had* to take it with her. Things, I mean, like complicated directions that she'd have to study. It was just 'Come to the usual place.' "

The Deputy Director said, "H'm. Yes. I see your point."

"I believe the only way he could have any hope she'd bring it along was by leaving it actually *in her car,* sometime during the day. And the later the better. To follow that up, we'll have to know exactly what her movements were on Friday. There's a lot of ground still to cover there. But if we could find someone who saw Limbery near her car during the afternoon, say, or the early evening, that should go a long way towards clinching it."

"Can't expect miracles," said the Deputy Director genially. "Any of those extra bits would be useful. Agreed. But they're only extras. You've got what matters. Motive, access and a string of lies afterwards. And remember this. The defense have got to put Limbery in the box. Or risk the most damaging construction being put on his refusal to give evidence. And once he gets into the box, from all I've heard of him, he'll hang himself five times over."

"A search warrant," said Mariner. "Certainly you can have one. My clerk will make it out for you. I should have thought, after what's happened, that you'd have every right to search his house without one."

"Better be on the safe side," said Knott.

"Are you looking for anything in particular? Or shouldn't I ask?"

"No secret about it. The buzz is that he had a collection of lethal weapons. There was talk of a revolver. He used to boast to the boys about it."

"Stupid," said Mariner. "Stupid as well as vicious."

Number 17 Lower Belsize Road was already a focus of local interest. Photographs of it had appeared in the press. Tradesmen and passers-by slowed their pace as they came to it, or stopped altogether to stare at the closed front door and the empty windows.

When Knott arrived, with McCourt and Esdaile in attendance, a crowd gathered as though by magic. Knott viewed his audience impassively. He knew that from now on most of his moves would have to be made under the stare of publicity. He said, "Does anyone happen to know who locked the house up?"

A woman said, "Parson did it. He's got the keys."

McCourt was already on his useful moped. He said, "I'll get them for you. Shouldn't take long."

The Reverend Bird was out, but his wife was at home and located the keys for him.

"Dicky thought it wasn't right to leave the house unlocked and the windows open," she said. "You know what people are like. They'd have been trampling all over it. Helping themselves to souvenirs, probably. I hope he did right."

"We're much obliged to him," said McCourt.

"He's taken this very hard, you know. He seems to think that something which happened in church might have upset Jonathan. You heard about that?"

"Aye. We all haird about it. It wasn't in any way your husband's fault."

"So I told him. But he's very worried. He went to Reading this morning, to the prison. To see if he could help."

"That was kind of him," said McCourt and managed to extract himself and the keys.

When he got back he found that the crowd had increased. Knott was sitting on the low front wall of the garden. A number of amateur photographers had already snapped him. He said, "You've been long enough. Come on, we'll go in round the back."

Although its owner had only been gone for twenty-four hours there was already a feeling of emptiness about the house, an impression of airlessness. No air coming through the windows, no air being breathed in the rooms.

Knott spent a few minutes instructing his assistants in the technique of searching and they then split up, taking a room each. It was Esdaile who unearthed the armory. No particular attempt had been made to hide the weapons. They were in an unlocked cupboard in the bedroom. A Japanese ceremonial sword, a Gurkha kukri, a German three-edged needle bayonet, a British pattern cavalry saber, a pair of foils.

"Just a big boy scout," said Knott. "I wonder where he kept the gun. If he had one."

The two sergeants resumed their search, but they found no gun. When they got back to the sitting room Knott was staring at a photograph in a leather frame which he had found on the mantelpiece. It was a family group, evidently taken some years ago.

"Do you know who they are?"

McCourt examined the picture and said, "Aye, that's Limbery on the right. The girls would be his two sisters. I've haird him talk of them. And the woman would be his mother. She's still alive, in a nursing home somewhere."

Knott pointed to the jagged edge of the photograph. "He's cut off a piece," he said. "Why would he do that?"

"That would be where his father was standing, no doubt."

"Why cut him out of the photograph?"

McCourt thought about it and said, "It might be because he disliked him. If you want something with his dabs on it, best place will be the kitchen."

The collection of weapons was taken back to the police station and locked in a cupboard. Knott said, "If we're to be ready for committal by Monday week we've got a lot of work to do. When I was talking to the Director I said there

161

were three gaps I'd like to fill in and I'm allotting one to each of you. Bob, I want you to concentrate on Katie's movements on the Friday. I understand she went up to town by train. When did she go? How did she get to the station? If she took her own car, where did she leave it? Was anyone seen hanging round it?"

"You're thinking about that note?"

"Right. The likeliest thing is that someone slipped it into her car. Even if it had been left locked it could have been pushed through one of the side flaps, or something like that. Then I want to know who she saw in London. It could have been that photographer chap Ruoff. I can't see, at the moment, how he fits in."

"He's got a guilty conscience about something," agreed Shilling.

"Eddie, I want you to chase that typewriter. We know the make and year of the machine. Look at all the machines in his office, of course, but it's too much to hope you'll find it there. Then ask round the various people he might have borrowed one from. And get an advertisement drafted for the local papers. Any person who possesses or has any knowledge of a Crossfield Electric to communicate with the police. I don't care how widely it gets known that we're looking for this particular machine. The wider the better."

He swung around on Ian. "I want you to concentrate on Limbery's movements that night. He was out in his car and he must have used it to put him within striking distance of the boathouse. Cars get noticed. So he'd have been careful to keep it some distance away. And he wouldn't have driven it through the village, that's certain. He'd have come in from the west."

McCourt said, "But if it was his car at the end of River Park Avenue—" and stopped. Knott was staring at him.

"What did you say?"

"I said, sir, if it was his car at the end of the avenue, then we *know* where he put it."

Knott said, "You're a trained police officer. You're working on this case. Am I to understand that you haven't even taken the trouble to read the file?"

"No, sir. I mean, yes, I have read it."

"Then since you took Mrs. Mason's statement yourself, you know that Limbery was on Streatley Common at ten past twelve. And since you took the statements of Miss Tress and Mrs. Havelock, you may remember that they both spoke of that car moving away from where it was parked at some time *after* twelve. Good going, don't you think? Thirteen miles in five minutes."

"I'm sorry, sir."

Having put Sergeant McCourt in his place, Knott relaxed a little. He said, "I'm not talking to Bob, because he knows all this. I'm talking to you two. Forget anything you've read about murder investigations and concentrate on this. You make your mind up who did it. You charge them. You put together the case you're going to set up in court. Then you put yourself into the shoes of the defense. You pick all the holes you can in your own case. Then you set to work and plug those holes. Right?"

"Right," said Sergeants McCourt and Esdaile in unison.

"Which reminds me. There's one little job we've got to do at once. Get into Reading, Ian, have a word with Farr and get the names of the officers who were on the traffic block on Pangbourne bridge that night. We'll want statements from them and certified copies of the records they kept."

As McCourt rode into Reading on his moped he was thinking about Knott. He didn't like him and was, in fact, afraid of him. But he couldn't help admiring him. It was the narrowness of his vision combined with the weight of his personality. It had the penetrating power of a thin but rigid blade driven by a massive force. The fact that it was driving at the wrong objective would not deter him for a moment. If he was wrong, it was for the opposition to prove him wrong. That was how justice in England worked.

When McCourt had finished his job in Reading he looked in at the general infirmary. The sister, who knew him well, said, "Not good news, I'm afraid, Sergeant. Inspector Ray had a bad hemorrhage last night. We've had to move him into the intensive care unit. No one can talk to him for a bit. Is there some message?"

"Not really," said McCourt. "Just to wish him luck."

SIXTEEN

That evening, a string of coal barges drawn by a tug plowed its slow way up the river. The first bow wave lifted the body clear of the snag, the next one carried it out of the rushes and started it on its stately progress downstream. Had anyone been there to see it they would have noticed that it floated in an odd manner, almost as though it was wearing an old-fashioned life jacket, which kept the chest clear of the water.

"I must confess," said Mrs. Havelock, "speaking as a magistrate, that I do get tired of having young tearaways brought up in front of me and someone saying, as though it explained every form of crime and violence, 'It must be

164

remembered that he came from a broken home.' Really, I fail to see the connection. If the father pushes off, the mother, with the help of the state, can usually cope perfectly well."

"Better than if she's spending all her time fighting with an unsatisfactory husband," said Georgie Vigors.

"Exactly. Now take Jonathan. Superficially he had a normal family background. His mother was a sweet and loving little woman. The only time I met her she reminded me of an apple dumpling. His father was a schoolmaster. Hearty, genial type. Being wise after the event, one can see that it was totally disastrous for Jonathan. His father bullied him until he was old enough to stand up for himself and hit back. Then he left him alone. I fancy Father was a bit of a coward. After all, he was only twenty-six when war broke out and perfectly fit. First he claimed he was in a reserved occupation. When that wore a bit thin, he scuttled off into the Ministry of Information. I got all this from my second husband, who loathed his guts."

"I do see," said Georgie, "that it could be about the most fatal relationship a boy could have with his father. He'd be apt to grow up disliking any form of authority."

"Not just disliking it. Hating it."

"It explains a lot."

"Funking the war didn't do his old man a lot of good in the end, because he was run over by a drunken lorry driver when Jonathan was starting at Bristol University. Johnno had to come away and get a job. His mother's still alive. I imagine some of what he makes goes to help her."

The two ladies paused to consider the unsatisfactory life of young Jonathan Limbery.

"Maybe it *explains* a lot," said Mrs. Havelock at last. "But it doesn't add up to an excuse for smashing Katie's head in."

Colonel Lyon, the Governor of Reading Jail, was a conscientious man. He made a point of visiting the remand wing every day and speaking to the inmates. "They're in my prison," he used to say, "but they're not prisoners. They haven't been convicted yet. Until they are convicted, I prefer to regard them as temporary visitors."

He had kept Limbery to the last. He hoped that his visit was going to be more productive than the two previous ones, during which Limbery had ignored the warder's order to stand up, had sat on his bed glowering and had refused to do anything but grunt.

On this morning he seemed to have recovered his powers of speech. He said, "It's no good keeping on at me. I've made my mind up. The state wants a sacrifice and I'm to be the scapegoat. All right. But if I'm going to be slaughtered, I'm going without bleating. The only thing I regret is the satisfaction my conviction is going to give to that bastard Knott."

The warder said, "Mind your language." Jonathan took no notice of him.

The Governor said, "That's all very well, Limbery. But if you're innocent—"

"Of course I'm innocent. I've said it often enough."

"You've said it often enough," agreed the Governor. "But if you're innocent, why not give people a chance to prove it? With the attitude you're adopting you might just as well plead guilty and have done with it."

"No you don't," said Jonathan. "You're putting words into my mouth. I didn't say I was going to plead guilty. Why should I plead guilty? I never touched the girl."

"In that case—"

"What I'm not going to have is a lot of lawyers fighting over my bones like sick jackals."

"Then do I take it you're going to conduct your own defense?"

166

"You're dead right I am. And I'm going to say exactly what I think of the lousy stinking police and their filthy bullying tactics."

"It's your privilege," said the Governor.

As they walked back toward his office the warder said, "Do you think he's putting it on?"

"Working up for a plea of insanity, you mean?"

"I thought he might be. You remember that man we had who stood on his head the whole time. Said he couldn't think unless the blood was running into his brain. He tried to stand on his head in court."

"It could be a try-on," said the Governor, "but somehow I don't think it is. He's angry and he's frightened. Like a small boy banging his head against the wall to show he doesn't care."

"Maybe the parson will talk some sense into him."

"I didn't know Father Michaels was planning to have a word with him."

"Not our chaplain, sir. The one from his village. The Reverend Bird. He telephoned last night."

"Well," said the Governor, "I hope he has more luck with him than I have."

The main offices of Vigors and Dibden, Solicitors, were in Market Street, Hannington. As the practice expanded, they had opened a branch office in West Hannington village. This was two rooms and an annex, just large enough for Noel, one managing clerk and one girl who doubled as receptionist and typist. Noel spent most of his time there. He knew that when his father retired he would have to take over the main office. Meanwhile he was enjoying his independent command.

It was six o'clock in the evening and he was finishing the day's work by signing a batch of letters, when Bird was announced.

"I wonder what he wants," said Noel.

"He didn't say," said the girl. "He just said it was urgent."

"Ask him in."

Noel's first impression was that the rector was ill. His face was drained of color and there were smudges under his eyes.

He said, "You look as if you could do with a drink."

"I'm all right. Just tired. Well, thank you. But put plenty of water in it."

"I often have one myself about this time of day," said Noel. "Take the comfortable chair. Or I should say the less uncomfortable one. This office really needs total redecoration and refurnishing." He went on talking about nothing much until his visitor had downed half his drink and was beginning to look a little more comfortable. Then he said, "What can we do for you, Dicky?"

"It's not me. It's Limbery."

"I thought that might be it. You went to see him?"

"I spent the afternoon with him. It was a most unhappy experience."

"It must have been hellish. Drink that up and have another."

"Thank you, Noel. But no. I very rarely touch spirits. This will be quite enough." He took another cautious sip and said, "It wasn't very pleasant. He didn't seem able to stop talking. For the first two hours—it seemed like two hours, it might have been longer—he was preaching me a sort of sermon. His text seemed to be that hatred was more vital than love."

"Poor Dicky."

"I couldn't stop him. I don't know that I even wanted to. I thought it was probably doing him good to get it off his chest. But it was terribly depressing. Like watching a man trying to plow up the sand. Futile, sterile, pointless. In the end some good did come out of it. I managed to make him change his mind about being legally represented at the trial."

"I wondered what he was planning to do about that."

"He'd told the Governor that he was determined to conduct his own defense."

"Good God! Why?"

"I gather it was partly because he doesn't like lawyers as a class and partly because he wanted to have an opportunity of telling the judge what he thought about the police. However, in the end I persuaded him to hand it all over to you."

"To me?"

"To you personally. No one else. He said he liked you and had found you a sympathetic character in the past and he was prepared to let you do it. If you wouldn't, he'd do it all himself."

Speaking slowly, to get his breath back, Noel said, "It's quite true that we used to see a good deal of each other at one time. We used to play a lot of squash. He usually won. He's very quick on his feet and he's got exceptionally strong wrists. When he hit the ball, he really did smash it —hold up." He thought Bird was going to pass out.

"It's all right. No, really. I'm quite all right."

"Stupid of me to say a thing like that," said Noel. "I didn't mean—"

"Of course you didn't. It's just that I visualized for the first time the sort of thing that happened. Someone positioning himself behind Katie in the dark and smashing—"

"We could both do with another drink," said Noel firmly.

"Well . . . a very small one. Thank you. You will take this on, won't you?"

"I'm not by any means an expert in criminal law, but if it's me or no one, I shall have to do it."

"If it's going to be terribly expensive, I could talk to his friends. I'm sure there are a lot of people who would help."

"I'm sure there are. And equally I can think of one or two people who certainly wouldn't. However, it may not be necessary. As far as I know, Jonathan hasn't got any money. We should be able to get him legal aid. When we've got that, we'll be able to brief top counsel. Cheer up, Dicky. You've done a good day's work."

SEVENTEEN

The Prince Albert Lock is on the river halfway between Pangbourne and Reading, serviced by a side road from Tilehurst village. The son of Mr. Baxter, the lock keeper, came bursting into the cottage at eight o'clock that morning and was sharply told by his mother to remove his Wellingtons and comb his hair or he wouldn't get any breakfast.

Ignoring these suggestions as being frivolous or unimportant, he dropped his fishing rod on the floor, said, "Where's Dad? Oh, there he is," and pelted out into the garden. Mrs. Baxter shook her head sadly.

"A corpus, is it?" said Mr. Baxter. "Then we'd better have'un out, hadn't we?"

"Can I help?"

"I don't think your ma would like that."

"It's not fair. I saw him. In the reeds, this side of the weir."

"Well," said Mr. Baxter, who was as weak-minded as his wife with their only son. "Mind you scrub up well afterwards."

The body was lying on its back. Mr. Baxter, who had seen many corpses in his time, looked at it critically. "Not been in more'n a few days," he said. "But what's that holding him up in front?"

His son, at the last moment, felt a distaste for the thing. He said, "I think I'll go and get my breakfast."

"That's right," said his father with a grin. "You do that."

It took him five minutes to disentangle the body from the weeds and drag it up onto the towpath. He unbuttoned the coat and then, after a brief hesitation, the shirt as well. He knew that the police disliked people meddling with a body until their own doctor had seen it, but he was puzzled by the inflated appearance of the chest.

The explanation was a stout square rubber wallet, almost the size of a small cushion.

"Funny sort of apparatus to carry about under your shirt," said Mr. Baxter.

He picked it out, dipped it in the river to wash off the dirt and slime that had accumulated on it and examined it again.

At first he thought there was no opening to it. Then he found the tiny head of the zip fastener countersunk in the thick rubber at the corner. It was too small for his clumsy fingers to get hold of. Curiosity had now got the better of discretion.

First he dragged the body by its heels through the back gate and into his garden, where it would be out of sight of passers-by. Then he went back for the wallet and carried it into his tool shed. He threaded a piece of fine wire through the eye of the zip fastener and pulled gently. The top of the wallet came open. The inside was still almost dry and the contents, which seemed to be pictures or photographs of some sort, were wrinkled at the edges but otherwise unharmed by their days of immersion.

Mr. Baxter carried them across to the door to examine them. Then he whistled softly. In the twenty years he had watched over the Prince Albert Lock a variety of flotsam and jetsam had been carried down on the broad bosom of Father Thames and deposited on his doorstep: contents of boats overturned in the upper reaches, furniture lifted from bungalows by the winter floods, on one occasion an upright piano. But, said Mr. Baxter to himself, as he separated the photographs gently and examined them one by one, blow him down if he had ever seen anything quite like this before.

He thought he had better let the police know straightaway.

Constable Leary from Reading, who respected Mr. Baxter's expertise in such matters, said, "Where do you think he went in?"

"Well," said Mr. Baxter, "it's not all that easy to say. Normally—that's to say usually—you can tell how long someone's been in by looking at his face. Being the softest exposed part, that's what the eels get at first. In this case that contraption he had under his shirt kept him floating on his back with his face clear of the water, so it's hardly been touched. You see what I mean?"

"Yes," said Constable Leary with a slight shudder. He was not as used to bodies as Mr. Baxter was.

"Another thing, see this?" Mr. Baxter disentangled a long branch of thorn from the belt at the back of the dead man's coat. "I'd say he'd been hitched up one time or another in the bushes at the edge of the bank. That makes it more difficult to judge. However, taking one thing with another, I'd say he hadn't been in above three or four days and that means he went in somewheres between Streatley and Hannington."

"Three or four days ago," said Superintendent Farr when this was reported to him. "And there was a cheap day-return ticket to Hannington in his wallet."

"That's right," said Constable Leary. "The date was washed away. But it was Hannington all right."

"The railway could probably give us the date if you gave them the serial number. Put an inquiry through to Paddington. And let Knott have a copy of your report. I don't suppose there's any connection with his business, but you never can tell."

He was looking at the photographs as he spoke. They were enlargements, fourteen inches by twelve. The wallet had evidently been custom made to keep them safe, and it had done its job well.

"Hot stuff," said Constable Leary. "That one of the two boys. I don't know as I've ever seen anything like it."

"It's what they call hard pornography."

Constable Leary was about to make a joke based on the word hard, but discretion prevailed.

"There's a special squad in the Met," said Farr. "They deal with this sort of thing. We'd better let them know. He came from London, didn't he?"

"Seems so. There was that return ticket from Paddington in his pocket."

"Nothing with his name on it?"

Leary shook his head.

"He'll be a runner for one of the outfits who peddle this sort of muck. You say the face is O.K. Get a photograph taken and send it up to Central with a report. Copy to Knott at Hannington."

Constable Leary departed reluctantly. There were one or two of the photographs he would like to have looked at again. Now they would be locked away in the Superintendent's safe and he wouldn't have another chance.

Mr. Beaumorris had reached an age when he did nothing impulsively. Every action had to be judged in the light of its reactions on himself, his comfort and his convenience. Naturally there were other considerations. He liked to help his friends. He liked, even more, to discomfort his enemies. Among them he ranked George Mariner, a self-made parvenu who behaved like a snob without any real grounds for being snobbish. He disliked Superintendent Knott, too, the brute who had driven his old friend Bill Connington to take his own life.

Recently a piece of information had come into his possession. If he passed it on to the authorities it might embarrass Mariner. On the other hand it might help Superintendent Knott. A difficult problem.

He spent most of the morning thinking about it and then decided, as a compromise, to telephone the friendly Sergeant McCourt.

Ian listened without comment to what Mr. Beaumorris had to say. He had a feeling that he was being presented with an important piece of information, but it was difficult for the moment to see how it was going to fit into the plan which had started to form in his slow Scots mind as he was standing in the upper room in the boathouse staring at a spyhole in the wall.

He said, "I suppose you got all this from your girl Myra?"

"That's right," said Mr. Beaumorris placidly. "I get most of my news from her."

"Then let me see if I've got it right. While the Mariners were out at the dance on Friday night, someone telephoned their house. Polly took the call. She says it was a man. She didn't recognize the voice, but she thought it was a Londoner."

"Correct. She also thought he'd been drinking. Not that he was drunk, you understand. But the voice was slightly slurred."

"And she's quite certain she didn't recognize it."

"Absolutely certain. It was no one she'd ever heard before in her life."

"This was about half past ten?"

"Just after."

"Did he say what his name was?"

"Yes. He said he was Mr. Lewisham."

"And he asked for Mariner by name?"

"He asked if Mr. Mariner was at home. Polly said no. He asked when he was coming back. By this time Polly was getting a bit bored with him. She simply said she hadn't any idea when he was coming back. The man said, 'Then I'll ring later.' She said, 'O.K., you do that.' And the man rang off."

"Did he say where he was telephoning from?"

"No, but Polly says it was a telephone box."

"And he didn't try again later?"

"Not while she was there. When the Mariners came back she told them about it. Before she could say much, George said, 'Wait a moment. I must get my wife to bed. She's very tired.' And he hustled her upstairs into her bedroom. Then he came down and said, 'All right. What was it?' Polly told him and he said, 'I don't know any Mr. Lewisham. It must have been a wrong number.' 'Can't have been,' said Polly. 'He asked for you by name.' To which George said, rather huffily, 'That doesn't prove anything. He probably got my name out of the phone book.'"

"But—"

"Yes," agreed Mr. Beaumorris. "It was a stupid thing to say. But Polly says he was quite clearly pretty shaken by the whole thing. However, it wasn't her business. So she pushed off."

Ian thanked Mr. Beaumorris. He said that it probably had nothing to do with the matter they were investigating, but he'd certainly ask Mr. Mariner about it. He declined a glass of sherry and went straight back to the police station. The operations room was empty, but the records of the case, now occupying two bulging folders, were on the Superintendent's desk.

He got out the transcript of Mariner's statement. The passage he wanted came toward the end. *Knott: But she took off as soon as you got back? Mariner: As soon as she heard our car in the drive.*

He sat staring at it for a long time. He was still sitting there when the door opened and Knott came in quietly. It was something Ian had noticed about him before. He never made much noise.

"That's right," he said. "Keep studying the record. Read it right through every day. Every word. Nothing like it for concentrating the mind." He seemed to be pleased about something.

Ian said, "I've got another report to add to it. It's on tape but I haven't had time to transcribe it yet."

"Important?"

"It could be." He told him about it.

Knott said, "The trouble is, son, you never know which bits belong and which bits don't. I remember once when I was investigating a case of arson, we kept getting reports about a man who thought he'd been brought up by a wolf pack. Used to call his father 'Baloo' and his mother 'Baghera' and went howling round the fields at night. Fascinating stuff. Nothing to do with the case, though." He opened an envelope on his desk, read the flimsy that was in it and said, "Here's another," and threw it across.

The body of a man, as yet unidentified, was recovered from the Thames at the Prince Albert Lock this morning. He appeared to have been in the river not less than three and not more than six days. Height five foot eight. Heavy build. Weight stripped fifteen stone. He was carrying a number of obscene photographs, clearly high-class professional work featuring girls, young men and boys. These were in a wallet specially constructed to hold and conceal them. It seems probable that he was a runner or traveler for one of the studios in London who produce or retail this type of work. A photograph, face only, accompanies this report. Details of fingerprints and dental work will follow. Information about this man required by Berkshire Police, Reading. Detective Superintendent Farr.

"It's an advance copy from Farr at Reading," said Knott. "He thought I might be interested."

Ian looked puzzled.

"The lock keeper who pulled the body out—he's by way of being a bit of an expert on Father Thames and his ways. He said the man probably went in somewhere around here at the weekend."

Ian said, "Yes, but—"

"I know. Just another wolf man. All the same, we'll add it in. You never can tell. Get a third folder from Eddie. We don't want to burst the seams of that one."

"You agreed to do *what?*" said Vernon Vigors, shaken out of his usual calm.

"To represent Jonathan," said Noel. "Why not?"

"Do you feel you are equipped to do so?"

"If you mean do I know anything about defending a man charged with murder, the answer's no, I don't. And I've had precisely two cases in the Crown Court."

"Then don't you think it would be more sensible to entrust the case to a London firm? One who have got some experience in that particular line. It's very specialized, I believe."

177

"There are two answers to that," said Noel. "The first is that the case will be masterminded by the counsel we choose, not by me. The second is that Jonathan adamantly refused to consider any solicitor except myself."

"He chose *you,* not the firm?"

"Apparently."

"But it's the firm that will be on the record."

"Naturally."

"Didn't it occur to you to ask me before you accepted?"

"Frankly," said Noel, "it didn't. Because it never occurred to me for a single moment that you might object."

Mr. Vigors considered this, chewing his upper lip with the teeth in his lower jaw. It was an unconscious trick, but Noel had seen it before and braced himself for trouble.

"Our firm," said Mr. Vigors, laying stress on the first word, "has built up a very sound practice in and around Hannington. We act for most of the respectable—and respected—families in the neighborhood. Did you stop for a moment to consider what they would feel when it became known that we were acting for an anarchist, who has already attacked and wounded a policeman?"

"No," said Noel.

"No?"

"I mean that I didn't stop for a moment to consider it. It seemed to me to be irrelevant."

Up to that point father and son had kept their tempers. Regrettably, Mr. Vigors Senior was the first to lose his.

He said, the color of his face contradicting the smoothness of his voice, "We happen to be a partnership. Not a one-man band. You may have overlooked the fact that in our partnership articles, to which you signed your name when you joined Richard Dibden and myself, there was a clause which stated that any important decisions had to be taken unanimously."

178

"No," said Noel. "I hadn't overlooked that."

"Possibly you don't regard this as an important decision?"

"Extremely important."

"Very well, then—"

"But possibly you may have overlooked the fact that when we set up our sub-office in West Hannington, it was agreed that in everything dealt with from *this* office I was to have an absolute discretion about clients and matters taken on. I may not have got the wording quite accurate, but that was the gist of what we agreed." Noel paused and added, "In writing."

His father stared at him. His face, normally pallid, was now scarlet. Since he seemed unwilling, or unable, to say anything, Noel continued: "Since Limbery has specifically applied for *my* help, it can hardly be disputed, I imagine, that it is a matter which comes under this office and in which I exercise my discretion."

His father said, "You're determined to go on with this."

"Yes."

"And to disregard my very strong personal wishes in the matter."

"I don't like doing that. But yes."

"In that case we can hardly go on as before."

"I'm not sure what you mean."

"I mean," said his father with calculated brutality, "that since you seem to have no regard for me and for what I stand for, we can hardly meet on the same terms as we did. I shall, for instance, find it embarrassing to share a house with you."

"I'm glad you raised the point," said Noel. "I meant to tell you before. Georgie and I are expecting an addition to our family. We may have to have resident help, for a time anyway. It would be much more convenient if you could find somewhere else to live. I'm sure you understand."

His father looked at him for some seconds and then swung around and left the room without a word.

"Did you *have* to do it?" said Georgie that evening.

"I couldn't see any way round it."

"It was a bit rough."

They were close together, sharing, as they sometimes did, a dilapidated armchair. Noel put his arm around her and said, "You've got to understand this. The alternative was letting Jonathan try to defend himself. If he was allowed to do that, examine the witnesses, address the court, can you imagine any sort of justice being done at the end of the day?"

"I suppose not."

"I'm going up to London tomorrow to see our London agents. We're going to brief the best barrister money can buy. And we're going to get at the truth of this matter, if it costs me every bloody friend I've got."

EIGHTEEN

"Have you ever sold anyone a Crossfield Electric?" said Sergeant Esdaile to Mr. Plumptree, who kept the business machinery and equipment store in Reading.

"Dozens of them," said Mr. Plumptree. "Two or three years ago—before the fashion for golf balls got going, that is—it was one of the most popular machines on the market."

"And you've got records of who you sold them to?"

"Not exactly."

"What do you mean?"

"If I looked at my purchase and sale cards and compared them with my stock cards, I could tell you how many I sold in any one year. It would take a bit of research, but I could do it all right. But that doesn't mean I could say *who* I sold them to. I never had any call to keep that sort of information."

"I suppose you don't remember selling one to anyone in these parts. In Hannington, for instance."

"Not offhand I don't. I'll think about it and I'll have a word with my lads. If I find out anything I'll let you know."

"Well, ta," said Sergeant Esdaile gloomily.

Friday morning found Noel Vigors in London. He went from Paddington Station by Underground to Covent Garden and walked to Norway Court, where Messrs. Crakenshaw, Solicitors and Commissioners for Oaths, had their office. It was within a stone's throw of Bow Street Magistrates Court, where they did much of their business.

The Crakenshaws were the London agents of Vigors and Dibden. Noel had written to them and spoken to them on the telephone, but this was the first time he had been to see them. He was received by Simon Crakenshaw, who was about Noel's age but looked much older, being prematurely bald.

He said, "I read all about it in the papers. I was hoping you'd get involved and rope us in. Tell me all about it."

Noel did his best. He said, "I am a bit worried about the financial side of it. Limbery really hasn't got any money. No capital at all, as far as I know, and a very small income from that paper of his, and a lot of that goes to his mother."

"Dependent relative?" said Crakenshaw.

"I suppose she is, yes."

"Then don't worry about the money side. The poorer he

181

is the better. We'll apply for legal aid. We ought to get a full certificate. Minimum contribution."

"Will it cover leading counsel?"

"Certificate for two counsel? Certainly. The committee will be falling over themselves to help. Charge of murder. Man with no money. The sky's the limit."

"Well, that's a relief," said Noel, "because I've a feeling we're going to need the sky."

Crakenshaw said, "If Knott's running the case you're going to need to pull out all the stops." He thought about the matter for a few moments. He said, "I think Mrs. Bellamy would be our best bet."

"Serena Bellamy? I've seen a lot about her in newspaper reports. Do you think we could get her?"

"She's the top of the tree. But I think we might. And I'll tell you why. She loathes Knott. They've had one or two fights in court already. If she sees half a chance of putting him down she'll jump at it. Murder cases aren't quite the glamorous occasions they used to be when there was a gallows at the end of the road, but they still grab the headlines and no counsel objects to a bit more of that, however well known they are."

"I see," said Noel. He found Crakenshaw's professional outlook both alarming and reassuring. "She'll find Limbery a very awkward character to deal with."

"She won't be dealing with him," said Crakenshaw. "It's you and I who have to do all that. She won't talk to him. She'll steer totally clear of him until they face each other in court."

"Why on earth—?"

"What she says is that it enables her to view the case dispassionately. It's also a complete answer to any suggestion of professional misconduct. No one can accuse her of suggesting a phony line of defense to the prisoner if she hasn't even seen him, can they?"

"But they might accuse us—"

"They might. But since we're not going to deviate one inch from the straight and narrow it doesn't arise. We've found that it's much better to stick to the rules. I know there are firms that don't. I don't believe it pays them in the long run. And once you get a name for it, the police can be real sods."

"I see," said Noel. He was beginning to realize that ten years of conveyancing and probate mixed with occasional motoring offenses might have presented him with a one-sided view of legal practice. "What do we do next?"

"I'll give you the legal aid forms to fill in. Limbery will have to sign a declaration of means. Then we'll have a word with Mrs. Bellamy's head clerk. It's Friday now. She won't be able to see us before Monday. And you say the committal proceedings are fixed for Monday week."

"So I'm told."

"That's Knott all over. Rush the opposition off its feet. Well, we can always apply for an adjournment."

Ten minutes later, Noel found himself out in Norway Court again. He was conscious of a feeling of breathlessness.

"I've established," said Sergeant Shilling, "that Katie went up to town that Friday morning. She called on her agent, Mark Holbeck. Incidentally, I think he ought to have mentioned the fact to me when I was talking to him. Perhaps it slipped his memory."

Knott grunted.

"However, he remembered it when I put it to him. Apparently she only looked in for five minutes around midday. She told him she had a lunch date with Venetia—you know, the A.C.'s daughter."

Knott grunted again.

"I had a word with Venetia. After lunch they seem to

have gone out on a shopping spree together. They had tea at Venetia's house and Katie pushed off saying she'd be just in time to catch the six twenty and she'd better not miss it, because she'd promised to go to a ghastly local hop and if she came in late everyone would think she was trying to put on an act."

"Shrewd thinking," said Knott. "When does the six twenty get to Hannington?"

"It doesn't. You have to change at Reading and get the slow train. That's scheduled to reach Hannington at ten past seven. Which it did. I've checked."

"Then she'd be home by half past?"

"She'd have to extract her car from the station car park, which takes some doing, as it's small and the cars are pretty well jammed together. But if she went straight home, she'd certainly be there by half past. Then, I imagine, bath and change."

"Eat?"

"Probably not. If she had a good lunch. There were refreshments at the dance."

Knott thought about it. It seemed straightforward. The connection with the Loftus girl might be tricky. On the other hand, if he pulled off this one it must do him a bit of good in quarters that mattered. He realized that Shilling had something else to tell him.

He said, "While I was at it I found out that Limbery was in Reading that morning. Mariner told me. He was there, too. He's still a consultant with his firm and goes up occasionally. Actually they were on the same train, both ways."

"Times?"

"Eight forty up. Two fifty back. Mariner first class, Limbery second. But even if they'd been in the same carriage I don't imagine they'd have chatted to each other."

"No love lost there," agreed Knott.

He was visualizing Hannington Station, which he had

184

already inspected. The opening in front of the nineteenth-century station building and the cramped car park to the left of it packed with commuters' cars. He said, "I imagine Limbery drove to the station?"

"We know he did."

"How?"

"Because Mariner, who came out of the station building at the same moment, saw him walking off into the car park to fetch his car. Correction. Assumed that he was going to fetch his car."

"Why didn't he follow him to get his own car?"

"Because his wife had taken him to the station and was meeting him."

"A pity. He might have told us how close to Katie's car Limbery's was parked."

Knott followed this reasoning without difficulty. He said, "You think that's when he slipped in the note?"

"If her car was parked next to his it would have been a perfect opportunity."

"We might be able to find out. The eight forty up is the regular commuters' train. Those two chaps who work in London—Tony Windle and Billy Gonville—chances are they'd have been on it."

"Find out."

Jack Nurse said, "It's an absolute scandal. I only heard the news this morning. I can't imagine what young Noel can be thinking of."

"What's he done now?" said his wife.

"What he's done is to take on, totally off his own bat, and without consulting anyone, the defense of that madman Limbery."

"Why not?" said Sally. "Someone had to do it."

"Why not? Because Vigors and Dibden is a respectable firm, miss. That's why not."

"You mean that someone who's accused of a crime has to go to an unrespectable firm."

Mr. Nurse sometimes found it difficult to cope with his daughter's logic. He fell back on generalities. He said, "Like all young people, Noel thinks he knows better than his elders."

"Perhaps he does, sometimes."

"I imagine I may be permitted to know more about legal topics than you do, young lady."

"I know one thing about the law. A man's presumed to be innocent until he's proved guilty. I think Noel was quite right to stick up for him."

"You do?"

"Certainly. That's what proper lawyers are for. To stick up for people who can't stick up for themselves."

"Then you think I'm talking nonsense?"

"In this case, yes."

"Now, Sally," said her mother hastily. "You don't really mean that."

It was too late. Storm signals had been hoisted.

"I certainly do mean it," said Sally. "I think it's absolutely foul the way vile old men like George Mariner and Vernon Vigors have assumed, without a particle of proof, that Jonathan killed Katie."

"Vile old men, eh?" said her father. His foot was tapping the floor. "Perhaps you'd like to add your father to the list."

"If you insist on joining the club, yes."

"I see."

"Sally," said her mother, "you mustn't talk like that to your father."

"I'll talk to him in any way I want."

"In that case," said her father, "you'd better pack up your things and take yourself off to somewhere you'll be appreciated."

"Jack!"

"Since you treat me like dirt," said Sally, "the sooner I stop polluting your house the better."

"You can't go away like this," said her mother. "Where will you go?"

"To London," said Sally, who was as close to tears as her mother was. "Patricia Cole will let me share her flat. She told me so."

"She won't want you at this time of night," said her father, who saw that he had gone too far. "Cool down. We'll talk about it in the morning."

"I've done all the talking I'm going to do," said Sally and slammed out of the room.

"Bit of luck finding you two here together," said Sergeant Shilling.

Tony Windle and Billy Gonville looked at him cautiously. Sergeant McCourt they knew and, to a certain extent, trusted. They were not so certain about this smooth-faced young man from London.

"Anything we can do for you?"

"Just to think back to Friday morning. I imagine you both went up to London as usual."

"As usual."

"That would be the eight forty."

"As usual."

"And both went down to the station in your cars."

"We both went down in Gonville's car. Mine was out of action."

"Yes. I remember. Your local practical joker had put yours out of action. By the way, have there been any other incidents of that sort?"

"If there have, we haven't heard of them."

"Odd. Mariner, Vigors and you."

"Not really," said Tony. "Most people round here lock their cars up at night. Vigors and Mariner hadn't got round to putting their cars away. The damage was done during the evening. That's why everyone thought it was kids. We haven't got a garage, so mine was easy meat. While he was at it, the joker might have fixed Billy's, too. They're parked together in our back yard."

Billy said, "Is Scotland Yard worried about it?"

"Not really. But it was cars I came to ask you about. When you parked yours at the station, did you happen to notice Limbery's car?"

They looked at each other. The conversation so far had been casual enough. Were they now getting to some point that mattered?

"As a matter of fact, I did," said Tony. "It's a ropy old Morris Traveller. A respray job. It was parked at the far end."

"By the pedestrian access?"

"Just beyond it."

"I understand that Katie went up to town that morning on the eight forty. I wondered if you happened to notice where *her* car was parked."

So that's it, said the two young men simultaneously to themselves. It was Windle who answered. He said, "We could hardly have noticed Katie's car. It wasn't there."

"Oh?"

"Walter ran her down to the station. I expect her mother fetched her. That was the usual arrangement when she went to town."

"But—" said Shilling.

"I know," said Tony. "She had a car of her own. But she doesn't seem to have been keen on using it. Lately, that is. She drove round in it a lot when she first got it. New toy. Then she seemed to get tired of it."

"The fact is," said Billy, "she liked other people to do things for her. If Tony's car hadn't been out of action she'd have expected him to drive her to the dance that night.

188

Although it was only four hundred yards straight down the road."

"Is that right?" said Shilling. An idea was beginning to shape itself in his mind. He thought he would try it out on Knott.

When he had gone, Tony heaved himself out of his chair, took two large glass-bottomed pewter tankards out of the sideboard and filled them from a cask in the corner. He handed one to Billy, who sank half of the contents in two gulps and then said, "It *is* odd, when you come to think of it."

"Very odd," said Tony. "For the first few months of this year she was hardly out of that car. Drove it all over the place, took it up to London. Then—it didn't happen gradually—she just seemed to stop using it."

"Do you think it could have been her? Young Roney—?"

"It might have been. He said it was a small red car. Of course, they're common enough."

He was referring to something that had happened in the first week of March.

Roney Havelock, walking home from school in the dusk, had been hit by a car driving on sidelights only. That part of the street, between River Park Avenue and West Hannington Manor, was unlighted. When he saw that the car was going to hit him, Roney had jumped for safety. Some outlying portion, possibly the driving mirror, had caught in his coat and hurled him onto the side of the road. He had cracked his head on a fencepost and knocked himself out. The next motorist to come past had been his mother, who had picked him up, taken him straight to the Hannington Infirmary and telephoned the police. By that time Roney, who was suffering from concussion, had been able to make a statement. He hadn't noticed the car until a moment before it hit him. It was small and red. That was all.

189

"There could be nothing in it," said Tony. "Katie's car is small and red—"

"Lot of them about."

"But it *was* then that she practically gave up using her car, particularly after dark."

"The police never pinned it onto anyone."

"That's right," said Tony. "They started making a lot of inquiries. I remember Ian coming to talk to me about it. My car's red and smallish. Luckily I'd got an alibi. Then, somehow, they seemed to lose interest."

"I notice," said Billy, "that you didn't mention any of this to the Sergeant just now. All you said was Katie had given up driving lately. March isn't exactly lately."

Tony finished his beer, took both mugs and refilled them. He said, "If Katie did knock young Roney down, she may not even have known that she'd touched him. And it can't have anything to do with her getting killed five months later."

"I suppose not."

"And anyway, I don't trust Shilling. And I don't like his boss."

"The White Rat."

"He's simply in it for what he can get out of it. I was talking to Pritchard at lunch yesterday. You know the chap I mean?"

"Conk Pritchard?"

"No. That's his brother. This was Dozey Pritchard. Their father's something in the Solicitors' Department at Scotland Yard. He was saying that if Knott pulls this off he's a snip for promotion to Commander. All he wants is a conviction. It doesn't matter to him whether he's got the right man. It's a race between him and another chap on the Murder Squad called Haliburton. He was the one who pulled off that kidnapping job at Exeter, remember?"

Billy considered this, staring into his tankard as though

he could see the truth rising with the bubbles from its amber depths. He said, "Do you think Johnno did do it?"

Tony said, "No, I don't. Do you?"

"It's out of character. Sticking poor old Eddie through the arm in front of an admiring audience. That was Johnno all over. But lurking on a dark path and beating Katie's head in. I just can't see it. And who the hell's that?"

The telephone was in the hall. Billy went out. A one-sided conversation followed, which consisted mostly of Billy saying, "What?" and "Oh" and finally "Hold on a second." He came back and said, "Well, what do you know? That's Sally Nurse on the telephone. She wants to know if she can come round and spend a couple of nights here."

"Has her house burned down?"

"She's had a fight with her father and walked out. A friend in London had offered her a share of her pad, but the friend's gone abroad and locked the place up. Won't be back till Monday."

"I don't mind, if you don't," said Tony. "She can use the sofa."

"Safety in numbers," said Billy with a grin. "All right. I'll tell her."

"I didn't get a lot out of them," said Shilling. "Except that it's clear Katie's car wasn't in the car park that day. I checked that with Walter. But I did get the beginnings of an idea."

Knott grunted. He preferred facts to ideas. But he had enough respect for his assistant to listen.

"It's that business about the practical joker. He drained old Vigors' radiator and he let down Mariner's tires and then, sometime on Thursday night, he immobilized Windle's car by pinching the distributor."

"Wolf man," said Knott.

"Well, it might be, of course. But it just occurred to me.

Suppose the first two were dummy runs and it was only the third one that mattered. If Windle's car hadn't been out of action, he'd have driven Katie to the dance. That's for sure. Since he couldn't, she had to use her own car."

"Couldn't Walter drive her?"

"Walter would be taking her mother. If she went with them, she'd be tied to them for the evening. No, failing Windle, I think she'd be bound to take her own car. Not a certainty, I agree, but highly likely."

"Yes," said Knott. And again. "Yes. I take your point."

"That was a perfect setup for the killer. Katie's up in London. Her car's standing all that day in her stableyard, which is easy to get at and nicely hidden from view. All he's got to do is to slip the note through the window. Katie finds it there *when she comes out to drive to the dance.* She wouldn't want to leave it lying about. Not with all that LYPAH business in it. Natural thing would be to tuck it away in her bag. It's almost the only way he could be certain it *would* finish up there."

Knott was thinking about it, twisting it this way and that, slotting it into the pattern he had created.

He said, "It's all right in one way. He'd have to know quite a bit about Katie and her habits. The fact that she'd probably get her brother to drive her to the station instead of taking her own car. And the supposition that if Windle's car wasn't available she'd take her own car to the dance. And that's the sort of knowledge Limbery would have. In another way it doesn't fit quite so well. It argues a very careful forward-thinking killer."

"Not a hotheaded fool," agreed Shilling. "A cold-blooded bastard."

NINETEEN

"I don't see why we shouldn't take it," said Mariner.

"Be your age, George," said Mrs. Havelock. "You know what you're told. If you have any personal connection with the accused, you can't sit."

"Is that right, Gerry?"

"On the nail," said Group Captain Gonville. "It would be quite impossible for any of us to sit. We all know Jonathan."

"Far too well," said Mrs. Havelock.

"Then what do we do?"

"Ask Henry."

Henry was their clerk. He was also their mainstay. He knew all there was to know about law and procedure. Mrs. Havelock sometimes thought that he would have made a very good judge.

"I'll give him a buzz," said Gonville. The magistrates were meeting in his drawing room.

When he came back, he said, "Henry's already fixed it. He's getting Appleton from Reading."

"Pity," said Mariner. "This was one case I was really looking forward to taking."

And that, said Mrs. Havelock to herself, is just why you're not going to be allowed to take it.

That same morning the weather broke. It was the first rain since mid-July and was generally welcomed. As Superintendent Farr came into the temporary operations room behind the Hannington police station a spout from a blocked drain above the door shot a cupful of water down his back. He took off his coat and said, "Well, that's a bloody friendly way to welcome a colleague."

Knott and Shilling were working at their desks. Knott said, "Come in, Dennis. I can see by that happy smile on your kisser that you've got something for us."

"I have and all," said Farr. "And seeing I was coming in this direction, I thought I'd give it to you myself." He extracted some papers from his briefcase. "First, the Met have put a name to that bod that was pulled out of the river. Lewson. Known to the criminal fraternity as Gabby. He and his brother Louie both worked for this photographer, Rod the Sod Ruoff."

"When I saw the photograph," said Shilling, "I thought it reminded me of someone. It must have been his brother I met when I went up to the studio to ask him about Katie. Chucker-out and general dogsbody."

"Right. And they both have a bit of form. Nothing sensational. Insulting behavior. Drunk and disorderly. Just a pair of barroom cowboys."

"An odd pair to be working for a studio," said Knott.

"It's an odd studio. Society beauties and television personalities and a sideline in porn. I'll send the photographs over and you can see for yourself."

Shilling said, "I suppose 'Gabby' was short for Gabriel."

Knott looked at him sharply. He suspected that his assistant sometimes pulled his leg. He said, "I don't get it."

"Gabriel was the messenger of the gods. Gabby seems to have been a messenger boy for Ruoff. Taking the merchandise round to the customers. I should think there was an element of blackmail about it, too, wouldn't you?"

"I thought the same thing," said Farr. "Some respectable citizen buys a few naughty photographs. Then he gets cold feet and doesn't fancy having any more. So Gabby turns up at his house one evening with a wallet full of prime stuff. The last thing our respectable citizen wants is a fuss on his own doorstep. So he buys the lot to keep him quiet."

"You could be right," said Knott. "But has it got anything to do with my case?"

"Next point," said Farr smoothly. "There was a ticket in Gabby's wallet. A cheap day-return ticket to Hannington. The date was washed off, but the number on the ticket was still legible. Paddington say that it must have been issued latish that Friday. They can't be certain of the exact time, but around five or six. Since it was a day-return, presumably Gabby planned to go back to London the same night. The last train back is the fast from Swindon, which stops at Hannington at ten minutes before midnight. That would give him about six hours. For whatever he was planning to do."

"All right," said Knott. "All right. That means that he was hanging around this part of the world at the time Katie was killed. That still doesn't mean—"

"Wait for it," said Farr. "I've kept the punch line for the last." He took out another sheet of paper. "We've got the pathologist's report on Lewson. Dr. Carlyle, from Southampton. He did the autopsy on Katie, too. He says, 'An examination of both wounds leaves me in little doubt that they were made by the same weapon. The shape and size of the fracture, which it was possible to measure with precision, suggests a thinnish steel pipe, with some protuberance, or knob, at the end of it. In both cases it was swung downwards and sideways into the head, and the fact that the depth of penetration was the same in both cases suggests that the same hand struck both blows, although that last point is, of course, only surmise.'"

The three men looked at each other. Knott's face was

ugly. The case, which had looked straightforward, seemed to be branching out in unexpected directions. It was an unwelcome development.

"Of course," said Farr, "it *could* still be unconnected. Or it could be connected in some way which doesn't make any real difference to your case. All the same, Charlie, I think it might be a good idea to sort it out before the defense starts sniffing round it. It'd be normal tactics for them to raise as many side issues as possible. Muddy the water. Put up a smokescreen. You know what I mean."

Knott grunted. He could see the force of Farr's suggestion. It was his belief that defense lawyers would try every dirty trick in the book. And the less plausible their case, the dirtier and trickier would their conduct of it be.

He said, "We'll have to tackle this from both ends. We want to know what Lewson was doing down here that evening. The first place he'd make for would be the nearest pub. That's routine stuff. One of Dan's boys can tackle that. We'll give him a photograph and tell him to start at the railway station. The London end must be your pigeon, Bob. I asked Division to keep an eye on Ruoff's place. See if they've got anything for us. If they could think up an excuse to look at his records, we might be able to find out who his customer in Hannington was."

Shilling said, "I've got any amount of things to finish here. I could go up on Monday."

"Soon as you can," said Knott. They all had a lot to do. He was beginning to regret that he had offered to open the committal proceedings so quickly. It would entail a loss of face if *he* had to ask for an adjournment. Probably the defense would save him the trouble by asking for one themselves. They must be further behind than he was.

Walter Steelstock was standing in the front doorway of West Hannington Manor staring down the drive. The rain

196

was sweeping across the lawns in a gauzy curtain. The farmers might want it, but it was a bore that it should have happened on a Saturday afternoon. He had organized a game of tennis with the two Havelock girls and Billy Gonville. If the game had gone well, he had thought of suggesting a trip into Oxford that evening. Certain plans, which involved Lavinia, were beginning to form in his mind. These followed the sequence which he had been taught in the Cadet Corps at school. Intention. Method. Movement of own troops. Movements of enemy. The enemy, in this case, was his mother. He heard a sound behind him and spun around.

Peter was coming downstairs and taking evident care to do so without making too much noise.

Enemy troops? His mother in the drawing room?

Peter jerked his head toward the dining room and Walter followed him in, closing the door quietly. He noticed that Peter's face was white. That was either excitement or fear. They affected him in the same way. When he was younger, in moments of stress he had sometimes passed right out. The doctor had talked about puberty and growing pains and had told them not to worry about it. In the last two years there had been no recurrence of the trouble. Now he looked ghastly.

Walter said, "For God's sake, sit down, Pete, or you'll fall flat on your back. What's up?"

Peter sat down, put his elbows on the table and said, "Will they ... will the court ... make out that Johnno killed Katie?"

"I should think it's quite likely."

"Why?"

"Why would they find him guilty, you mean?"

Peter nodded. Walter, observing the staring eyes and the sweat standing out on his forehead, thought that he looked like a frightened horse. He lowered his voice and spoke slowly. He said, "It's the note that was found in Katie's bag."

"You mean a note from Johnno asking Katie to meet him that night."

"That's the obvious assumption."

"But—" said Peter. And then evidently changed his mind. "Is that all?"

"The rest seems to be circumstantial. The fact that he was known to be a wild character and that he had been very keen on Katie and had quarreled with her that time at the Tennis Club."

"That was my fault."

"Why?"

"He was coaching me at tennis on our court. I kept saying to him that there was plenty of time. And then—there wasn't."

"I don't see that it's anything to get worked up about," said Walter. "He's such a casual chap that he's always late for everything. If it hadn't been you, it'd have been some other reason."

Peter hardly seemed to be listening. He said, "Is that all they've got against him?"

"There's a sort of theory—I'm not sure where it came from—that he's put up a cock-and-bull story about where he actually was that evening and the police can prove that he's lying. It's something to do with the job he says he was on for the paper. That's all I know about it. We shall have it served up piping hot when it comes to court."

"And then it'll be too late to do anything about it."

"Anything about what?"

"I mean, once he's sworn to his account of what he says he was doing it'll be too late to go back on it."

"A lot too late," said Walter grimly.

198

"It's quite extraordinary," said Dicky Bird, "but it looks as though we shan't have a single treble in the choir to-morrow. They've fallen by the wayside, one after the other. Two of them have got bad colds, another one's going out with her parents. Tina Gonville says she's sprained her ankle, although I'll swear I saw her skipping down the street this morning—"

"There's nothing coincidental about it," said his wife.

"What do you mean?"

"Roney and Sim Havelock have been going round saying they'll scrag anyone who sings in your choir."

"Why on earth—?"

"It's something to do with what you said in church last Sunday. They've got the wrong end of the stick, of course. But they've convinced themselves that because you were sympathetic about Katie, you must be antagonistic to Jonathan. He's their hero."

He stared at her. "I didn't mean—"

"Of course you didn't. It's mad."

"It's very unsettling," said her husband.

When Knott wanted his assistants he summoned them on the internal telephone. As they got up to comply, their own outside telephone rang and McCourt stopped behind to answer it. When he reached the operations room he found Dandridge and Esdaile examining a dozen photographs which had been spread out on the table. He said, addressing himself to Dandridge, "That was Superintendent Farr on the telephone. Bad news, I'm afraid. Inspector Ray died this morning."

"I was afraid of that," said Dandridge. "I had a call from his wife last night." Shilling and Esdaile gave a sympathetic murmur. Knott grunted.

By this time, McCourt had reached the table and Esdaile moved aside to let him see the photographs. McCourt stared at them bleakly for a moment, then swung around, walked to the door and went out.

"What's up now?" said Knott.

Esdaile said, "Ian's upset."

"You mean that stuff turned him up?"

"That's right," said Esdaile.

Shilling said, "When he was with the Met, his first posting was West End Central. He got his face shoved into a lot of shit there. I guess it upset him."

Knott seemed more interested in the feelings of Sergeant McCourt than he had been in the death of Inspector Ray. He said, "Do you mean that sex upsets him? Is that it, Bob?"

"Not straight sex. I mean, he's quite O.K. as far as that sort of thing's concerned. He had one or two rather smooth girlfriends when he was up in London, I seem to remember. They rather go for that ascetic Scots look. What he couldn't take was perversion. Maybe it was being brought up in a manse."

"It takes them both ways," said Knott. "I remember one youngster—I was in recruit class with him—his father was a canon and I wouldn't have trusted him with my sister *or* my kid brother. I suppose that's why Ian pulled out of the Met?"

"I guess so," said Shilling. "I think it was the Pussycat Case that finished him. It was about that time, if you remember."

"I remember it," said Knott with a faint grimace of distaste.

"He asked for a transfer soon after and got himself a job down here. I believe his folk live down here."

Knott said, "I thought they were Scotch."

"His father was. His mother's English. She came down here when the old man died."

"I think he's O.K. now," said Eddie.

"Better put those photographs away," said Knott.

McCourt came back. He looked pale, but otherwise collected. He said, "Sorry about that, sir," addressing the apology to Dandridge, and sat down quietly by the table.

"Right," said Knott. "Now I want to recap. We've got a certain amount of information about this porn peddler. I'm not at all sure how he fits into our case, or whether he fits into it at all. But if the pathologist is right and he was killed at the same time as Katie and by the same weapon, we've obviously got to fit him in somewhere. Over to you, Dan."

"Well," said Dandridge, "we've discovered that he got here by the seven forty. That's one of the through trains from Paddington. It wasn't crowded and anyway the man on the gate knows most of the regulars, so he spotted this chap at once. He seems to have drifted off into the town and gone on a pub crawl. He put in an hour at the Station Tavern, moved on to the Masons Arms, where he had something to eat, and finished up at the Crown."

"Where's the Crown?" said Knott. He had got up and was examining the large-scale map.

"It's on the corner of Eveleigh Road," said McCourt. "It's near my lodgings. I often drop in there in the evening for a bit to eat and a pint."

"Is the landlord reliable? I mean, would he make a good witness?"

"Old Scotty. Yes, I would say he'd be all right."

"What time did this chap leave?"

"Apparently he went out twice. Once to use the phone. At least he asked where the nearest box was. So that's the supposition. The second time was when the pub was closing. He was about the last man out."

"Which would be when?"

"Officially eleven o'clock."

Ian said, "Scotty's fairly strict about that sort of thing. It wouldn't be later than a quarter past."

Knott was still examining the map. He said, "It's beginning to add up. In parts, anyway. Eveleigh Road runs down to the river. Lewson rolls out at a quarter past eleven, not exactly drunk, but tolerably full of whisky. Wherever he was making for, and I guess that's fairly obvious now, he'd be likely to use the towpath in preference to the main road. If he'd looked at the map he'd know he could get back to the main road easily enough by using Church Lane or River Park Avenue. But for that pathologist's report—and pathologists are sometimes too bloody clever by half—I'd guess that he slipped on the bank, which is pretty steep there, cracked his head on something sharp, rolled into the river and was drowned."

"He wouldn't be the first," said Dandridge. "Is something bothering you, Ian?"

McCourt had been trying to speak for some time. He said, "Did you say the man's name was Lewson?"

Knott grinned at him. "It's all right, son," he said, "we've all noticed it. Lewson. Lewisham. I don't doubt he was planning to call on the chairman of your Bench and sell him a few more dirty photographs."

TWENTY

"Well, Mr. Vigors," said Mrs. Bellamy, "we've got a lot of work to do and not much time to do it in."

The sun was shining directly into her south-facing chambers in Crown Office Row, lighting up the spines of the law books which crammed the shelves, focusing on one patch of blinding scarlet which Noel could see was a set of *Famous Criminal Trials.*

"I'm afraid that's right," said Noel. "I was only consulted late last week. I imagine we could ask for an adjournment."

"We could," said Mrs. Bellamy, "but I'm not sure that I shall advise it. We'll keep our options open for a little longer, I think."

Ever since he came into the room, Noel had been teased by a resemblance. It was some minutes before he placed it. Mrs. Bellamy was a perfect female counterpart of Oliver Cromwell. There was the same calm sagacious face, the heavy jowls, the impression of rustic, kindly competence, a kindliness qualified by the steel of the eyes and flatly contradicted by the rat-trap mouth, a mouth which had said, *I would cut off his head, were he three times king.*

On this occasion this formidable woman was doing no more than studying a long list of names and was seeming to find it puzzling.

"We shall need your local knowledge, Mr. Vigors," she said. "What we have here is a list, seemingly arranged in alphabetical order, of the witnesses the Crown intends to call. Rita Black, Fire Officer Burt, Dr. Carlyle, Joseph Cavey, Arnold Cowie . . . A more considerate opponent than Detective Chief Superintendent Knott would at least have set them down in the order in which he intended to call them. We might then have had some notion of the parts they were intended to play in his carefully staged melodrama. Detective Sergeant Esdaile, Dr. Farmiloe—that's a name I remember. What's Jack Farmiloe doing in your part of the world?"

"He retired there last year."

"Anything he says will be gospel. Sim Havelock, Detective Chief Superintendent Knott, Police Constable Luck, George Mariner, Mary Mason, Sally Nurse, Olivia Steelstock, Walter Steelstock. Olivia is the mother, Walter the brother, I take it? Quite so. Noel Vigors. Hullo! Slightly unusual to call the solicitor acting for the defense as a Crown witness."

"I noticed that," said Noel. "Maybe because I can give evidence of when Katie left the dance—or maybe to talk about a quarrel that took place in the Tennis Club."

"We shall have to think about that. Anthony Windle, Chief Superintendent Wiseman and that's the lot."

"I can place the locals for you," said Noel. He ran his finger down the list. "Cavey's the caretaker of the village hall and part-time barman at the Tennis Club."

"The man who found the body?"

"Right. Arnold Cowie is editor of the Reading *Sun*. Limbery covered local features for him. Including that fire. Which no doubt accounts for Fire Officer Burt. Sergeant Esdaile is local C.I.D. Sim Havelock is a small boy, son of Mrs. Havelock, one of the Hannington magistrates."

"How small?"

"Eight or nine."

"I detest child witnesses," said Mrs. Bellamy. She looked as though she could have eaten two for breakfast. "You can't cross-examine them, and the court believes everything they say. P.C. Luck? Is he one of yours?"

"Not that I know of."

"You and Sophie had better check the local forces. Reading, Swindon and Oxford for a start."

Sophie was one of the two girls who had been introduced to Noel when he came into the room. She nodded and made a note. Both girls were dressed in the formal black and white of the profession and he assumed that they were pupils in the Chambers. The masculine formality of their dress did not conceal the fact that they were both easy on the eye.

"George Mariner's the local bigwig. I know nothing about Mary Mason. Sally Nurse is the daughter of our managing clerk, Jack Nurse. She was at the dance that night and was thought to have had a crush on Katie. Copied her clothes and getup. The Steelstocks you know about. Tony Windle was a rather casual boyfriend of Katie's. Superintendent Wiseman—I don't know him."

"He is the number-one fingerprint expert at Scotland Yard," said Mrs. Bellamy. "A very competent man. Dr. Carlyle is the pathologist. He's attached to the Southampton General Hospital. Haven't you got a friend in those parts, Laura?"

The second girl said, "I know one of the sisters at the hospital. She helped us in that abortion case last year."

"See if she can get alongside Dr. Carlyle. I'd very much like to see a copy of the autopsy report *before* it's produced in court." She returned to the list. "It looks as though the jokers in the pack are Rita Black and Mary Mason. Unfortunately two rather common names. Local directories might help."

"Couldn't we ask Knott?" said Noel.

"We could. And he could tell us. He could even give us copies of their statements. But we can't force him to do so. And since I'm sure he'd refuse, I don't intend to ask him. He is not a man who believes in making life easy for the opposition."

Simon Crakenshaw, who had been sitting quietly in one corner of the room, caught Noel's eye at this point and winked at him.

"All we've got to work from," said Mrs. Bellamy, "is the statement of the accused. Unless Rita Black and Mary Mason are surprise witnesses who actually saw the crime committed, which I doubt, they must be connected in some way with Limbery's account of what he did that night. The editor fits in with that. He'll probably be called to say that Limbery's story of the fire was so superficial that he needn't have been there at all. Or not for very long. One of the others could be connected with the roadhouse where he says he had a snack. Better check on that, Laura."

Laura made a note.

Mrs. Bellamy put both documents down and sat back in her chair, which creaked in protest. She said, "We've got one other line which has got to be followed up hard. Katie was a client of a well-known—I should say notorious— London photographer called Ruoff. I was involved in a case with him about four years ago."

There were numbered box files on the shelves inside the door. Sophie had one out and open on the desk almost before Mrs. Bellamy had finished speaking. Her fingers rifled through the papers and found the one she wanted.

"He ran a series of parties which were described, with more accuracy than usual, as orgies. Young people of both sexes were given drinks which had been hocussed with some drug which left them barely conscious. They were then stripped and photographed in interesting positions. Oddly enough the objective didn't seem to be blackmail. At least that was never suggested. The photographs were sold to private clients who were prepared to pay highly for them and to fringe magazines which specialized in that sort of thing. The victims didn't complain. One imagines they were ashamed of having gone to that sort of party at all. They may not even have been sure of what had happened to them. It was the prosecution of one of the magazines which brought the matter to light." She closed the folder.

"What happened to Ruoff?" said Noel.

"He was bound over and had to pay a heavy fine. Most people thought he should have gone to prison. He was very ably defended. By me."

Noel was on the point of making a comment, but noticed that Sophie and Laura were looking particularly impassive and decided not to.

"However, he was punished. In another way. As the hearing went on, the names of some of his victims became known. And their friends laid for Ruoff. He was beaten up at least once and he had to hire two barroom bullies to look after him. Men with criminal records. Names here, somewhere."

"In the newspaper clippings," suggested Sophie.

"Right. Here they are. The Lewson brothers. Now you see where we're going?"

Noel saw nothing, but managed to look intelligent.

"Superintendent Knott is a man who likes to keep his cases simple. From the witnesses he's calling, it's clear he sees this as a local killing. He'll want to cut the London end right out. That makes our tactics clear. We plug the London connection for all it's worth. And it's worth a good deal. This is a case of violent crime. Down at West Hannington you've got a lot of nice people?"

Noel said, "I certainly wouldn't have described any of them as violent criminals."

"Right. While up in London, in what we might call the

other half of Katie's life— Quite a good expression that— the other half of Katie's life . . ."

Noel saw her mentally trying it out on the jury.

"As I was saying, up here we've got a pornographic photographer who's already been in trouble with the police, two professional criminals and others, for all we know, in the background. That's a hotbed that's more likely to spawn a murder."

"How do we investigate it?"

"We use private detectives. Captain Smedley will be our best bet. He'll put a couple of good men onto it. They'll find out anything that's there."

"I know Katie's agent, Mark Holbeck," said Sophie. "I could have a word with him."

"Good girl. The more we can dig up the better. I'll be frank with you, Mr. Vigors. Nothing we find may have any connection with the killing. But we have to fight with what weapons we've got. And where we have no weapons to our hand, we have to manufacture them. In the Mancini case —you remember it?—the Brighton trunk murder—Norman Birkett had to defend a pimp who was found with the body of the girl he'd been managing stowed away in a trunk with her head bashed in. What did he do? He started to talk about morphine. Got Roche Lynch, the Home Office analyst, to admit that owing to the putrefaction of the corpse it was impossible to tell *exactly* how much morphine there was in the body. By the time he'd finished, the jury didn't know whether she'd died of an overdose of drugs or had fallen down the steps or been hit on the head with a hammer. A masterly performance. Well, we mustn't sit round chatting. We've all of us got a lot to do."

Simon Crakenshaw walked back up Middle Temple Lane with Noel. He said, "Did you see her eyes light up when she observed that Knott was going to give evidence? She's been waiting for this opportunity for months."

"I did wonder," said Noel, "whether her main object was to get Limbery off or to put Knott down."

"Oh, both," said Simon. "Both, I think."

The car which drew up outside the Hannington police station was a black three-and-a-half-liter Rover. The man who got out of it matched the car. He had the air of distinction which derives from height, leanness and a military cast of countenance. In fact, although Mavor was known by his friends at the bar as "Brigadier Mavor," he had been too young for the war and had never been in any branch of the Army. His father had been a master printer from the Midlands and a notable trade union organizer.

Dandridge brought him through into the back room and both Knott and Shilling jumped up when he came in. He shook hands with them.

"This is a surprise," said Knott. "We were told that Davenport was going to take the committal."

"So he was," said Mavor. "There's been a change of plan. I'm going to take it. The Director felt that Davenport wasn't quite up to Mrs. Bellamy's weight."

"Do you mean to tell me," said Knott, "that that lesbian bitch has got in on the act? For God's sake! How's Limbery going to pay for her?"

"Legal aid."

"The criminal's charter. Is there any other country in the world as daft as we are? Law-abiding citizens pay money out of their taxes for lawyers to fiddle acquittals for the criminals who rob their houses and rape their daughters."

"You ought to stand for Parliament, Charlie," said Mavor. "Let's sit down, get the papers out and do some work. Better have the troops in as well."

Dandridge and the two sergeants were brought in and introduced. Papers were spread and Knott expounded the case of the Queen against Jonathan Limbery, interrupted from time to time by questions from Mavor. These were not always directed at Knott. All five of them came under fire from time to time. When some fact was not clear, Mavor seemed to take it in his teeth and shake it until he had worried his way to the center of it or, as happened occasionally, decided that there was no hard center to it, when he would spit it out.

At the finish he said, "The main outline's clear enough, Charlie. The only piece I can't make out is how Lewson comes into it. If it wasn't for the pathologist's report, I'd write it off as coincidence. But Carlyle's not a fool. If he's convinced that both wounds were caused by the same weapon, he'll stand up in the box and say so."

"Always supposing he's asked."

Mavor thought about this. He said, "You mean, leave the second body out of it altogether?"

"It's no part of our case. We haven't been asked to investigate it. Why should we bring it in?"

"Logically you're right. But I don't like it. It's a loose end. You leave a loose end lying, someone's bound to trip over it."

"Is there any reason," said Shilling, "why it shouldn't fit into our case quite neatly? We know that Lewson left the Crown at about a quarter past eleven and probably went along the towpath. He probably meant to turn up Lower Church Lane. That would be the logical way to get to Mariner's house. But suppose he missed the turning. It was a dark night and he was fairly full of whisky. That would bring him to the boathouse at the exact moment when the murder was taking place. Limbery has killed Katie and has the weapon still in his hand when Lewson lurches onto the scene. Curtains for Lewson."

"I think that's almost certainly what did happen," said Knott. "In fact, if we have to bring Lewson into the story at all, that would be my explanation. But I still think it would be better to keep him out of it."

Mavor swung his head slowly, looking at each of the men around the table in turn, as though they were a jury and he was estimating their response to some proposition which he had put forward. His eyes came to rest on McCourt. Here he seemed to sense an element of resistance.

"You've been very quiet, Sergeant," he said. "Let's have your ideas. Don't be bashful. Imagine that you're counsel for the defense. If there *is* another theory which fits the facts, much better have it out now and push it around."

McCourt shot a quick look at Knott, who remained unresponsive. Then he said, "It was that car, sir. The one that was parked at the end of River Park Avenue. The wheelbase corresponds exactly with Mr. Mariner's Humber Diplomat."

"How do you know that?" said Knott. "You been round measuring it?"

"No, sir. I got the specifications from the factory."

"And that's all?"

"Not quite."

"Let him have his head," said Mavor, who had been studying McCourt.

"It seems that Lewson was planning to call on Mr. Mariner with those photographs."

"A fair assumption."

"Well, I don't think our Mr. Mariner is a nice sort of man at all. For instance, he's made a sort of spyhole in his office at the Boat Club so that he can watch what goes on. It looks straight down onto that pile of punt cushions under the window. Even at night, if there was a bit of moon, he'd be able to see clear enough."

"You mean he's a voyeur," said Mavor. "It's very likely.

It fits in with the dirty pictures. But it doesn't mean he killed Katie."

"No, sir. Not by itself. But I think he did."

There was a short silence. Out of the corner of his eye McCourt could see Sergeant Esdaile gaping at him and Shilling with the beginnings of a smile on his face.

Knott said, "How? And why?" He said it with no more apparent feeling than if he had been opening a debate on some theoretical subject.

"He could have got there in time. In fact he's almost the only person at the dance who could have done so. He was first away, just as soon as he saw that Katie had taken the bait. It would be a matter of minutes to drive back to his house. The business of the telephone message maybe held him up for a few minutes, but no longer."

"Wouldn't his wife hear him driving off?" said Mavor.

"She's very deaf, sir. And she takes sleeping pills. You'll find Miss Tress mentioned it in her statement. They're quite strong. You can only get them on a doctor's certificate."

"I suppose you checked this, too?" said Knott.

"Aye. I'd a word with Dr. Farmiloe."

"Go on," said Mavor. "Mariner drives down to the river, parks his car, walks along and smashes in Katie's head. Now why would he do a thing like that?"

"It's a bit difficult to be sure about that, sir, without knowing exactly what the relationship between them was."

Knott grunted and said, "If there was a relationship."

"Oh, I think there was," said McCourt. He seemed to be gaining confidence as he went along. "If you remember what Windle said—it's in his statement there."

"Don't read it," said Mavor. "Play it to us. It's always clearer that way."

It took a minute to fit the tape into the machine and

212

locate the place. Then Tony Windle's voice came out, startlingly lifelike: " 'The most you'll ever end up as is something in insurance. That's no good to a girl like me. What I need is people with influence. People who can help me out when I get into trouble. I've got friends like that up in London. And I've got at least one *very* useful friend down here.' I asked her who it was and she wouldn't tell me."

McCourt clicked off the machine. Mavor said, "Fill me in, please. That was Tony Windle, the local boyfriend, talking? And he was reporting something Katie had said to him?"

"That's right, sir."

"Play the last bit again."

Tony's voice said, " 'And I've got at least one *very* useful friend down here.' I asked her who it was and she wouldn't tell me."

Mavor said, "And you think this *very* useful friend was George Mariner?"

"I know he was useful to her once."

"Oh? Tell us about that."

"It was the time when a boy was knocked down by a hit-and-run motorist last March. A small red car. I'd been told to look into it. I'd eliminated a number of other possibilities and I'd concluded there was enough evidence to question Katie. I told Inspector Ray."

"Ray?"

"He was in charge of C.I.D. here," said Dandridge. "He died last week. Stomach cancer."

"And Ray told you to lay off?"

"That's right."

"And you think Mariner had been leaning on him?"

"I think so, sir."

"It's only supposition."

Unexpectedly, Sergeant Esdaile said, "The Inspector

and Mr. Mariner were very close. If anyone could influence him, it would be Mr. Mariner."

"Suppose you're right. It puts Katie in Mariner's debt. What was the payoff? Did she give him a turn or two on the punt cushions?"

"That might have been the way it started. But I don't think it stayed like that. Katie was a girl who didn't like anyone to have a hold over her. She preferred— Well, sir, it's all in Mark Holbeck's statement."

"Then I'd better reread it," said Mavor. During the three minutes that it took him to do so there was silence in the room, broken only by Sergeant Esdaile's heavy breathing and an occasional creaking as Dandridge shifted uncomfortably in his chair.

"What Holbeck's statement tells us," said Mavor, "is that Katie was a girl who liked to have the whip hand."

"That's right, sir."

"And how did she get the whip hand over Mariner?"

"I think that's in Holbeck's statement, too, sir. You remember he said that Ruoff was angry because Katie had stolen something on one of her visits to him. Suppose what she stole was evidence that Mariner was one of his customers. His name in an address book, an account, something like that. It didn't mean that Mariner was doing anything criminal—"

"He started as Mr. Mariner," said Knott. "I think I prefer it that way."

"I'm sorry, sir." McCourt's face was as scarlet as if it had been slapped. "It didn't mean that Mr. Mariner was doing anything criminal. But if the story had got out—"

"Chairman of the Bench," said Mavor, "churchwarden, big white chief. You've made your point, Sergeant. Do you think she was blackmailing him?"

"Not for money. She had plenty of her own. I think what she had was a sort of power complex. She liked to have people on the end of a string and give it a tweak from time to time."

"And you think she tweaked Mariner once too often? So he typed out this come-hither note, laid for her and killed her?"

"I thought he might have done."

"It's a theory. Like the case we've been working on so far. They're both theories. That's right, isn't it?"

Not knowing what was coming, and not caring to risk another rebuff, McCourt contented himself with nodding.

"So what we have to do is to compare them. Like the washing powders on television. Give them a practical test on Junior's soccer shorts and see which of them washes whitest."

In the next few minutes McCourt realized one fact clearly. It was not his impressive appearance alone which had elevated Mavor to the position of Senior Treasury Counsel.

"So far as motive goes, you'd agree that the motive you put forward for Mariner will work equally well with Limbery? If Katie had proof of some homosexual activity —there are hints of this in a number of the statements— then it would give her the same sort of hold over him. And since he was the more violent character of the two, he was more likely to have reacted by killing her. All right? So far as motive goes, we'll call it fifteen–all. Now let's think about opportunity. Your timetable is feasible, but it's damned tight. Dr. Farmiloe, who doesn't make mistakes about things like that, gave the *likely* limits as eleven ten to eleven forty. When he says that, he's really putting his money on sometime halfway between. Say eleven twenty-five or eleven thirty at the latest. It was *after* eleven when Mariner left the dancehall. He had to get his car out, get his wife on board, drive home, get her out again and install her in her bedroom. Then cope with the maid and the

215

telephone call. Then, I imagine, take a peep at his wife to see she really was asleep. Then get the car out, drive it by the back way, I imagine, to River Park Avenue and park it. Then walk two or three hundred yards to the boathouse. If I'd been asked, I wouldn't have put him there before twenty to twelve."

"If he didn't go there to kill Katie," said McCourt, "why did he go?"

"That's obvious," said Knott. "He saw her slipping off, guessed she was going to meet Limbery and decided to treat himself to an eyeful. Bang in character."

Mavor nodded. "So he arrives sometime after half past eleven. By which time Limbery could have killed Katie *and* Lewson and got clear. Mariner waits at his spyhole for twenty minutes or so. No luck. Nothing for peeping Tom this time. He pussyfoots back to his car, arriving there a few minutes past twelve, and drives off, being heard by Miss Tress, whose extrasensory perception tells her that a dirty old man is passing her bedroom window, and is noticed driving back *without lights* by the vicar and his wife. All right so far, Sergeant?"

McCourt said, "Aye, it'll work that way, too."

"Thirty–all so far? Right. Now I'll give you three reasons why your theory of Mariner as murderer doesn't work at all. First, because the murderer, as we suppose, visited Katie's house later that night and broke open her desk to find the note which he hadn't found when he ransacked her bag. Or what he thought was her bag. Why should Mariner have bothered? The note didn't incriminate him. It pointed away from him. It pointed to Limbery."

"The breaking in could be unconnected with the killing. There'd been an attempted burglary once before."

"Ingenious, but unconvincing. Take the next point. The latest reasonable time for the killings was half past eleven. Here's Mariner with two corpses on his hands. So

216

tell me this. Why did he hang around for half an hour?"

"Searching Katie's bag."

"Twenty seconds."

"Hiding the weapon."

"If he didn't throw it into the river higher up, he'd take it home with him."

"Perhaps Dr. Farmiloe was wrong about the time."

"It's not a supposition I'd bank on myself. But let me show you the third hole in your case. To my mind it disposes of it. Haven't you forgotten that telephone call?"

McCourt started to say something and then stopped.

"Work it out, Sergeant."

"You mean the call Lewson made to Mariner's house? The one that Polly took?"

"And told him about. He may or may not have known who Lewson or Lewisham was, but he knew this much. *Someone had telephoned him asking for him by name and proposed to call on him later that evening.* If he was proposing to go out and treat himself to an eyeful of what was going on in the boathouse he wouldn't necessarily have put it off. Suppose the man does turn up. His wife's in bed, deaf and drugged. There's no one else in the house, which is an isolated one. He can ring the bell and thump the knocker as much as he likes. In fact, if he does know who Lewson is, all the more reason for being out when he calls. He knows Lewson can't hang around too long. He'll be planning to take the last train back to town. Another reason, incidentally, for not coming back until after twelve. *But now try it the other way round.* Imagine he's going out to commit a carefully planned murder. Knowing that a man is going to come to his house and will stand up afterwards in court and say, 'Wherever else Mariner was at half past eleven he wasn't at home. I thumped on the knocker for five minutes. I could hear the dog barking. If he'd been there he must have heard me.' "

"You started at fifteen–all," said Knott with a grin. "I think we've reached game, set and match. Retire gracefully, Sergeant."

McCourt was saved from answering by the telephone. It was the outside line on Shilling's table. He listened with a look of mild surprise on his friendly face.

"It's for you, Ian," he said. "Walter Steelstock on the line. He wants a word with you. He says it's urgent."

"Me, personally?"

"You, by name."

Knott said, "If it's urgent, you'd better jump on your fiery steed and gallop round there."

After he had gone, there was a moment of silence, broken by Mavor, who said, "He's a bright lad. There were one or two very good points in that theory of his. Got a logical mind. Only wants a bit more experience."

"He told me," said Esdaile, "that he was planning to be a lawyer. It didn't work out. His father died."

"Wouldn't there be more scope for him up in the Met?"

"He tried it," said Shilling. "It went sour on him. He got dipped head first into the cesspit of Soho and it didn't mix well with a simple Scottish upbringing."

Knott said, "As if this case wasn't complicated enough, without detective sergeants thinking for themselves." He said this with ferocious good humor. "Don't you start getting ideas of your own, Eddie."

"Me?" said Esdaile. "I just do what I'm told. I spend most of my time looking for typewriters."

"The machine that note was written on," said Mavor thoughtfully. "If you could find that, it really would be a clincher."

When McCourt reached West Hannington Manor, Walter had the front door open for him. He said, "Come in

218

quietly, if you don't mind. Mother's in the drawing room. We didn't want to disturb her."

He led the way up the broad thick-carpeted staircase and along a passage to a door on the left, at the end. It was a bedroom which had been converted into a mixture of study and workshop, a boy's room full of books, papers, trophies, toolkits, records, posters and photographs.

"I've got the Sergeant for you," said Walter and backed out, closing the door quietly but firmly behind him.

Peter, who had got up as they came in, indicated the only chair and said, "Won't you sit down." He sounded as breathless as if he had just finished a hundred-yard sprint.

McCourt said, "Thank you," and seated himself with deliberate slowness. His hand on the side farthest from Peter slid in his coat pocket and switched on the recorder. "I gather you've something you wanted to tell me."

"I heard," said Peter, "that is, Walter told me— Is it true that no one knows where Johnno—where Limbery—was that night?" He was speaking in a high, unnatural voice.

"If it's the Friday night of the killing you mean, we have had an account from Limbery of his movements."

"But he can't *prove* where he was?"

"His story is unsupported at the moment."

"Well, I can tell you where he was. And I can prove it. He was with me."

McCourt said in his most unemphatic voice, "Aye. Well, perhaps you'd like to tell me about that. Before we start, why don't you sit down. I'll have to ask you a few questions. It'll maybe take a little time."

Peter squatted on the end of the bed. The action of sitting down seemed in some sense to relax him. He said, "It was about ten o'clock—a bit later. Mother and Walter had gone out to this dance and Mrs. Basset always has Friday evenings off, so I was alone downstairs when the telephone rang. It was Johnno—Mr. Limbery."

"Let's call him Johnno," said McCourt.

"He told me he'd been sent out to do a story on a fire. He was going straightaway. Would I like to come with him for the ride? I said yes, I would. There's a door in the wall at the bottom of our garden. It leads out into Brickfield Road. We keep it locked, of course, but I knew where the key was. And I left the scullery window unlatched. I'd often got in and out that way before." He smiled, in a way that made his sullen face suddenly attractive. "I guessed we might be late getting back, you see, and I wanted to be able to slip in without disturbing the others."

McCourt nearly said, Would your mother have minded you going out like that? but he had the sense not to interrupt. Peter was talking more easily now, but there was explosive material not far below the surface.

"When we got to Streatley we could see the fire. It was the other side of the river, just outside Goring, blazing away like anything. We drove up as close as we could and parked the car and Johnno got out and talked to one of the firemen. They were doing what they could, but until the other brigades arrived they couldn't do all that much."

"That would be the local brigade?"

"I should think so. I don't know exactly what was happening, because I stayed in the car. Johnno made a few inquiries and we pushed off."

"You realize, don't you," said McCourt, "that if your story's going to be a help to Johnno, we have to be a wee bit careful about times. For instance, you said Johnno rang you about ten o'clock, or a bit later. How much later?"

"Not more than a minute or so. The ten o'clock news had just started. I turned it off when the telephone rang."

"Then he drove straight round? So you'd have been on your way by ten past ten and that would get you to Goring —when? By half past, assuming you went straight there."

"That would be about right, I think. I couldn't swear to the exact time."

"As a policeman, I'm always suspicious of people who swear to exact times. About how long were you at the fire?"

"Well . . ." said Peter.

He's tightening up, thought McCourt. To help him, he said, "I imagine you must have been away before the roof fell in, or Johnno would have put it in his report?"

"Yes, we were away before that happened. I shouldn't think we were there much more than half an hour."

"That brings us to eleven o'clock. What next?"

"Then we drove back to Streatley Common and parked there for a bit. Johnno was writing up his notes. He'd brought his battery-powered record player with him. He usually carried it round in the back of the car. The kids liked playing it."

"So you had a pop concert and he wrote his article for the paper?"

"That's right," said Peter. Easier now.

"And this lasted how long?"

Tension again. "I think it must have been an hour. Perhaps a bit more."

"Well, that takes us to around a quarter past twelve. What happened then?"

"Then we drove back to a telephone box. It was quite funny actually, because soon after he'd started a woman came out of one of the houses and she wanted to use the phone and she got absolutely furious and started hammering on the glass and Johnno took no notice at all."

"You'd be able to identify the house this woman came out of?"

"Yes. I think I could. I think it was the one opposite the telephone box, on the other side of the road."

"Did she see you?"

Peter thought about this one. He said, "I'm not sure. I

was sitting quietly in the car. I think perhaps she didn't see me. She was concentrating on getting angry with Johnno."

"What then?"

"Then we put on a few more records and talked for a bit and drove home."

"How long was the second session?"

"I can't remember exactly. I was pretty sleepy by then."

"It's important, so let's see if we can work it out. We know Johnno got home at a quarter to two. He'd have dropped you a few minutes before. Right? That would get you home sometime after half past one. I suppose everyone was in bed."

"There was a light on in Mother's room. I wondered why. Of course, I didn't know—"

"Of course not. Let's say twenty minutes for the drive back. That means you'd have left Streatley at one fifteen, near enough. How long was Johnno on the telephone?"

The question seemed to jerk Peter back from some secret place into which his thoughts had wandered. He said, "How long? Well . . . I don't know. I don't think it can have been much more than ten minutes. I expect it seemed much longer to the lady."

"I expect it did. That would mean that your second session was a bit shorter than the first one. Half past twelve to a quarter past one. Say, three quarters of an hour."

"Yes, I should think that would be about it."

McCourt was planning his strategy carefully. He said, "You're fond of Johnno, aren't you, Peter?"

"Yes, I am." A touch of defiance.

"And I guess he's fond of you."

"You'd know soon enough if Johnno *wasn't* fond of you."

"Not a man to hide his feelings, I agree," said McCourt with a smile. "I suppose you first got to know him when he taught at Coverdales."

"He didn't teach the form I was in. But he ran a sort of

unofficial music club. A pop group, really. I was a member of that. The boys all liked him. He didn't get along too well with some of the masters, though."

"And then you saw more of him, of course, when you were at home."

"He came round here a good deal."

"To see Katie."

"To see both of us, I guess. Mother froze him out after a bit. She didn't approve of him at all."

"Different generations, different points of view," said McCourt easily. He was coming to the point now and he had to tread with care. There was a question that must be asked. He knew it and he fancied Peter knew it too. Chief Superintendent Knott would have had no doubts and no hesitation. He would have banged the boy over the head with it and gone on banging until he had got the answer he wanted. Looking at Peter's flushed but obstinate face, he thought that a slow approach might be more productive than brutality.

He said, "I'll tell you frankly what's worrying me, Peter. You're a great friend of Johnno's. In fact you're one of his fan club. Like all the boys round here, as far as I can make out. Everyone will know that. If you come forward now with this story, people are going to ask two obvious questions. First, if your account is correct, why is it totally different from Johnno's own account?"

Peter said, "Is it?" It was either good acting or his astonishment was genuine.

"It certainly is. You won't expect me to go into details, but really your account doesn't tie up anywhere at all with his. But the second question is even more important. *Why haven't you said something before?* You know—everyone's known—for the last ten days what Johnno's accused of doing and when he was supposed to have done it. Why didn't you come forward at once? Why didn't you say, 'He couldn't have done it. He was with me the whole time'?"

Peter said nothing.

"Don't you see, it makes what you're doing now look like a last-minute effort to save Johnno's skin."

Peter still said nothing. He seemed to be enmeshed in his own thoughts.

With genuine compassion in his voice, McCourt said, "I expect I oughtn't to be saying this, but I will. If you want to go back on what you've told me, now's the time to do it. Before you get involved to a point where you *can't* go back."

Peter seemed to be nerving himself. McCourt waited patiently as the seconds ticked by in silence. Then Peter said, "Unless I can answer both those questions, you're not going to believe what I've told you. No one's going to believe it. Is that right?"

McCourt said, "Aye. That's about the strength of it."

"The answer to both questions is the same. Johnno wouldn't tell you and I couldn't. Because of what went on in the car."

For a long moment McCourt didn't seem to understand him. Then he said, in a voice suddenly hard, "Be careful what you say now."

"You wanted the truth. I'm going to give it to you. I've always been in love with Johnno and I think he's always been in love with me."

"Love?" said McCourt. The single syllable spat out like a small explosion.

"Yes, love. Why shouldn't he love me? What's wrong with it?"

McCourt said nothing.

"People thought he came round to our house to see Katie. It wasn't true. He came to see me. I don't think I realized how far it had gone. I mean, he hadn't actually done anything to me before. Being together there in the car that night, it just happened. He put one arm round me and started to kiss me. I kissed him back."

"Was that all?"

"No, it wasn't all."

"Did he undress you?"

"Yes."

"And you let him do that?"

"I didn't let him do it. I helped him." The defiance was back in Peter's voice.

"I don't think we need the details right now," said McCourt. He put a hand into his jacket pocket and switched off the tape recorder. Then he got up and said, "You called it love. I call it filth."

He walked across to the door and went out, leaving Peter sitting on the end of the bed with fat tears rolling down his cheeks.

"Well," said Mavor, "and what do you make of that?"

Shilling had departed for London and the Superintendent was alone with Mavor. McCourt's tape recorder stood on the table between them.

"I'd been expecting something of the sort," said Knott. "When a case stirs up a lot of local feeling, you're always liable to get it. Someone comes forward with a last-minute alibi."

"Then you don't believe the boy's story?"

"Not a word of it."

"You realize it can't have been a last-minute effort. They must have concocted it together, before you pulled Limbery in. Otherwise Peter couldn't have known about the episode at the telephone box."

"At first sight that was a convincing touch," agreed Knott. "But it doesn't necessarily mean they concocted the story together. I think what happened was that Limbery told Peter about the woman wanting to use the telephone box and dancing with rage and banging on the glass. Told it to him as a good story, maybe they had a private laugh over it. When Peter had to invent his version he fitted in that bit. Limbery couldn't use it himself. He needed a story which kept him at the fire much longer. Well past the time of the murder. And he stretched it a bit further with that snack at the motel—where no one seems to have remembered him, incidentally."

"Friday night crowd. Quite possible."

"Perfectly possible. And if he hadn't come back, by bad luck, across the wrong bridge we might never have been able to shoot his story down at all."

Mavor thought about it. He said, "There was one point in Peter's version that I found almost totally incredible. Did you notice? *He said that he didn't get out of the car when they arrived at the fire.* Can you believe it? Sparks flying, timbers falling, men rushing about. Damn it all, he'd come out to see the fire. Can you imagine any boy staying shut up in the car?"

"Exactly," said Knott. "You find me a single independent witness who saw the boy at the fire, or anywhere else that night, and I might pay some attention to it."

"We shall have to give it to the defense," said Mavor.

"Even if we're not going to use it?"

"Unless you want to go into the Court of Criminal Appeal and come out on your ear. It's an alibi defense. Normally it comes the other way round. This time we've got it first. Certainly it goes to them. And if you feel inclined for a bet, I'll give you two to one in pounds that they don't use it."

Knott considered this generous offer, but said, "No. I've a feeling you're right. It's a messy enough case as it is. They won't risk messing it up further."

Inspector Dandridge at that moment was saying the same thing, in different words, to McCourt. "It's a nasty

226

case," he said. "You don't want to make it any nastier by being too clever. Our job's to put one side of it. The prosecution side. We play that straight down the middle. Sure there are alternative solutions and little bits that don't fit. That's a job for the defense. They'll produce them quick enough, don't you worry."

McCourt, who had been unusually silent since his return from the Manor, said he would bear this advice in mind.

It was past nine when Sergeant Shilling reached London, and the dusk of a late August day was clouding over with a threat of more rain. As he parked his car a flurry of drops blew along the street. He turned up the collar of his raincoat and trudged back along the pavement to Ruoff's front door. A hammering with the bull's-head knocker produced no answer.

In the silence which followed, he thought he heard a very faint sound inside the house. It was an indeterminate noise which might have been made by feet going up or down stairs.

He hammered once again on the knocker. This time the silence was complete. He tried the door handle. The door swung open.

Shilling was conscious of a prickle of apprehension, a capillary reaction to a situation which was abnormal and might be dangerous. Normal householders do not leave their front doors on the latch after dark. Nor do they retreat upstairs when a visitor announces himself. The street was a quiet one, one of London's backwaters, with a privacy and a seclusion that must have suited Ruoff's dubious trade.

No point in hanging about, said Shilling to himself. He went in, but left the front door ajar, giving himself enough light to see the foot of the stairs and the photograph of the giant hand pointing upward.

227

"Excelsior," said Shilling. He climbed the stairs and paused on the first landing to listen again. In the silence he heard a single very faint creak, as though someone had shifted his weight from one foot to the other, trying to make no noise as he did so. The fact that it was so cautious encouraged Shilling. The man who was ahead of him had as little right in the house as he had. Less, possibly. Shilling climbed the next flight. He was now on the bedroom floor. The door on his left was wide open. Shilling looked in.

This was the master bedroom. The blinds were drawn, but enough light from the streetlamp outside filtered in around the edges for him to see the outlines of the room: the row of white painted cupboards along one wall, the big double bed, a table by the bed and an ornate brass lamp on it.

He saw something else, too. A bundle lying on the bed, a shapeless inanimate bundle. Sergeant Shilling knew what it was and cursed under his breath. Then he stepped up to the bed, felt for the switch and turned on the light.

The man was dressed in vivid orange and green pajamas. His hands had been tied, his wrists lashed together with a dressing-gown cord and pulled up into the middle of his back. His ankles had been hobbled with a second cord which was attached to the rail at the foot of the bed. He was lying half on his side, with his face turned away.

Shilling walked around to the other side of the bed. He had known the truth before he saw the engorged face and staring dead eyes. Whatever secrets Rodney Ruoff had possessed, they were not going to learn them from him now.

A noise made him look up.

Three men had come into the room.

TWENTY-ONE

Shilling knew one of them, a man with close-cropped gray hair and a red face, who said, "Good God, Bob, what the hell are you doing here?"

"I came to ask him some questions," said Shilling, looking down at what lay on the bed.

"Too late now," said the gray-haired man, who was Detective Chief Superintendent Forster. "I suppose it was something to do with what's happening down in Berkshire. It was Charlie Knott who put us onto watching this place."

"What happened to *him?*"

"No mystery about that. One of his boyfriends did it. Kid called Billy. Real age eighteen, mental age eight. Like I said, we had the place under observation. Sergeant Lillee here saw the kid leaving late last night."

"Early this morning," said Sergeant Lillee.

"We knew all about Rod's little games, so there was nothing unusual about it. However, when there was no sign of life, no one going in or out all day, blinds still drawn, we began to wonder what was going on and we went in to look. The Sergeant found him about half an hour before you arrived. He left young Parrish in charge and came for me."

"So it was you pussyfooting about on the stairs, was it?" said Shilling.

"That's right," said Parrish. "Tell you the truth, I thought at first it was Billy, come back to have a look. Mind you," he added hastily, "it was pretty dark."

"What are you going to do now?"

"We're pulling in Billy. No difficulty there. He'll tell us all about it. We shan't even have to ask him."

"You can't help feeling sorry for the stupid bastard," said Shilling. He looked at the bundle on the bed. "I suppose this is an occupational risk with an old poof."

"That's right," said Forster. "He lets the boyfriend tie him up. Master and slave scene. Then the boyfriend gets a bit too excited and finishes him off. It's happening all the time."

"It couldn't have happened at a worse time. I badly needed to ask some questions and he was the only one who could give me the answers."

"There *is* a tie-up with Charlie's business, then?"

"There could be," said Shilling. "But God knows whether we shall ever find out now what it was."

"I'll tell you something," said Sergeant Lillee. "You weren't the only people who were interested in this outfit."

Shilling and Forster stared at him.

He said, "When I was watching the place on Friday night—I was using a room opposite—I saw a man hanging about. I thought I recognized him, so I said to myself, I'll go down and take a closer look. Might have a word with him."

"For God's sake," said Forster. "This isn't a six-part serial. *Who was he?*"

"Chap called Blaine. Works for Captain Smedley's outfit. Used to be in X Division."

"Captain Smedley?" said Shilling.

"Private inquiry agency," said Forster. "Only uses ex-policemen. Very hot stuff."

"Bloody hell," said Shilling.

"It's not going to please Charlie, is it?"

"That's the understatement of the year," said Shilling. "This is going to be apple pie for the defense. Their tactics are obviously going to be to muddy the water, and here's a dirty great stick to do the muddying with. What we must do now, no way out, is find out what the tie-up really was. We can't ask Rod, but there is another possibility. We go through his papers."

Forster thought about it.

He said, "I don't see why not. As long as we do it together. The technical whiz kids will be here any moment now. They'll want to take over this room, and the pathologist will want the body. You and I could start working on his papers."

"There's a sort of office upstairs in the studio," said Parrish. "Lot of books and papers there. Photographs, too."

"Then let's get started," said Forster. "Take us all night, I wouldn't wonder."

"I *had* got other plans for tonight," said Shilling. "I'll have to do some telephoning. She'll be bloody furious."

"Tell her you're saving it up for next time," said Forster.

The second telephone call which Shilling made was at seven o'clock the next morning. It caught Knott as he was shaving. He washed the soap off his face and sat on the edge of the bed swinging his stubby legs and listening to what Shilling had to say.

"Tell me again about those names," he said.

Shilling told him, reading them off a list he had in one hand.

"He seems to have been in touch with half the celebrities in London. Not all stage and screen people, either."

"He was a well-known photographer," said Shilling. "They meet all sorts."

"And the only names which connect up in any way with

231

this business are Katie herself and George Mariner. We already knew he was a customer."

"And Venetia Loftus, as was."

"Yes," said Knott thoughtfully. "And Venetia Loftus. Who is she now?"

"Venetia Arkinshaw. Married to an artist. Lives in Putney."

"Yes," said Knott. He was in no hurry about that one. He was turning over the possible ramifications of involving, even indirectly, the daughter of the Assistant Commissioner in a case which was, God knows, messy and complex enough already.

He said, "She was a particular friend of Katie's, wasn't she?"

"They were at school together. And kept up afterwards."

"And Katie was lunching with her on the day she was killed."

"That's correct," said Shilling, and added, to himself, Not my decision, thank God.

"All right," said Knott at last. "Go and have a word with her. I needn't tell you to go carefully. Don't lean on the fact that Venetia was one of Ruoff's clients. There could be dozens of innocent reasons for that. Keep it general. Anything she can tell us that might help."

"Right."

"And one other thing. *Tell her father what you're planning to do.* If he objects, don't do it."

The door of the house in Putney was opened by a young man wearing a beard and a smock.

He said, "I gather you've come to grill Venny. Her old man's been on the telephone to her for hours. Has she done something frightful?"

"She hasn't done anything at all," said Shilling with elaborate cheerfulness. "It's just that we think she may, indirectly, be able to help us with some information that she may have picked up at second hand."

"When you wrap it up like that," said the young man, who was Philip Arkinshaw, "it sounds absolutely terrible. However, I gather her father's told her she's got to spill whatever beans there are. Come on up."

He led the way to the first-floor drawing room and left Shilling with Venetia, a pleasant-looking person, of Katie's age and type, but with more than a hint of the maturity that marriage and housekeeping seem to bring.

She said, "Dad's been on the phone. I gather you want to know about Rodney Ruoff."

"Anything you can tell me."

"Is it right he's been killed?"

"Yes."

"Who did it? One of his boyfriends?"

"The local police seem to think so."

"He had it coming to him. He really was a sod."

"In the original sense of the word," said Shilling with a smile.

"That's right. In the original sense of the word. He's no loss to anyone. How does he fit into your business? What was his connection with Katie's death?"

"That's where we hoped you could help us, Mrs. Arkinshaw."

"Well, I'll do what I can. It was—let me think—three or four years ago. I can't remember the exact date. It was when Rodney was starting to promote Katie. Show her photographs around and talk to people who could be useful. And in case you're thinking anything else, Sergeant, so far as Katie was concerned, that was all it was. He hadn't got any other ideas about her. To start with, he hadn't much use for girls as girls. Only as models."

"Strictly for show and not for use."

"Right. And it *was* a sort of safety factor when you went to one of his parties."

"Wild parties, I imagine."

"Orgies, Sergeant. No other word for it. Fun though, in a creepy sort of way. You met all sorts. Upper crust and lower crust. You were always encouraged to bring guests. As long as they were young and beautiful. Going to them was the thing to have done among the young of our set at that time. It was a sort of dare, if you understand me."

She spoke of it, thought Shilling, as though it was thirty years ago, not three.

"Katie and I reckoned that if we brought our own drink with us and kept together we'd get away more or less intact."

"Your own drink?"

"That was the important thing. If Rod had his eye on anyone he used to fix their drink. God knows what he put into it. Some sort of drug, I imagine. So what we used to do was take a medicine bottle full of something fairly harmless in our evening bags—outsize evening bags being rather the fashion at that time. Then, if the drink looked suspicious, we'd tip it quietly into a vase and refill from our own supply."

"You could do that?"

"When Rod's parties got under way you could do anything. Even if someone had noticed you, they wouldn't have batted an eyelid."

"And what was Ruoff's idea?"

When Venetia hesitated, Shilling said with his most candid smile, "It's all right, Mrs. Arkinshaw. I'm older than I look. And I did spend a year at West End Central."

Venetia said, "You sound like an S.S. boy saying, 'I did my year at Buchenwald.'"

"It wasn't quite as bad as that. But we did have to deal with some fairly incredible perversions."

234

"This wasn't incredible. You might call it commercial. He'd get some boy or girl hooched up to the eyebrows and take them off into one of the bedrooms. Maybe a boy on his own, or two boys, or two girls. He'd get them to take off their clothes and pose for him."

"The commercial angle being?"

"Certainly not blackmail. I don't think that was ever the idea. What he wanted was photographs he could sell to the porn merchants here and abroad. A lot of the really way-out pictures went to Denmark and Sweden. Another thing, if the person concerned *was* at all well known—I don't mean a celebrity, but someone who might have friends who'd kick up a fuss—he usually managed the picture so that the face was unrecognizable. He was a good enough photographer to do that. He couldn't always manage it. It was when he slipped up on that, once, that he got into trouble, I believe."

"That's right," said Shilling. "And got off with a fine. Which no doubt the sale of the photographs paid for ten times over."

While he was saying this, he was thinking that a lot of what he was hearing he knew before. Some of it was new. But none of it really took them much further. Venetia was offering information readily enough. But his instinct told him that she was keeping something back. There was one locked room in the house. One secret cupboard that hadn't been opened. And the tantalizing thought was that if he could see into it he would see the whole truth.

He said cautiously, "When I was talking to Katie's agent, Mark Holbeck— I expect you know him?"

"Yes. I know Mark. I thought Katie rather went for him at one time, actually."

"Not reciprocated?"

"I gather not."

"Well, Holbeck mentioned some occasion when he'd met

Ruoff at a party. This was fairly recently, I gather. When he mentioned Katie's name, Ruoff blew up. He said she'd stolen some of his property and refused to give it back. The implication was that he couldn't take any steps to get it back either. I don't suppose you'd have any idea what it was?"

"No," said Venetia slowly. "But I could guess."

"Yes?"

"It's what I was telling you. About the photographs Rod took. If the face was recognizable—particularly if it was someone . . . well . . . someone who was normally rather respectable—Rod couldn't flog it to a porno magazine. But the chances are he'd keep it. Suppose Katie was at the studio one day on business and was left alone for a moment. It would have been just like her to open drawers and cupboards and poke about to see what she could find. She was noted at school for being light-fingered where other people's property was concerned."

"Yes," said Shilling. "Yes."

The door of the secret cupboard was half open.

"If it happened to be someone she knew. Someone at Hannington, say. Someone respectable. Naturally she'd have kept it. And as like as not she'd have let the person concerned know she'd got it. Not to make money out of him. Just to feel that he was in her power and had to dance when she pulled the strings."

"Yes," said Shilling again.

"But I'm afraid that's only guesswork. I don't really think there's anything more I can tell. It was a long time ago and in retrospect rather silly, I'm afraid. I'm a sober married woman now."

A gesture indicated the nicely furnished drawing room, the photograph of the infant on the mantelpiece, the carapace of respectability.

Shilling accepted that he was being dismissed. He said,

"Thank you very much, Mrs. Arkinshaw. What you've told me could be very valuable. If you do think of anything else, telephone Hannington 343. Direct dialing. You'll be put straight through to Superintendent Knott or myself, or if we both happened to be out, Inspector Dandridge, or one of the sergeants, Esdaile or McCourt. Don't bother to show me out, please. I can find my own way."

Venetia held the door of the drawing room open and watched him make his way down the narrow but elegant stairs toward the front door.

It was as well for Sergeant Shilling's peace of mind that he was unable to see the expression on her face.

"It's plausible," said Knott. "But it needn't necessarily have been Mariner. Lot of respectable people in Hannington."

"Although we already know there *was* a connection between Mariner and the Ruoff crowd," said Mavor.

"I know, I know," said Knott. He sounded both angry and obstinate. Shilling recognized the tone of voice. He had heard it before in other cases.

"But it doesn't *prove* anything. Suppose everything we think is true. Suppose he's a dirty old man and Katie found a picture of him with his clothes off. Suppose she used it to tweak him. Suppose she even used it to get him to lean on Inspector Ray about the hit-and-run case. Suppose all of that. It still doesn't make him a murderer. He's not the murdering type. Limbery is."

"There's only one objection to that," said Knott. "I can't imagine why Mariner would agree to take his clothes off, or even more why anyone would want to take a photograph of him when he had."

"You can't tell with men of that age," said Mavor. "One of our high court judges— Well, no, I'd better not tell you about that."

There was a knock on the door and McCourt came in. His face was whiter than usual. He had a slip of paper in his hand. He said, "A message has come through from Central. They've had a report from the Forensic Science people who've been working on those prints we sent them. The ones from the door of the cupboard above Katie's desk."

"Well?" said Knott impassively.

"They're sending you a written report. I jotted down the gist of it. They've managed to bring up two prints, a thumb and an index finger, sharp enough for identification. Neither of them corresponds to Limbery's prints."

"I see. Anything more?"

"They tried them on the main computer. No record."

"Well, that's that. Thank you, Ian."

McCourt placed the paper quietly on the table and went out. Mavor had been watching him. He said, "I've got two pieces of advice for you about that young man. The first is that Dandridge ought to find him something to do. Something quite unconnected with this case, I mean. There must be plenty of routine work piling up. The second is, don't call him as a witness."

"I wasn't thinking of doing so," said Knott. "But why? Do you think he's turning sour?"

"Not sour exactly," said Mavor. "But he's got a very Scottish conscience. Abstract notions of right and wrong. It makes him an uncomfortable bedfellow in a case like this where there's a lot of wrong and not much right."

TWENTY-TWO

By the time McCourt had crossed the yard and reached the room he shared with Esdaile his face had changed from white to red. He shut the door with explosive firmness and said, "I see."

"See what?" said Esdaile.

"I see," said McCourt. "That's all he said: 'I see.' I tell him that the bottom's knocked out of his case and that's all he can say: 'I see.' "

"I wouldn't go as far as that," said Esdaile placidly. "I never thought that burglary at Katie's place had necessarily got anything to do with her killing."

"Not necessarily," said McCourt. "But it seemed pretty clear. The killer searched her bag for the note he'd sent. He couldn't find it, so he went to her house to look for it."

"Maybe," said Esdaile. "Maybe not. Don't forget, she was burgled once before."

"All right," said McCourt. "Let's suppose it was just a coincidence. I don't believe it. But suppose it was. Are we going to give the facts to the defense? Are we going to say to them that when we started we thought this fingerprint was so important we took the door right off its hinges and sent it up to the Science Laboratory and wasted their time on it for a fortnight and now it doesn't turn out to be the one we wanted, we're going to forget about it?"

"No need to get worked up," said Esdaile. "It's nothing to do with you or me."

"Of course it is. It's to do with us and everyone else in the police. If we don't play the rules, who is going to?"

Esdaile looked at him curiously. He said, "If you feel like that, you ought to resign."

"That would just be running away."

"For God's sake," said Esdaile. "What *are* you going to do?"

McCourt relaxed and grinned. "What I'd like to do is to catch the killer and hand him to Superintendent Knott on a plate, clearly labeled and garnished with watercress. And there's only one way to do that. We've *got* to find that typewriter."

"Don't talk to me about typewriters. I've started dreaming about typewriters." Esdaile opened his desk and took out a thick file. "I worked out the other day, I've asked two hundred and ten people if they've ever owned or sold or seen a Crossfield Electric. I've actually traced two dozen of them and none of them produced a sample which looked anything like that bloody note. It wasn't worth sending them up to the Documents Division. Even I could see they were no good."

McCourt seemed to be thinking of something else. He said, "When you were making these inquiries, Eddie, how did you do it?"

"How?"

"I don't mean with the shops. They'd know what you meant when you talked about a Crossfield Electric. I meant with private people. Look. Say the husband was out and you asked the wife whether her husband used to have one. She'd say, 'Oh, I know he *had* a typewriter, but I can't remember exactly what sort it was.' "

"I showed her a picture, of course."

"Have you got a picture?"

"Dozens of them." He fished out a handful of catalogues and pushed one across. McCourt examined it. It seemed to fascinate him. He stared at it for so long that Esdaile said, "What's up? The bloody thing isn't even beautiful. Now if I'd been going round with the photograph of some smashing girl—"

"Eddie," said McCourt, "I've seen a machine just like this one."

"I've seen two dozen. I told you."

McCourt ignored him. He said, "Do you remember? I told you two or three weeks ago I had to go and see the Master Mariner. It was when that joker tried to wreck his car. He kept me waiting for twenty minutes in what he calls his business room. I had plenty of time to admire the fixtures and fittings. *I'll swear he had a typewriter just like this one.*"

Esdaile said slowly, "He must have bought it up in London, then. Because if he'd bought it anywhere local I'd have been given his name by the shop that supplied it. Are you sure?"

"Absolutely sure."

"Another thing," said McCourt. "There's been a lot of publicity about this. A notice in the press and so on. If he really has got a Crossfield Electric, why hasn't he come forward to say so? If he was innocent he'd have told you about it and you'd have gone up and taken a sample of the type face and cleared it and that would have been the end of it."

The two sergeants looked at each other.

"What are you going to do about it?" said Esdaile at last.

"Think up some excuse and go up and have a look for myself. If he keeps me waiting, which he usually does, I'll slip in a piece of paper and run off a sample."

"Suppose he hears you?"

"If it's an electric typewriter it'll be pretty quiet."

"I hope so," said Esdaile. "Because if he catches you taking samples behind his back and if they turn out to be innocent samples, he really will have a stick to beat you with. He plays golf with the Chief Constable, too."

McCourt said, "If the samples match, it'll be a long time before he plays golf with anyone."

"We have quite a few points to consider," said Mrs. Bellamy, "and one or two very useful leads." Her voice had a purring quality. She's a cat, thought Noel, a big well-muscled tabby cat, sleepy-looking, but murder to any mouse that strays within reach of her claws.

"First of all, we've got Captain Smedley's reports. There's no doubt at all that the killing of Ruoff has got some connection with Katie's death. Otherwise why would Sergeant Shilling, who must have more than enough work to do down at Hannington, be snooping around Chelverton Mews?"

"The papers this morning," said Simon Crakenshaw, "all carried the same story—some sort of official handout, I suppose. That a man was assisting the police with their inquiries and a charge was expected shortly."

"No doubt," said Mrs. Bellamy. "But it still leaves my question unanswered. Here's another one. What was Lewson, one of Ruoff's bodyguards, doing down at Hannington? And how did he come to fall into the river with a hole in his head which had been made by the same weapon which killed Katie? Your pathologist was absolutely clear about that, Laura?"

Laura showed her pretty teeth in a grin and said, "Absolutely, Mrs. Bellamy. As a matter of fact he was rather annoyed about that. Apparently Knott didn't entirely trust his opinion. He sent his report up to Summerson for checking. That's the sort of thing that just isn't done among top-class pathologists."

"Knott never had an ounce of tact. What did Summerson do?"

"He sent the report back with a scribble at the bottom of it. 'I agree with every word of this report and wonder why it was necessary for me to see it.'"

"Excellent," said Mrs. Bellamy. "That gives us several different lines of attack. Next we have to think about this last-minute alibi that the prosecution has kindly presented us with."

"I'm not too clear about the rules," said Noel. "I suppose they passed it on to us because they had to."

"In theory," said Mrs. Bellamy, "the Crown has to present the defense with any relevant information. However, there's no need for them to do so before the committal proceedings. Then they must expose the whole of their case. But they'd have been severely criticized if they hadn't passed on this particular piece of information as soon as they got it. And I think they had another reason. They were fairly certain we wouldn't dare to use it."

Noel said in tones of incredulity, "But I thought—"

"You thought that the boy's story was a complete defense to Limbery, Mr. Vigors."

"Well," said Noel. *"If* it's true, surely—"

"Whether it's true or not is unimportant. In the last analysis what matters is whether the court believes it. He'd be savagely cross-examined, asked for prurient details, which he'd be ashamed or unwilling to give, contradict himself at half a dozen points and finish by bursting into tears. And at the end of it all, when he'd been publicly crucified, do you know what conclusion the court would come to? They would conclude that conduct of this sort *had* taken place, possibly more than once, but *not* necessarily on the night in question. And this presents the Crown with one enormous advantage, one ace in their hand which they didn't possess before. You might almost call it the ace of trumps. Motive, Mr. Vigors. Motive."

"I suppose so," said Noel unhappily. Although no hint of expression had appeared on their well-drilled countenances, he felt certain that Sophie and Laura were laughing at him.

Mrs. Bellamy said, in more accommodating tones, "You mustn't believe all the nonsense that's talked about motive. Every judge in a murder case tells the jury that there's no onus on the prosecution to prove motive. I sometimes wonder how he can say it without laughing. There may be no onus, at law, *but motive is the one thing the jury understands.* They don't believe that people commit murder for no reason at all. Show them a reason and you show them a guilty man. So far the only motive they've got is a piffling one. A lovers' quarrel! Six weeks before! No one in their senses is going to believe in that as a motive for murder. But give them a real motive. Let Peter tell his story and suggest that Katie had got to know about it. Hell hath no fury like a woman who's been thrown over for another woman. But a girl who's been thrown over for her own brother! A girl like Katie, who had a tongue like a whipsaw and enjoyed using it and watching people squirm. There's a background to murder that any jury could understand."

Simon said, "I see the force of that. But can we do without Peter's evidence? The court *might* believe him. And it *is* an alibi."

Mrs. Bellamy considered the point, her thick white hands resting on the table in front of her. She carried an armory of rings on both hands thick as knuckle dusters.

"It's really a balance of chances," she said. "If the Crown case was a strong one, I'd agree with you, we'd have to use the boy. But I don't think it is a strong one. The more I look at it the weaker it seems. Are you by any chance a bridge player, Mr. Crakenshaw?"

Simon, who knew that Mrs. Bellamy was a bridge player of international repute, thought it safer to say, "I play a little."

"Then you know that the secret of good defense lies in working out what cards your opponent holds. So let's see what cards the Crown has got."

She ticked them off, one point at a time, the rings on her fingers sending out flashes of blue light as she did so.

"They've got the note. That's their strong card. I imagine they hoped to spring it on us, but luckily we know all about it."

Noel nodded. It was Walter who had given him that useful piece of information.

"Forewarned is forearmed. The evidence that it came from Limbery is internal and we know that they're not too confident about it. If they had been, they wouldn't have wasted all that time looking for the typewriter. What else have they got? Opportunity. Limbery wasn't at the dance. Five hundred other inhabitants of Hannington weren't at the dance. Is that a reason for suggesting they killed Katie? His account of his movements that night is inaccurate. Suppose that it is. People aren't always meticulously accurate when talking to the police. Particularly when they haven't been charged and have no reason to suppose they are going to be. Motive? As things stand, so weak as to be unbelievable. I'm really surprised at Knott risking a charge if that's all the ammunition he's got."

Surprised, thought Noel. But pleased, too. She's looking forward to her old enemy making a fool of himself.

He said, "Do I gather from what you've said that you propose to go the whole way in the Magistrates Court?"

"And lift restrictions on reporting?" said Simon.

"We've asked for an old-fashioned committal," said Mrs. Bellamy. "No need to make our minds up on the other points until the last moment. We'll keep our options open."

McCourt had decided that a simple and adequate excuse for calling on Mariner was to take along a copy of the photograph of Gabby Lewson and ask him if he recognized it. This could reasonably be tied into an inquiry about the telephone call from the mysterious Mr. Lewisham.

Two things prevented him from carrying out this plan immediately. The first was that he suddenly seemed to have a great deal of work to do—routine matters which had been pushed to one side while the murder investigation was proceeding. It was not until late on the Wednesday evening of that week that he managed to get away and visit the Croft. Here he met the second difficulty. Polly, who answered the door, told him that Mariner was not at home.

"Gone up to London for two days," she said. "Left this morning. Coming back Friday night."

"Do you know what he's up to?"

"Search me," said Polly. "I heard him telling Mrs. Mariner something about business."

This was awkward. If he asked to be allowed to inspect Mariner's study, Polly would be bound to ask him why he wanted to and he could think of no plausible excuse for doing so. Not that Polly would have objected. He suspected that she disliked Mariner almost as much as he did.

She said, "If it's urgent, he's staying at his club. You could get hold of him there."

McCourt said, "It'll keep. I'll try again on Friday evening."

The thought of what he had to do worried Noel Vigors so much that he found it difficult to get to sleep. He was desperately sorry for Peter. He had known and liked him ever since he was a shy six-year-old wincing under his father's hearty verbal onslaughts. He suspected that what

246

had brought Peter and Limbery together was the fact that they had both been afflicted with bullying and inadequate fathers.

Peter's statement of what had happened on that Friday night when Katie was killed had had the ring of truth. Noel was more than half inclined to believe it. That, as he informed his pillow at two o'clock in the morning, was personal feeling; and it was his duty as a professional man to be impersonal and dispassionate. Intellectually he accepted the arguments put forward by Mrs. Bellamy for not calling the boy. He accepted that she was more experienced in these matters than he was. He tried not to be influenced by the fact that he disliked her.

Georgie grunted sleepily and said, "Wassup?"

"Too hot."

She said, "Take off one of the blankets," turned over and went to sleep again. He wished he could have discussed the problem with her, but that was professionally impossible. He turned onto his other side and started to count sheep going through a gate until these became clients going through the door of his office. He got a couple of hours of unrestful sleep.

Next morning when he reached the Manor, Peter, who had been warned of his visit, was waiting for him. They walked down together to the wooden shack beside the tennis court which was a repository for tennis and croquet gear and they sat on a bench in front of it.

Peter said, "I heard you'd taken on this case. I was glad about that. Johnno would have made an awful mess of it if he'd tried to do it himself. Is it true you've got a Q.C. from London?"

"Quite true. I saw her yesterday."

"Her? You mean it's a woman? Funny. I always thought of Q.C.'s as men. Do you think a woman will be able to stand up to the police?"

"I can't think of anyone Mrs. Bellamy isn't capable of standing up to."

"I expect you wanted to talk about my—about me—giving evidence."

Noel thought that there was no point in trying to break it to him gently. He said, "As I told you, we had a conference on the case yesterday. Mrs. Bellamy has decided that it would be better not to call you."

He had wondered how Peter would take it. Many people, having offered to give evidence, evidence which would involve them in public ridicule, if nothing worse, might have been relieved when their brave offer was refused. The reaction he had not looked for was anger.

The blood mounted in the boy's face, coloring his pale and freckled skin. He said, "Why, Noel? Why? Why?"

Noel said, "The police don't usually try to help the defense in a case like this. So when they told us what you'd said, we came to the conclusion that they *wanted* you to give evidence. That it would actually help their case. You'd be cross-examined viciously about exactly what had taken place between you and Limbery. They'd ask you for a lot of details. You understand? Then they'd suggest that this part of your evidence was very likely true. *But that it hadn't happened on this particular occasion.* That you'd made all that up, to help him. Do you see?"

Peter muttered something under his breath. His mouth was set in a hard line that reminded Noel of Mrs. Steelstock.

Noel said, "If they could convince the court that their version was right, it supplied a sort of motive . . ."

Noel was aware that he was getting into deep water. Fortunately for him, Peter didn't seem to be listening. He was busy with his own bitter thoughts. He said, "When I told Sergeant McCourt what had happened, I thought the police would have to drop the case. All he's done is tell everyone about it."

"Not everyone," said Noel. He was listening more to the tone of voice than to the words. He wondered if there was any age at which you could be more deeply hurt than at sixteen. "I know about it. And our counsel knows. They wouldn't—they couldn't—say a word to anyone else."

"All right. I trust you. But I don't trust the police. They'll talk about it and make jokes about it and soon it'll get out. Johnno warned me, never trust the police. Never, never, never. They'll always do you down if they can. I hate them. All of them. Particularly that smug Sergeant. I thought he'd understand. He's always been friendly. And he—he looked at me as if I was a piece of dirt he wanted to scrape off his boot."

When Noel got home to lunch, as he did on most days, Georgie said, "What's up? You look as if you'd been run over by a traction engine."

"Not a bad guess," said Noel. "I can't tell you about it now, but I will when it's all over."

"It's this bloody case, isn't it?"

"Yes."

"I wish to God, if Katie was going to get murdered, she'd had the decency to do it up in London, where she really belonged."

This made Noel laugh, which may have been what Georgie had intended.

TWENTY-THREE

"I wish Peter wouldn't spend all his time cooped up in that room of his," said Mrs. Steelstock. "He's hardly come out of it for the last two days. It can't be healthy. Couldn't you get him to take some exercise?"

"I've tried," said Walter. "He just tells me to leave him alone."

"What about a game of tennis?"

"He doesn't want to play tennis."

"What can be wrong with him? He's been like this ever since that policeman came to see him. Do you think he can have said something to upset him?"

"I think he may have done," said Walter. "The only things he's said to me have been about the police. He's very bitter."

"About all of them?"

"Yes. About Sergeant McCourt in particular."

"Odd," said Mrs. Steelstock. "He always seemed to me to be one of the nicer ones. Nicer than that horrible Superintendent from London, anyway. Whatever can he have done to him?"

"Term will soon be starting. He'll have to snap out of it then."

It was late on Friday evening when McCourt arrived at the Croft and rang the bell. Polly opened the door to him.

She said, "His Majesty is taking his bath. As soon as he emerges I will inform him of your presence. Perhaps you would care to await him in his throne room. I mean his study."

"O.K. I hope he won't be too long."

"Fifteen minutes minimum, I should guess," said Polly. "He's a careful washer."

That should be long enough, said McCourt, but this was to himself.

As soon as he was alone in the study he moved across quietly to the desk where he knew the typewriter was kept. The desk was locked. It did not look like the kind of lock that would respond to such simple methods as were available to him. Moreover, if he succeeded in opening it he was far from certain that he would be able to relock it. One thing he did notice. If there was an electric typewriter in the desk, it was no longer plugged into the wall socket.

It was a full twenty minutes before George Mariner appeared. Even before he began to speak, McCourt noticed the change in him. His face seemed to have lost some of its smooth rosiness and his eyes were deeper in his head. He looked like a man who has sustained a shock. A man who was unused to shocks and lacked the resilience to deal with them.

Mariner said, speaking hurriedly, "Sorry to keep you waiting, Sergeant. Something about this case, I suppose. Is it true that the committal proceedings are starting on Monday?"

"Unless the defense asks for an adjournment."

"That's unusually quick, isn't it?"

"It is quick," agreed McCourt. "No doubt there will be a considerable delay before the case can reach the Crown Court. If it goes forward."

"But I suppose it means that the Superintendent is very sure of his ground."

McCourt did not feel prepared to comment on this.

Mariner said, "Well, now, what can I do for you?"

"There are one or two loose ends we would like to tidy up, sir, if we can. This is one of them."

McCourt slid his hand into his pocket and laid the photograph of Gabby Lewson on top of the desk. Mariner looked down at it. His eyes flickered for a moment. He said, "It's not very pleasant, is it?"

"Well, you see, he'd been two, three days in the water. He'll have had a little cosmetic treatment, I don't doubt."

Mariner was still staring at the photograph. He said, "It's difficult to be sure, with him in that state. But I don't think— No, I'm quite sure. I've never seen him before."

McCourt repocketed the photograph. Mariner seemed glad to see it go. He said, speaking more normally, "Was there any reason to suppose I should have known him?"

"We did at one time connect him with that telephone call that came to your house on the night Katie was killed. Polly thought he called himself Lewisham. This man's name is Lewson. It would have been easy for her to make a mistake."

"Polly doesn't make mistakes. If she said Lewisham, that's what it was."

"And the name meant nothing to you?"

"Nothing at all. Might I ask why the police should attach such importance to this particular telephone call?"

"It's like this," said McCourt. "*Any* stranger who was in this neighborhood at just the time Katie was killed and is unaccounted for is bound to be a subject of inquiry. If our first idea had been right and 'Lewson' and 'Lewisham' were one and the same person, then you might say that he *was* accounted for. In the river. On the other hand, if Mr. Lewisham exists, as a separate person, we're bound to try to locate him."

McCourt wondered, as he said it, if this would sound as

252

thin to Mariner as it did to him. Apparently not. Mariner had followed the explanation carefully and now said, "Yes. I see that. But I find it difficult to help you."

"You're quite sure that the name means nothing to you? You have so many different interests. If I might make a suggestion, why not have a look in your address book? A busy man jots names down and forgets them."

"If it'll set your mind at rest, Sergeant," said Mariner. He took a bunch of keys out of his pocket and unlocked the desk. McCourt moved unobtrusively up behind him. There was a typewriter in the desk. It was a new portable machine and bore no resemblance whatever to the typewriter that McCourt had seen there three weeks before.

"Lamprey, Levett, Ligertwood, Livingstone. No Lewisham, I'm afraid, Sergeant."

"Another dead end, I'm afraid," said McCourt politely. "But thank you for trying."

"Really," said Colonel Lyon, "I don't think I've ever read such a letter. I hardly know what to do about it."

In times of doubt he was used to consulting his head warder, a reliable and experienced officer.

"Might I have a look at it, sir?"

"Certainly."

The letter had arrived at the prison that morning, addressed to Jonathan Limbery and marked "Personal and Confidential." These words were three times underlined.

"I had to open it, of course."

"Of course, sir."

"From West Hannington Manor and signed 'Peter.' That would be the dead girl's brother."

"That's right, sir."

The head warder was experiencing some difficulty with the handwriting, which had started reasonably enough but had deteriorated as passion took hold of Peter's pen.

253

"The police are playing their usual dirty tricks. Sergeant McCourt is the worst of the lot. I used to like him, but now I hate him more than all of them. When he came to see me I told him about what happened in the car that night. He spat in my face.

"Really, sir! That doesn't sound like Sergeant McCourt. A very steady officer, I'd always understood."

"There's worse to come."

"I'm sure he was the one who persuaded them not to call me as a witness, so if they do convict you and send you away, you'll know who to blame. For that and anything else that happens. I hardly know what I'm writing. Perhaps they won't even let you see this letter. Goodbye, my dearest, dearest Johnno.

"Might have been written by a girl, sir."

"It's a very curious letter altogether," said the Governor. "I don't think I can show it to him."

"Certainly not."

"Then what am I going to do with it?"

"If I were you, sir, I should tear it up and forget about it."

"I don't think I can do that," said the Governor unhappily.

The Reverend Bird looked sadly around the church. The congregation was an unusually large one for Sunday evensong, but the front row of the choir stalls on each side was empty. Although the local boys had refused to join the choir he had had a happy little group of girls, including his own daughter. Now even she had refused to perform. "I should be all by myself and look silly," she had said.

He had prepared a sermon on Church Unity, a subject which was being much canvassed by his bishop at that time. But before plunging into ecumenical argument he felt that he must say something more directly to his troubled flock. He had sensed that they were deeply divided, young against old, children against parents. He had heard of the discords in the Vigors family and of the sudden departure of Sally Nurse for London. He had caught a glimpse of Peter, white-faced and miserable, coming out of the gates of Hannington Manor and had felt an impulse to run up to him and put an arm around his shoulders, an impulse which he had been just sensible enough to resist.

The committal proceedings hung like a black cloud across all horizons.

He said, "Long before I was born and before most of you were born, a man called Wallace was tried and convicted of the murder of his wife. It was a well-known case. Criminologists still argue about whether he was guilty or not. There is still doubt. But one thing about which there is no doubt at all is that owing to the intense local feeling which the case aroused he didn't get a fair trial. He appealed against his conviction. On the Sunday before his appeal was heard the Anglican Bishop of Liverpool prescribed a prayer to be read in all the churches of his diocese. I should like to read it to you. It ran, 'You shall pray for the people that their confidence in the fair dealings of their fellow men may be restored and that truth and justice, religion and piety, may be established among us. Finally you shall pray for all who await the judgment of their fellow men and commit them to the perfect justice of Almighty God.' "

After a brief silence, during which the congregation seemed to be holding its breath, he said, "And now to my text . . ."

Walking back after the service with Mr. Beaumorris to pick up her car, which she had parked in the open space between his cottage and the Rectory, Mrs. Havelock said, "I thought Dicky Bird was better than usual tonight. All the same, I think he might have told us the end of the story. Did the man get off?"

"I rather think that he did," said Mr. Beaumorris. "And died less than two years later of a very painful disease."

"So much for the justice of God," said Mrs. Havelock.

Mr. Beaumorris was surprised to see a light in his front room, and even more surprised to find Sergeant McCourt waiting for him, with Myra in attendance.

McCourt said, without preamble, "I fear that this visit is totally irregular. But I am here to ask for your help."

"Then won't you sit down. Are you asking for Myra's help as well?"

"Yes."

Mr. Beaumorris, who made it a rule of life never to be surprised at anything, said, "Very well, then let us all sit down."

"First I ought to explain why what I am doing is irregular. I am doing it without consulting my superior officer, Inspector Dandridge. And without informing Superintendent Knott. In fact, what I am doing may turn out to be contrary to his interests."

"My dear Ian," said Mr. Beaumorris. "You don't mind me calling you Ian, I hope, particularly as we are meeting on such an irregular basis." The old man snuffled happily. "If what you are proposing to do is likely in any way to discommode or embarrass Superintendent Knott, you are assured of my unstinting help. Of Myra's, too, I am sure."

"It's kind of you to say so. Then this is what I want. It would be difficult for me to go to Mariner's house and speak to Polly. Do you think you could persuade her to come down here for half an hour? I take it there'd be no objection to her coming out with you on a Sunday evening."

"We're not slaves," said Myra. "Of course she'll come, if she wants to. What am I going to tell her?"

"Tell her," said McCourt, "that there's one piece of information which may affect the result of the case tomorrow and that she's the only person who can give it to us."

"Don't be too long," said Mr. Beaumorris, "or I shall be dead of unsatisfied curiosity before you get back." He added, "You can take my bicycle if you like." But Myra was already hurrying down the street.

When Polly arrived, McCourt said to her, "On the night Katie was killed, the night of the Tennis Club dance, I had to go round to some of the bigger houses and warn people to be careful about locking up. You remember?"

Polly nodded, her face impassive.

"I waited for Mr. Mariner in his business room. There was an electric typewriter on his desk. It's no longer there. He's got a much smaller portable machine."

"That's right. He bought it in Reading, about a week ago."

"Then what happened to the other machine?"

Polly thought about it. McCourt said, "It's a heavy brute of a thing. He couldn't have walked out with it. It might still be in the house, of course—"

Polly shook her head. She said, "It's not there. I'd have seen it if it was."

"Then if it's gone, either he took it away in his car or someone came and fetched it. Can you remember whether he's had a visitor, with a car, in the last ten days?"

Polly said, "I don't think—" And then, "Oh yes. There was one. Commander Bellairs."

The name meant nothing to any of them.

"He's not in the Navy now. In fact, he's quite old. He runs that boys' club up in London. The one that Mr. Mariner is boss of. And come to think of it, that was rather funny. Usually he's fussy about visitors. He doesn't like going to the door himself."

"So I noticed," said McCourt.

"They ring the bell and I let them in and fetch him. Even if he sees them coming, he likes to do it that way."

"Stuffy old pig," said Myra under her breath. The others ignored her. McCourt said, "So what was funny about this occasion?"

"What was funny was I didn't see him come or go. I just happened to notice his car parked outside the front door. That's how I knew it was the Commander. Mr. Mariner must have let him in and out himself."

"And when was this?"

"Sometime last week."

"Can you remember which day?"

"Thursday, I think. Yes. I'm sure it was Thursday. I was cleaning the silver when the Commander arrived and that's the day I do it."

"And it was *after* the Commander's visit that Mr. Mariner bought the new typewriter."

"That's right. He went into Reading on the Saturday morning and brought it back with him. Why is it important?"

"I'm not entirely sure yet," said McCourt. "But if what I think is true, it might be the most important thing that's happened so far."

TWENTY-FOUR

"You are charged," said the clerk "that you did on the fifteenth day of August last at West Hannington in the County of Berkshire murder Kate Louise Steelstock."

"Absolute nonsense," said Jonathan.

"The accused pleads not guilty," said Mrs. Bellamy.

"You are further charged that on the twenty-third day of August at West Hannington aforesaid you did wound Detective Sergeant Edward Esdaile with intent to commit grievous bodily harm contrary to Section Eighteen of the Offenses Against the Person Act 1861."

"Nuts to that and any other charges you can dream up," said Jonathan.

Mrs. Bellamy, who had remained on her feet, said, "The accused pleads not guilty to both charges. Might I add that we have asked for committal proceedings in the old style under Section Seven because it is our intention to demonstrate, to your satisfaction I trust, sir, that there is no case to answer on the first charge and that there was such provocation on the second charge as to render a charge under Section Eighteen untenable. We have requested that reporting restrictions should be lifted so that this may be demonstrated publicly at the earliest possible opportunity."

Mr. Appleton nodded. The reporters scribbled.

The Reading Magistrates Court was a large one, which was lucky, since it was packed to suffocation point. Intending spectators who had thought, by arriving at eight o'-clock, to be certain of getting in had found a queue already stretching down one street and around the corner into another. The constable on duty had advised them to go home. "Some people have been here all night," he said, "and a lot came down by the six o'clock train from Paddington."

The only people from West Hannington who got into the courtroom were Mrs. Havelock and Group Captain Gonville. As magistrates they had been given privilege tickets and were wedged into a narrow space between the Bench and a much enlarged press box. Mrs. Havelock had left Sim in the witness room with Roney to keep him company.

Mavor rose as Mrs. Bellamy subsided. ("Just like the

259

weatherman and his wife," whispered Mrs. Havelock. "One goes in when the other comes out.")

"It is not my intention," said Mavor, "to make an opening speech. I shall call the witnesses before you, only reserving the right to intervene from time to time in order to place their evidence into its proper context so that the charges may be better understood. Broadly speaking, they will cover three different topics. First, matters directly connected with the charges. Secondly, matters arising out of a certain note, which I will put in evidence at the appropriate time. Thirdly, matters referring to the account given by the accused of his movements on the night of August fifteenth and the early morning of August sixteenth. Sergeant Esdaile, please."

Sergeant Esdaile produced the plans he had drawn and the photographs he had taken and these were explained to Mr. Appleton, who placed them carefully on the table in front of him. Mavor then said, "I should now like to turn to the second charge. Would you please tell us, Sergeant, what happened on August twenty-third."

Sergeant Esdaile did his best, but Mrs. Havelock couldn't help thinking that he succeeded in turning what had been a fast-moving and exciting episode into something which sounded curiously dull and unconvincing.

Mrs. Bellamy said, "I understand, Sergeant, that you have fully recovered the use of your arm."

"That's right."

"And have been back on duty for the week past."

"That's right."

"Could you tell the court what you have been doing?"

Sergeant Esdaile looked surprised.

"I don't mean all of it. What have you been mainly engaged in?"

"Mainly I've been pursuing inquiries about a typewriter."

"And have your inquiries been successful?"

"No, ma'am."

"One of the places you looked would have been in the office of the accused."

"Yes."

"And you would have inquired of the friends and acquaintances of the accused whether they possessed the particular machine you were looking for. Again without success."

"That is so, ma'am."

"Did you dislike the accused?"

The sudden switch threw Sergeant Esdaile completely. He gaped at Mrs. Bellamy, who repeated the question.

"I didn't like him or dislike him. I didn't really know him very well."

"If you didn't dislike him, why was it that, on the occasion you have told us about, when you were told to bring the accused in for questioning, you called him"—Mrs. Bellamy looked down at her brief for a moment—"a long-haired communist agitator and a bastard who did nothing but stir up trouble?"

"I never did."

"Did you consider it part of your duty to use expressions of this sort?"

"I told you I never said anything like it."

"I shall be calling two witnesses who heard the words," said Mrs. Bellamy and sat down.

"Remembering that you are on oath and that you are a police officer," said Mavor, "I should like to have your assurance that you never used the expressions we have just heard."

"Certainly not," said Sergeant Esdaile. He sounded more surprised than indignant.

"Thank you. Mr. Joseph Cavey."

Mr. Cavey described his discovery of the body. He produced no surprises and was not cross-examined.

He was followed into the box by Dr. Farmiloe, who gave his evidence in the clear, unhurried manner of one who has performed the same function many times before. He referred from time to time to a sheaf of notes which he held in his hand.

"In summary, then," said Mavor, "your conclusion was that the girl had been killed by one blow, on the back of the skull, at a time which you estimate, on the grounds which you have explained to the learned Magistrate, to have been between a quarter past eleven and a quarter to twelve."

"My possible estimates were rather wider than that. But that is the most probable timing."

Mrs. Bellamy said, "Your experience, Doctor, entitles your estimates to be received with respect. But I should like to clarify one point. Your post here, and your post when you were in practice in London, is that of Police Doctor."

"I'm not sure that officially there is any such position. I am on call to the police and receive a small fee for my services. They could, of course, use any other doctor if they wished."

"Having you on the spot," said Mrs. Bellamy with a slight smile, "they would be very foolish if they did call in anyone else. But that is not my point. You are not, I think, a pathologist."

"That is correct."

"And there are a number of pathologists in the country —the leading ones, naturally, are in London—whom the Crown habitually calls on in murder cases."

"In cases involving death or severe bodily damage."

"Quite so. They are usually referred to in the press, again incorrectly, as Home Office pathologists."

Dr. Farmiloe nodded.

"If I might make their respective functions clear, sir," said Mrs. Bellamy, turning to the Magistrate, "since they are sometimes misunderstood. The main duty of the Police Doctor is to certify the fact of death. It was extremely sensible that Dr. Farmiloe also turned his attention to ascertaining the time of death, since you will understand from the explanations he has given you that the sooner this is done the more accurate the result will be. But"—Mrs. Bellamy paused for a moment and looked around the crowded room—"it is no part of his function to determine the cause of death. That is a matter for the pathologist?"

Since there seemed to be a question mark at the end of this statement, Dr. Farmiloe nodded again and said, "I think, in fact, it went to Dr. Carlyle at Southampton."

"Then I can defer questions on it until Dr. Carlyle produces his report for us."

Mavor, who had been fully aware for some time of the direction in which Mrs. Bellamy was heading, rose to his feet and said, "In view of the fact that Dr. Farmiloe, who has great experience in these matters, was able to tell us that the cause of death was a blow on the head, we saw no reason, sir, to trouble you with an additional report."

Mr. Appleton thought about this. He was a large red-faced man who, when he was not dispensing justice, looked after four hundred acres of mixed arable and sheep farm. He said, "I don't follow this. Has Dr. Carlyle made a report?"

"Yes, sir."

"And he is the Crown Pathologist for this district?"

"Yes, sir."

"Then I would like to see it."

Mavor already had it in his hand. He said, "Certainly, sir. Before putting it in, perhaps I might read you the passage which is in point. 'The cause of death was severe damage to the brain tissue from a single deep and well-marked fracture of the skull.' There are other comments, but that is the main conclusion."

He handed it to the usher, who handed it to the clerk, who passed it up to Mr. Appleton. Mrs. Bellamy, who had remained standing, said, "Might I suggest that it would be better if the learned Magistrate saw *both* Dr. Carlyle's reports."

A moment of silence.

"As far as I know," said Mavor, "he made only one report."

"If those are your instructions, then I can only say that you have not been instructed fully. I have here a copy of a report on a second death which occurred at about the same time and approximately the same place, in which Dr. Carlyle makes a most instructive addendum to his first report."

Mavor looked at Knott, who shook his head like an angry bull tormented by gadflies.

"If you have *not* been supplied with a copy," said Mrs. Bellamy sweetly, "I have several here." She extracted a number of documents, handed one to Mavor and one to the usher, who looked inquiringly at the Magistrate.

"I should like to see it," said Mr. Appleton. He felt that an attempt was being made to pull the wool over his eyes and resented it.

"The passage is at the end," said Mrs. Bellamy.

Mr. Appleton read it through and said, "I think this is most relevant. Why was it not produced?"

Mavor, who had been conferring with Knott, said, "I understand that the police view is that since there was no connection between the two deaths there was no point in troubling you with it."

"It's not a question of troubling me. My function is to arrive at my best estimate of the evidence. How can I do that when part of it is kept from me?"

"There was no intention—"

"This report says, 'On close examination of the depressed fracture in this case, I was struck by the marked similarity to the fracture in the earlier case and concluded that they had both been made by the same instrument.' "

The press box was drinking this in with the gratification of puppies presented with an unexpected meal. Mr. Appleton glanced at them and said, "Since these proceedings are being publicly reported, I should perhaps explain that this second report concerns a body, since identified as a Mr. Lewson, which was recovered from the river some miles below Whitchurch. There seems to be evidence that it entered the water at Hannington on the evening that Miss Steelstock was killed." He turned to Mavor. "Did that not seem to you to be important?"

"Having considered the matter carefully, sir, we came to the conclusion that Dr. Carlyle must have been mistaken."

"I see."

"Although," said Mrs. Bellamy, "his conclusions were supported by Dr. Summerson, who is possibly the most experienced pathologist in the country. There is a note by him to that effect, at the foot of the report."

"In spite of that," said Mavor stolidly.

"I have said this before and I will say it again," said Mr. Appleton. "It is not the job of the police to pick and choose what evidence they will give. It is their duty to present all the evidence. Have you any more questions, ma'am?"

"No more questions," said Mrs. Bellamy, subsiding gracefully.

"George Courtenay Mariner."

Mr. Mariner took the oath in a confident voice, identified himself and proceeded to describe the quarrel which had taken place in the Tennis Club bar. Mrs. Bellamy appeared to be so far uninterested in what he was saying that she spent most of the time in a whispered colloquy with

Sophie. It was clear, however, that her attention had not wandered, for when Mavor said, "Was there, to your knowledge, an earlier occasion when the accused engaged in an altercation with a Mr. Windle?" she was on her feet in a flash.

"I must object to that," she said.

"If your objection," said Mavor, "is that evidence about the earlier occasion would better be given by Mr. Windle himself, I can assure you that it is my intention to call him."

"My objection, as my learned friend well knows, is that the earlier episode can only be referred to as evidence of the general character and disposition of the accused. It cannot be adduced in committal proceedings."

Mr. Appleton looked lost. His clerk rose to his feet and said something to him. Mr. Appleton nodded several times and said, "The objection is supported."

"I have no questions for this witness," said Mrs. Bellamy. She managed to say it in a tone of voice which implied that his evidence was unimportant and irrelevant. Mariner looked surprised and left the box. It was difficult to say whether he was relieved or disappointed at not being cross-examined.

"I should explain," said Mavor, "that my next witness, Arthur Simpson Havelock, is a boy of nine. His mother is in court and if you feel it advisable that she should stand near the boy, we should have no objection."

"He'll be all right," said Mrs. Havelock, "as long as you don't frighten him."

Sim, looking minute but quite self-possessed, took the oath. The Magistrate, who knew Mrs. Havelock and all her children, said, "Look at that gentleman, Sim. The one standing up. He's going to ask you some questions."

"All right."

"How old are you, Sim?"

"I'm nine."

"And you're old enough to understand that this is a law court and that you're giving evidence and must speak truthfully."

"O.K."

"You see Mr. Limbery. Over there. You know him, don't you?"

"Yes."

"Did you ever see him with Miss Steelstock?"

"With Katie?"

"Yes."

Mavor waited patiently. His training and his instincts had been against calling the boy, and if his evidence had not been vital to his case he would not have done so.

Sim said, "Do you mean about seeing them at the boat-house?"

"If you saw them at the boathouse, then you can tell us about it."

"Well, we did." Sim paused and added, "We saw them twice. Once was in May and once was in July."

"And what were they doing?"

The court held its breath.

"They were lying on the ground. The second time we didn't see much because they went into the boathouse."

"When you did see them, Sim—on the first occasion—can you tell us what they were doing?"

"Not really. It was getting dark."

"I see. So it would have been sometime about nine o'-clock."

"About then."

"Were they lying close together?"

"Quite close, yes."

Out of the corner of his eye, Mavor could see Mrs. Bellamy watching him like a hawk. He thought that the last answer was almost what he wanted. If he went any further he might spoil it. He said, "Thank you," and sat down.

Mrs. Bellamy said, "When you were answering the gentleman, Sim, I couldn't help noticing that you said, 'We saw them.' Was someone with you?"

"Roney was."

"Is Roney your brother?"

"Yes."

"I suppose he's younger than you?"

For the first time Sim smiled, exposing a gappy set of front teeth. He said, "Roney isn't younger than me. He's eleven. Nearly twelve."

Mrs. Bellamy looked at the Magistrate, but he already had the point. He said, "I take it that the other boy is being called?"

Mavor's sigh was almost audible. He said, "I understand, sir, that there was some sort of difficulty about the older boy."

"What sort of difficulty?"

"He wasn't willing to give evidence."

The Magistrate looked puzzled. He said, "If the two boys were together on both occasions, surely it would have been preferable to have called the older boy. There's no rule that I know of against issuing a subpoena to a minor."

"It would be unusual," agreed Mavor. "But I know nothing against it."

"Is the boy available?"

Mrs. Havelock said, "He's in the waiting room."

"I should like to hear his evidence."

Mavor hesitated. He said, "I shall have to take instructions, sir."

"Very well."

Two whispered conferences began. The first between Mavor, Knott and the solicitor acting for the police; the second between Mr. Appleton and his clerk.

"Like amateur theatricals when something goes

wrong," said Group Captain Gonville. "The only difference is they haven't got a curtain to lower. Are they going to let Roney loose on us?"

"They're in for trouble either way," said Mrs. Havelock grimly.

As the conferences came to an end, the Magistrate said, "I'm told that I've got no right to call for any particular witness. That's not my job. It's up to the prosecution to produce exactly what evidence they wish. I'm going to say this, however. If the older boy, who could clearly corroborate his brother, is *not* going to be called, I shall have to regard what the younger boy says as being, to a certain degree, suspect. I don't mean that I shall disregard it altogether, but I shall accept it only with considerable caution."

Mavor said smoothly, "We have decided that there is no reason why the other boy should not be asked to give evidence. If he refuses to speak, no doubt the court will have to decide whether it has any power to make him do so."

"Obdurate witnesses used to be pressed between heavy weights," said the Group Captain. "Perhaps he'll be too nervous to say anything."

"Don't you believe it," said Mrs. Havelock.

After this preamble, Roney's entrance into the witness box had something of the effect of a star actor whose entrance onto the stage has been carefully delayed and prepared for him by the supporting cast. He smiled cheerfully at the crowded court and took the oath in a clear and confident voice. A murmur from the female members of the public, although not formulated into words, clearly expressed the mass view that he was a sweet little boy.

"We have one or two questions to ask you," said Mavor. "I'm sure you realize the importance of giving truthful answers."

"Yes, sir."

"Your brother has told us that you were with him on two occasions, once in May and once in July, when you saw Mr. Limbery with Kate Steelstock near the boathouse."

"That's right, sir. We saw them there."

"Could you tell us what they were doing?"

"Just sitting together talking."

"Sitting?"

"Sitting on the ground."

"They weren't lying down?"

"Oh no, sir. Just sitting. Talking and laughing."

"You're sure they weren't lying down."

"Quite sure."

"You realize that you are giving evidence on oath."

"Yes, sir."

"And if you don't speak the truth, the consequences can be very serious."

"That's right," said Roney. "It's called perjury and you can be sent to prison."

"Then let me repeat the question. Are you sure that they weren't lying together on the ground quite close to each other?"

"I won't have this witness intimidated," said Mr. Appleton. "He's told you once. What's the point of getting him to say it again?"

Roney flashed a grateful smile at Mr. Appleton and said, "He isn't frightening me, sir. Mother told me that if I had to give evidence, I'd only got to tell the truth and no one could do anything to me."

The crowd loved this. Mavor said, "Very well," and sat down. Mrs. Bellamy said, "I'd like to ask you a question, Roney."

"Yes?"

"You were just outside Mr. Limbery's house in Belsize Road when a policeman came to ask him some questions."

"Sergeant Esdaile. Yes, I saw him."

270

"Were you close enough to hear what the Sergeant said to Mr. Limbery?"

"Oh yes, quite close enough."

"Then could you tell us what he said?"

A slow flush crept up over Roney's pale cheeks. He said, "It was rather rude."

"We're quite used to hearing rude words in this court," said Mr. Appleton. "No one's going to be shocked. Just see if you can remember."

"Well, sir, he said something like Johnno—I mean Mr. Limbery—being a long-haired nuisance. Then he called him a bastard. I can't remember what came before bastard, but it was a sort of rude word."

"Thank you," said Mrs. Bellamy. "Thank you very much."

At about this time, Sergeant McCourt was looking for the Surrey and Berkshire Dockside Mission. He knew of its existence and like other charitable-minded inhabitants of Hannington had contributed small sums toward its upkeep. He had stopped doing so when he discovered that George Mariner was running it.

The mission house had not been easy to find, being tucked away in a back street in Stepney; and when found, it had not been easy to enter, since the front door was locked and bolted. Exploration down a side street had led him to the missioner's flat and persistent hammering on the door had produced the missioner's assistant, an earnest young man with a crew-cut, wearing overalls liberally splashed with fresh whitewash.

"Excuse my appearance," he said. "Just trying to smarten the place up. Police? Good heavens, what have they been up to now?"

"Nothing to do with your young charges," said McCourt.

"I just wanted to find out if you had recently come into possession of an electric typewriter."

"Quite recently. Last week, in fact. Don't tell me it was stolen. Mr. Mariner—"

"It was Mr. Mariner gave it to you?"

"That's right. He knew our old one was broken. He'd just bought himself a new portable and told Commander Bellairs to come down and collect his old one. Why?"

"It's just a matter of checking a lot of local machines. We want to find out how one particular note came to be typed. That means elimination of all other possible machines."

"Elimination?"

"That's right."

"It sounds mad to me. But come in."

If McCourt had looked back as he followed the young man in he might have noticed an inconspicuous person busy lighting a cigarette ten yards down the pavement. Had he been even more alert, he might have noticed that the same person had been hanging about outside the barrier of the arrival platform at Paddington, but his mind was fixed on his quest.

As the door shut behind McCourt, the person showed signs of activity. He moved quickly back into the High Street and without actually running, but without wasting any time at all, reached a telephone box, dialed a number, said, "Blaine here," and asked for Captain Smedley.

The Captain listened to what Blaine had to say, thought about it for a moment and said, "Good show. I guessed it would be worth keeping an eye on that young man. Stay with him."

Most of the excitement in the afternoon was caused by one man and two women fainting. They were carried out of the packed and stifling hall, but this had not diminished the crowd, since three more people from the head of the queue were allowed in.

Mavor had been dealing with the discovery and identification of the note. Listening to him as he pieced together the evidence of Sally Nurse, her father and mother, Sergeant Shilling and Walter Steelstock, Mrs. Havelock had appreciated for the first time how a prosecution case had to be built up. Not by one or two dramatic witnesses but by a lot of humdrum people contributing each their own small share, a brick at a time in the edifice of the Crown.

The only light relief had been Walter's bashful explanation of what he understood LYPAH to mean. The press had enjoyed that.

As the afternoon drew toward its close, Mrs. Steelstock was in the box. She had identified her own signature on the envelope which contained the note and Mavor was now moving on, cautiously, to a different topic.

"Can you tell us," he said, "from your own observation, something of the relationship between your daughter and the accused?"

"To start with, they seemed to be good friends."

"Yes?"

"More recently I should have said that any feeling my daughter may have had for Mr. Limbery had ceased."

Jonathan, who had appeared to be dozing in the dock, sat up.

"You mean that he had ceased to be friendly?"

"Yes."

"How had this happened?"

"I'm not sure I follow you."

"I mean that where a friendship between a young man and a girl ceases, it is usually because one of them cools off."

"It was Kate who dropped Mr. Limbery."

"And that," said Jonathan, "is a damned lie."

273

Mavor ignored him.

"Could you suggest a reason for her doing so."

"Certainly. She had come to the conclusion that he was an immature and self-important young man."

"And that is a bloody lie. What does an old crumb like you know about young people, anyway?"

Mr. Appleton said, "You must not interrupt the proceedings."

"Have I got to sit here and listen to a lot of crap talked about me by people whose heads are stuffed with maggots?"

"There's a remedy for that. I can have you removed from the court and the proceedings can go on without you."

Jonathan subsided with a grunt.

Mrs. Bellamy said, "Tell me, Mrs. Steelstock, would you have described Kate as a confiding girl?"

Mrs. Steelstock circled around it for a bit and then said, "Sometimes."

"I am right in thinking that she didn't live at home."

"She had her own house. Yes."

"Did she tell you about all that happened up in London? All about her television program and her friends up there."

"Well, no."

"Did she discuss Mr. Limbery with you?"

"Not in so many words."

"If she didn't discuss him in words, how *did* she discuss him?"

"I meant," said Mrs. Steelstock coldly, "that I gathered what her feelings were by her conduct."

"What conduct?"

"She no longer invited him to the house."

"But she could, of course, have been meeting him elsewhere?"

"I suppose so."

"Thank you."

"No doubt at all," said Mr. Mapledurham. "Not a scrap of doubt. Capital 'T' slightly worn at the foot, lower-case 'b' tilted. 'S' fractionally out of alignment. Those are the obvious ones. A careful analysis would probably give you half a dozen more."

"You're quite certain it's the same machine?"

"Swear to it in any court of law."

"You might have to do just that," said McCourt.

A quarter to four. The first day's proceedings would be coming to an end soon. The quicker he got back to Hannington the better.

A quarter past four. The Magistrate looked at the clock. He said, "I understand from your opening remarks, Mr. Mavor, that you will next be calling what you described as your third set of witnesses, dealing with the movements of the accused on the night of the killing."

"That's right, sir," said Mavor. "I shall call Superintendent Knott to put in a statement made by the accused and follow that with three or four witnesses who will deal with various aspects of that statement."

"I normally rise at four thirty, but in the circumstances—" The Magistrate looked around the room at the public—overheated, drooping and sated.

"It would perhaps be convenient to start with this new section of evidence tomorrow," agreed Mavor. He was unaffected by the heat. Like a naval officer, he did much of his work on his feet in uncomfortable surroundings.

The usher said, "The court will rise."

As they were going out, Mrs. Havelock said to Group Captain Gonville, "I should call that level pegging so far."

"A lot's going to depend on Knott. I could see that female gorgon licking her lips when she heard he was going to be called as a witness."

"It's odd, isn't it, how the whole thing seems to have developed into a private battle between the two of them. Jonathan seems to have been relegated to the role of extra."

"An extra, if you like," said Group Captain Gonville. "But not a non-speaking part."

"It's interesting," said Knott shortly, "but it's not conclusive."

McCourt stared at him. The Superintendent's face was more gray than white and the lines of fatigue and strain were bitten into it, but his voice was as flat and as expressionless as ever.

"The Documents Division was quite definite, sir. They're reporting in writing. It'll be with you first thing tomorrow."

"I'll read it with interest, son. But what does it actually prove, except that the note was written on Mariner's typewriter? Anyone could have got at it. He made a habit of keeping people waiting. I could have typed it. You could have typed it. The Chief Constable could have typed it. So what's to prevent Limbery snatching a chance when he was alone there?"

"Why would he do that?"

For a moment Knott looked as though he wasn't going to answer. Then he said, "If you were planning to send a note and you didn't want it found, but there was a chance it might be, wouldn't you type it on someone else's machine? Particularly if you loathed his guts." He climbed to his feet and lumbered out.

McCourt turned on Shilling, his face set in unusual lines of anger. He said, "So the charade goes on."

"Curtain up at ten sharp tomorrow."

"And nothing can stop it?"

"I don't say it couldn't be stopped," said Shilling, carefully, "but it's going to take more than this last bit of evidence to do it. After all, there's some truth in what he said. Almost anyone could have used the machine. All you had to do was ring the bell. Polly lets you in and you've got anything from two to twenty minutes available, according to who you were. When I called recently I was kept waiting for twelve minutes."

"Yes, but why did he—?"

"I know what you're going to say. The answer's panic. When he heard that inquiries were being made, he had to get rid of the machine. Stupid thing to do, but understandable. And his conscience wasn't all that clear if he'd been out doing a spot of voyeuring. And a word of advice. I don't think I should try any more bright suggestions on the old man. Not just at this moment."

"I heard he had some rough handling in court."

"That wouldn't worry him. It's something else."

He stopped and McCourt noticed that his face was unusually grim.

"The Steelstock boy has killed himself. His mother found him when she got back from court. He'd cut his throat with one of his father's old razors and made a filthy mess of it. He left a note, too. Blaming the police in general and you in particular."

TWENTY-FIVE

It might have seemed impossible that the crowd should be larger, but on the second morning the waiting line stretched far back, down the street beside the court building, along the back of the building and fifty yards out into the road beyond. The people at the head of the queue had been there all night. They had left the court at the end of the hearing and had immediately taken up their positions outside the door. There were half a dozen policemen on duty now.

The crowd was not only larger. It was in a different mood. Somehow the news of Peter's death had got out. It was a garbled account passed by word of mouth. Katie's kid brother had killed himself. It was something to do with the police. They hadn't wanted him to give evidence (or, in another version, they had wanted him to give evidence). They had bullied him. They had tried to break him down. The boy could take no more and had cut his own throat.

The crowd was angry.

When the police judged that the courtroom was full and tried to shut the door of the public entrance, there was a scuffle. A woman said, "Why won't you let us in?" A big red-faced man who had his foot in the door preventing it from being shut said, "We know why. You don't want us to hear the truth, do you? How many more kids are you going to kill?"

The policeman at the door summoned help and they got it shut. The crowd outside refused to disperse. When Knott arrived he was recognized and a storm of hissing and boo-ing broke out. Knott ignored it and pushed his way through toward the side entrance. The policeman on duty there held the door open for him. He said, "I don't know what's come over them."

"Mass hysteria," said Knott.

"I understand, Superintendent," said Mavor, "that the accused made a statement."

"He made two, sir. An earlier statement in answer to some questions which I put to him in the course of my investigation. A later and more formal statement after he had been charged and cautioned."

"The second statement was taken down?"

"In his presence, sir. And signed by him as being cor-rect."

"Then perhaps you would read it out to us."

" 'As the result of a telephone call from the news editor of the Reading *Sun,* I left my house at approximately ten o'clock that evening—' "

"The evening he referred to being August fifteenth?"

"That is correct, sir. '—at approximately ten o'clock that evening and drove over to Quantocks Paper Mills outside Goring to report on a fire which I was informed had broken out there. I proceeded to the scene of the fire, arriving at about half past ten. I was engaged in making notes and conversing with the fire officers until about a quarter to twelve, when I drove to a call box on the Oxford road and dictated my report over the tele-phone to the newspaper. I then had a quick snack at the King of Clubs roadhouse, which is also on the Ox-ford road. I left the roadhouse at approximately a quar-ter to one and proceeded back via Whitchurch and

Pangbourne, getting home at about half past one.'
Signed and witnessed."

"Thank you, Superintendent. I'll put in a copy of this
statement." A document was handed up to the Magistrate,
who added it to the pile on his desk. "Now tell us, Superintendent. Did this statement coincide with the earlier informal statement which you mentioned?"

"It was a good deal shorter, sir. But it coincided in every
material particular."

"Then I would like to draw your attention, sir, to three
points in it. First, that the accused says he spent an hour
and a quarter at the scene of the fire. Secondly, that he
telephoned his account to the paper from a call box on the
Oxford road. Thirdly, that he returned home through
Whitchurch and Pangbourne, which would involve crossing the Thames at this point. It is the contention of the
Crown, sir, that the accused has lied, and lied deliberately,
on all these three points. The remaining witnesses will be
directing their testimony to those matters."

Knott made a move to leave the box, but Mrs. Bellamy
was already on her feet.

"I have one or two questions which I should like to put
to this witness. I was not clear whether this was to be his
only appearance, or whether he is to give evidence on
other points later."

"If you have any questions to put to the Superintendent,
do so now by all means," said Mavor.

"Thank you."

Mrs. Bellamy had brought out a pair of old-fashioned
pince-nez glasses, which she perched on her nose, alternately looking through them at her notes and over them at
the witness. There was something mesmeric about the
bobbing up and down of her head.

("Like a wasp eating marmalade," whispered Mrs.
Havelock.)

280

"Could I direct your attention to the pathologist's reports which we have had read to us. *Both* reports, Superintendent. Particularly the second one. You remember it?"

"Yes."

"A report by one eminent pathologist, endorsed by a second, a very eminent one, which stated that *two* people had been killed by the same weapon, at about the same time and probably by the same person."

"It was not a statement. It simply suggested the possibility."

"When two eminent experts suggest a possibility, you don't think it becomes a probability?"

"I think it remains a theory."

"But it was a theory based on facts. The shape and depth of the wound."

"Yes."

"Relevant facts."

"If you like."

"And is it not your duty to inform the defense of all relevant facts which come to your notice?"

"It would only have been relevant if the accused was charged with the second killing."

A man at the back of the court said loudly, "Nonsense."

The Magistrate looked up. Then he said, "I'm afraid I don't understand that myself, Superintendent. If there was evidence that the same man had killed two people, surely this was relevant."

"All that we had to go on was a theory put forward by Dr. Carlyle that the blows could have been produced by the same instrument. We did not consider this to be strong enough evidence definitely to connect the two."

"In other words," said Mrs. Bellamy, "you thought you knew better than Dr. Carlyle."

"If you want to put it that way."

"And than Dr. Summerson."

"Yes."

"Who are acknowledged experts in their own field."

"I agree."

"And what training in forensic pathology have you had, Superintendent?"

"I have listened to a lot of pathologists giving evidence and have believed exactly half of them," said Knott.

("Not bad," said Group Captain Gonville.)

"This second man, whose death you regarded as unimportant, has been identified, I believe, as being a certain Gabriel Lewson, employed as a runner by a society photographer named Rodney Ruoff. Is that right, Superintendent?"

"That is so."

"And did you also regard it as totally irrelevant that Ruoff was himself murdered a few days ago?"

"We hardly thought it likely that the accused had had any part in that killing, since he was in custody at the time it occurred."

"Quite so. But did it not occur to you as a relevant fact that *three* people, all of whom were closely connected, should have been killed within a few days of each other?"

Knott said, "There was no connection known to us—" and stopped.

"You were going to say that there was no connection between Miss Steelstock and Ruoff?"

"No close connection."

"Although he was her photographer and the man who had set her on her way to stardom."

"No close connection," said Knott obstinately.

A murmur came from the crowded listeners. It was difficult to distinguish words, but "rubbish" was certainly among them. Mrs. Bellamy listened to it with her head cocked. The reporters wrote, "Raking cross-examination," and "Police witness under fire."

"Let me repeat a question I put to you earlier," said Mrs. Bellamy. "You do agree, I hope, that if facts *are* relevant, it is the duty of the police to share them with the defense?"

"Yes."

"The object of a criminal trial is to elucidate the truth, not to secure a personal victory for a particular policeman."

"The object of a trial," said Knott, "is to determine whether the accused is guilty of the crime he is charged with. Not to examine any other crimes which may have taken place in the neighborhood at the time."

It was a good answer, in a debating sense, but, thought Mrs. Havelock, it was too long. It was the first small sign that the Superintendent was getting rattled.

Mrs. Bellamy said, "Of course. That's right. And that is what I meant by the word 'relevant.' Relevant to this crime. Now am I not right in thinking that a considerable part of the police investigation was devoted to trying to trace the typewriter on which this famous note was typed?"

"It was one of the things we tried to do."

"Was not one of your sergeants sent round all office suppliers in the neighborhood with a description of the make of typewriter?"

"Yes."

"And an advertisement put in the press?"

"Yes."

"Would you not describe that as a persistent investigation?"

"All our investigations in a murder case are persistent."

"And were they all as successful as this one?"

Knott looked at her for a long moment. The color was creeping into his face. He said, "I'm not sure that I understand."

"Then I must make myself clear. Did not one of your

283

officers go up to London yesterday and visit a certain mission house in South London? Did he not find a typewriter there and take a sample from it, which he subsequently handed to the Documents Division in your own Science Laboratory for testing?"

"I believe that is correct."

"And what was the result?"

"I'm afraid I can't tell you."

"Why not?"

"I have not yet received an official report."

The noise from the courtroom was like the hiss of expelled breath which has been held too long. Someone shouted, "The man's a liar." A woman sitting close behind Mrs. Havelock said, "Make him answer," in tones of such venom that Mrs. Havelock looked around startled. It was a woman she knew quite well, a mother of three children and normally as placid as an apple dumpling. Now her face was transformed by fury.

Mr. Appleton looked around the room, from side to side, waiting until the noise had died away. Then he said, quite pleasantly, "I have no doubt you are as anxious as I am to hear the rest of the evidence in this case. But I have to warn you that if there is any further interruption, I shall adjourn the hearing and continue it with the press in attendance but with no members of the general public there at all. Have you any further questions for this witness, Mrs. Bellamy?"

"There is one further matter which I should like to explore. It concerns the statement which we have heard read out to us. A statement alleged to have been made by the accused."

"A statement which was made by the accused," said Knott. He was back on balance again.

"Could you explain to us exactly how it was obtained?"

"The accused was asked if he wished to volunteer a statement. He did so. And it was written down."

"Sentence by sentence, as he spoke it?"

"Yes."

"I am only raising the point because certain parts of it sound more like a police version of what the accused *might* have said than a verbatim record of what he *did* say. For instance"—Mrs. Bellamy adjusted her pince-nez —" 'I proceeded to the scene of the fire, arriving at about half past ten . . . and conversing with the fire officers.' That hardly sounds to me like something the accused would actually have said."

"He did say it."

" 'I left the roadhouse at approximately a quarter to one and proceeded back via Whitchurch and Pangbourne.' Did he say that, too?"

"Yes."

"I thought it was only policemen who 'conversed' and 'proceeded.' Ordinary people 'talked' and 'went.' "

"That's what he said."

"You're sure this wasn't the sort of statement which is obtained by the police asking a series of questions which suggest the answers they want."

"Quite sure."

"More lies," said Jonathan.

"I am pressing the matter because I am going to suggest that at this point you inserted two or three words which the accused never said—'via Whitchurch and Pangbourne.' "

"He said them in his formal statement and in his earlier informal statement."

"Which was not taken down verbatim?"

"No, but it was tape-recorded."

For the first time Mrs. Bellamy looked taken aback. She recovered quickly. She said, "If this was done without the knowledge and consent of the accused, I do not see that it can be referred to in evidence."

"I understand," said Mavor, "that the tape itself will

demonstrate that the accused was informed that his words were being recorded."

"Before or after he made his statement?"

"The passage occurs towards the end."

"And until then he knew nothing about it and had not consented to a recording being made?"

"He had not consented, but he made no objection."

Mr. Appleton conferred with his clerk. He said, "When the accused made this earlier statement, had he been charged?"

"No, sir."

"Then I don't think it can be given in evidence in this court."

Mavor said, "We accept your ruling, sir." He had not thought they would get away with it, but it had been worth trying. And the intervention had robbed Mrs. Bellamy's cross-examination of some of its sting.

"I shall resume at two o'clock," said Mr. Appleton. "And might I ask spectators, if they intend to remain in court over the interval, not to leave a quantity of debris on the floor. Yesterday it took the attendants half an hour to sweep up."

"It looks as though we should finish this afternoon," said the Group Captain. "I thought Mrs. Bellamy made the best of the running this morning. How do you think the chances stand now?"

"Still fifty-fifty," said Mrs. Havelock. "Thank God it's Appleton who has to make his mind up and not us."

At three o'clock that afternoon, Sergeant Shilling, who had been left in charge of the operations room, sustained two shocks, both of them severe.

The first shock arrived in the form of a telephone call. Shilling recognized the voice. It was a detective sergeant called Whittaker who worked in the Fingerprint Section at

Central. Wrong. Not Whittaker. Whitmore. He seemed to be amused about something.

He said, "You remember that print you sent up to us?"

"The one off the cupboard door."

"That's the one. Well, guess what!"

"Tell me," said Shilling. Already he could feel a faint tickle of uneasiness.

"You know we tried it on the main computer. No luck there at all. Not a chirrup. This morning, just for laughs, we put it on the Sock List."

Shilling's hand tightened on the telephone. He understood well enough what Whitmore was talking about. The Fingerprint Section maintained a separate record, known as the "Scene of Crime," or "S.O.C. List." On it were recorded the prints of all those people who might have legitimate business at the place where a crime had been discovered. Not only police officers in all the forces in the country, but pathologists, police surgeons, photographers and the like. It was useful as an eliminator and could be keyed, if necessary, into the main print computer.

"Looks like he's been a bit careless," said Whitmore "He'll collect a rocket from Knotty." Shilling was hardly listening to him. His mind was racing ahead, trying to absorb and work out the shocking implications of what he had heard.

"Don't be too hard on him," said Whitmore. "We all make mistakes. We'll be sending you a written report by hand this evening."

Shilling said, "Thank you," and rang off. He was still staring blindly at the telephone when a second and greater shock followed.

He had been aware that something was happening across the other side of the courtyard. Someone had arrived. He heard Sergeant Bakewell's voice saying, "It's just across here, sir. I'll show you the way."

Then the door was opened and Terence Loftus, Assistant Commissioner of the Metropolitan Police, stalked into the room.

Mrs. Mason said, "Of course I'm sure. You don't stand for twenty minutes outside a lighted telephone box without being able to recognize the man who's deliberately keeping you waiting. I can assure you it fixes his face very firmly in your mind."

She glared at the man in the dock. Jonathan rewarded her with a charming smile.

"And you're quite certain about the time?" said Mavor.

"Perfectly certain. You see, my sister doesn't like being dragged away from her television set before midnight. Then she has to put the dog out. We have a standing arrangement, that if I want to ring her I do so at five or ten minutes after midnight. That suits us both. I don't go to bed early myself."

Mavor was on the point of saying, "Thank you very much," when he noted that a disturbance was taking place near the side door. A uniformed policeman was forcing a passage through the crowd for a tall gray-haired man whom Mavor had no difficulty in recognizing. By this time everyone in the room realized that something was happening.

Mavor said, "It seems there may have been a development of which I ought to be apprised. I wonder if you would allow me to hold up the proceedings for a moment."

"Certainly," said Mr. Appleton courteously. He, too, had recognized the newcomer, who was talking to the solicitor for the police. Mavor joined the conference. Most of the talking was done by the gray-haired man. He had a gesture of chopping the desk in front of him with the edge of his hand, a karate blow.

Mavor returned to his place, placed the last paper he

had been using neatly on top of his brief and said, "I understand that the Crown will offer no further evidence on the first charge."

A curious sound broke from the packed ranks of the spectators. It was like a communal gasp, followed by an outbreak which started as a murmur, escalated into something more menacing and died away suddenly when it was observed that Mrs. Bellamy was on her feet.

She said, "I should like to understand that. Does it mean that the charge is withdrawn?"

"The first charge, yes."

"In that case, since, as I have indicated, there is evidence of considerable provocation on the lesser charge, I should like to make an application that the prisoner be released forthwith on bail."

The response from the courtroom made it clear that there was strong popular backing for this suggestion.

Mr. Appleton turned to Mavor, who had Knott now at his elbow, whispering fiercely.

Mavor said, "The second charge may be a lesser one. It is nevertheless a very serious one. Wounding a member of the police force. It would, I submit, be most unusual to afford bail on such a charge. However, the decision must be left to you, sir."

"Has he surrendered his passport?"

"I haven't got a passport," said Jonathan. His voice was so high-pitched as to be almost out of control.

"Something missing up top," said the Group Captain. "*I* wouldn't let him loose. Not for a minute."

"On condition, then," said Mr. Appleton, "that you report every evening before six o'clock to the Hannington police station and if you break that condition your bail will be automatically canceled, I am prepared to grant the application."

Jonathan had listened to this with a smile twitching his

lips. Now he threw back his head and laughed. It was a horrible sound, part spite, part hysteria, with very little humor in it. Fortunately it was drowned by the roar of cheering which broke from the court.

There was a scene of confusion as the reporters fought to make their way out through the side entrance and the people at the back shouldered and elbowed their way through the slower spectators. The police had bolted the door to prevent a further invasion from the street and it took some seconds to get it open. Then the crowd belched out and the noise of the cheering spread down the waiting queue and flowed out into the streets of Reading, flowed down a dozen telephone wires into the offices of great papers and out to millions upon millions of readers.

The police had blundered. The man they had accused of the killing of Katie Steelstock was free.

TWENTY-SIX

"Thirty years of police work," said the Assistant Commissioner, "have convinced me that it is always the most trivial causes which lead to the most disastrous results. If my daughter, Venetia, had known that Sergeant McCourt was stationed at Hannington, she'd have told me a fortnight ago what she told me yesterday morning and most of our troubles would never have happened."

Knott grunted. They were alone in the Assistant Commissioner's office. Knott's face was still gray, but some of the life had come back into his eyes.

"It appears that she got friendly with McCourt when he was in London. They met over some trouble with a dog. A nice-looking boy, with an easy manner. She took him along to one of Ruoff's parties. Ruoff gave him the full treatment. Hocussed drink and private photographic session in the bedroom. My daughter went looking for him and came in right at the end. McCourt was pretty well flat out by that time, though he realized afterwards what had happened and this must have been what finally decided him to change the filth of London for the clean country-side. When Ruoff gathered that his latest model was a police officer he was scared stiff. He'd just had one brush with the law and lucky to get away without a prison sentence. He assured my daughter he'd destroy the photograph."

"But he didn't," said Knott.

"He didn't," agreed the Assistant Commissioner. "He kept it and Katie found it when she was rummaging through his cabinet and took it away. It was apple pie for her. She had that puritanical young man on the end of a string, with a hook in his mouth she could twitch whenever she felt like it."

Knott was thinking it out slowly. He said, "Then it was really the photograph and the note that he was looking for when he broke into her house late that night."

"It was the photograph he was looking for, though I don't doubt he'd have been glad to destroy the note, too. He'd had to word it to make it seem as though it came from Limbery. He knew Katie was still hot for him and would come running. On the other hand, he'd no wish to get Limbery into trouble."

Knott said, "He must have known it might be found. That's why he typed it on Mariner's machine."

"That's what all his later maneuvers were about. Shifting the blame onto Mariner. If anyone had to be a scapegoat for his crime, he'd rather it was someone he loathed than someone he liked."

Knott was still thinking back. He said, "There was an earlier attempted burglary at Katie's house. I suppose that was him too."

"I imagine so. He simply *had* to destroy that photograph. Once it was gone he'd be safe, or so he thought. He reckoned that Ruoff wouldn't dare open his mouth. He didn't realize my daughter knew about it. Another thing he didn't know was that Ruoff had kept the negative. Forster found it when he was going through his effects. It's not a pleasant picture."

There was a long silence.

"I'd guess," said Knott at last, "that if she'd just used that photograph to tease him he wouldn't have killed her. It was when she forced him to lie and cheat about that running-down case that she signed her own death warrant. He suggested, you remember, that Ray had taken him off it at Mariner's instigation. But he didn't make the suggestion until he knew that Ray was dead."

"A ruthless, single-minded young man," said the Assistant Commissioner.

"Well placed to do what he had to do. Out and about at all hours on that moped and no questions asked. Put Windle's car out of action on the Thursday night and the other two as well, no doubt. Called on Mariner, who was sure to keep him waiting, and used his typewriter. Dropped the note in Katie's car. He'll have done that when he called at the Manor that evening."

"Right. And walked down the towpath, in the dark, from his conveniently placed lodgings in Eveleigh Road and waited for Kate. If she didn't turn up, no harm done. But she did."

"So did Lewson," said Knott. "That's clear now. Maybe he recognized McCourt, maybe he didn't. McCourt was taking no chances. So he killed him, too. And went home to bed."

"A cool customer."

"But not so cool right now."

"How is he?"

"The doctors say he'll live."

When Jonathan was released he had gone back to the remand wing for bail formalities. There he had been given back his belongings, and the letter from Peter. He had read it, gone straight back to his house, dug up the revolver he had buried in his back garden, met Sergeant McCourt in the road and shot him three times through the body. He had then given himself up.

"A pity he didn't shoot a bit straighter," said the Assistant Commissioner. "Now we shall have it all to do over again. If he'd worn a thicker pair of gloves when he broke down the door of Kate's desk I don't believe there'd be even a prima facie case against him."

Knott said, "I remember telling him that he ought to keep up to date on the techniques of his profession."

"It'll be the devil of a case to run," said the Assistant Commissioner. "A lot of assumptions but no proof." He thought about it for a bit. "I think I'll give it to Jim Haliburton."

The grunt which Knott gave might have meant anything, or nothing at all.